Advance Praise for
Communicate with Confidence!

"Many of the world's most talented and ambitious people fail to achieve their potential simply because they haven't mastered the art of effective communication. With clarity, conciseness and great wit, *Communicate with Confidence!* teaches you everything you always wanted to know about being a great communicator but didn't know how to ask."

Michael LeBoeuf, Ph.D.
Author of *Fast Forward* and *How to Win Customers and Keep Them for Life*

"The biggest career boost you'll ever give yourself. Read and master these principles."

Ralph O. Doughty
Major General
U.S. Army Reserve

"Those in the workplace cannot survive, much less excel, without superior communication skills. *Communicate With Confidence!* delivers everything anyone will need to know—period. It is *the* definitive work."

Dr. Judith Briles
Author of *The Confidence Factor* and
Show Me About Book Publishing

Other Selected Titles by Dianna Booher

Communicate
with
Confidence!

*How to Say It
Right the First Time
and Every Time*

REVISED AND EXPANDED EDITION

DIANNA BOOHER

New York   Chicago   San Francisco   Lisbon   London
Madrid   Mexico City   Milan   New Delhi   San Juan
Seoul   Singapore   Sydney   Toronto

5 6 7 8 9 0   DOC/DOC   1 0 9 8 7 6 5

ISBN   978-0-07-177013-2
MHID   0-07-177013-5

Communicate with Confidence is a registered trademark of Booher Consultants, Inc.
SEER Format is a registered trademark of Booher Consultants, Inc.
Platinum Rule is a registered trademark of Anthony J. Alessandra.

McGraw-Hill books are available at special quantity discounts to use as premiums and sales promotions, or for use in corporate training programs. To contact a representative please e-mail us at bulksales@mcgraw-hill.com.

This book is printed on acid-free paper.

To

Vernon

Jeff, Jennifer, Courtney, Grant, Jake

Lisa, Kevin, Mason, Elena, Spencer, Abby

Angie, Kevin, Anna, Sarah, Matt

Sandy, Leanne, Aaron, Lauren, Andrew, David, Jackie

Dad and Mother: Alton and Opal

In Memory of Keith

Communication is the soul of management: analysis and solid decisions translated into clear messages that influence people to act and feel good about their performance.

Language is a wonderful thing. It can be used to express thoughts, to conceal our thoughts, or to replace thinking.

—Kelly Fordyce

Words are what hold society together.

—Stuart Chase

Men govern with words.

—Benjamin Disraeli

The greatest problem in communication is the illusion that it has been accomplished.

—George Bernard Shaw

The ability to deal with people is as purchasable a commodity as sugar and coffee. And I pay more for that ability than for any other under the sun.

—John Davison Rockefeller

You show me the person who can communicate wel . . . They can have an enormous impact, and they will jump out of the pack.

—Warren Buffett

I speak to millions every day, but it's different one-on-one when people have paid to hear you say something meaningful.

—Oprah Winfrey

Contents

Acknowledgments

The principles of communication have been of interest since the Greek philosophers Aristotle and Socrates wrote; and graduate students, management consultants, and Gallup pollsters still find the subject to be worth covering. I'm indebted to all the philosophers, researchers, and writers who have published their findings and thoughts in this broad field, and I encourage you to examine the bibliography for an extensive list of their works.

Specifically, I want to thank my clients for their help in conducting research in their organizations. I'm also grateful to the many individuals in my workshop and speech audiences. When they single me out after a program to share their own experiences of success or failure in communication, they always reconfirm my central theme: communication skills can make or break a relationship, a career, or an organization. They keep me on target by asking for practical, usable tips, and they continually provide me with new anecdotes on the fundamentals. Thanks to each of you who has passed on your experiences to me.

Finally, I'd like to thank those on my staff who worked with me specifically to gather this research during our work among clients and to prepare this manuscript, both the original version and this second edition: Polly Fuhrman, Kari Gates, Vernon Rae, Cinda Benton, Janet Houston-Spore, Nancy Koenig, Sally Luttrell, Chris Casady, Nancy Ross, Robin Hutchins, Steve Winkle, and Bill Strong. These people have been the most encouraging teammates an author could have.

Introduction

Communication Is a Life-or-Death Matter

That's not an overstatement. In corporate offices, in courtrooms, in Congress, and in bedrooms and boardrooms around the world, "miscommunication" surfaces as an issue—the cause of economic crises, poor job performance, lost sales, lawsuits, broken relationships, or even death. More than any other skill, communication determines people's success in sales meetings, marriage, or management.

Maybe that's the reason that Communicate with Confidence®, our trademarked phrase, continues to crop up everywhere and create headaches for me. Let me explain. When the first edition of this book came out almost 18 years ago, my editor suggested the title.

My response was, "That's too . . . ordinary. It needs to be catchier and have a bigger benefit than just 'confidence.' Most people think they already communicate well. The title needs shock value. With that title, it'll never sell."

My editor promised to take my concerns back to the publishing committee.

She called a week later to say, "The committee doesn't agree. I'm afraid that's going to be the title."

"It'll never sell, then." I hung up the phone, disappointed.

Fortunately, I was wrong. (Hey, I never claimed to be a positive thinker at that point in my life.) Sales took off. Book club sales. Foreign sales. Media coverage galore. We developed our interpersonal skills training course to match and trademarked the title for that purpose. For the past 18 years, my trademarked phrase has popped up repeatedly—on other people's e-books, courses, columns, speeches, and websites. Thanks to Google Alerts and a good intellectual property attorney, we've discovered that people do want to communicate with confidence.

Whether because it's a great title, a great benefit, or a great big gap in the workforce or at home, communication heads the list of reasons for people to do things—reasons that people join an organization, leave an organization, love their boss, hate their boss, find their soul mate, divorce their soul mate, win an election, or lose an election. In survey after survey, from senior executives reminiscing about their career success to recruiters hiring college graduates, communication always tops the list of skills needed for success. Whether it is a valid or invalid measure, the lack of communication skills tags people as being less competent, less attractive, and less qualified as leaders.

Where communication is concerned, some people think they've got it made because they have an extroverted personality. But that's not necessarily the case. An outgoing, life-of-the-party personality doesn't necessarily equate to sensitivity to others, which is the core of goodwill. Both introverts and extroverts need specific skills.

That's not to say, of course, that either personality type doesn't know how to communicate. We all communicate up to a point—up to the point where our habits set in. Until someone makes an insensitive remark. Until someone asks us for our advice and then argues against it. Until we feel that our ideas are routinely being ignored in meetings. Until we're tongue-tied when we have to deal with a group of complainers. Until we feel defensive about how we're handling a current project. Until we fail to persuade our team or our customer to take action. Until a friend tells us that we need to learn to negotiate rather than dictate. Until someone won't accept no for an answer. Until we get a flaming e-mail. Until a trusted friend deletes us on Facebook. Until a spouse wants out of the marriage.

When you find yourself in any of these situations, you may feel the need to change the way you're communicating—to increase your skill with a specific technique that jump-starts you and gets you past a limiting habit and on to progress. You want to stop hoping that you "get through" to the other person and ensure that you do.

That's the "why" of this book.

WHAT'S IN IT FOR YOU?

Ask lawyers, engineers, or system analysts which creates the most frustration and failure—the technical part of their job or dealing with people? They'll agree on the latter. Samson of biblical fame killed 10,000 Philistines with the jawbone of an ass. Similar destruction occurs on a daily basis with the same weapon.

Consider these benefits of communicating well. You'll

- Get the correct information more quickly.
- Build credibility with customers and colleagues.
- Develop more intimate relationships.
- Build loyalty in a supportive climate.
- Unleash the creativity within yourself and others by building on each other's ideas.
- Improve your teamwork.
- Facilitate problem solving.
- Build consensus for decisions.
- Motivate others to work more effectively.
- Lead and participate in more effective meetings.
- Save time and energy, reduce rework, and increase productivity through clear instructions and discussions.
- Avoid needless arguments.
- Reduce hurt feelings—yours and those of others.
- Overcome paralyzing anger, fear, or shyness.
- Give constructive feedback and coaching.
- Respond to feedback and criticism appropriately.
- Solicit helpful advice when it's not readily forthcoming.
- Negotiate for what you want without diminishing the other person.
- Win more cooperation when others' response is voluntary.
- Stand firm in your opinions without giving offense.
- Give and accept appropriate praise and compliments.
- Manage your own conflicts without escalating them.
- Mediate others' conflicts without getting burned yourself.
- Exercise more power over decisions that affect you.
- Influence and motivate others without strong-arm tactics.
- Find ways to "work around" difficult personalities.
- Generate enthusiasm for your ideas and proposals.
- Receive more invitations to accept leadership roles—both formally and informally.
- Receive more invitations to speak publicly to influence others.
- Increase your own and others' job satisfaction.

- "Pick other people's brains" profitably: for ideas, experiences, habits, attitudes, and hard-core facts.
- Broaden your network of friends.
- Build your self-esteem and confidence by learning to be assertive.
- Defend your rights without manipulating or offending others.
- Handle insults, sarcasm, or other verbal assaults with style.
- Reduce your fear of vulnerability and decrease feelings of loneliness.
- Listen better so that others feel understood and valued.
- Generate meaningful or entertaining conversations.
- Reduce cross-gender misunderstandings and conflicts resulting from style differences.
- Understand the meanings and intentions of those of other cultures.
- Improve your physical health by reducing stress caused by misunderstandings and conflicts.
- Improve your mental health by growing as a person and developing more supportive relationships.
- Lead others to mutual benefits and goals.

Are there hard data to back up these "wishful thinking" benefits? Yes. In 2010, Watson Wyatt Worldwide, a global management consulting firm, released a comprehensive study (covering 328 organizations representing five million employees) that reported that companies with effective communicators had 47 percent higher total returns to shareholders over the prior five years than the firms considered to have the least effective communicators.

How *important* are the goals and skills just listed? The American Management Association surveyed more than 2,000 senior managers in 2010 as part of its Critical Skills Survey. Respondents predicted that communication skills would be the top employee development priority for the immediate future; this priority was cited by 41 percent of the managers surveyed. Now, more than ever, you have to be able to

- Use a variety of media and formats to gather information and communicate your message.
- Communicate and build rapport with globally diverse groups.
- Establish your credibility and expertise in a larger context and be accountable to more people for results. That is, you can't just focus

on welding a widget and going home. You have to understand why that widget meets the customer's needs and continually come up with ways to make it better, faster, and cheaper—or the organization will be looking for somebody who can keep the big picture in mind.

Wherever you work and whatever you do, you have to be able to gather information, analyze it, summarize it, and present it so that others can digest it and use it for decision making.

When it comes to communication and connection, the question isn't, "Who needs help?" The question is, "Who doesn't?"

I coach executives primarily—those with exceptional skills in their areas of expertise and industry. But at some point in their careers, almost all successful professionals either realize that better communication skills can increase their ability to lead more effectively or understand that poor communication habits are limiting their influence and results. I've never had anyone tell me that she couldn't improve her communication; like fitness, better communication is an ongoing process.

HOW TO USE THIS BOOK

Here are some suggestions on how to improve your communication skills in general and use this book specifically:

- *Skip to a chapter that addresses an immediate challenge you're facing.* Review the headings for quick tips on techniques, approaches, or phrasing to address your specific issue. For example, if you've apologized to someone, but the relationship hasn't improved, go to the chapter on apologies and see if your apology came across as insincere for some reason. If you need feedback on your career, but you aren't getting it, turn to that chapter to identify ways to ask for usable feedback and discover why people may be hesitant to give it.
- *Listen to the conversations of others.* Be an eavesdropper. You'll hear hilarious stories and arguments that will make you want to take sides even when you don't know the players. And you'll also learn how tone affects others' reactions and how ambiguous words create confusion. You'll notice what works and what doesn't work for other people. Then compare your observations with the tips given in this book.

- *Consider your options and alternatives for saying things before you speak.* Try to become aware of the various responses open to you when someone accuses you, angers you, praises you, or motivates you. Simply being aware of your options and ways to express those options will expand your communication horizons. No single comment is always appropriate. Aim to develop flexibility in responding to different people on different occasions. Look for the options outlined here.

- *Identify the level at which most of your relationships rest, determine which ones you want to deepen, and consider how to go about creating a stronger connection.* For example, do you recognize or acknowledge others as mere acquaintances, making a perfunctory comment such as, "How are you doing this morning?" or, "How are things going?" Are you a step closer as casual friends in that you know each other well enough to chat about a conflict with a family member or to discuss upcoming events or facts of common interest? Are you close friends who share deeply held opinions, beliefs, and values? Or has your relationship progressed to the intimate friendship stage that permits you to share feelings and thoughts about yourself and others and pass on judgments. In other words, have you as friends granted each other the freedom to say things that will improve your character? With awareness of the levels of intimacy, you'll develop your sense of what's better said and left unsaid in spur-of-the-moment situations with others around.

- *Select tips to follow and practice.* If people don't seem to give you appropriate attention when you're leading a meeting, for example, review the associated tips in this book and then try them out at your next meeting. The more you practice these guidelines, the more confident you'll feel and the less mechanical the techniques will seem. Or, if you fear that you're falling behind in the social media area, turn to that chapter and pick up some pointers to develop your online presence. Within 24 hours, you can make yourself as vocal and vibrant online as you are face to face.

- *Use the book as a refresher.* If you're attending an upcoming convention, party, family reunion, or industry meeting where you fear you'll be ill at ease in networking, reread the tips associated with small talk, such as conversation starters or exit lines for leaving a small huddle.

How do you know if you're successful at communicating? Consider the responses you get. Are you having the desired effect on people? In other words, are you making them think, feel, or do something that you want? What seems to be their impression of you? Do others try to dominate you, control you, ignore you, or abuse you? How easily do you connect with others online using Twitter, Facebook, or LinkedIn groups?

Can you work effectively in groups? Does your team accomplish its goals with a minimum of clashes? Do you weigh others' words and understand and evaluate their messages appropriately? Effective communication involves both the messages you send and those you receive—what you say, what you hear, and what each of you *thinks* the other said and heard. Do others say that you listen to them? Do you feel that others always give your ideas a fair hearing? Can you sell your ideas effectively?

Failure to communicate is the frustration of modern management, the dating scene, and the family dinner table. Over time, all human relationships depend on the sum total of your interactions, stacked end to end. Personally or professionally, communication becomes a life-or-death issue.

1

Establishing Your Credibility

Trust is the glue of life. It's the most essential ingredient in effective communication. It's the foundational principle that holds all relationships.

—Stephen Covey

If I only had three words of advice, they would be, Tell the Truth. If I got three more words, I'd add, all the time.

—Randy Pausch

When you break your word, you break something that cannot be mended.

—No attribution

When gamblers go to the racetrack, they consider the horses' prior performance when placing their bets. When investors buy stocks, they look at the past performance of the mutual fund or the corporation. When voters go to the polls, they consider the voting record of the candidate before casting their ballot for or against. Yes, hunches and name recognition play a part in all these situations, but over the long haul, performance profoundly affects our decisions about whom we believe. The same is true in leading, learning, or loving: credibility counts.

Tip 1. Find Commonalities.

People like people who are like them. And people believe and trust people they like. Try to discover attitudes, likes, dislikes, family backgrounds, experiences, personality virtues or quirks, careers, goals, or values that you have in common with others. Researchers tell us that attitudes and morals are what matter most to the majority of people. So those are the

1

commonalities you want to emphasize. People reason that if you're like them in one of these key ways, you're probably like them in other ways. Therefore, they begin to transfer trust to you as friend to friend.

Tip 2. Show Concern and Compassion.

People tend to trust people who show concern for them. When they bleed, they want to know that others are bleeding with them. Even companies have to show concern rather than self-interest in times of crisis.

During the Pepsi needle-syringe-tampering reports, you may recall the criticism that some expressed concerning the company's handling of that crisis. When the public asked about the possibility of recalls, Pepsi officials fell back on logic: the cans were bottled at different plants in different parts of the country, and there was no logical pattern to the alleged tampering incidents. So, there were no recalls: a logical decision. But Pepsi received criticism not for what it said, but for what it didn't say: some believed that it failed to show concern about public safety.

With the more recent reports of accidents involving acceleration problems with Lexus cars, the same issue arose. The first reaction from executives at Lexus? "Let's investigate." The public outcry: "Show some concern, *then* investigate."

The BP oil spill off the Gulf of Mexico generated the same reaction: Outrage at the executives in charge at the time of the spill because of their public comments that showed more regard for the intrusion on their personal time to handle the accident than for the loss of life and property.

The same sentiment is true on an individual level. People have to feel your concern before they hear your words.

Tip 3. Demonstrate Cooperation with Good Intentions.

To be credible, you must demonstrate that you are acting in good faith to the best of your knowledge and ability. People must believe that you want to cooperate to help them achieve their personal and career goals. People will forgive you for poor judgment, but they will rarely forgive you for poor intentions.

Tip 4. Be Consistent.

"He's flip-flopping again. Yesterday, he announced to an audience in Detroit that blah, blah, blah. Then this morning in San Francisco, he told a group that he intended to blah, blah, blah." Politicians will do anything to sidestep that charge of being inconsistent. Inconsistency can be disastrous to a candidate, an advertising campaign, or a child.

Have you ever been around a household with young children who have a hard time going to bed at night? At 8:00, Mom says, "Johnny, time to turn off the TV, pick up your toys, and go to bed." Johnny makes no move. At 8:05, Mom says, "Johnny, I'm not going to tell you again to turn off the TV and pick up your toys. If you don't obey me, I'm not going to let you watch TV tomorrow night." At 8:10, Mom says, "Johnny, pick up your things, turn off the TV, and go to bed now! I'm not going to tell you again. If you don't mind me, you're not going to watch TV tomorrow night." Johnny picks up a couple of toys and continues to watch TV. At 8:20, Mom turns off the TV for Johnny. "Here, I'll help you. It's time for bed." She picks up most of the toys and gets Johnny in bed at 8:30.

The next night, same routine. The third night, same routine. The fourth night at 8:20, Mom says, "Johnny, put away your toys, turn off the TV, and go to bed!" As usual, Johnny ignores her. Mom explodes, spanks him, and sends him to bed wailing. She's thinking that the problem is all Johnny's when in reality she's trained him to ignore her by her inconsistency. Her words do not match her actions.

The same thing happens at work. We communicate by our actions and inactions as well as our words. We communicate by which policies we enforce and which policies we don't enforce; by what we allow work time for and what we don't allow work time for; by what we fund and what we don't fund; by what behavior we reward and what behavior we punish; by what we do and what we criticize others for doing; by what we ask for and what we're willing to give in return.

To be credible, our words have to match our policies, performance, and plans. Otherwise, we create a Mom-and-Johnny situation.

Tip 5. Demonstrate Competence.

People flock to experts, star performers, wise decision makers, and winners. People don't intentionally invest their money in poorly performing stocks; neither do they want to invest their trust in people they doubt can achieve what they claim. To be led, either by words or actions, followers need to have faith in your competence to perform. They want to know that you can win the game. They want to know that you can finish the project successfully. They want to know that you can turn the company around. So how do leaders inspire confidence in their abilities while seeming modest and likable as people? They acknowledge their accomplishments as leaders, but avoid arrogance. Difficult, but not impossible. How? The attitude behind the talk turns the tables.

Tip 6. Be Correct.

Few people set out to be incorrect; it's just that when they are missing information, they make assumptions or reason wrongly. Instead of informing, they unintentionally misinform. Whether or not people routinely ask for the source of your information or conclusions, be ready to provide it. If they ask for sources, rather than being offended, welcome such testing questions as credibility checkers. Why would people want sources for relatively insignificant information? Because we test validity on *all* important matters by considering the source. How do we test the source of important information? By checking the credibility of *all* information coming from that same source. Credibility is circular. Credibility in the insignificant breeds credibility for the significant. Once you're caught in an error, credibility creeps back ever so slowly.

Tip 7. Admit What You Don't Know.

When people smell blood, they dig. Here's a conversation that illustrates the fervor generated by the smell of bluff:

"How much does your company contribute to charity each year?"
"Hundreds of thousands of dollars."
"Is most of it to the United Way, or to individual causes?"
"Both."
"What amount goes to the United Way?"
"I think our goal was $240,000."
"Did you meet it?"
"I'm sure we did."
"Many companies don't meet their goals, you know. They just tout the goal as PR and never come through with the money."
"Ours does."
"Were you on the United Way committee?"
"Not exactly."
"What do you mean 'not exactly'?"
"Not this year, I wasn't. But I have a friend who was. And I've served in prior years."

"So you're really not sure of the exact figures this year?"

"Not exactly."

"So you don't know the exact figure donated to the United Way this current year?"

"No."

"So can you tell me the other specific organizations you contribute to regularly?"

"Not without checking."

"So you're guessing at the total amount given to charity each year, right?"

People push when they smell bluff and guff. Witnessing such a conversation feels like watching a shark go after fresh bait. Admitting ignorance is a simple principle, easy to remember, easy to accomplish, but difficult for some people to swallow: nothing makes people believe what you *do* know like admitting what you don't know.

Tip 8. Be Complete.

Are you telling all you know? You need to recognize the difference between lies, half-truths, omissions, and cover-ups. True, but incomplete, statements can lead to false conclusions; literal truth, when offered without complete explanations, can lead to literal lies. Knowing smiles accompanied by long silences can elicit wrong conclusions. Lying happens in numerous ways. Intentions stand center stage here. Ultimately, questionable intentions cast doubt on character.

Tip 9. Stay Current.

Give up outdated data, opinions, and stereotypes. Given today's information overload, data more than two or three years old can't support your decisions. Correct, but outdated, statistics soon become incorrect. Recollect.

Tip 10. Be Clear.

Sometimes the better we understand something, the worse job we do of explaining it; our familiarity makes us careless in describing it. It's difficult to remember when we didn't know something that has become second nature to us. Ambiguity creeps in when we least expect it. Meanings depend on context, tone, timing, personal experience, and reference points. The best test of clarity is the result you see.

Tip 11. Avoid Doublespeak.

The previous tip referred to unintentional ambiguity caused by carelessness or incompetence. With this tip, I'm referring to intentional gobbledygook explanations meant to obscure rather than enlighten, convoluted details and irrelevant facts simmered together to make mush for the ear.

A financial consultant related this situation to me about his audit firm: "We have two boilerplate formats for our reports to clients. When we go into banks and find several ways we can help them, we use the first format. That report gives our findings and list of recommendations right up front. But if we go into banks and can't find much wrong—we don't have many recommendations for improvements and have charged them a big fee for the audit—then we use the second boilerplate. We begin the report with background on our company, the credentials of our auditors, the various audit procedures used, and then we finally get around to the findings and recommendations." He ended with, "But I don't think we fool anybody." He's right. Purposeful gobbledygook only brings one's intentions into question.

Tip 12. Use the Language of Credibility.

When you talk about data or give technical explanations, use factual words, not opinion words. Example: "The data collected on these pumps are *accurate* because ...," not "The data collected on these pumps are *credible* because ..." or "The data collected on these pumps are *comprehensive* because. ..." Of course, both statements could be either true or false. But the words *credible* and *comprehensive* sound like opinion, whereas the word *accurate* sounds factual.

Tip 13. Skip the Confessions of Honesty.

When someone says, "To be honest, I think the project involves far too many suppliers," it makes me think, Are you typically *not* honest with me? "Frankly," "candidly," "to be truthful"—all such phrases imply that what follows—the truth—is the exception for you. That's not a good announcement to build credibility.

Tip 14. Avoid Exaggeration.

Was the score 50 to zip or 30 to 10? Did you have to wait half an hour or half a minute? Did the caller slam down the phone or hesitate to talk? Did the supplier raise the prices on your raw materials 10 percent or 2 percent? Exaggeration makes great humor but destroys credibility.

Tip 15. Evaluate Criticisms and Objections.

If you reject or refute criticisms and objections out of hand, without hearing them out and giving yourself time to consider them fully, you lose credibility. People identify you as a reactor rather than a reflective, credible thinker. The more thorough your consideration of contradictory information, the more credible your final opinion or decision.

Tip 16. Accept Responsibility for Decisions, Actions, and Results Where You Have or Had Some Control.

Watch comments such as the following, unless they are absolutely true: "We had no control over that project in our department." "Upper management made those decisions." "Competitors forced us into those arrangements." "Those policies are set by the government." "If it were my decision, I'd handle it differently." "I wasn't given a say in the matter." Shirkers suffer credibility gaps.

Tip 17. Keep Confidences.

When people know you share personal, confidential matters about others with them, they'll fear that you'll do the same thing where they're concerned. Keeping confidences when "nobody would know you told" speaks volumes about your character. Those who observe your discretion in deciding to keep quiet about hurtful or personal information involving others bridge to other favorable conclusions about your credibility in times of stress.

Tip 18. Avoid Lying "Offstage."

When you lie to a third person in front of a second person (for whatever reason) and that second person knows you're lying, you lose credibility with the second person. Once observers have recognized your willingness to lie to others, they will doubt that you are telling them the truth when you're in a tight spot.

Tip 19. Be Sincere and Genuine.

Sincerity is easy to fake and hard to make. That is, people who pretend to be sincere can pitch an earnest plea, look at you with pleading eyes and a straight face, and promise plums that dance in your head. But genuineness comes from character and is therefore harder to generate on the spot. You either are or you aren't. What you experience is what you share. What you value is what you give. What you say is what you believe.

Tip 20. Be Vulnerable.

Believing people requires risk on the part of others. If others risk trust, they want to know that you share their risk: the risk of being honest; the risk of exposing your own weaknesses and foibles; the risk of telling things that might hurt you if they were used against you; the risk of stepping up to the plate and giving it all you've got when you swing. Taking the risk of being transparent inspires others to risk taking you at face value.

Tip 21. Be Attentive to Perceptions.

I've known people to say, "I'm my own person. It doesn't matter what others think." Yet they feel disappointed when others don't treat them courteously, fail to respect their time, ignore their input, or disregard their information. These same people complain when they don't get the job they want or the salary they expect. They don't understand why the best employees hate to work for them or why their colleagues fail to give their best efforts on team projects. Other people's motivations remain a mystery to them. Gaining buy-in and excellent performance from others always seems like a hit-or-miss situation when they're leading the effort.

Before falling into that same trap, consider this: other people's perceptions create their reality. Your *own* facts, intentions, and motives do not. People can't see how you think and what you intend. Be aware of how your actions *look* to other people. Is that the perception you want to leave?

Tip 22. Make Your Appearance Work for You.

Picture yourself lying on the operating table in a hospital emergency room. A guy in sweats and Nikes jogs toward your bedside and says, "I'm Kelly, the brain surgeon. I'll be ready to operate in a moment. Just let me give you this shot first." Would you have a few second thoughts? Appearance counts. Physical appearance, dress, grooming, posture, presence, and poise either underscore your credibility or damage it. Look the part you want to play so that others will believe you and applaud your lines.

2

Conversing One on One

The way we communicate with others and with ourselves ultimately determines the quality of our lives.

—Tony Robbins

The real art of conversation is not only to say the right thing in the right place but to leave unsaid the wrong thing at the tempting moment.

—Dorothy Nevill

The vacuum created by a failure to communicate will quickly be filled with rumor, misrepresentations, drivel, and poison.

—C. Northcote Parkinson

Blessed is the man who, having nothing to say, abstains from giving in words evidence of the fact.

—George Eliot

Sometimes you have to be silent to be heard.

—Stanislaw J. Lee

Tact is something that if it is there, nobody notices it. But if it not there, everybody notices it.

—No attribution

Think as wise men do, but speak as the common people do.

—Aristotle

It would not be so bad to let one's mind go blank—if one always remembered to turn off the sound.

—No attribution

The meaning of your communication is the response you get.

—John Bandler and Richard Grinder

R are is it for a day to go by without our having to communicate. We even have a special term for people who choose not to participate: hermits. Dialogue in our day-to-day lives creates the difference between misery and defeat, on the one hand, and success and satisfaction, on the other. The following guidelines will help you communicate what you intend in committee meetings, hallway briefings on the state of a project, explanations of your expense account, trade-show-floor exchanges, or dinner with your boss and spouse.

Tip 23. Recognize That Those in Less Powerful Positions Want to Win Your Goodwill; Interpret Their Words and Behavior Accordingly.

If you're the boss, you're going to get more attention to your preferences, quicker responses to your requests, and overt approval of your ideas. Don't, however, jump to the conclusion that all this happens because you're necessarily an excellent communicator, that your requests have more merit than those of others, or that your ideas are necessarily better. If you want honest feedback in your position of power, you'll have to work hard for it.

Tip 24. As a Powerful Person if You Want to Build Rapport with Others, Remove the Status Symbols and Power Barriers.

Be aware of the kind of power you have with different groups. You have *reward* power if you can somehow positively influence what will happen to another person. You have *coercive* power if you can negatively influence another person's future. You have *positional* power if by your position as boss or director or police officer or flight attendant you can force your will upon another. You have *expert* power over someone if you have knowledge that this person needs. You have *referent* power over people if you can influence them through your personality. Being aware of these power pockets forces you to take your interactions with certain people more seriously. They will.

   If you want to minimize this power and relate to others on an equal footing—if you want an honest opinion that they may be reluctant to give—remove the status reminders. You may want to sit beside them, not across the desk from them. You may want to arrive at the cocktail party in your own car, not in a limo. You may want to take off your name badge and introduce yourself without the title. You may want to join them in the lounge rather than invite them to the country club.

Rapport building hinges on such small steps.

Tip 25. Assess Others' Knowledge and Experiences Exactly.

If you assume that your listeners are more knowledgeable than they are, they may misunderstand your message, give up on trying to understand your explanations, or become frustrated or angry because they think you're "putting on airs."

A vice president at a large oil company attended a session where he'd asked the controller to explain to the first-line supervisors and managers how to complete a specific form justifying their annual budget requests. During the opening session, the controller illustrated the budget form using a figure of several million dollars for the purchase of equipment. At the break, the vice president wisely took the controller aside and asked her to lower the dollar amounts so as not to make the supervisors feel small because their responsibilities did not involve such large expenditures. That vice president picked up on an important subtlety.

On the other hand, you can err in the opposite direction. If you assume that your listeners know less than they actually do, they may feel that you are insulting their intelligence, boring them, or wasting their time on information they already know. Aim to meet them exactly at their knowledge and interest level. To do that, ask yourself five questions: What is their primary interest in this situation, event, or issue? How much do they already know, and from what source and perspective are they likely to have received information? How will they use the information for themselves? Why would they want to know this? What reaction will they have to the subject: Skepticism and doubt? Loss of face? Defensiveness? Support? These answers will help you reach them appropriately eye to eye.

Tip 26. Set a Level Playing Field.

Before you speak, make sure that what you're about to say doesn't contain words or phrases that imply your superiority. Example: "I want you to meet Jana Jones, who works for me" versus "I want you to meet Jana Jones, who works *with* me." Example: "Haven't I told you not to bother me with those kinds of details?" versus "I'd prefer that you handle those kinds of details without involving me." Example: "I try to spend as much time abroad as possible when my job allows it" versus "I like to travel when I have the time."

Tip 27. Avoid Coming Across as a One-Directional Communicator.

Several years ago, I was standing in a trade-show booth when a man walked up, stuck out his hand to shake mine, and began: "My name's _____. I notice we're competitors here at the show. We have a booth over the way, number 399. You probably remember that Ford RFP that came out about four months ago. Well, if you're wondering about it, we've got it sewed up. I understand your people bid on it. That was really a formality, because one of the VPs there had already made contact with us and wanted us in. That was an easy sale for us. You know what I mean? Don't you wish all of them were that easy? It's going to be a big contract. Three hundred thousand before they're through. Well, nice to meet you. Just wanted to stop by and say hello."

All of this came out without his ever taking a breath and without my ever having an opportunity (or inclination) to cut in and respond. Don't be a hit-and-run speaker.

Tip 28. Avoid Getting a Reputation as a Manipulator.

People with strong personalities sometimes take advantage of less able communicators—or those with no goal for a particular conversation or meeting. They manipulate others before their victims realize what's happening. They outsmart people by seducing them with flirting. They deceive them with misused facts. They pretend to feel something that they don't. They shame others into acting against their best interests. They dominate others through sheer tone. They play martyr when it suits them. They tempt others with unkept promises and false power. Over time, such tactics work against the people who use them.

Tip 29. Be Interested, Not Just Interesting.

The heart of this principle involves putting aside self-interest long enough to devote attention to someone else. Yes, we are attracted to life-of-the-party people because they amuse us. But interested people win us. They make us want to stick to them like glue. Nothing is so flattering as to have someone show personal interest in our job, our background, our experience, or our views.

Tip 30. To Express Interest in Someone, Soften Whatever It Is You're Doing.

Soften your voice, soften your tone, soften your smile, soften your posture, soften your touch, soften your eye contact, or soften your nod. Softening communicates openness.

Tip 31. Use Radical Language to Be a Leader.

You have to shake people out of complacency in order to lead them in a new direction. Focus to inspire followership. Intrigue others to tempt them to make a change with you.

Tip 32. Have a Sense of the Dramatic When You Talk.

Would you rather have someone tell you about a movie or see it for yourself? So would I. We like action—in the voice, in the face, in the body, in the scene. Add a funny twist to the story. Use description to set the scene. Add gestures to give a story a sense of place. The only benefit you as a conversationalist have over a manual or an e-mail is animation. Use it.

Tip 33. Learn to Self-Disclose.

People feel loyal to you only when you're willing to let them get to know you. They can't like someone they don't know. If you consider the closest, most meaningful relationships you have in the workplace, they're most often based on self-disclosure. Those initial conversations and invitations are often overt: "Let's spend some time together after work—I'd like to get to you know you better," or, "Well, I've told you my life story. Tell me about yourself. You have family?"

Practice disclosure by sharing facts about yourself—where you work, projects you've handled, hobbies you enjoy, trips you've taken, sales you've lost. The subject doesn't matter as much as the fact that you're willing to share the information. Over time and with practice, you'll gradually feel at ease when sharing your values, opinions, and goals. The relationship will develop accordingly.

That, of course, doesn't mean you're going to have the energy to unload in every conversation. However, if a friend self-discloses and you fail to do so, that friend may suddenly feel that you're no longer interested. He feels an imbalance in the conversation. Therefore, when you're too tired or preoccupied to share mutually, at least let the friend know that it's a lack of time or energy rather than unconcern.

And don't think that self-disclosing will necessarily make you more vulnerable to attack and hurt. Just the opposite is true. Self-disclosure can bring you the protection of friendship and loyalty from those who come to understand and appreciate your values, ideas, and intentions. Emotional distance creates mental illness. To disclose improves your mental health.

Tip 34. Confess Your Weaknesses.

If you want to be approachable, you have to present yourself as human. You have to be willing to let others see your weaknesses and your blunders. If you admit a weakness, you are demonstrating to the other person that you trust her to keep your secret. That person, in turn, will feel that she can trust you with personal confidences. Under this principle, I've heard people own up to eating a whole pie, losing a deal because of arriving too late for a meeting, and not liking their moody teenagers. Rather than pounce on such secrets, most people will take a peek at your deficiencies and then help you hide them you so that you won't be embarrassed. Your willingness to appear open before others allows them to identify with you as a kindred human being.

Tip 35. Keep in Mind That Being Logical May Be Ineffective.

Communication involves the emotions as well as the intellect. Emotional arguments have proved very successful where logic has failed to move people. An appeal to someone's self-interest may ensure more buy-in than a logical explanation of fairness to all concerned.

Tip 36. Visualize the End, and Then Construct the Means.

Decide what reaction you want from your audience, and then decide how to structure your message so that you get that reaction. Do you want your audience to be emotional about the decision? Then choose anecdotes and stories. Do you want them to come to a rational conclusion? Then choose facts and logic to develop your idea. Do you want them to get involved personally in implementing your plan? Then apply your ideas to the work in their own departments. Picture the goal, and then decide how to develop your idea to get people there.

Tip 37. Pay Attention to the Meta-Message.

Gerard Nierenberg coined the term *meta-message* to describe those messages that come through between the lines; they come from the context, relationship, timing, tone, purpose, and person speaking. For example, Susan calls her colleague Jack for the third time in one day. She says, "Hi, it's me again." He responds, "I'm working on the Caliver report; it's due in half an hour." His message is not intended as an update on his progress. His words and tone mean, "Why are you bothering me again? I don't have time to talk now."

Another example: A husband comes home with a new sports car. The wife asks, "Why did you buy that car?" He responds, "The gas mileage is as good as anything else on the road." Her tone and words didn't ask for his reasons for the purchase. Given their earlier conversations about his being selfish and never considering her opinions, she meant, "Why did you not include me in your decision?"

If you've ever wondered why someone responds negatively to "positive" words, consider the meta-message. A senior executive walks into a meeting and says, "Sorry to keep you waiting. A call came through from London that I simply had to take." Another executive in the corner may greet the late arriver's apology with a scowl; to him, the meaning was, "I outrank you, and I have the power to keep you waiting."

A boss says to a subordinate, "I simply can't approve that transfer for you. It's not in your best interest in the long run." The subordinate may reject the seemingly "caring" statement and instead get the meta-message that he is a child in need of protection for his own good.

We deal with some meta-messages every day and recognize them as such. You say to a good friend who tosses out a ridiculous idea: "You're crazy—that's off the wall." Given your big smile and strong relationship, she knows you really mean, "Thanks for the laugh." We understand such.

With other meta-messages, we walk away from a conversation feeling disappointed or "zapped," but we don't understand why. With any meta-message, a response to only the words is insufficient. If an argument or a discussion follows, it will most certainly be off the subject. Listen and respond to the meta-message; that's where the action is.

Tip 38. Hide Behind the Words if You Want to Avoid Hearing the Message.

Because meaning comes from relationships, timing, circumstances, and intentions, words play only a small part—but they can serve as an excuse if you want to pretend not to understand the message.

> HUSBAND: (To wife at convention.) When are you coming home?

> WIFE: Probably sometime Saturday. (Pretending not to understand that his tone says, "I think you're staying longer than necessary," she simply answers the question.)

Tip 39. Match Your Tone to Your Intentions.

Different linguists and psychologists have provided a variety of labels to describe habitual styles or tones of communicating:

Accusing/blaming. "It's your fault we missed that deadline." "Don't ask me why we didn't hire more people to start with—I knew better." "Well, I was only reacting to what you said earlier about not having sufficient budget."

Appeasing/placating. "Please, let's just forget it. It doesn't really matter." "Would you please consider changing the deadline?" "Just tell me what you want me to do now, and I'll get on it."

Computing/disassociating. "The deadline is August 1." "Two people cannot get the job done." (There are no personal references, no feelings, no emotion.)

Analyzing/diagnosing. "The contract did not really call for an August 1 deadline. You, as manager, selected that date. Was your intention to test our commitment? To force us to abandon our quality procedures?" "Why are you saying that to me?" "You know, the reason you're feeling that way is that you're insecure yourself."

Dogmatic. "We will lose the business if we miss that first deadline." "It can't be done that way." "You're wrong." "It has to be blue."

Dramatic/Effusive. "We kill ourselves and you're still not pleased." "This is the stupidest plan we've ever used—there's not a company on earth that could meet that deadline." "Either give me an answer today, or I quit." "I wouldn't transfer her out of here for a million dollars; she knows all there is to know about inventory management."

> *Straightforward/leveling.* "I'm disappointed that we missed the dead-
> line. I had two people helping, and I thought that would be suffi-
> cient, but evidently it wasn't. We need to hire more help."

Do you recognize any of these as a habitual style of yours (or someone you know)? If so, is that the way you intend to come across?

Tip 40. Avoid a Patronizing Tone.

Patronizing people sound as though they're doing you a favor by enlightening you. Whether such a person knows anything about the subject or not,
he always expresses an opinion—and makes those with more expertise feel
stupid for bothering to have such expertise. You get a strong urge to argue
with this individual, even if you don't disagree with him, just because of
his superior, haughty manner.

Tip 41. Don't Talk Down to People—Even Kids.

Instruction manuals that contain statements such as these make users think
they were written for an idiot. If so, the idiot certainly wouldn't be reading the manual! "Plug the appliance into the electrical socket." "Accidents
frequently happen." "Make sure your computer is turned on." "Make sure
your smartphone is charged."

Tip 42. Avoid Moralizing.

We like "lessons," but generally not when they come from someone who
adopts a mother-superior tone.

> EMPLOYEE: "We found four widgets that had the threads stripped."

> MANAGER: "Every time you skip the inspection, you have things
> like that happen. Your people are careless."

Habitual moralizing responses grate on people's sensitivities, particularly if the messages come from peers.

Tip 43. Hear Silence the Way It's Intended.

There's the old adage, "Silence is consent." People who believe that are in
for a big disappointment. When you make a statement that's met with
silence, it can have several meanings:

- The person is reflecting on what you said and considering your
  opinion.

- The person is in complete agreement and thinks that no response is necessary.
- The person thinks that she understands what you said (and is unaware of not understanding it).
- The person agrees and intends to act immediately.
- The person agrees but has no intention of acting.
- The person is too angry to speak.
- The person is reflecting on what you said and rejecting your opinion.
- The person is too overcome with revulsion to speak.
- The person is giving you an immediate rebuke.
- The person wasn't listening and is nodding with his mind in neutral.
- The person hears you and is confused, but doesn't want to appear ignorant by asking you to elaborate further on something that you think is perfectly clear.
- The person is so confused that she doesn't know how to ask for clarification.
- The person is in a state of shock.
- The person is depressed.
- The person is stalling.
- The person feels too powerless to respond.

If you want to confirm what the other person's silence means, stick around long enough to read further body language or hear further comments to get confirmation.

Making a statement in a staff meeting that is greeted with silence can mean total opposition or total agreement. It's better to find out which than to have the project, policy, or procedure sabotaged later. It's up to you, the talker, to probe for the meaning of the silence.

Tip 44. Recognize the Implications of What Isn't Said.

"You really did a superb job this time" can bring questions about what was wrong with the job completed last month. When you congratulate people for their accomplishments, consider who in the meeting didn't receive congratulations. When you don't hear from a key client who typically calls in December to ask about anticipated price increases for the coming year, consider why not.

Simply recognize that not all messages are delivered with words. Messages that are expected but never heard sometimes carry more weight than spoken words.

Tip 45. Use Silence to Your Advantage.

If you don't want to commit yourself with an oral response, you can use silence to mask your own opinions or emotions. With practice, you can gain attention with silence (by a long pause before you respond—one that builds suspense and adds weight to what follows), or you can avoid attention with silence (as if you've "moved on" mentally).

Silence can build intimacy. Only when people don't know each other well are they uncomfortable with silence between their exchanges. People who feel intimate with each other understand silence as a "communion of thought."

Comfortable silence gives you time to reflect on what has been said, to make a decision, to change the subject, to create psychological distance from the past, and to get ready to move on mentally. Silence is a very versatile conversational tool.

Tip 46. Eliminate Contradictory Body Language and Words.

Your customer asks you if you can expedite the order "this one time," and you grimace while saying yes. Your colleague asks if you've got time to lend an ear about a problem he's having in closing a sale. You say, "Okay, yeah, sure" while glancing at your watch and texting a friend. Your boss asks if you're sure you can have the report finished by 5 o'clock. You say it'll be no problem while sighing heavily, running your fingers through your hair, and then beginning to massage your temples as if you've got a splitting headache. Either say what you mean or act out what you mean. But don't make the messages contradictory.

Tip 47. Check for the Hidden Agenda Before You Bite Hook, Line, and Sinker.

Does the other person's body language support or contradict her words? If so, why would she want to conceal the truth? Does this person's message contradict common sense or contradict what the person has said or done in the past? Does this person seem to be beating around the bush with a small stick rather than landing it in the middle? Do you have a "gut feeling"—racing heart, sweaty palms, knots in the stomach, dry mouth, tense shoulders, a pounding headache? If so, your body is telling you to look behind the words for a hidden motive.

Tip 48. Believe Body Language over Words.

Body language trumps words. Unless someone is a superb actor, his body language will display the truth of the matter.

Tip 49. Don't Polarize People.

Some people get great joy out of driving a wedge between people rather than bringing them together. They bring up controversial issues at cocktail parties. They play devil's advocate in every meeting and recruit associate demons to side with them. They pass on thoughtless comments that one group or person says about another "just to make them aware." Such a person's mission in life is to cause division; as a result, she usually gets knee-jerk reactions and decisions based on emotion rather than solid reasoning.

Tip 50. Voice Your Disagreement After, Not Before, Asking the Other Person's Reasons for an Opinion.

If someone expresses an opinion and you immediately express an opposing view, you both lose. Why? Because the person who first expressed an opinion will often consider your contradiction rude or the beginning of an argument. A typical response will be for the person to refer to the earlier statement and begin delineating reasons as support.

You both win, however, if you hear an opinion with which you disagree and then immediately ask the person expressing that opinion to elaborate on the reasons behind it. Then, if you feel comfortable with the situation, you can state that you hold a different opinion and give your reasons. At the end of the conversation, both of you will have learned something about the other side, and neither will feel as though you've had an argument/disagreement.

Quite possibly, if you had stated your disagreement early on, the other person would simply have kept quiet, preventing a valuable exchange of ideas.

Tip 51. Bring Up a "Touchy" Subject Only with a Warning.

Prepare people with a lead-in. "I know this isn't a popular topic and some of you don't want to make a commitment one way or the other, but...," or, "I know most of us hate prejudice in all its forms, and it's not my intention to pinpoint ....," or, "Some people definitely do not share my concerns about X, but I want to express them anyway...."

Otherwise, with such an abrupt change of subjects—and introducing a touchy one at that—others may "pop off" and embarrass themselves or "can" you in the process.

Tip 52. Use Indirectness to Test the Waters Before Diving In.

Toss out a comment indirectly, get the other person's reaction, and then go ahead with the comment or claim that you were unclear about your meaning. It's a face-saving ploy to get the other person to commit to his attitudes, feelings, or opinions first.

Tip 53. Avoid Dogmatic Pronouncements.

"That's not the way it happened at all." "You're being ridiculous." "You can't do that." "Are you crazy?" "Everybody knows that..." "That'll do no good at all." "You're wrong." "That's not true." "You misunderstood." Such statements make enemies of friends or followers.

Tip 54. Consider "I" Messages to Make Others Less Defensive.

If I say to you, "You're wrong about that contract!" you'll probably be taken aback and feel defensive. If, on the other hand, I say, "I disagree with your interpretation of that contract," you're likely to respond, "Oh, where?" or, "Well, you're entitled to your opinion and I'm entitled to mine."

If the store owner says to the customer, "You must sign this agreement before we will process the order," the customer may respond, "Oh, yeah? I don't have to do anything with your paperwork. I can walk out of here." But if the store owner says, "I need to have this paperwork signed so that our processors can set up the delivery date," the typical customer will respond internally, "Okay, I need to sign it if I want to get delivery without a hassle."

The difference between an "I" message and a "you" message sounds enormous.

Tip 55. Substitute *And* Statements for *But* Statements.

A *but* statement negates the first part of your sentence. The hearer ignores the first part and focuses on what comes after the *but*.

But statement: "I respect your work, but I don't agree with this new idea."

And statement: "I respect your work. And I have reservations about this new idea."

But statement: "I hear what you're saying, but I don't agree."

And statement: "I hear what you're saying. And I have a different view."

But statement: "I understand your point, but you're missing mine."

And statement: "I understand your point, and I'd like you to understand mine."

But statement: "You're dependable, but you're impulsive."

And statement: "You're dependable. And you're also impulsive."

Tip 56. Respond Rather Than React.

Reacting to comments or a situation implies a knee-jerk, uncontrolled response without thought to the implications or results. Responding to someone's comments or a specific situation means a deliberate, thoughtful response that leads to the result you intend.

Tip 57. Defend Your Ideas Without Being Defensive.

Defending ideas shows commitment and analytical forethought. Defending your position to others in such a way as to convince them to come around to your view is almost always appropriate, as long as you are straightforward in your words and even-tempered in your tone.

Being defensive, on the other hand, puts people in a negative light. The defensive person steps into the arena of emotion, responding with excuses and fears. Moving away from logic, a defensive person moves away from credibility with listeners.

Tip 58. Don't Make Arguing an Ego Trip.

When you attach ego to disagreement, you typically stop listening and start planning your counterattack. You often miss what the other person is really saying; "winning the argument" becomes your mission rather than hearing an opposing view and honestly deciding whether you might agree with some of it or whether you are even more convinced that you're right. In other words, don't go after a win as if you're playing tennis. Look at the difference as an opportunity either to confirm your own thinking or to change it.

Tip 59. Dig for the Bigger Problem Beneath Arguments About Trivialities.

A buyer says to the sales rep, "I thought you told me you'd call Wednesday morning?"

"Yes, I did. But the management meeting lasted all the way to noon. I hope the hour's delay didn't inconvenience you."

"Yes, it did. I've already placed my order with another firm."

You can be sure that the problem was bigger than this one hour's delay.

An assistant says to the boss, "Do you or do you not want coffee inside the conference room?"

"Just put it outside the door so that we can get to it at breaks."

"Well, last time you wanted it inside the room."

"Yes, but we have a different purpose and group for this meeting."

"I've got sugar, not Sweet'N Low."

"Please buy artificial sweetener, like I told you."

"I'll have to go to the store myself; the cafeteria here is out."

"Then go to the store."

You can be sure that the difficulty is over something larger than the coffee details for the meeting. The person who seems to be "unreasonable" or "difficult" is usually hurt on a deeper level. The trivial argument represents a symptom.

Tip 60. Be Firm, but Not Inflexible.

You want to state your opinions convincingly and forcefully so that you can influence others—if that happens to be your goal. Be firm enough that people don't consider you wishy-washy, but don't disregard what others say or feel. Your topic, timing, and temperament should display the appropriate firmness and flexibility in any given situation.

Tip 61. Adopt a Problem-Solving Orientation When Presenting a Problem.

Before going to a customer with a problem . . . or to a boss with a mistake . . . or to a spouse or friend with a disappointment, spend some time working on

a solution. You don't want to hide a problem, of course, if delay will only com-
pound it. But rather than focusing on how a mistake, problem, or disappointment occurred, focus your conversation on resolving, improving, or
altering the outcome.

Tip 62. Define Things in Terms of Cooperation Rather Than Competition.

Look for ways to cooperate on projects, decisions, or goals rather than
focusing on differences. "Well, it's clear that we both want to keep the customer happy. You think it's by price, and I think it's by better service. Let's
weigh both of those." With such a statement, you focus on cooperating to
win, not competing to see who's "right" and who's "wrong."

Tip 63. Recognize Unanswerable Questions.

Ever since we were in fourth grade and Ms. Witherspoon asked us the capital of Louisiana, we've felt compelled to answer questions. And if we are
in a position of leadership or authority, we feel the urge even more strongly.
But some questions defy answers. Identify which they are, and save yourself the frustration.

Tip 64. Don't Rain on People's Parades.

Some people go through life focused on telling people what won't work
for them, what they should or should not have done, and what will create trouble for them. When people share a dream, they most often want
support—not caution. Think twice before becoming the naysayer about
people's ideas, plans, and dreams.

Tip 65. Frame the Positive Angle.

How can you position what you want to say so that people accept the message in a positive light? A manager at a large computer company had as
his mission to put together an online database that would make life easier
for all his telephone support people, but he could get no cooperation from
them. Here was the situation.

As part of a licensing agreement and fee, users received telephone
support by calling an 800 number. The problem was that when a call came
in on a complex question, the reps would spend hours researching the
answer, but the system kept no record of that call or answer. Therefore,

there was a lot of duplication of research effort, a big backlog of customer calls, and numerous complaints about delays. The manager's goal was to have the reps record their answers and send him a copy so that he could put the answers into an online database. But, despite his explanation of how this would help, he got absolutely no cooperation from the reps.

After reading his email to solicit their written answers, I understood why. The email began: "As you know, we are legally obligated to provide a four-hour response on all customer calls. Currently, we are backlogged with customer calls and making little or no progress; complaints continue to grow...." A negative approach.

I suggested this rewording: "How would you like to get through your stack of backlogged customer calls quickly? How would you like to have all the researched answers to customer calls at the tip of your fingers? Help is on the way. For the next 30 days, I'm asking you simply to record and forward to me a copy of...." This positive approach generated a much better response.

Positive framing means to say what you're for, not what you're against. Say what you're going to do, not what you're not going to do. Say what you can do, not what you can't do.

The positive angle takes a little thought, but the results are well worth the effort.

Tip 66. Use Positive Rather Than Negative Words.

Clinical psychologists say that we hear and remember positive wording better than negative wording—particularly instructions. When someone reads a sign that says, "DO NOT DUMP TRASH HERE," that person has to switch tracks. "Hmmm. I can't dump trash here. Then where? Oh, I can dump trash over there." However, if the sign reads, "DUMP TRASH IN THE BIN NEAR THE BACK DOOR," the person can avoid the switching technique.

Not: "I wasn't able to reach him on the phone."

But: "We never spoke to him by phone."

Not: "I don't know whether I should make that purchase."

But: "I question the wisdom of that purchase."

Not: "I don't know many people here."

But: "I know none of the people here."

Not: "I can't have this ready until Friday."

But: "I can have this ready for you on Friday."

Not: "They can't correct that problem until they redesign the motor."

But: "When they redesign the motor, they're going to correct that problem."

Not: "Our managers don't communicate with one another."

But: "Our managers should find ways to communicate about cross-departmental projects on a regular basis."

Not: "We'll have to go into debt."

But: "We will issue bonds."

The positive message or instruction sinks in more easily, further, and faster.

Tip 67. Place Positive Statements Before Neutral Ones.

A husband and wife sit down to the dinner table for a bowl of soup. She tastes the soup and says, "Did you put oregano in this soup?" He responds, "Yes, I certainly did. But not enough for you to taste it—you're so particular. You're going to know the next time I volunteer to cook dinner." She would have gotten a much better response with a positive lead-in: "This soup tastes different somehow. I like it. Did you put oregano in it?"

When people hear a neutral statement, they may be tempted to "read into it" past conversations or react defensively for any number of reasons. It's better to use the positive statement first so that the person knows how to interpret what follows.

Tip 68. Express Your Opinions as Opinions Rather Than as Irrefutable Facts.

The difference is usually one of tone and word choice. *Fact:* "The contract will turn on delivery date. We'll lose them." *Opinion:* "I think the contract will turn on delivery date. I'm afraid we'll lose them." *Fact:* "Gary will resign if we don't give him this raise." *Opinion:* "Gary has been interviewing with other firms. I think he'll resign if we don't come through with this raise." Others will be less defensive when you use such wording, and you'll save face if you're wrong.

Tip 69. Express Your Opinions as Statements, Not as Questions.

"Don't you think that restaurant is too expensive?" is likely to get a response such as, "No, not really." The other person will continue with her plans, and you'll feel as though your opinion was ignored. Instead, respond to the statement of plans with, "I think that restaurant is too expensive." Then other people can agree or disagree, but at least they'll understand that you were stating an opinion for consideration.

Tip 70. Identify Your Own Feelings, Needs, and Opinions so You Can Permit Others to Do the Same.

If you're in the habit of suppressing what you really want to say, denying yourself the opportunity to stand up for your rights, or squashing your opinions for the sake of harmony, then you'll gradually lose your ability to read other people's verbal cues. You'll lose your sense of listening between the lines. Claim your rights and need to express yourself so that you can feel comfortable when others claim those same rights with you.

Tip 71. Own Your Statements.

Put yourself into your wording. State your opinions as if you own them:

Not: "This food isn't good."

But: "This butter tastes rancid to me."

Not: "You get so hyper about money."

But: "I think you get supercritical about how I spend money."

Not: "That office next door is too loud."

But: "I find it hard to concentrate with that hammering going on next door."

Not: "Just drop the subject, please."

But: "I don't think we're getting anywhere with this discussion. What do you say if we just table this discussion for another week?"

Not: "Relax, there's no problem."

But: "I think you should relax until next week when you know for sure if there's a problem."

When you stake a claim to an opinion, people give it respect.

Tip 72. Say What's on Your Mind Without Shifting to a Hostile Tone.

When anger threatens to overcome you, breathe deeply, slow down, and lower rather than raise your voice. Your words and opinions will sound firm and factual, not emotional and irrational.

Tip 73. Don't Switch from "You" to "Me" and Back to "They" When You Want a Response About Your Own Situation.

A colleague met me in the hall after my speech about communication and productivity with this comment: "You know what you ought to do when you start to work here? You ought to tell them you have to have your own laptop and setup at home because otherwise they won't let you switch to flexible hours. I've told them that I set personal goals like you advocate in your speech, and I can be very productive working alone at home. But my boss is old school; they just don't see how they can manage an at-home employee. Never mind that almost a third of the workforce works from home these days! You have to be someone they want to hire badly and then use that as a bargaining chip before you accept a job these days."

Meaning? When he began the conversation about *me*, I thought he was commenting on the possibility that *I* personally might want employment with his company. Then I gathered that he might be talking about his own personal frustration with not getting approval for at-home work. Finally, I concluded that he was expressing a general opinion about how to bargain for approval to work at home—and offering that opinion for me to share in my next speech.

The principle involves ownership. It's better to talk *to* me, *about you*, or *about others*. People can't tell the players without the proper pronouns—*I, me, you, they,* and *we.*

Tip 74. Don't Tell Others How to Think or Feel.

People resent those who presume to read their minds—even if those presumptions are correct. Example: "We know you'll like the carpet we're shipping equally as well" generates an "Oh, yeah?" Example: "Certainly you can appreciate the situation you've put us in" generates, "No, I can't." Example: "As I'm sure you're aware" triggers "No, I wasn't." Example: "We know you'll find the trip exciting and profitable for all your staff" elicits, "I'll be the judge of that."

Tip 75. Let Others Vent Their Emotions so That They Can Hear You.

When people "charge" you with angry words, you'll do better if you let them have their say rather than trying to stop the flow in midstream. When they get cut off, they can't listen to the other side of the story or to your explanation, because they want you to hear how they feel. Think twice before making these comments: "Please take a few moments to compose yourself, and then we'll talk," or, "Just wait a minute, now," or, "Stop yelling at me." Instead, encourage others to flush themselves of emotion. They'll be drained of the anger or excitement and better able to hear your response.

Tip 76. Seek Out the Causes of Behavior; They'll Be More Worthwhile and Revealing Than the Behavior Itself.

When there's a dispute or problem that leads you to question somebody about what was said, to whom, about what, and in what circumstances, the tendency is to dwell on the chronological sequence. To resolve the issue more quickly and more effectively, focus on the "why." Use probes such as these: "Why do you think Barack said that to you?" "Why did you think I wanted the calendars today?" "What did you think would happen if you told Jerry about the delay?" "Why did you think replacing the machine would be a better solution than repairing it?" The "whys" are a preventative measure; they tell you how to work around future misunderstandings.

Tip 77. Express an Opposing Viewpoint to Build Credibility, to Entertain, or to Do Someone a Favor.

Most people get bored with those who always agree with them. Can you imagine trying to read a novel without all the repartee between hero and heroine? Differences of opinion stoke the fire. The same holds true even in a live social setting. My son, who was contemplating dumping his current girlfriend for a new one, once remarked: "I can talk to Patty even better than Carole. Carole just says what she *thinks* I want to hear. Patty really tells me what she thinks."

It's not an opposing opinion that upsets most people; they react negatively only when the differing opinion comes across with a hostile or superior attitude.

Tip 78. Be Tactful, Not Offensive or Insensitive.

To be more specific: When you're brief, be polite. If you're aggressive, smile when you say it. If you're emphatic, be pleasant with the command or opinion. If you're negative, be diplomatic with your word choice. If you're right, don't rub it in.

Tact calls for two essentials: Be alert enough to know when tact is called for, and be quick-witted enough to find graceful wording.

Tip 79. Don't Ask Others to Cover for Your Insensitivity.

Administrative assistants will have a special place in heaven for their role in softening the blows to others' self-esteem caused by insensitive bosses who "can't be bothered about feelings when there's work to be done."

Tip 80. Consider the Price of "Nice."

When you, for whatever reason, decide to be "nice" as a way of life, you may be doing yourself and another person serious harm. If you make a habit of not speaking up to disagree, not stating your feelings, or not making waves about actions that involve you, you may grow resentful. And that resentment frequently leaks out in other ways—by your sabotaging projects, by creating emotional distance from another person, by doing less than your best, or by exploding over minor issues.

As a result, when you later respond with reasoned resentment, your behavior is labeled "irrational." Worse, feelings on both sides of the relationship grow cold, and the relationship withers.

Tip 81. Verify Assumptions—Your Own and Those of Others.

A manufacturer's rep was puzzled by a client who refused to accept a "line through" on his quotation for office furniture. When the customer changed his mind about the color of a product, the rep told him simply to ink through the change and return the contract, thinking the customer would value the speed in getting his furniture ordered and delivered. On the contrary, the customer delayed placing his order for another three days while the rep sent a clean contract with the one-item change. Why neatness over speed? The purchasing agent's boss valued neat paperwork and considered inked changes to be "sloppy work." So much for assumptions about what customers value.

We make similar invalid assumptions almost daily. As a newlywed, I stumbled to the kitchen at 4:00 a.m. to cook my college student husband a full breakfast before he went off to his summer roofing job. About two months into the routine, I left the kitchen for a moment and then returned to see my husband scraping his scrambled eggs into the disposal. "What's the matter? They weren't done right?" I asked.

"Sure, they're fine."

"Then why didn't you eat them?"

"Honey, I'm sorry. I just have trouble eating eggs and toast at 4:00 a.m."

"But I thought you said you liked a big breakfast—that your mom always cooked you a big breakfast."

"I did. But that wasn't at 4:00 a.m."

No more early mornings for me in the kitchen.

Of course, we don't become aware of our assumptions until something happens to let us know that those assumptions are not shared. It's impossible to verify all assumptions before taking action or responding, and it's impossible to trace assumptions back to what exactly led us to make them. The goal is to be alert to the pitfalls.

For example, "I noticed that you didn't turn in any referrals for prospects on the new accounts. Does that mean you're upset about the compensation program?" Such a probe gives the other person responsibility for denying or verifying such feelings.

If someone winked and said to you, "I heard the pilot had a difficult time landing the plane because of a 'temporary physical condition,'" what would you think? That the pilot was intoxicated? Maybe asleep? Or pregnant and suffering morning sickness? Did you consider that the pilot might be female?

We typically assume that everybody sees things the way we do, values the same things we do, and wants the same things we do. Assumptions blind us, limit our thinking, and bring us to wrong conclusions.

Tip 82. Check Out Inferences.

We hear words, and we draw conclusions from those words. That can be a critical communication gaffe. Make a habit of checking out what you think the words, tone of voice, body language, and context mean. You could be right; you could be wrong.

> MANAGER: "I still have not seen your report." (The statement could be an observation, yet it contains the word *still*, as if the manager might be exasperated.)

> EMPLOYEE: "I'm sorry. We had three people out this week. Are you wondering if the project is going to be finished on time?" (The employee checks out the manager's real concern.)

Tip 83. Read Others' Cues and Clues to Determine the "So What?"

When people make statements about "they" or "other people" when presenting a sorry state of affairs, you may be puzzled as to the significance. Why are they telling you this? To determine the answer, use "so what?" probes: "What does this mean to you and your job?" or "So how does this policy affect you personally?" or "So, are you concerned personally about the results?" With your probing question, you're giving people "permission" to be open with you and get personal about their feelings or concerns. Then you can personalize your response and be appropriately empathetic.

Tip 84. Check Out Hunches When Someone Denies Intentions.

People often reveal things that they don't intend to reveal. Then, when you question them directly about whether they feel this way or that way, they become vulnerable, cautious, and guarded. If you tip your hand with a comment such as, "Are you saying you think Bill was wrong in firing that consultant?" the other person often becomes suddenly aware that the feeling he intended to hide has become transparent. People will deny such sentiments if you push them. Before you tip your hand, check out hunches by asking less direct questions to verify the person's true intentions.

Tip 85. Challenge Generalizations.

"The marketing people never consider the credit risks involved when they make those offers." "Management doesn't give a whit about the long-term effects on our families." "Customers won't pay extra for a feature like that." Always dig for the basis in reality. Collect the specifics as evidence before you accept the generalization as truth.

Tip 86. Test Old Axioms.

Conventional wisdom can be dangerous to your future if you accept axioms at face value. Besides, they're often contradictory: "He who hesitates is lost" versus "Fools rush in where angels fear to tread." "In the counsel of many is wisdom" versus "YOU can never please everybody." "Don't make waves" versus "Be a risk taker." Don't accept truisms out of hand simply because they've been around a long time. Any truth has its exceptions. Rather than pass off some glib cliché as your own opinion, reconsider its truth in the light of each new situation.

Tip 87. When You're Listening, Have a Penchant for Details; When You're Speaking, Take Your Cue from the Listener and Your Purpose.

If you're the listener, consider yourself the leader. After hearing the big-picture message, sift through the details to see if they really support the conclusion you just heard. Look for nuances of meaning, gaps in logic, and further application in other tasks or situations. On the other hand, if you're the speaker, let the listener lead. Give as much or as little detail as the listener's interest and your purpose dictate. No more and no less.

Tip 88. Differentiate Between Showing Deference and Being Patronizing.

The difference is one of attitude and choice. People show deference when they consciously choose not to embarrass someone, when they keep quiet so as not to offend someone, or when they respond with respect because of someone's position or age. The attitude that others hear through the words shows respect, acceptance, and graciousness.

A patronizing attitude, on the other hand, comes through in facial expressions, sighs, knowing winks, or direct comments that "excuse" the other person: "Of course, operators, we don't expect you to be able to understand the inner workings of these machines. We'll worry about a failure should that occur." The attitude that shows through the words or gesture is patient tolerance and superiority.

Tip 89. Avoid False Courtesy.

"Do you mind if I speak up?" "May I say something?" "If you'll allow me to state an opinion..." "If you're open to suggestions, I think..." "Not that my opinion is worth much to you, but..." Such phrasing has nothing to do with courtesy; it's thinly masked hostility.

Tip 90. Get People's Attention First if You Really Want Them to Hear You.

Conversation is common. If you want people to really pay attention to what you're saying, you have to rise above the norm. Here are four options:

Make a sudden move. If you're sitting in the doctor's waiting room reading and somebody beside you stands up, you automatically look up—even if you know who that person is and why she is standing up. Movement attracts attention. If you want someone who seems preoccupied to listen to you, stand up and move across the room to speak. Lean forward at the table to present your ideas. If you're standing in the hallway, ask the person to follow you into an open office space. Just move.

Repeat. If you're puzzled by a road sign, you reread it—maybe several times. People sometimes need more than one hearing before things sink in. Repetition represents the backbone of commercials. Repeat in several ways or in multiple formats what you want others to hear. Tweet it; post it on your Facebook page; post it to your LinkedIn discussion group.

Be novel. People have short attention spans. If you want to extend their attention beyond the typical 20 seconds, you have to get your point across in a unique way. Be flippant, make a joke, startle with an aggressive statement, make a gross overstatement or understatement, use a unique analogy, or carry on two sides of a dialogue. Just be novel to expand attention to your idea.

Be emotional. Raise your volume, soften your volume, plead, or laugh. Emotion attracts attention to straightforward statements.

Tip 91. When Someone Constantly Interrupts You, Stop Talking Immediately and Abruptly to Make the Interrupter Aware.

You can also courteously call attention to someone's habit of cutting you off: "Pardon me, I'm not finished." "May I finish this thought?" "I didn't get to finish what I was saying." "I need another few seconds to explain why I feel that way." "I didn't get to elaborate a moment ago about my reasons." Making people aware that they're crowding you makes a dramatic impact on them without sounding rude.

Tip 92. Don't Step on Others' Sentences.

Sometimes we so closely identify with or confirm what another person is saying that we jump right in while he's expressing himself. That rapport-building identification should not concern you. But you want to watch habitually crowding others when they speak—not giving them an opportunity to respond, interrupting them, or talking over them with an intent to dominate.

Interrupting can become a bad habit. And some people are not so gracious as to let you get away with it. If you catch yourself frequently interrupting or overlapping other people, get someone to help you with the annoying habit. Ask that person to signal you with a raised hand or the sliced-throat gesture to make you aware when you cut her or others off.

Tip 93. Signal the Other Person When You Receive a Message.

On occasion, the most hurtful response is no response—particularly when the other person has shared deep feelings. At home, probably more often than at work, we are tempted to "sit tight" on a message and not acknowledge that we heard it.

WIFE: I think we should take a four-day weekend soon.

HUSBAND: *(Silence.)*

WIFE: It has been six months since we've been away together.

HUSBAND: *(Silence.)*

WIFE: What do you think?

HUSBAND: Okay, okay, okay. I'll check my calendar tomorrow. What do you expect me to do about it tonight?

The husband doesn't realize that he escalated the conversation simply because he gave no acknowledgment that he heard the first comment. Acknowledge another person's comment to you and you'll be surprised how quickly the "nagging" from a parent, peer, or spouse stops.

Tip 94. Avoid Playing Tour Guide Through Your Own Conversation.

This habit surfaces after each statement: "Am I not right?" "Correct?" "You follow me?" "You understand?" "Okay?" With me?" "Clear to this point?" Such hand-holding comments lend an air of false patience with a slow learner.

Tip 95. Give Glib Reassurance Sparingly.

"Don't worry; it'll turn around for you." "You win some, you lose some." "Aw, they'll come around—give it a week or two." In effect, a comment such as, "We'll work it out later," often means, "I don't want to get into that discussion, so let's change the subject," or, "I've got problems of my own right now, and I don't have time for yours." Such comments cut people off from feeling understood.

If the person felt it necessary to pass on the problem or concern, he'd like the chance to go into the details. It's not that he's necessarily looking for a solution; he may simply want to feel that someone appreciates the difficulties he's facing. Moral support doesn't come through thoughtless clichés; it comes from having someone say or demonstrate that she understands the circumstances.

Tip 96. Develop Your Memory.

Yes, you can blame some forgetfulness on age. But most of us forget because we don't make an effort to remember. We tell ourselves things like, "I'm not good at remembering names," or, "I'm a little fuzzy on the details, but I never forget a face." These attitudes are nothing more than giving ourselves permission to forget.

Practice remembering things by forcing yourself to note details and then recalling them later, just for the heck of it. Exercise your memory muscles by memorizing axioms, quotations, number sequences, or instructions. Use mnemonic devices such as repetition, rhymes, acronyms, acrostics, or chain linking as an aid. I make up sentences out of such cues and recite the sentences until I can grab my iphone, notepad, or a scrap of paper to jot down the information. My best ideas come when I'm listening to self-help recordings while exercising.

Why do we remember some things and not others? Because of the relative value we attach to the information. For example, if someone throws you a sales lead, you'll remember the name—dollar signs are attached. When you receive certain information, you immediately have to attach some importance to it so that you advance that information to long-term memory. Otherwise, you'll throw it out with the rest of the memory trash in a matter of moments. Simply be more conscious about what you want to retain as you take it into your head.

Do, however, continue to dump your memory trash daily. There's no use cluttering your memory with things you can record somewhere and retrieve at will from paper, the computer, or the Web. People who have good memories never trust them. But because they've attached a value, forced the information into long-term memory, and taken the extra step to record something, their memories take over and they rarely have to refer to the documented record ever again.

Tip 97. Don't Tell Others What They Already Know.

Yes, you can repeat for emphasis, but don't state the obvious. Examples: "I see you've already called a taxi." "You're limping." "The cord has to be plugged in before it will work." "Statistics can be misleading." "We're experiencing a lot of change during this downsizing." At best, others will think you're unimaginative.

Tip 98. Don't Overload Yourself with Information to the Point of Distortion.

Yes, your brain is a complex computer, but even computers run out of storage space. If you've attended a meeting or listened to a recording where information flows freely, stop long enough to digest what you've heard before you lose everything.

Tip 99. Don't Overload Your Listener with Data That Has to Be Processed Before It's Usable.

Raw computer printouts of numbers are of little use to a senior executive unfamiliar with reading such data in that format. Most people find themselves in similar situations. To be usable, information has to be interpreted. Don't tell me that most of the business development managers in your territory sell an annual volume of $900,000. Is that typical of the industry? An incredibly successful job? Cause for alarm? Interpret.

Tip 100. Relate the Unknown to the Known.

It's difficult for most of us to comprehend the national debt. However, consider the following analogy to bring the debt into perspective: If Warren Buffett were a corporation, he'd rank high on the Fortune 500 list. If he were financing the national debt, he'd be penniless in seconds. Now that's understandable.

Talk about health care in terms of football injuries if you're addressing high school students. Relate the inner workings of a spacecraft to those of a car for people at General Motors. If you're talking to dietitians, put the quality movement in terms of meat loaf.

Tip 101. Make Information Easy to Access.

When a new chief information officer joined our company, he was anxious to show me all the ways he could slice and dice data. After setting up a more functional inventory system, he handed me a binder with a copy of all the reports that the system could produce, along with a written description of each. Exasperated that I seemed to have difficulty remembering what data each report showed, he gave it a second shot: He decided to set up the report menu with questions: "What is the price for each video?" "Which books need to be reordered when?" "How many copies of which titles have been sold in the last 12 months?" Finally, we were speaking the same language.

Tip 102. Reduce the Number of Interpreters.

Consider how often instructions get distorted when they pass through several people on the way to the user. Recently, I asked an assistant to check on prices and procedures for some photography: sitting fees for portraits, makeup and wardrobe staff, product shots, and prints for both portraits and products. My assistant had to talk to the photographer's receptionist, who talked to the photographer, who talked to the studio manager, who talked to corporate headquarters. Then the answers all got relayed back down the line. Needless to say, the answers we finally received did not match the questions.

Tip 103. Interpret Facts and Statistics Rather Than Serving Them Raw.

In a recent meeting with a speaking bureau, I overheard someone discussing a meeting planner's $80,000 budget for an upcoming convention. One account executive commented, "Speaker Smith charges $7,500 for a keynote speech." (Meaning: *Maybe we should recommend him to the meeting planner, who will be delighted to get such a good speaker at such a low cost.*) The second account executive commented, "Yeah, you're right; the client will think the guy's no good unless his fee is at least $15,000. Maybe we should recommend Speaker Jones."

Statistics get jumbled even more easily than facts. "Our survey indicates that employees want more control over discretionary vacation days and more time off during the 8-to-5 day. Twenty-nine percent said they wanted 'more control,' and half said they wanted 'more time off.'" Is that half of the total displeased employees? Or half of 29 percent? Or are 79 percent displeased about vacation and time off? How displeased? How many vacation weeks did the typical displeased respondent have this year? What were the other survey questions and answers?

Statistics and facts do not speak for themselves. They need interpretation.

Tip 104. Get Acronyms and Abbreviations Right.

Some people pepper their conversations with acronyms and other technical jargon to let their audience members know that they're one of the "in group" and to sound knowledgeable. That's good—if they're accurate. But nothing makes an individual look more foolish than to be throwing around an acronym like an insider when he has the letters reversed.

Tip 105. Don't Use Jargon as Snobbery.

For some people, jargon is an attempt to show superiority, to exclude others, or to confuse others. Take it as a sign of insecurity and a cover-up for not being able to communicate at the appropriate level with a larger, lay group of people. In today's workplace, we're all technical—only on different subjects. Not knowing how to step outside the boundaries of one's own jargon-filled job to express an idea so that others can understand is an inadequacy to be overcome, not a sign of superior intelligence or know-how.

Tip 106. Avoid "As You Are Aware" Statements Intended as Put-Downs.

People sometimes use such a phrase when they know that the listener is not aware. The phrase often implies superiority and directs attention to their difference in knowledge of the subject. Any time you purposely make another person feel unknowledgeable, she will be looking for an opportunity to return the insult.

Tip 107. Use the Simple Word When the Simple Word Will Do.

Why do otherwise intelligent people use the biggest word possible to express a simple idea? Take your choice: They're trying to show off their education; they're trying to impress someone they think is more educated than they are; they're trying to obscure rather than clarify; they feel that it's their responsibility to enlarge everyone else's vocabulary; they're trying to build their own vocabulary by practicing a new word.

Mark Twain quipped, "I never write 'metropolis' when I can get the same price for 'city.'" Good writers and orators have known for centuries the value of using the simple word. In Lincoln's Gettysburg Address, of the total 268 words, 190 have only one syllable.

Tip 108. Substitute New Words Permanently for Those You Can't Pronounce.

When I was recording an audio series for Nightingale-Conant, I discovered—after about 10 tries with the producer at my shoulder—that I can't pronounce the word *error*. So I've learned to live happily ever after; I say *mistake*. An acquaintance of mine misspeaks *relevant;* instead, she says "revelant" and seems unaware of the mispronunciation. Ask a trusted friend to point out such mispronunciations in your own conversations so that you can make a permanent correction or substitution.

Tip 109. Select Powerful Verbs.

Verbs carry the weight of your thought. Don't bury them or string them out.

Lackluster: I don't know if the test results are conclusive.

Powerful: I doubt the validity of the test.

Lackluster: This is an exciting product line for our customers.

Powerful: These products will excite our customers.

Lackluster: We should offer a higher level of service even if we have to charge our customers more for that service.

Powerful: I recommend better service at a higher cost.

Tip 110. Cut Adjective and Adverb Clutter.

"Haste makes waste." These are words of fact, or at least they sound like fact. Nouns and verbs bear the weight of your message. "Too much speed in carrying out tasks results in extra time being spent to redo things that were done inefficiently to begin with." These are words of opinion, adjectives and adverbs. "You should carefully consider a variety of alternatives" sounds stronger this way: "Consider your alternatives."

Unless you intend to hedge, develop the habit of speaking with nouns and verbs, omitting descriptive words when possible. They weaken your words—just like pouring water into tea.

Tip 111. Avoid Using *Et Cetera* as a Catchall.

When you cite a list of items, objects, procedures, or activities, be precise. *Et cetera* has a precise meaning: "in the same manner." Correct use: "10, 20, 30, 40, et cetera." In this case, the *et cetera* means "continue numbering as in this pattern." *Et cetera* doesn't mean, "and-what-have-you stuff I don't want to take the time to say." Other lazy-thinking, catchall phrases include these: "any way, shape, or form," "by any means whatsoever," "by any manner or means," "other considerations too numerous to mention." Ask yourself whether you're throwing in a phrase as a substitute for precision.

Tip 112. Rid Yourself of Junk Words.

"Sort of," "a lot," "okay," "right," "type of," "more or less," "you know what I mean," and "you get the picture" add fat and sugar to the communication menu. They lead to a vocabulary deficiency in conversation.

Tip 113. Be Specific.

Often, tasks go uncompleted, questions fail to get answered, and promises are broken because people are not mind readers. Lack of specificity causes more customer-service problems than defective products ever could.

Other examples of mind-reading exercises: "I'd like you to research this problem and propose a solution by the end of the month." Does this boss want a lengthy questionnaire distributed to all employees? Does he want to hire a market research firm for an industry survey? Does he want to telephone a few key supervisors involved with the problem?

"You did a great job!" What was great? The analysis? Keeping it under budget? The customer's reaction?

"Give me some feedback on the seminar." Bluntly? Diplomatically? Did it help me personally? Do I think others from the department should attend? Did I think it was worth the cost? How helpful or entertaining were the speakers?

Such requests and statements grope in the darkness of abstraction. Notice improvement in the following:

Nonspecific: When you talk so rudely to me,...

Specific: When you tell me I'm unfocused in my work,...

Nonspecific: When you don't talk to me,...

Specific: When you don't talk to me about your work projects,...

Nonspecific: You don't seem to care about your work anymore.

Specific: You have missed four deadlines this month.

Nonspecific: Do you know why you can't get along with people?

Specific: We've had three people ask to be removed from your team. Do you know their reasons?

Tip 114. Push Other People to Be Specific.

Don't overlook the most straightforward approach to getting people to be specific so that you can understand what they mean. Use some of the following probes: "Could you be more specific?" "Please fill me in on the details." "Do you have a particular situation in mind?" "Can you give me a specific example of what happens?" "For instance?" "Such as X or Y?" "How many are you talking about?" "To what extent is that the case in your department?" "Can you put a percent to it?" "Can you give me a specific number to work with?" "When does that happen?" "Where is that happening?" "How is that happening?" "Why is that happening?" "Who exactly is involved?" "So what's your assessment of the situation?" "So what exactly do you want me to do?" You'll be surprised at the gulf between first mention and the answer to these probing specifics.

Tip 115. Choose Precise Words.

We demand precision in most professional situations. A doctor uses the exact scalpel size to perform an appendectomy. A pharmacist fills a prescription to the exact gram. A machinist runs the lathe to the one-hundredth of an inch. Even a Sunday driver has to stop behind the white line at the intersection. Yet we often accept communication as an "art," an imprecise activity that can't possibly be error-proofed. Reexamine the idea that just any word will do. Choose the most precise words and you may be surprised how little rework is required.

Tip 116. Use Concrete Words Rather Than Abstract Ones.

Concrete words describe those activities, objects, or people that you can visualize: *car, house, pocketbook, teenager.* Abstract words can be used in so many contexts that their meanings becomes muddled. *Meaningful results, on-the-job crises, employee freedom, management support*—each of these phrases will have different meanings to different people in different situations. Many people find themselves in arguments when their words are so vague they don't realize that they actually agree.

A husband says to his new bride, "Honey, I really want a large family."

She looks a little apprehensive. "Uh, I was thinking small."

He says, "But large families have more fun. Kids help each other out. They learn to give and take, and to sacrifice for each other. And holidays are so much fun with a houseful."

She says, "Yes, but small families are nice, too. The relationships are closer, more intimate. And the kids have to get along—there's nobody else to run to. And you can afford to give them a better education and all the advantages."

He says, "I'm disappointed that you feel that way."

"Me, too. I . . . didn't know you felt that strongly. I guess we should have discussed this long ago."

The next day on the golf course, he complains that his wife won't agree to three kids. She calls her mother to confide that two kids are all she can handle. Two? Three? One extra toothbrush between a large family and a small one? Large and small are relative terms.

Prefer concrete words rather than abstract ones.

Tip 117. Beware of Misleading with Connotation and Denotation.

Is a "feisty" woman powerful or amusing? Is a "hulk of a man" intimidating, forceful, or just big? Is an "adequate performance" worth a raise, or does it need improvement? The *denotation* of a word is the dictionary definition. The *connotation* of a word is the associated meaning given in context and culture.

Between denotative and connotative definitions, there's a world of misinterpretation and swayed opinion. Of great concern to social scientists is that the use or misuse of a single word can change the entire results of an opinion poll. If you intend to subtly lead others to your way of thinking, select your words carefully. If you prefer a neutral opinion, select the denotative word or phrase.

Denotation	Connotation
house	mansion, hovel
price	investment, fee
agreement	opportunity, contract
low cost	a real value, cheap
temporary	alternative, makeshift
strong	tenacious, obstinate
initial	pioneering, primitive
odorous	fragrant, foul smelling
change	stimulate, agitate
firm	confident, opinionated
satisfactory	ample, adequate
end, finish	abort

Tip 118. Make Semantics a Big Concern.

People often use a disclaimer such as, "Well, that's just semantics," to downplay the importance of their word choice. See if you get a completely different message from each of the following versions.

"Robert is meeting with the lawyers this afternoon."

"The lawyers are meeting with Robert this afternoon."

"The lawyers and Robert have scheduled a meeting this afternoon."

"Both Robert and the lawyers are getting together on this issue this afternoon."

Who initiated the meeting? Is it formal or informal? Will the decision be official or not? Is Robert in trouble? Much of the interpretation
comes from the word choice and sentence structure.

"How was the seminar?" Answer: "Not bad." Isn't "not bad" a different message from "quite good"? Semantics.

Entire businesses have renamed their employee titles because of the crucial importance of semantics to convey a new management philosophy,
changing from "salespeople" to "associates" to "advisors" and "consultants."
Semantics is no small matter.

Tip 119. Remember That Personal Experience Affects Interpretation.

I grew up on a cotton farm in the South, where we defoliated for boll wee-
vils and other vermin regularly and where we had neighbors who bought
bees for their hives and baby chicks for their hatcheries. As a preteen driving across country with my family on vacation, someone pointed out
the car window to a "flea market." I glanced at the warehouse-looking
structure, expecting to see a breeding lot for fleas. When I use the phrase
"storage facilities" in our business writing workshops for a Houston
client, people think about "oil tanks." In Silicon Valley, "storage facilities" conjures up either storage space on their in-house server or websites "in the cloud."

Tip 120. Remember That Meaning Comes from Context.

When a patient in a mental hospital says to you, "I want to go home," you
don't necessarily take it seriously or try to help her get the paperwork and
permissions completed. However, when a college student is talking about
"going home" for the holidays, you feel supportive and offer encouragement. When a manager wants to "go home" after a long day of work, you
know that the trip is short and that he will be back the following day. When
a psychologist talks to you about "going home" mentally to heal childhood
wounds, you may begin a new thought process that lasts for years. Meaning
doesn't come from words. Meaning depends on who says the words to
whom, when, and for what purpose. The more common the word, the more
meanings it probably has.

Tip 121. Don't Attach Too Much Significance to a Less Than Well-Chosen Word Used Carelessly.

Have you ever caught yourself stewing over one little word in a bigger context—turning that one word over and over in your mind and chewing it up for all the misery it provides? Let's say your spouse comments, "We have briefcases and paperwork all over the house! This fit you've been in over that Delco project is wrecking your entire schedule. You're bringing more and more work home lately. You're going to be so stressed out and tired that you're going to get sick."

Response? "Fit, huh? So she thinks it's a fit, huh? I'd like to see her keep her cool if she were in my shoes!" The word *fit* sets you off. A better-chosen word might have been *dither* or *predicament*. You've got a choice—take the comment for its full context and message, or play off the one poorly chosen word that brings up an entirely different message and emotion.

When pinched with the poorly chosen word, don't blow the comment out of proportion. Consider the entire context.

Tip 122. Use Honest Words.

Have you ever read a tourist brochure enticing you to a vacation getaway that disappointed you? Once there, you understand that "sun-drenched" means "hot," that "tucked away in the valley" means "inaccessible except by donkey," that "relaxed atmosphere" means "no room service," that "surrounded by water activities" means "two lakes with a paddle boat," and that "moderately priced" means "creaky furniture and no maid service." Be as honest with your words as with your pocketbook.

Tip 123. Never Say *Never, None, All, Everything, Totally,* or *Constantly*.

When you use one of these absolutes, the other person will typically focus on the exception rather than on the general rule you meant to discuss.

Assessment: "You never come home in time for dinner with the rest of the family."

Response: "I don't know what you mean. Last Thursday I was home in the middle of the afternoon."

Assessment: "You always complain about where we eat lunch, Charlie."

Response: "No, I don't. Yesterday we ate seafood. I hate it, but I didn't say a thing."

Assessment: "You're constantly late with your status reports."

Response: "I don't know what you're talking about. I turned in the report a week early in June."

Steer clear of the exceptions, and focus on the real issue that needs attention.

Tip 124. Minimize Times When You Use *Should, Must, Will,* or *Ought* Statements.

All four words sound abrupt, intimidating, or even condescending in situations where you might be perceived as "telling people what to do." Even if you intend your comment only as friendly advice, the words make listeners feel inadequate or stupid, as if they should have known better or acted more wisely. These "hot" words make people say, "Oh, yeah? Who are you to tell me what I should/must/will/ought to do?" Even if you do have to tell someone what to do, why not wear a velvet glove rather than a boxing glove?

Tip 125. Recognize Weasel Words as Escape Hatches.

Guard against the weasel words that can slip into sentences: *maybe, possibly, could, sometimes, wish, may possibly cause, could attribute to, seems to, appears to be,* or *might be a consideration.* The most frequent customer-service problems involve what the customer considers "unkept promises." When there's a problem, customer-service reps insist that they never made the promise the customers thought they heard. Service reps focus on the *may, might,* or *sometimes,* and customers overlook such hedge words.

When you're on the receiving end of promises, question people about the escape hatches. When you're on the giving end, state as much as you can verify or promise—no more and no less. Of course, you can't state absolutes that aren't absolutes. But realize that weasel words drain the power from your claims; predictably, people pounce on them.

Tip 126. Don't Destroy Your Position with Disclaimers.

A consulting firm that inspects property in distant cities for potential investors and then reports on the condition of the property asked me to review some of its reports for format, organization, and persuasive appeal.

After reading the first few, my reaction was, "Why would I hire this firm for an opinion?" Its boilerplate included an appendix full of disclaimers that said in effect, "We make no judgments about the investment value of this property." The disclaimers invalidated the contents and value of the rest of the report!

The same thing happens in conversation: "You're not going to agree with what I'm about to say, but . . ." The conversation that follows sounds invalid and full of holes.

Tip 127. Avoid Ending Statements with Questions.

"I thought the speaker was boring, didn't you?" "The lounge should be renovated also, don't you think?" "The customer knew of the price increase, right?" "Let's hold the meeting outside the city; what do you think?" Tag questions at the end of statements make you sound tentative and unsure of your opinions or the facts.

Tip 128. Recognize the Royal "We" as an Epithet.

When someone doesn't want to own up to decisions, he can always hide behind a committee decision. "We have decided this benefit is an unnecessary expense." "I have decided . . ." takes more courage. Leaders use it to own their decisions; managers frequently shun it to avoid accountability for and repercussions of their decisions. Others notice the distinction.

Tip 129. Pay Attention to the Stress on Words.

Notice how the meaning of this sentence varies as I change the stressed (italicized) word(s).

> Rosita said Sonya heard the client complain about the price.
> *Rosita* said Sonya heard the client complain about the price.
> Rosita *said* Sonya heard the client complain about the price.
> Rosita said *Sonya* heard the client complain about the price.
> Rosita said Sonya *heard* the client complain about the price.
> Rosita said Sonya heard *the client* complain about the price.
> Rosita said Sonya heard the client *complain* about the price.
> Rosita said Sonya heard the client complain about *the price.*

Inflection often carries the message. Learn to recognize the stresses in your own words and in those spoken by others.

Tip 130. Eliminate Redundancies.

Here's a list to start your thinking. Choose one or the other, but not both: *fitting* and *proper, workable* and *feasible, absolutely* and *positively, accurate* and *correct, beneficial* and *helpful, hazardous* and *unsafe, sick* and *unhealthy, disadvantaged* and *underprivileged, the powerful* and *the elite, serious crisis, important essentials, desirable benefits, basic fundamentals, final outcome, separate* and *distinct, alternate choices, past history, joint partnership, advance warning.* And the list goes on with each nightly news broadcast.

Tip 131. Grapple with Grammar.

Here are some common mistakes and a shortcut or simple rule to help you avoid each:

> *Correct misused verbs. Gone-went, do-don't-doesn't, lie-lay, sit-set, affect-effect, was-were.*
>
> *Use -ly on adverbs.* The boss writes quickly. They decided promptly. The committee meets regularly.
>
> *Differentiate between* good *and* well. *Good* describes an object, place, idea, person, or thing. *Well* describes how something performs. Fido is a good dog. Fido eats well.
>
> *Drop unnecessary prepositions at the end of sentences. Not:* "Where's the paper at?" *But:* "Where's the paper?" *Not:* "These are the designs I worked on." *But:* "I worked on these designs." *Not:* "Which team is Jason on?" *But:* "Jason is on which team?" *Not:* "Where did the contract go to?" *But:* "Where did the contract go?" Some prepositions sound fine at the end of sentences; others sound limp. Let clarity be your guide.
>
> *Eliminate double negatives.* The following words mean no/not/negative; use only one of them in any sentence: *no, not, never, none, no one, nowhere.*
>
> *Choose correct pronouns.* When you come to a confusing sentence using who or whom, here's a trick: substitute *he* or *she* for *who* and *him* or *her* for *whom* and you'll make the right choice. When the choice involves a list of other people, leave out the other names and you'll choose *me/he/him, she/he,* and *us/we* correctly. Example: "Give the order to Jim, Joanne, or me." Leave out Jim and Joanne: "Give the order to me." It's a fail-safe system for choosing correctly.

Tip 132. Use Poor Grammar Only for an Intended Effect.

Ain't can mean, "I'm just one of you people—forget I'm the regional VP." Don't use it when you're not sure if your audience knows that you know better. Make a conscious choice for an intended effect. Then think about it twice more.

Tip 133. Use Up-to-Date Slang.

Nothing makes a 40-year-old manager look more foolish than using teenage slang. And the problem with picking up slang from your kids is that as soon as you've learned it, they've changed it. Either stay up to date or give up the effort and speak plain English.

Tip 134. Overcome Sloppy Diction.

Avoid dropping the ends of words, running words together, and otherwise making it difficult for people to understand you. If you've ever dialed a company and had a receptionist respond as unintelligibly as a robot on fast-forward, you understand the irritation.

Tip 135. Avoid Being So Overly Precise That You Sound Like a Stuffed Shirt.

We shall? We will? He proceeded to tell me? He continued? Is it I? Is it me? Let clarity versus awkwardness be your guide. Of course proper grammar is important, but remember that grammar rules are not static. Usages become archaic. And some things people remember as "rules" never to be broken have never been rules at all; they are matters of style. Such word choices and phrasing may make your conversation or your writing seem awkward and stiff. Be precise in meaning and proper in grammar where clarity is concerned, but less formal in matters of style.

Tip 136. Use Your Speaking Voice, Even When You Write.

As a rule, talkers *include* the people. After conducting business and technical writing courses for corporate clients for the past 30 years, I've discovered that people have two voices: a writing voice and a talking voice. They'll say to you, "I suggest that we terminate the project." You say, "Why don't you put that in your report?" A week later you receive the report, which says, "It is recommended that this project be terminated."

The "recommender" has disappeared. When you pass the report on, the next reader wonders who made the recommendation.

Another difference: Writers use a stiffer vocabulary than talkers. A salesperson will say on the phone, "I'll check to see if we have that chair in stock and call you back tomorrow." She then e-mails you, "Your preference for item #AG349 has been received. After verification of the availability of that merchandise, you will be notified no later than September 12 as to whether your order can be processed immediately." You'll notice that the salesperson used the coldest, longest, vaguest word possible for each concept.

If you want a helpful technique for testing the proper voice, read your own documents aloud. If they sound stilted to your own ear, they will sound the same way to someone else.

Tip 137. Speak with the Appropriate Degree of Formality or Informality.

After some introductions, "Hello" or "How do you do" is appropriate. Others call for a "Hi, nice to meet you." Colloquialisms like "We've been fightin' this tooth and nail" are in order in some groups, but not in other groups. To be unduly stiff in your word choice can be as inappropriate as showing up at McDonald's in a tux or arriving at the symphony in a swimsuit.

Tip 138. Take Cues About First-Name/Last-Name Preference from How the Other Person Answers the Phone.

Assuming that everyone welcomes being called by her first name is arrogance by the powerful and a put-down to entry-level employees. Using their last names may set up a formal, impersonal tone to some people. Far more women are called by their first names than men, particularly among those with titles such as "Dr." It is generally up to the people of higher status or position to give lower-status individuals permission to use their first names. They are announcing equality, an act that by its very nature underscores their power and status.

To know others' preferences, listen to how they answer their own phones: First name only? Last name only? Both first and last? If still unsure, ask them politely what they prefer. Err on the side of formality until you are told otherwise.

Tip 139. Recognize Name-Dropping as an Attempt to Gain Status.

Dropping the names of the great, the near-great, the powerful, and the near-powerful sends a message to listeners that the speaker is making a stab at gaining admiration and increasing his own stature by association. It demonstrates insecurity.

Tip 140. Avoid Sexist Language.

Eliminate nouns that are gender-specific and metaphors understood primarily by only one gender: for example, football analogies or ballet analogies. Use *police officer* rather than *policeman; flight attendant* rather than *stewardess; chair* rather than *chairman*. To say, "The troops were led by a female colonel," or, "They hired a male nurse" is no more appropriate than saying, "The troops were led by a male colonel," or, "They hired a female nurse."

Suggestions: (1) Prefer speaking or writing the plural rather than omitting half the human race. *Not:* "An employee will need *his* badge to get into the building." *But:* "Employees will need *their* badges to get into the building." (2) Alternate references between the genders. (3) Omit the pronouns altogether: "An employee will need a badge to get into the building."

Tip 141. Know the Value of Understatement.

When you overstate your case, others dig for the gaps. If you don't believe this, notice your reaction the next time someone says to you, "The most bizarre thing just happened. Hilarious. You won't believe it. This person walks in and . . . " The typical reaction after such a lead-in is a letdown, a that-was-not-so-bizarre-or-hilarious reaction. You're set up for disappointment.

As a speaker, I'd much rather the introducer understate the benefits he expects my audience to gain than to overstate them. Otherwise, I'm traveling uphill.

Tip 142. Don't Exaggerate.

Did you get "dozens" of calls on the ad, or did you get six? Did you have a "fabulous" job offer, or was it just generous enough to make you consider a move? Did the warehouse barrel "go up in flames," or was it just smoldering? Exaggeration for a good story is acceptable; people understand "creating the mood" to generate a good laugh at the party.

But when people exaggerate routinely in business settings, over time they destroy their credibility. Others will not accept "problems" as problems. They will not greet "successes" as successes. They will not use "facts" as facts.

Tip 143. Fight the Urge to Top Off the Tank.

Just as though they're topping off the gas tank before heading cross-country, some people feel as though they have to "top off" everybody else's point. They always have a "can-you-top-this?" story or comment after everyone else's. A funnier joke. A worse problem. A heavier workload. Fight the urge to always top what anybody else says.

Tip 144. Avoid Overqualifying.

Have you ever walked into a lawyer's office and asked for an opinion about whether you should go to court on a particular issue? And after an hour, you walked away still not knowing what the lawyer's expert opinion was? Some lawyers fear making an outright statement. They fear being taken out of context. They fear being misquoted. They fear that the consequences will be more severe than they predicted. Some people walk that same legal tightrope on every issue. Nothing is a yes-or-no question. It all depends.

Tip 145. Cut Long Prefaces to Your Points.

Ever since teachers first assigned students oral book reports back in elementary school, people have tended to tell things "from the beginning." A colleague catches you in the hallway: "Hey, I've got a great idea; you're going to love it. First, let me give you a little background." Wrong approach. People never understand the background until they hear the point. Prefaces confuse and lose people.

Tip 146. Avoid "Speaking with Footnotes."

Don't let yourself get sidetracked by minor issues. My grandfather's stories rambled on in this fashion: "The other day—I guess it was Wednesday—no, it must have been Tuesday because that's the day I went by to feed the horses—one of Harold's boys came over, or maybe it was his cousin. Name's Christopher. About six years old. And Harold had told him not to cross the street by himself. Of course, he plays out in the front all the time, but there's usually somebody at home to watch him. Well, they weren't bidding much on my horses that day...." You get the picture. When you know a great deal about your subject, it's tempting to continue to toss in tidbits, but remember that people follow a straight path more easily than they follow a circuitous one. Where do you want to lead them? Go straight there. If they want an excursion later, they'll ask.

Tip 147. Self-Edit Your "Thinking" Details.

Some people talk through details to analyze a situation, and by the time they come to the end of their discussion, they know what they think. The problem with that process is that others may not want to follow the same thinking route. They typically prefer that you cut to the chase.

Maybe the habit of dumping the details comes from having been graded on the curve in the school system. The more students recite or write, the greater the evidence that they've read the assignment and the better the resulting grade. Not so in conversation.

Tip 148. Unwind Motormouths.

When people who have a reputation for long-windedness ask, "Do you have a minute?" agree with their phrasing: "Yes, I do have about three minutes before I have to make a call/attend a meeting/get back to my X project." You've put them on notice that your time is not unlimited, while also saying yes to them.

A second technique involves continually bringing them back to their point. "So what was it you wanted to tell me about the insurance form?" "I'm not following what this has to do with the issue of X." "So, can you help me on the Y problem?"

Finally, you can always interrupt their monologue with a brief question that elicits a one-word answer from them. Then when they interrupt themselves to answer your question, you have regained the floor.

Tip 149. Use the One-Minute Gag Rule.

If you speak for longer than one minute at a turn without giving the other person a chance to respond, the chances are great that you're becoming long-winded and that you're going to lose the other person's attention. Make it a habit to relinquish the floor every 60 seconds until someone invites you to continue.

Tip 150. Distinguish Succinctness from Bluntness.

The difference is tone. Yes, you want to be succinct with the details, to choose words well. But a one-word answer often sounds blunt, curt, insolent, surly, or discourteous. At best, it can be misinterpreted or unclear. Add a sentence elaboration just for the sake of tone, if not clarity.

CALLER 1: Do these staplers come in black?

CALLER 2: No. *(Sufficient, but blunt.)*

CALLER 1: Do these staplers come in black?

CALLER 2: No. They come only in gray and brown. *(Succinct.)*

CALLER 1: What did you think of his report?

CALLER 2: Boring. Long. *(Sufficient, but blunt.)*

CALLER 1: What did you think of his report?

CALLER 2: It contained little of value to me personally, but others found useful information in it. *(Succinct.)*

Tip 151. Challenge the Expert When the Expert Is Obnoxious.

Try a little splash of irreverence. Instead of holding court with the rest of her admirers, confront an obnoxious expert with the confusion she has created: "I'm sorry, but you've lost me." "Can you explain this so that someone outside your field can understand it?" "I'm afraid I couldn't agree to something I don't understand. I need to have an explanation without the acronyms, the abbreviations, and the footnotes." If such directness does not persuade the know-it-all to be clearer, question her until you get the answers you need. After enough interruptions like, "And what does that mean?" "So what does that refer to?" "So why is that number significant?" most such people will usually come down off their lofty perch and speak plain English.

Tip 152. Judge Ideas on Their Own Merit.

Stories abound about the shabbily dressed "guest" who turns out to be the owner of the entire hotel chain. And we know that physical appearances can be deceiving—whether we're talking about athletic prowess, political clout, or wealth. However, we fail to remind ourselves of the same principle in our conversations. The shop supervisor who suggests a new process may pepper his speech with poor grammar and repetitious details but come up with money-saving ideas. Pay attention to content without being distracted by delivery.

Tip 153. Don't Reject What Someone Is Saying Out of Hand Solely Because the Words He Uses Seem Technically Incorrect.

Many people know what they mean—they just can't say it well. For example, a prospective client called one day to ask if I did keynotes on negotiation. I started to tell him no and refer him to a colleague better known for "negotiation" programs, but I decided to probe further. After he began to elaborate his objectives for his sales conference, it became clear that he really wanted a talk on *persuasion.* His sales representatives needed to consult with prospects about needs and then persuade them that their company was the best provider of the service. Big difference. I almost missed a profitable engagement by simply taking his term *negotiation* at face value without investigating.

Tip 154. Resist the Urge to Nitpick.

"I read in the paper this morning that something like 16 banks have gone under in Texas alone this year." Response: "Yes, I saw that. Actually, it was 18."

"I heard that Janie resigned to go back into advertising—Chicago firm, I think." Response: "She's been wanting to get back in the ad biz for years. She told me the job was in Pittsburgh."

The correction may be subtle or overt, but the effect is the same. People feel "corrected"—and they won't necessarily appreciate it. Avoid the temptation to nitpick about facts that don't matter.

Tip 155. Avoid One-Up Phrases.

These one-ups are common put-downs: "Oh, didn't you already know that—I guess I should have told you." "It may be of interest to you that ... " "I guess you had no way of knowing, but ... " "As you'll soon discover ... "

Tip 156. If You Must Correct Someone, Do So Gently.

If you think you must correct someone's statistics or "facts"—that the person would be glad to know the exact, correct number, name, or location—then do so with tact. Try these tactful turns: "The actual figure is X; however, your conclusions are exactly right," or "You've interpreted very closely; only one minor correction: the location was Y," or: "It was my understanding that X is the exact figure, but you're so right about Y," or, "I read an updated report on that today; the final story is that..."

Tip 157. Don't Make Judging Other People a Hobby.

People watching can be an amusing pastime—how they walk, talk, dress, eat, or work. But passing judgments can cast the commentator in a bad light: "Look at her jacket. Brown and taupe have been out of style for at least three years," or, "Look at the way he cocks his head to the left when he talks to people. He always comes across as such a know-it-all," or "Her desk looks like a cyclone hits it every weekend. No wonder she's always asking for an extension on her deadlines." Yes, we all make personal observations about people, but voicing them to others can be habit-forming.

Tip 158. Avoid Doormat Statements.

Common routines: "Nothing is wrong, and I don't want to talk about it." (Meaning: "Something is wrong, but I want you to have to wait to know what it is.") "Don't bother about me—I'll be okay." (Meaning: "Please consider me.") "I guess I'll have to live with it." (Meaning: "I don't intend to live with it.") Such attempts aim to put the other person in a bind; the words say, "There's no problem; take no further action," but the tone means, "You'd better take some action." So, should listeners keep probing or drop the issue? Either way, they usually lose and resent it.

Tip 159. Avoid Sour-Grapes Lines.

Do these have a familiar ring? "I don't think I'd accept such an award." "I'm glad it's not me." "I'm glad I wasn't put in the position to say no." "I don't have time for that sort of thing." "Honestly, I'm relieved to have lost that contract." If lying to yourself eases the pain, go ahead. But others will probably smell sour grapes.

Tip 160. Watch for Diversionary Tactics.

People can create a distraction and sabotage a project in three ways: (1) Make light of a serious request, situation, or concern. (2) Simply stall by changing the subject. (3) Steal someone's thunder by delivering the punch line for her presentation before she gets to it. Any of these tactics create a lasting, unfavorable impression on the speaker and on the observers.

Tip 161. Don't Bark Orders.

Adding courteous words helps: "please" and "I'd appreciate it if you would..." Adding an explanation to the order makes it even more palatable: "Do not use this entrance. The inside roof is under construction." "Do not use this copier; it is out of toner."

Tip 162. Never Issue an Order That You Can't Enforce.

Words come easily; enforcement does not. And once you've put your commitment into words for the world to read or hear, you have to be committed to follow through. Without that commitment and resources, credibility goes out the window.

Tip 163. Squelch Automatic Put-Down Responses When Somebody Presents a New Idea.

"So what's your complaint with the way it's done now?" "So what's your gripe?" "Come again?" "Where did you get that idea?" "I think you've misunderstood something along the way." These "welcoming" comments sound as though they're coming from a person on a hot wire fence. The person may appear to be receptive, but the reaction feels like an electrical jolt.

Tip 164. Make Only Promises You Intend to Keep.

Once retailers have someone on their hot-check list, it's difficult for that person to pass another bad check in that store. Likewise, people who promise action that they don't intend to take get labeled. If you don't mean the following statements, don't use them: "I'll see what I can do." "I'll try to find time." "I'll check my files and get back to you." "Maybe we can get together sometime." "Let's chat about that later." Once people learn these are empty offers, it will take a major reconstruction effort to restore your credibility.

Tip 165. Make Invitations Specific.

"Why don't we get together for lunch sometime?" comes across as, "I might possibly want to spend some time with you, but I'm not sure. Why don't you call me with a specific time and I'll see if I've still got the urge?" If you really do want to spend time with someone, be specific: "Why don't we have lunch next week? How about Wednesday at Reno's Deli at about 1 o'clock?" Or, if you honestly don't know your schedule: "Let's have breakfast together next month. I'll check my calendar this afternoon and call you to see if you're available after the first week." Or, "What day next week works for you?" Only a specific invitation sounds sincere.

Tip 166. Make Invitations Vague if You Think You Should Spend Time with the Other Person, but You Don't Really Want to Badly Enough to Make a Commitment.

I've had an acquaintance who has been saying to me for two years when we meet at parties, "Call me for lunch sometime." After about five such invitations, I phoned with an invitation to breakfast or lunch any day of the week for the next month. It seems that he was "behind, rushed, overextended" for an indefinite period of time. Had he really wanted to get together, he would have responded with something like, "Gee, I'm really behind with several projects this month. But what if I phone you on Monday the 22nd, and let's set a date then."

If you don't want to make a commitment of time, be vague. People will get the message—all of it.

Tip 167. Avoid Challenges to Someone's Integrity.

A sure way to make enemies in a meeting is to challenge someone's integrity with statements or questions like these: "What is your agenda for getting this done so fast?" "Who asked you to do this?" "What's in this for you?" "What are you not telling us?" "Whom should we ask for the other side of the story?"

Tip 168. Judge Others on Their Intentions as Well as Their Actions.

Have you ever known a satisfied customer to give a testimonial that actually dissuaded another prospect from buying? Or have you seen someone take up a collection for a gift when the small amount embarrassed the recipient? Have you ever heard an emcee introduce a speaker, minimizing rather than maximizing the speaker's credentials? Even the best intentions don't ensure success.

Sometimes people just don't have the knowledge or skills they need to perform the way they intend, and correcting their mistakes can cost more in time and effort than if you had done the task yourself. So the tendency is to judge others on their results and ourselves on our intentions. Give people the benefit of the doubt when they talk. Look at their heart.

Tip 169. Make Your Own Intentions Known, Even if Your Action Doesn't Hit the Bull's-Eye.

If what you do flubs, people are left on their own to interpret your intentions by looking at your results. If the awards ceremony somehow left the recipients feeling put down rather than praised, explain the intentions behind your words. If the meeting ended in anger and with no decision, explain that your intention was to offer opportunity for input. Help people give you the benefit of the doubt.

Tip 170. Beware of People Who Swear They're Telling the Truth.

Watch for people who insist: "Trust me—we're not the kind of vendor who gouges in a crisis." "You can trust us to give you an honest opinion, no matter what the fees involved." "I swear he said it." "Can I be frank with you?" "We don't make this information readily available to all our customers, but I want to be up front with you." Such lines indicate something other than the truth. Those who always tell the truth never think to call attention to the fact that they're telling it.

Tip 171. Show Total Belief to Ferret Out Liars.

When someone starts a whopper and you show obvious disbelief (with a raised eyebrow or a questioning tone), he'll grow cautious and often tone down his story. On the other hand, if you doubt that someone is telling the truth, show no signs of skepticism. Your demeanor and accepting attitude will entice him to continue until the statements become so outlandish as to be obviously a lie.

Tip 172. Don't Hide Behind "They Didn't Ask Me Not To."

A shared confidence is a trust. When people don't have the good sense to know that something should be held in confidence even when they were not specifically asked to do so, others will question their judgment. Good judgment about such issues generally reflects good character.

Tip 173. Be Authoritative if You Want Control.

Your manner, appearance, speech, and writing should all work in tandem. Don't tell us what you're going to try to do; do it. Don't stand to the side looking contemplative; command space. Be sure; act the part.

The most famous experimental studies on the subject of obedience to authority were those conducted by Stanley Milgram, who used a "shock generator" with a panel of 30 switches supposedly controlling electric shocks from 15 to 450 volts. The volunteers were taken into a room and told that they were part of an experiment on teaching learners. Each time a learner, strapped in a chair in the next room, gave a wrong answer, the volunteer was supposed to administer a shock. With each "learner error," the volunteer was supposed to increase the voltage. No matter what the screaming and the pleading of the "learners" next door, the volunteer was asked to continue the shocks. The idea was to see how long these volunteers would continue to administer what they thought were painful or even dangerous shocks when told to do so by an authority figure—a doctor in a lab coat in charge of "scientific research."

The results? Although they were physically free to leave the room and quit the experiment, fully 65 percent of the volunteers were obedient to the end, giving screaming "learners" the maximum of 450 volts. Such is the power of our ingrained social pressure to obey authority. If you act like an authority figure, people will generally comply.

Tip 174. Sound Logical if You Want to Deliver Powerful Messages.

Make sure that your message includes analytical statements, that you organize your points well, that you use transitions from idea to idea, and that you have a goal for meaningful conversation. When your words sound like you know where you're going, people can follow you to your logical destination.

Tip 175. Feel Free to Be Illogical.

To an engineer, the charge, "That's illogical" may be the kiss of death. The rest of the world doesn't necessarily cower under the weight of that accusation. "Thou shalt be logical" is not one of the Ten Commandments. The trick to minimizing the frustration of defending yourself is to acknowledge openly and quickly that your decision or behavior was not based on logic.

You're off the hook. People can accept that not all decisions, conclusions, or actions rest on logic. Feelings are fine.

Tip 176. Be Ready to Justify Any Decision You Make.

Although feelings are fine, people may work harder and cooperate better when they have reasons. Although someone may hold a powerful position to command, real leadership calls for motivation. Rather than feeling annoyed at having to justify their decisions, leaders accept such challenges to inspire and motivate others to follow.

Tip 177. To Be Quotable, Speak in Bumper Stickers or Tweets.

Have you noticed that the media quote some celebrities or authorities more often than others? Two doctors may have the same credentials and the same knowledge about laser surgery, but one will be interviewed in six magazines or journals, while the other will never be asked for an opinion at all. If you want to be remembered by others, if you want to be quoted by your friends to their friends, if you want to be mentioned from the lectern as a leader, pepper your speech with pizzazz. Learn to turn a phrase so that it's amusing and provocative—not just adequate to cover the subject. Visualize your opinion as a five-word bumper sticker. Or, make it tweetable and retweetable.

Tip 178. Don't Assume Another Person Has Power to Control Your Destiny.

Do you remember the age when you thought your parents could fix whatever happened in the world? We sometimes assume those in positions of authority have that kind of all-encompassing power to make or break us. As a result, we get angry at "what *they* don't do and could if *they* would." Respect the influence of powerful people, but don't attribute to them the power to control events or circumstances out of their reach. You'll wear a grudge in your manner and voice.

Tip 179. Don't Create Obligations Among Others to Enhance Your Sense of Power.

Have you ever bought someone lunch when it was raining and nasty outside so that she would "owe you one" in a meeting later that day? Presidents buy congressional votes on legislation by offering to play golf with senators or appearing with them in their home states. Large or small, the problem with such implied arrangements is that they build resentment in those who feel obligated. It's like being a tax cheat and worrying when you're going to find the IRS on your doorstep.

Tip 180. Credit Your Source for New Ideas.

It's not a matter of split-the-appreciation pie. Others may get credit for the idea, but you get credit for knowing when, where, why, how, and if to use the idea in any given circumstances.

It's much safer to make your source known up front than to take credit and have others discover the truth later and point out the idea's true origin. Preachers, playwrights, and politicians throughout the years could have headed off charges of plagiarism had they taken this tip to heart. Those who can push their ideas through to the top via another individual and still get credit continue to flood ideas on those who shower them with praise in return.

Tip 181. Ask for Others' Opinions.

Asking for an opinion from someone doesn't obligate you to act on that opinion. However, the fact that you have asked others to contribute to decisions has value both to you and to the other person. The president's multiple advisors for every decision feel honored to offer him their views whether or not he acts on them. Consider the pride with which citizens talk about being asked to testify before Congress about a personal experience or career expertise. Simply having someone ask for an opinion is a compliment.

Tip 182. Respond to What's Right with Suggestions Even if You Can't Use Them.

Consider it a sign of interest and helpfulness when others offer you suggestions. Respond in kind: "Thanks for mentioning that. You've got a good idea. Let's mull that over when we get together again," or, "You may be right. It's a different way of looking at things. We should give it serious thought," or "Your idea has real merit. We'd have to investigate further to make it workable for us. It sounds intriguing however," or, "You have a valid point—particularly on the pricing structure," or simply, "Thanks. I need all the ideas I can get. Hearing how others have done this is very helpful to prevent mistakes and learn what has worked for you."

Tip 183. Tell People How Much You Need Them.

People want to feel needed. Your staff won't stay with you nearly as long when they need you as when you need them—and they feel it. Put that sentiment in words often: "You're very good with technology issues. It's a good thing we have you," or, "I don't know what I'd do without you to keep me organized," or, "I need your help—again. I'm always calling on you, aren't I?"

Tip 184. Give People All the Glory They're Due When They Know the Inside Scoop.

What good is shaking hands with a celebrity if you can't tell anybody about it? What good is a commendation if nobody hears or sees it? What good is a secret if nobody knows you know it? Enjoyment comes in the telling. So, if you want to know what somebody else knows, you have to pay your dues. Tell him you understand that he must have an inside track to be trusted with such information. Then watch him let those confidential details slip right out his lips; he has to give you information to verify that he really does know something important. Your strokes simply bait him to tell you what you want to know.

Tip 185. Show Pleasure in the Success of Others.

Envy rears its ugly head prominently in silence. When someone tells of her good fortune or another person brings up that achievement in your presence, join in with your commendation. "It sounds like things are going well for you," or, "That's terrific. You should have told us sooner," or, "Wow. I can say I knew you when …," or, "So come on, tell us. What kind of hoops did you have to jump through to pull that off?" or, "Say, that's difficult to accomplish. I've tried it myself with very little success. Tell me how you did it." While lifting others into the limelight, you'll also raise yourself in the process. That's called class.

Tip 186. Let Another Person Know She Is Superior to You in Some Skill.

My husband, who has mastered this principle, always has more advice than he can use on fishing. He simply lets others know that he respects their expertise about bait, gear, fishing depth, and the best places to go, and they're glad to show him how much they *really* know. For hours. At personal cost. People enjoy being helpful when they know the admiration is genuine.

Examples: "Could you help me out of this mess I've created for myself?" "You have far more experience in these situations than I do. What would you suggest?" "I know this seems simple to you, but it's complex to me." "Thanks for making me look good with this. You did a fine job." All such expressions give credit where it's due and make people feel good about themselves.

Tip 187. Let Others Impress You if You Want to Make a Good Impression Yourself.

Dale Carnegie introduced this principle decades ago—we win friends by making others feel important. People like to talk about themselves, so encourage them to do so. Let them know that you admire or respect them for some insight, talent, skill, philosophy, or attitude. We like those who like us. On the other hand, we don't appreciate those who say, by word, tone, or expression, "So what? I'm underwhelmed."

Tip 188. Think About the Imposition and the Options Before You Ask for a Favor.

Ask yourself the following questions before you ask for a favor: Is the favor a real imposition? Are you asking the other person to spend time, effort, or money that you wouldn't be willing to spend on the project yourself? Will the other person say yes out of guilt? Are you giving the other person an option to say no without feeling guilty? Only a yes to the last question qualifies you to ask the favor.

Tip 189. Don't Presume on a Friend; Ask for Permission.

Friends will love you even more for the courtesy you've shown when you don't impose on the relationship. Use the following when the occasion calls for it: "Do you agree that we should do X?" "Will it be an inconvenience if . . . ?" "Don't let me speak for you—do you agree that . . . ?" "Do you have a problem with my doing X? I can certainly wait if you think that's best." Never substitute friendship for thoughtfulness.

Tip 190. Use the Ben Franklin Technique to Win a Friend.

Ben Franklin grew frustrated with a rival printer who seemed always to oppose him on any issue that he favored in legislative gatherings. But Franklin determined to make a friend of him. Books in those days were hard-to-come-by treasures. So Ben Franklin knocked on his rival's door, explained that he did not own a copy of a particular book, and asked his enemy if he'd be so kind as to lend his copy. Quite shocked at the humility and request, the enemy loaned him the book. Franklin took the book home, kept it for a week, and then returned it with his thanks. The rival became his friend, proving Franklin right on an effective way to win people over.

Asking for favors takes humility. Showing humility allows the other person to feel benevolent and/or powerful. With those ego strokes, much of the hostility in a relationship melts. An additional reminder: Be sure the favor is one that requires little time, money, or effort.

Tip 191. Take the Pressure Off Others When They Make an Unintended Gaffe.

Someone says to you, "Did you see that new brochure they came out with? It looks like something out of a 1960 catalog—fine print, no color." When that person discovers that you designed the brochure, he'll feel as though somebody had punched him in the stomach. And the pain of embarrassment will be associated with you—even though the words came from *his* mouth. In such cases, be magnanimous. Laugh it off. Use a light retort, such as "Yeah, it won only honorable mention at home as well."

If the gaffe is serious enough, share your own blunders to let the other person know you identify with the embarrassment. The offender will be grateful for a long, long time. To any other observers, you'll look like a class act.

Tip 192. Select the Setting That Suits Your Purpose.

A conversation in the hallway around the water cooler takes on a more ominous tone if it's held in the boss's office. A phone complaint doesn't sound as serious as a written one. A challenge from the lectern packs more punch than one behind a golf club on the green.

Tip 193. Change Your Physical Environment to Promote the Interactions You Want.

Notice the difference in how you interact with a doctor as you get shuffled around her office, from bed to X-ray lab to the comfy desk-and-chair conference room. Notice the difference in speaking manner and audience reaction to a speaker behind a lectern as opposed to the same speaker in the aisles. Buyers and sellers take on different postures and purposes, depending on whether they're sitting across a desk or sitting on a sofa in the lobby.

Use this environment-body-mind link to promote the interactions you want. As boss, if you want to decrease your status to be "one of the gang," sit down rather than stand up to speak. If you want to encourage interaction among the office staff, change the traffic patterns in your open space. Literally build the interactions you want.

Tip 194. Measure Your Relationship with Others by the Kind of Conversation They Share with You.

On the shallowest level, people pass on clichés: "The project's going slowly." "I've seen better days." "Hang in there." "There's always the weekend."

On the next level, people care enough to share meaningful facts: "Jeevan said he was going to hire three engineers before the fourth quarter if we won the Hyatt contract."

On a more intimate level, people feel free to share their opinions and judgments: "Even if Jeevan hires more engineers, I still think we're in trouble on this project. You're going about this in the most expensive way. It's a short-term view of the whole customer relationship, and Lucille's going to be angry."

On the most intimate level, people share their feelings: "I'm discouraged with trying to set up a health-care plan that suits everybody. Frankly, I wish I'd never accepted this leadership position. All I'm getting from my peers is animosity, and all I'm getting from my family is anger about my weekend work."

If you want to gauge the progress of a relationship from the other person's point of view, listen to what he is willing to tell you: Clichés and perfunctory remarks? Facts? Opinions and judgments? Personal feelings?

As the relationship grows, you'll notice these verbal cues along the way: You'll begin to use "I," "you," "we," and "us" more often. You'll develop verbal shorthand between you—inside jokes and references to your history together. You'll notice that you've been collecting commonalities: shared assumptions, expectations, and values. You begin to "interpret" for each other. "So what you're really saying is that you want to dump the project?" If you want the relationship to grow, all these verbal clues become welcome signs.

Tip 195. Recognize That Intimacy Breeds Distance.

As you spend more time with someone and intimacy develops, you discover "sore spots"—things you can't talk about. Why? Because you've come to value the relationship, and you fear that if you open your mouth to disagree and offend that person, you'll damage the relationship. Intimacy means that you have more to lose. That's why the pendulum continually swings from intimacy to distance and back to intimacy. Expect and accept that cycle.

Tip 196. Don't Mention That You're Nervous.

Whether you're giving a big presentation, picking up a VIP at the airport for an important event, or briefing your teammates about a project, you may understandably get a case of nerves. You may even be tempted to confide in a colleague about your nervousness because it sometimes elicits empathy. On the other hand, others may become so worried about your nervousness that they can't focus on what you're saying.

You're likely to get either of two reactions. The "parent" may feel as though you're a child she must protect—rather than respect. Or the person may "smell blood," and you may become a victim of his attacks in your nervous state.

Tip 197. Make Sure Your Dress Doesn't Distract.

Anything that distracts detracts. Dangling noise from your jewelry shouldn't announce your arrival or departure. Ill-fitting clothes shouldn't tempt people to suggest that you go up or go down a size. An odd hairstyle shouldn't make people point and giggle. Sexy attire at a business meeting may suggest something other than what you had in mind for the close.

My preschooler embarrassed me as he walked along beside me in Manhattan years ago. In a sea of strangers, we met a rather oddly dressed and coiffed man coming toward us. My son pointed at the stranger directly facing us and yelled: "Mommy, *what's* that?"

If dress is the message, make it a fashion show.

Tip 198. Prepare Talking Points or Questions for Important Conversations.

Like almost anything else in life, important conversations can profit from preparation. If you plan to attend a networking event, and you want to meet a key person to discuss a specific issue, prepare talking points or key questions to guide the conversations. If you're invited to a dinner or a luncheon organized around a cause, anniversary, or fund-raiser, go with key points you'd like to make when you meet the host or organizer.

For a job interview, consider the three key attributes or areas of experience that you'd like to emphasize, with examples to support each. Then, in response to the interviewer's questions, you can bridge to those points when appropriate. At the end of the interview, employers almost always ask if you have further comments or questions. That's when you sum up with those talking points again.

Never walk into a meeting in which you think you might be called upon "for a quick project update" without your talking points. Be ready, be brief, and be brilliant.

Tip 199. Glow, but Don't Gloat.

Kids act cocky when they win the soccer game or the debate tournament. They tease the losers unmercifully: "Should have been on our team! We're going to State! Na-na-nah-na-nah!" Adults shouldn't mimic them when they get their way in a meeting or on a project, get the promotion, win the award, or squeeze out the competition to make the sale. Let your language and tone convey humility. Act cocky, and your colleagues will see that you lose next time—whatever it takes.

Tip 200. Be a Yes-Man or Yes-Woman.

Despite all the books written and all the speeches given on positive thinking, most people lean toward the negative. For several years, an author friend of mine has been collecting massive amounts of evidence on this natural bias toward negativity. Consider this: You and your significant other start to go out to dinner, and he looks nice. You say nothing. But let him dress in something unusual, and you say, "Are you wearing that?" Negative focus. Kara has a rental car and invites Robert to ride from the airport to the hotel. She selects an easy route. There's no traffic, and they make good time to the hotel. Robert offers no comment. But let them get stalled in traffic, and Robert says, "This probably wasn't the best way to come. Loop 219 would probably have been faster." Negative focus.

The negative focus in a meeting sounds like: "Tried that idea last year—didn't work." "Vice President Rodriquez would never sign off on that." "They won't let us do that—it's against company policy." "Do you realize how much time that would take?"

If you want to stand out in a crowd, try positive, encouraging comments when someone brings up a new idea. Look for the good before you focus on what's wrong with the idea.

Tip 201. Try the "Am I Wrong?" Approach to Point Out Errors.

On occasion, you may need to point out someone's error with more than the usual sensitivity. For example, you've just negotiated a great discount with your favorite supplier—and then she's made an error on the paperwork. Or, you're trying to get an appointment with a prospect, and he gave you the wrong address for his building. Or maybe you're talking to your future mother-in-law, and she miscalculated the wedding charges that you promised to reimburse.

Here are some tactful phrases that soften the you-are-wrong message: "I may be wrong, but it seems to me that..." "I might be mistaken here—and it wouldn't be the first time—but..." "I myself could be confused here, but it looks as though there's a mistake in..." Make your statement and then end with, "Am I wrong?"

With such wording, you're letting the other person confirm his own error, a face-saving maneuver for him.

Tip 202. Confess Your Ignorance to Connect With Another Person's "Best Self."

My husband will be the first to tell you that he's not a fixer-up kind of guy. He can change a lightbulb, but if anything else goes wrong around the house, we have to call Roger, our handyman. And if Roger can't do it, then it's a plumber, electrician, carpenter, exterminator, roofer, landscaper, or cable guy to the rescue. But we always get excellent service and good prices—and more after-the-service help and questions answered than you can ever imagine.

Here's why: When the repair person shows up, my husband immediately confesses his ineptness as a handyman. He'll typically say something like the following: "I'm totally ignorant when it comes to this sort of thing. Do you mind if I watch you do this? I'd like to learn. Consider me your gofer. Just tell me what you need."

The repair person may use him to help, send him to Home Depot for parts, or tell him just to leave her alone for a few hours, then she'll report back on what she's done and teach him how to prevent the problem in the future. But in all cases, the repair person's attitude changes dramatically.

My husband's confession puts her in a one-up position. It appeals to ego. People like to explain what they know.

You may ask, "Won't others take advantage of you in such situations?" Some may, but we haven't found that to be generally true. Such a confession appeals to a person's nobler self.

Tip 203. Ask Rather Than Command.

"Gary, take these by the copy office when you leave." "Get us another fork over here, please—and more bread." "Have that report to me before you go on vacation because I need to see those numbers for my update." Such commands make people bristle, even if you're the boss or the customer and the other person has to comply.

You'll typically get a faster response with a better attitude when you *ask* someone to do something: "Gary, would you mind taking these by the copy office when you leave?" "We need another fork and some bread, please. Can you help when you get a moment?" "Will you please have that report to me before you go on vacation because I need to see those numbers for my update." Even if you're in a position to give a directive as a supervisor, asking improves attitude. People will get the message.

Tip 204. Make It Personal.

For the past couple of decades, we've heard the refrain, "Hey, it's not personal; this is just business." That was the mantra when someone got negative feedback, got passed over for promotion, got downsized, or got crossed off an invitation list. Today, the trend is to personalize everything. On Tuesday, a blogger may protest a dictatorship around the world, and on Wednesday she blogs about her dachshund digging around in the backyard.

Just a few years ago, large organizations tried to prevent their employees from responding to customer comments online; today, they encourage employees to jump into the fray and tweet responses to questions and complaints.

Marketing letters used to be written from the corporate "suits" and sent en masse by the millions to clients. Today, these same corporations encourage each business development rep to write her own e-mails tailored to specific prospects and clients.

So follow the trend. Loosen up. Whether you're making a formal presentation, e-mailing, or simply chitchatting about your organization, aim for the personal touch. People do business with people—not with organizations. Make it personal.

Tip 205. Interject Rather Than Interrupt.

Interjecting implies finding an open spot in the flow of conversation. Interrupting implies an unexpected trounce that *breaks apart* the flow of ideas in a conversation. Interjecting a comment *adds* to the plethora of ideas in a conversation. Interrupting comments distract from the main ideas under discussion. People who interject ideas typically enliven a discussion, while those who interrupt generally offend.

Tip 206. Do Not Assume That Others Know "The Backstory."

Think how wealthy you'd be if you had a dollar every time someone said to you after a major foul-up, "But I thought they'd surely know that blah, blah, blah." They don't know. Really. The details of our lives loom so large to us that we expect others around us to be familiar with and up to speed on our client issues, employee crises, quarterly commitments, and team projects. So we fail to communicate the full story when a crisis develops and dictates a sudden change of plans. That change often means that other processes have to be altered or stopped. But frequently the word doesn't travel fast enough. The situation becomes a train wreck. The common explanation from the person who didn't pass on the change of plans? "Well, I assumed they'd know." Take it from me—they don't know.

Tip 207. Don't Babble On.

Candidates in presidential debates get two minutes to lay out their case in response to a question. Advertisers shoot for 30- to 60-second spots. Spokespersons hit the airwaves with 20-second sound bites prepared to drive home their key points. Tweets run 140 characters. People have short attention spans. Tailor your message accordingly, or your colleagues will begin to consider conversations with you tedious.

Tip 208. Wade In, Rather Than Jump, to Create Anticipation.

The principle of supply and demand comes into play in conversations. Some people feel compelled to jump into any and all discussions, no matter how unqualified they may be to express an opinion on the topic. Others linger and listen before leaping in. Those who listen before they speak— and even delay speaking until they're asked directly for their opinions— often get the best hearing and most respect for their ideas.

I belong to a mastermind group where this plays out monthly. On almost any agenda topic, Phil speaks up first or second, and his ideas often seem conventional and predictable. On the other hand, Andres rarely opens his mouth until everyone else has spoken. But when he offers his opinion, all eyes focus on him. The long wait builds anticipation. When he does decide to deliver the goods, the group listens in awe.

Tip 209. Dig for the One Thing Positive in Those You Don't Like.

Novelists know that even their worst characters have to have at least one good trait to be believable. Otherwise, the book reviewers call them "cardboard" characters. The bank robber helps little old ladies across the street, the abusive husband makes a darn good living for his family, and the prostitute gives her last fifty dollars to an orphan. Nobody can be all bad and still be believable.

Your challenge is to probe for that "one positive thing" in a person you don't like. Does he meet deadlines? Does he pay attention to detail? Does he have a commanding voice with customers and is able to calm them when they're upset? Find that skill, attitude, or trait and focus on it. Ask for details about it. Solicit the person's opinions relating to that skill. Think about how those opinions or that skill benefits you, your team, or your organization in the long run. To get along, keep your communication and attention on "the one thing."

Tip 210. Turn Off Your Cell Phone in Their Face.

How often do you see just the opposite? Jorge walks into the restaurant to join his friend for lunch. He sits down at the table and plops his cell phone and keys right on the table between them. The message: "I may get a call, and that call is likely to be more important than you. If so, I want to know who it is immediately so that I can make a decision about taking the call or continuing my conversation with you."

If you want to send the opposite message when you join your friend or client, pull out your cell phone and let her see you silence the thing or power down. You're sending this message: "You're my top priority right now."

Tip 211. Stop the Luxury-Dropping.

You've probably known and grown a distaste for name-droppers. Equally off-putting are those who, when talking to the less fortunate, refer to their exotic vacations, their summer home and their winter home, their gardener, their tailor, and their private plane. This misguided attempt to earn admiration most often results in alienation. Emphasizing what you have that others cannot afford only magnifies differences and creates distance. Why do that?

Tip 212. Know When to Play Supporting Actor.

In many situations, conversations, and events, you are the star. It's all about you—the plot, the dialogue, the characters, and the theme all exist to make you look good. But on other occasions, it's all about someone else—your administrative assistant, the design team, your spouse, your kids, the host, the charity, or the cause. It's your turn to play supporting actor in their scene. Don't step on their lines. Don't try to steal the spotlight. Don't take their bows. If you do, the audience will resent you, and the real star may never forgive you.

Tip 213. Recall and Recap a Detail.

Business development people have been using this technique for years to build rapport. As they interact with their clients and prospects, they learn little details such as their birthdays, their children's names, or their hobbies and record them. Then they remember to send a card or an e-mail on the birthdays, ask about their kids, or forward them an article related to their hobby.

Of course, your intention isn't to sell anybody anything, but you want to make people feel special. So as you're talking to them, mention something you recall from a previous conversation: "How did that project ever turn out where you had to ship all those mock-ups to Brazil?" "So how did you enjoy your ski trip last winter? The last time we talked, you were telling me you were going to give in and take lessons before doing cross-country." Guaranteed, your colleague will walk away from the conversation feeling extra special that you remembered.

Tip 214. Clear the Clichés from Your Brain.

Well, okay, maybe ridding yourself of all clichés would be an impossible task. But try to get the most egregious of them out of your veins: "Have a nice day." (Gee, I was planning on having a rotten day.) "Safe travels." (No way! I was going to go right out into traffic and try to kill myself.) "I'm either on the phone or away from my desk." (No kidding.) "If I can answer any further questions, please do not hesitate to call." (Really? I feel relieved. I was so nervous about calling you.) "Thank you in advance." (Too busy to bother afterward, huh?)

Fortunately, the responses will not be as sarcastic as those in parentheses here—but then again, you can't see what people are thinking. Express the concern or sentiment, but choose original phrasing.

Tip 215. Don't Use, Like, Words Instead of, You Know, Pauses.

For some people, word fillers (*like, you know, uh, hmmm, you follow me?*) become a form of punctuation. Dropped into sentences, these word fillers, like, give the speaker or writer time to stop, right?, and think about where he wants to go next. But, you know, it's like, these people can't understand, like, how much these words interrupt, like, the smooth flow of the sentence. You follow me? So, uh, just pausing, like, to gather their thoughts about the topic, you know, and then continuing seems awkward to them. You follow me? In essence, they're punctuating, like, with a word rather than a comma. You know?

Tip 216. Shush Those Who Share Too Much.

You've heard of buyer's remorse. That's typically the situation when someone buys on impulse and then regrets it on later reflection. A related condition, sharer's remorse, sets in when a colleague starts to relate personal information in a situation in which her best judgment has been altered—for example, after a few drinks, or after an emotional break-up or scene with a spouse, or after a run-in with the law. In such an emotional or depressed state, people pour out details. But when they feel better, they're embarrassed at what they've told you and avoid you in the future.

Unless your relationship has progressed to the level of intimacy, at the point when a colleague starts to share embarrassing personal details, either change the subject or end the conversation. The friend may miss you at the moment, but she will love you in the morning.

Tip 217. Refrain from Rattling Off Excuses; Offer Explanations.

When you miss a deadline, join the conference call late, or rush into a meeting after it has begun and start spitting out excuses, you sound insecure. Whatever you say will typically sound like the schoolchild's, "The dog ate my homework." Generally, you'll sound more seasoned, decisive, and credible if you first speak up on the subject at hand and then in some way allude to the reason for your earlier tardiness. At that point, the reason comes across as an explanation rather than an excuse.

Tip 218. Make Promises Public Only if You Plan to Keep Them.

For the same reason that you shut people up when they start to tell you embarrassing things about themselves, you'll want to speak up about your commitments. Consider why couples share marriage vows in front of family and friends, why CEOs share the year's goals with employees, or why the president makes pledges in the annual state of the union speech. Accountability.

Words spoken in public carry more weight than those said in private for several reasons: They focus attention, gain support, inspire others, and make the speaker accountable. So give careful consideration to your public statements of what you plan to do. Your credibility depends on it.

Tip 219. Select the Implicit or Explicit Channel with Care.

Have you ever heard anybody say, usually with pride, "I'm just the kind of person who says what's on my mind." Get out of the way. Yes, that person may be honest, but he's often brutally honest, leaving wounded people in his path. This person rarely becomes a leader. What is proper and acceptable, we say explicitly. What might offend, we imply. Why? Because we're civilized. People matter.

Tip 220. Do Not Converse to Compete.

Some people compete in marathons; others drive race cars; still others write 25-word jingles about why Brand X is their favorite cereal, soap, or soup. And if you observed them over a few days or weeks, you'd discover that some people compete when they talk. They enter a conversation to win—when it matters, when it doesn't matter, and when it's totally beside the point. They feel the need to correct people. They must provide the missing detail. They have to have the last word. They must bring everyone around to their point of view.

Conversation is not about competition. If fact, if you always win, you lose.

3

Making Small Talk a Big Deal

During the Samuel Johnson days they had big men enjoying small talk; today we have small men enjoying big talk.
—Fred Allen

Talk to anyone about himself and he will listen without interrupting.
—Herbert V. Prochnow

The minute a man is convinced that he is interesting, he isn't.
—Stephen Leacock

A bore is someone who has no small talk.
—Michael Korda

One of the troubles of small talk is that it usually comes in large doses.
—No attribution

Wit is the salt of conversation, not the food.
—William Hazlitt

The trouble with a fellow who talks too fast is that he is liable to say something he hasn't thought of yet.
—Calvin Coolidge

Inject a few raisins of conversations into the tasteless dough of existence.
—O. Henry

Small talk means having a little loose change in your pocket. Like pennies in the checkout lane, quarters at a tollbooth, or dollar bills in a taxi, it'll come in handy when you least expect it. When it comes to small talk, you need to know when to jiggle it, spend it, or save it.

Tip 221. Work at Building Rapport.

Not all small talk is the same. With some people, you walk away having killed a few moments. With others, you feel a real connection and a desire to get to know them better. What's the difference? The effort that one or both of you have made at building rapport. What helps make the connection? Calling the other person by name several times during the conversation; mentioning other things you have in common (mutual acquaintances, places you've lived or visited, experiences you've shared, or career or personal goals); showing interest in that person's views or pastimes; and matching the other person's delivery style, voice volume and tone, emotion, and body language as you talk.

Basically, people like and feel a kinship with others who like them, appreciate them, enjoy the same things they do, and are helpful to them. Time and attention make the connection that lasts.

Tip 222. Know When Small Talk Is Appropriate.

Be sensitive to the other person's mood and circumstances. On an airplane, if your seatmate is obviously preoccupied, leave him alone. Neither would you try to engage someone in small talk when he's dashing down the hallway to make a meeting. On other occasions, small talk is inappropriate because of the person involved. If the CEO has unexpectedly called you in for "a little chat," this is not the time for you to take the lead. Let her dictate the topic and the pace with which you get down to business. The same is true with customers. Develop a sixth sense about those who appreciate small talk and those who don't.

Tip 223. Accept the Fact That Some People Don't Want to Make Contact at All.

Some people see small talk not as an opportunity for rapport building but as an infringement and an inconvenience. A salesman who was waiting for other registrants at a seminar asked an older guest nearby if he knew of a good Italian restaurant. The older guest turned away without answering. The salesman repeated the question louder, and the older guest again turned back to his conversation with his wife.

After the salesman gave up and stepped onto the elevator, the wife turned to her husband and asked, "Why didn't you answer him?" The husband mumbled, "If I'd named a restaurant, he'd have wanted to know how to get there. If I'd have told him how to get there, he wouldn't have understood and I'd have had to go with him. And if I'd have had to go with him, you would have been left here alone. And if you'd been left alone, you would have griped and complained. And you know how I hate a griping, nagging wife. We'd have been in divorce court before you know it, and I couldn't bear the thought of you on the street being picked up by the likes of that salesman."

Reading the signals from those people isn't difficult; simply respect their wishes.

Tip 224. Think Twice About Small Talk on the Phone.

Your timing for small talk is more, not less, crucial when you phone someone. When you're face to face, another person can use closed body language to signal you that she's busy, distracted, or involved in an intense conversation with someone else and prefers not to be disturbed. Not so on the phone. If you've placed the call, the rules of etiquette say that you're in control. But in reality, your call may be an intrusion at that moment. Therefore, don't assume that people expect or welcome a little chitchat before you get down to business.

Picture yourself in your office. A colleague brings in express mail from a customer who has rejected your latest contract and wants an addendum by the end of the day. A meeting that you're leading starts in five minutes, and you're still working on the agenda. An e-mail from your boss has just popped into your inbox; he wants to talk to you about Geraldine, who's threatening to resign at the end of the day. Your phone rings and the caller says, "So, Larry, how's it going? Your football team didn't look so good last weekend. What do you think happened?"

Feel like chit-chatting?

Remember that you have a one-up position when you place a call, and the other person can't make a quick getaway. The timing can be devastating to your reputation. Know where you're going with the call and be prepared to get there. If the other person sends you a cue that small talk is in order, you can always change course and accommodate the lighter mood.

Tip 225. Make the Small Talk on a Teleconference Inclusive.

When you log on to a teleconference five minutes early, don't exclude or bore people with details of your trip to Spain last month or zero in with questions about Ralph's recent school-board election. Instead, if you choose to chitchat while you're waiting for others to come on the line, toss out inclusive comments or questions: "Does anybody know how our stock prices are doing today?" "We're hearing rumors here in our Atlanta offices that the new Zooko product is doing extremely well in the Asian markets. Anybody hearing details on that?" Or: "We're having terrible snowstorms out here in the west this week. What's the weather like in your regions? Everybody on your teams make it in to work all week?" Let everybody play.

Tip 226. Risk Being the First to Say Hello.

You can narrow your odds of being snubbed if you look for someone with open body language and a timid expression, somebody who is "in between" conversations, or somebody who makes eye contact and returns your smile. Somebody has to risk rejection, and it might as well be you as the next person.

Tip 227. Introduce Yourself in a Way That Allows People to Respond or Connect.

"Hello. I'm Ty Wycosky, one of the team from San Francisco," or, "I'm Maria Garcia. Bill Thomas is one of my customers." Just add one other phrase in addition to your name that gives people a clue about what you might have in common so that they can ask about it or comment on it.

Tip 228. Help People Remember Your Name.

When others look panic-stricken about not being able to remember your name, take the pressure off: "I'm George Stallings—we met last week in the bank lobby when the lady in front of us brought in 17 jars of pennies." They'll be grateful, and you'll feel less embarrassed.

Better yet, give people a permanent way to recall your name. Here's my shtick when people have difficulty remembering or pronouncing my name: "My name's Dianna Booher, as in BOO-her, except I hope they applaud rather than boo."

Tip 229. Remember Others' Names.

Listen to a name the first time you hear it. Repeat it aloud, and ask the owner to verify that you have it correct. Use it immediately in the conversation during the next three minutes. Study the person's face. Take a mental snapshot. When he isn't looking at you, note tiny details that make him memorable. Fix his face, body structure, hairstyle, or mannerisms in your mind just as though you were studying a mug shot to identify the person who robbed your house. Details are what make it easy to connect people with their name.

The next step is to associate the name with that visual picture or a concrete item the name conjures up. Like a cartoonist, pick out one outstanding feature and exaggerate it in your mind. The next time you see that person, that feature will "jump out" at you and trigger the name. A big, lumbering guy named Jack might trigger the association of a lumberjack because of his size and manner. Associate "look-alikes" with celebrity names, features with animals, mannerisms with occupations, and so forth.

Another link may be to associate the name with the person's voice or an activity or habit. Bart has a barking voice. Katy flies a kite. Mike needs a microphone. Tucker tucks notes in his briefcase.

If necessary, write the name down as soon as you can do so without being obvious about what you're writing. Names are important—listen to them, repeat them, attach them, and fix them in your mind for later recall.

Tip 230. Personalize Your Greetings.

Instead of using typical perfunctory comments when meeting people, make them feel special by adding their names and mentioning specifics that apply only to them. *Not:* "How's it going?" *But:* "Tina, how's it going with your latest project?" *Not:* "Good morning." *But:* "Good morning, Rita. Looks like you and I are stuck in a rut with these same cafeteria muffins every morning." *Not:* "How's the world treating you?" *But:* "Jack, how're those engineers treating you over in Marketing?"

Tip 231. Gain Partial Credit by Recalling the Meeting if Not the Name.

When someone approaches you and you recall the face but not the name, at least prove that you haven't forgotten the person totally. "It's nice to see you again. I believe we met at the BBA convention in Anaheim. You had just changed jobs at Kellogg. Help me with the name again."

You can often get people to help you by introducing them to others in your group; they'll supply the name before you have to. Bingo, you've got the name. Be honest if you draw a complete blank on both the name and the person, and she offers no help. She'll know the truth, and you'll gain another strike by lying about it.

Try humor: "Your name again? I have trouble remembering my own sometimes. The aging process, you know." Or: "I'm sorry but I'm terrible with names—I even run through my kids' names like a laundry list before I get to the one I want."

Tip 232. Recall to the Person Your Topic of Conversation the Last Time You Were Together.

Others will be flattered that you remembered, and your comment serves as proof that you did indeed pay attention and consider them important. "John, you gave me so many tips about mutual fund investing last month. I enjoyed our talk very much."

Tip 233. Arrive Early Rather Than Late to an Event.

Arriving fashionably late makes it doubly difficult for you to feel confident as you enter a party in progress. Instead, arrive early and meet the small group who will gladly welcome and grab and shake the hand of anyone else who shows up a little early or just on time. You'll probably get assigned a task: to welcome others, hang up coats, do name tags, tell people where to put gifts, and so forth. And that's perfect. It puts you in a high-traffic area with a reason to meet and talk to everyone on the guest list! An extra benefit is that the band of early arrivers often becomes a sisterhood of sorts itself—your "group" for ongoing conversation and check-ins during the event.

Tip 234. Stop, Look, and Listen as You Enter an Event.

As you come through the door at a party or a networking event, don't slip in. Like the game-show host waiting offstage, enter with excitement. Then stop inside the doorway to scope out the scene. Look around the room to see what's where and who's doing what. Stand confidently with a big smile on your face. Wave at a few people or workers across the room—it can be the guy serving drinks behind the bar or the wait staff carrying platters. Nobody knows or cares whom you're waving to or which group of friends you're trying to spot. Listen to where the laughter and the voices are coming from. Where's the action? If you're shy, you'll be inclined to join the edges of the group. Instead, move confidently toward the noisiest group.

Tip 235. Go Play in the Traffic.

Don't warm the wall. If you do, you're likely to remain there all night—or, at best, be with one or two other lonely souls. If you have trouble entering groups and breaking into a conversation, position yourself in the high-traffic areas near the food, the doorway, the band, or the dance floor. People will surround you, and you'll have many opportunities to start conversations. When you find someone you want to spend longer than two or three minutes with, you can always move to the side and continue the conversation on a less superficial level than "opening lines."

Get in a food or drink line. Hand a plate or glass to the person behind you and strike up a conversation. Move to a standing-only table so others can join you easily. When you refill your drink or snack plate, offer to bring something back for others at the table as well. Don't sit down; others will think you're waiting for companions to surround you. Introduce the two people standing on either side of you. Go where people congregate and make yourself of service to them.

Tip 236. Comment on Unique Accessories.

Jewelry, scarves, and pens—people buy such things and wear them to events as conversation pieces, so use them to make a connection. Ask for details about them; compliment them.

Tip 237. Investigate the Sponsor; Check Out the Literature.

Visit the information table or rack. Typically, when events are sponsored by charities or other nonprofits, the sponsors have their literature displayed. Ask questions of others collecting literature there as well. What is their connection to the group? What have they learned so far, and what do they find intriguing and worth further investigation?

Tip 238. Strike Up a Conversation with Someone Who Looks Shy.

That person will be grateful for someone to talk with and will respond to almost any topic you toss out. As you and the other person build up your confidence, you can either part ways or bring others into your circle.

Tip 239. Play Host Rather Than Guest.

Friends of mine, Bob and Jane Handley, always seem to circulate well and know everybody at every party. Finally, I discovered their secret for being in the middle of every huddle. They simply took it upon themselves to play hosts rather than guests. They join a quiet group, introduce themselves to the person beside them, and then turn to another person on the right or left or passing by and say, "Mike, have you met Sam? He's with Allied. A chemical engineer." Bob listens to them talk for a few moments and then is off to make the next introduction, to freshen someone's drink, to show someone to the coatroom, or to beg someone to sing or play the latest hit.

Those who consider themselves guests, on the other hand, take a passive role and often feel either trapped by a bore or neglected by the most entertaining group.

Don't wait for others to introduce you, offer you food, suggest that you tell a story, or lead you to meet the new manager. Instead, play host yourself and look for things to do: music to play, food to replenish, people to introduce, traffic to monitor, tickets to sell, entertainment to encourage or praise, name badges to make, people to hug.

Tip 240. Bring Along Your Own PR Person.

If you feel immodest singing your own praises, but your purpose is to get attention from the "right" people, consider making the rounds with a friend who can make the offhand comments that you can't. "Hey, guys, I've got someone with me that you should meet: Marguerite. She's leading the new development team for the StarFish package. That's the project that's going to fund all our retirement condos in Hawaii!" or "Al, have you met Rosalinda? She's just sold over a quarter million worth of widgets in her first four months. Pretty impressive, huh? I'm standing close so it'll rub off on me."

Tip 241. Don't Intrude.

Be aware of groups that seem to be involved in an intense, confidential conversation. They'll be standing nose to nose and toes to toes, and they'll glare at anyone who approaches. If you enter such a conversation by accident, you can excuse yourself with, "I'm sorry. I didn't know you were involved in a confidential conversation" and move on.

Tip 242. Choose a Topic Appropriate to the Group, the Atmosphere, the Relationship, and Your Purpose.

Begin with one of the three options open to you: ask a question, state a fact, or voice an opinion. Generally, you're safe in discussing the other person's area of expertise or your own, the current affair you're attending, or the day's news.

General Topics

- Vacations—most interesting, least interesting, most rewarding
- Career goals for the next 10 years
- Job (What do you like most about your job? What do you enjoy the least?)
- Company culture
- Promotions or awards—who's getting them
- Hobbies
- Sports
- Current projects
- A specialty or unique skill
- Happenings that were embarrassing, amusing, or meaningful to you
- Your/his hopes or beliefs for the future about an issue, problem, or fear
- Community activities, causes, problems
- Current newspaper headlines
- Current court cases
- The arts—movies, plays, books
- The latest exploits of your favorite cartoon strip
- A funny thing that happened to someone you know
- New restaurants or amusement parks
- Her hometown (new features, likes, dislikes, leading industries, sources of shame or pride)
- Game playing:

  "If you could change occupations without any retraining, what would you like to do?"

  "If you could have dinner with anyone in the world, whom would you choose?"

  "If you had a million dollars to donate to charity, where would it go?"

  "What do you like or dislike most about this city or /state?"

  "Who was the most influential person in your life or your work?"

  "Who was your favorite boss or teacher?"

  "What was your most embarrassing moment?"

  "What's the funniest clean joke you know?"

  "So whom do you admire the most?"

- Poll taking:
  "So how do you think the ruling should go?"
  "So how high or low do you think taxes or interest rates will go?"
  "So how many people are you guessing will accept the retirement package?"

Talking with a Child

- School subjects he likes or hates
- One new thing she's learned during the week
- The culture of the school—what's fun there
- His parents' work
- Her favorite teacher
- What he does after school
- Her best friends and what she likes about them
- His favorite TV programs

Talking with a VIP

- Do you dread being away from your family?
- Does changing time zones so frequently bother you?
- How do you manage to keep your schedule straight?
- When do you find time to shop?
- To what do you attribute your success?
- To whom do you attribute much of your success?
- What's the most rewarding thing about your career?
- What advice would you give to someone just starting out in your field?
- Would you do things differently if you had to start over?
- Who gave you your first break or job?
- What was the best career decision you ever made?
- Do you try to keep your personal life and business life separate, or do they mesh well?
- Does your spouse appreciate your success?
- What does your family think about your success?

Talking with the Ill or Bereaved

- I imagine he had such a wonderful/full/interesting life.
- So tell me about the happy times with her.

- So tell me what kind of person he was.
- John has told me so much about your mother. He said she was ...
- So, are others involved in his care?

Tip 243. Ask About the Person's Most Recent Few Moments or Hours

People tend to be wrapped up in their most recent experiences—the traffic jam they just escaped; the project they left behind at the office; the client who's breathing down their neck for the new proposal. Let them dump it by asking, "What's your day been like?" or "You look as though you've just escaped from a pressing problem. What's on your mind?" They'll love the opportunity to pour out the details. Tomorrow the same conversation would be stale, but at the moment their head is swirling with the minutiae of the last event, struggle, mishap, or triumph.

Tip 244. Use "TALK" for a Topic Tickler.

Generally, the following four categories will help you recall areas of interest for conversational topics and questions to connect with others:

T = Timelines (What does your schedule look like next week, month, or quarter? Follow up on the events, projects, and activities mentioned.)

A = Activities (What are your hobbies? What causes are you involved with?)

L = Likes and dislikes (What do you like about your job? What do you dislike?)

K = Kids (*or parents or spouse*) (Tell me about your family . . .)

Tip 245. Toss Out Topics Like Bingo Cards.

In bingo, every player gets a card. When the caller announces a number, every player stays engaged, even though he may not get to cover a square. Similarly, in conversation, a single comment may rule out some of the players, but the general topics should be inclusive enough to engage everyone. If you bring up genetic engineering, chances are that you may have only one expert in the group who can contribute. But when the discussion deteriorates into a monologue of facts, energy escapes and people drift away.

Select general rather than esoteric topics—the NFL rather than the Washington Redskins, gas prices rather than the service station on Highway 288, the Olympics rather than pole vaulting.

Tip 246. Use Opening Lines That Lead Some Place.

Try a few of these as staples:

"What's this economy doing to your business or industry?"

"What do you think about the party?"

"Did you read the paper today?"

"How do you fit into the picture they're discussing?"

"What's your role in this project/group/crowd?"

"What experience have you had in this arena?"

"I'm not familiar with your industry/group. Will you give me a little background?"

"How's life treating you this month/this week/today?"

"Am I interrupting a personal conversation?"

"So tell me who won today—you or the lions?"

"Someone told me you were the one to ask about X. I need advice."

"Jim told me to be sure to come talk to you."

"Sherry wanted me to say hello for her."

"It's certainly pretty/noisy/cold/fun in here, isn't it?"

"The atmosphere here reminds me of my junior prom/our last sales convention/our board meetings."

"Doesn't Ginny look gorgeous/happy/excited/pleased/proud tonight?"

"Isn't this food delicious? Do you know what's in it?"

"I don't know a soul here, so I'm going to barge right in and eavesdrop."

"What do all these people here have in common?"

"How was the traffic/parking/weather on the way in?"

"How do you know the host/group/boss/couple?"

"People seem to be enjoying themselves, don't you think?"

"So what do you do for a living?"

"So what do you do when you're not working?"

"Are you enjoying the cruise/party/project/seminar?"

"Your clothes are fascinating/classy/so colorful."

"Where do you call home?"

"So, have you spent your entire career in this industry?"

"Do you come here often?"

"Do you know many of these people?"

"This group sounds like the one that's having the most fun. May I join? I could use a laugh."

"You people look like movers and shakers. May I join you?"

"This group looks so intense. I'm wondering what the topic is?"

"I've just been standing here listening, but you've touched a passionate chord in me. I think . . ."

"I've got a question. Do you know if . . . ?"

"I need help. Can you tell me where I could find . . . ?"

"I've always been interested in X, but I know very little about it. Can you tell me more about it?"

"I've always wished I knew more about starting a business or managing people. What's the most difficult thing you face?"

"I'm always interested in unusual names. Tell me the origin of yours."

"So what's going on in your life now?"

"We haven't talked in a while. Give me an update on X."

"You know, I see you often, but I don't think we've met. My name's Barbara."

Tip 247. To Stir Quiet People to Expression, Select a Topic About Which They Can Feel Passionate.

Such conversational options as patriotism, gratitude, respect, generosity, hatred, or integrity issues tug at the shy person's heart, leading her to speak up and offer feelings, opinions, and personal experiences—or at least reactions to yours.

Tip 248. Know Which Topics to Avoid.

Proceed with caution on these: religion, politics, race, frightening probabilities, criticisms of others, personal tidbits about others, or personal news, such as your ex-spouse's shenanigans or your daughter's drug problem. Avoid any subject that equates to a rut—don't be known as the person with the one-channel chat.

Tip 249. Play the Part of the "Stranger in Town" with Class.

If you seem to be the only one in a group who doesn't know the others or know much about a event or purpose, ask questions about the city, group, features, history, accomplishments, or future plans. People love to talk about themselves, and their city or professional or social group is an extension of themselves. Never comment negatively on the person's city or group affiliation. Negatives earn the same response as pointing out mustard stains on someone's clothing.

Tip 250. Develop Your Timing Instinct.

Check to see who is entering or leaving your group. How long do you have before you'll be interrupted to move into the serving line or hear the entertainment? Do you read the body language as boredom or impatience? It may not be the topic but the timing of your small talk before getting down to business that makes others seem stiff and ill at ease.

Tip 251. Read the Other Person's Mindset by His Opening Line.

If you ask, "How are you?" and the other person responds with, "I'm hanging in there," you can assume that this person wants to talk about a current problem. If the person answers, "Great, how about you?" she's in an exuberant mood. The same "Good, how about you?" spoken in a flat tone says that the person wants to avoid the discussion altogether—it's business as usual.

Tip 252. Cue Off Someone's Business Card or LinkedIn Profile.

When someone hands you a business card, examine it carefully for a conversation cue. For example, read the brand slogan aloud: "Increasing Productivity Through Effective Communication—How exactly do you do that?" Comment on the address: "I noticed from your Linked In profile that you're located in the Greenway area. How far is that from downtown? What other businesses are located nearby?" Refer to the person's title: "How long have you been in that position? What exactly does that entail?" Again, people like talking about their favorite topic—themselves.

Tip 253. Personalize Your LinkedIn Introductions.

Rather than send a LinkedIn message with a generic introduction or an offer "to help in any way I can," you'll make a far better impression in your online small-talk situations by sending a message with a question or comment that indicates you've read the person's profile and found it of specific interest. For example, "Jill, I noticed that you've been affiliated with several financial organizations and now run your own audit consulting firm. If you have occasion to need audit reports for South American clients, I can help you get translations of your boilerplates." Here's another LinkedIn comment that a "networker" sent me recently: "I notice you're an author. Love your book titles. Could you answer a question: What's the difference between a literary agent and a book packager?"

Tip 254. Cover for Someone's Memory Lapse with a Repeated Question.

Before I speak to a group, I often arrive early and meet a few people as they walk into the room. Generally, there's a systematic way to do this because people are seated in rows, and I can meander down a long row across the front or back of the room or shake hands with people seated along one of the aisles. The problem arises when people don't sit down immediately, but instead are milling around the room before the program begins. That makes it difficult for me to recall whom I've met and what I've asked them.

Recently, I had an embarrassing situation happen in which I asked one of these wandering people in my pre-speech moments the same question twice. "So what do you do?" I asked.

"We're a translation company—to the health-care industry," he responded.

About ten minutes later, I turned around, and the same man was standing in front of me again. Absentmindedly I asked, "So what does your company do?"

He glared at me and responded the second time: "We're a translation company. To the health-care industry."

The moment he said it, I remembered—and grew appropriately embarrassed. What he could have done—and what you can do to help your colleagues save face in a similar situation—is to answer a repeated question more specifically the second time around. Here's an example of how he could have answered the second time:

"So what do you do?"

"Well, sometimes we translate for a second-language speaker in ER. We have either someone on site or someone who's available by phone. We also translate signs in multiple languages for hospitals or doctor's offices. We also translate training materials and lead classes for the nursing staff."

With that different answer, I would have immediately remembered his first response and assumed that he thought I was probing for more detail. Both of us would have looked better in that encounter. If your client or customer feels good about the conversation, you win.

Tip 255. Relax Your Body Language if You Want a Relaxed Conversation.

When people stand erect, tense, and "on guard," those talking to them unconsciously begin to mirror that posture. As a result, the entire conversation becomes uneasy, stiff, and formal. If you want to be light and amusing, relax your body and the tone of the conversation will follow.

Tip 256. Recognize That the Response You Get Will Often Reflect Your Own Tone and Delivery.

If you toss out an opener with an amused smile and a light tone, people will usually respond in kind. If, on the other hand, you have a furrowed brow and look depressed when you ask their opinions on the economy, they may think you expect a serious dissertation on the subject. Rather than tackling the topic, they'll often give an offhanded comment and move on.

Tip 257. Ask Easy Questions First to Relax People.

People have a fear of being sucked into conversations that are over their heads and then left to drown. When introducing a new topic, toss out a question that requires an easy response, not an essay. As the other person relaxes in your presence, you or others can develop the topic with more specific questions and leads.

Tip 258. Ask for Opinions Rather Than Information.

When you ask others for information, such as, "What is the latest news on the XYZ case?" either they can tell you or they can't. If they can tell you, it's no big ego stroke for them to simply share common information. If they can't come up with the information, they'll feel uninformed or ignorant. When you ask for an opinion, however, people feel complimented. No matter whether they're informed or up to date, people always feel free to express their opinions, and flattered that you asked for them. They'll talk longer and more eloquently if your question touches issues about which they feel passionate. The more interest you show in that opinion, the more complimented they'll feel.

Tip 259. Don't Ask Questions That Are Too Broad to Answer.

"What do you think we need to do to get a handle on poverty?" "What do we need to do about TV violence?" "What's wrong with the youth of today?" Such questions sound too global for anyone to be interested in tackling them. Owners of LinkedIn groups have learned this principle the hard way when they post discussion questions and no one responds. Generally, the problem is that the question is too broad rather than too narrow. Narrow the focus to one aspect of an issue, and you'll find that more people have opinions and information to share.

Tip 260. Tickle People's Creative Fancy.

If you know that someone has special expertise in your topic, or if your topic is of general interest, toss out a project or problem that you "might" do or solve someday: "I'm thinking of recovering all the windows in my house. Got any ideas?" or "I'm toying with the idea of writing a book for my grandchildren—sort of a legacy. What kinds of things do you think I should include?" or "I'm planning a roast for an upcoming retirement luncheon. Got any gags or appropriate one-liners?" or "I'm planning my parents' twenty-fifth wedding anniversary celebration. Somebody give me ideas." Asking for input compliments others and gives them an enjoyable creative workout.

Tip 261. Pique Others' Curiosity with an Incomplete Comment.

Choose a subject that people will have some interest in, even though they may lack knowledge about it, and toss out a half-baked but intriguing observation. Try something like: "I'm planning to sell everything I own within six months," or "Kids are smarter than their years these days," or "I just saw Kim racing up 14 flights of stairs," or "Give me a moment to calm down. I'm considering murder at the moment," or "Teenagers— I've come to the conclusion that they're not real people." Such a comment will spur others to ask you to elaborate, and you're into a new topic. If it doesn't work and they either show no interest or miss the cue, shake your head as if still intrigued by a past conversation and then move on to something else.

Tip 262. Avoid Questions That Lead People On When You Have No Interest in Their Answers.

I call this the you-talk-while-I-look-around-and-see-what-else-is-happening ploy. "Tell me what you think about the state of communism today." "You read a lot, don't you? Tell me about the kinds of books you enjoy." "Are smartphones taking over the world? What do you use yours for?" That kind of question puts the other person on the spot to take the conversational ball while knowing you're going to tune out. This dishonest baiting question makes the other person feel downright foolish.

Tip 263. Echo Their Words to Bridge to Your Topic.

An abrupt change of subjects feels rude to the other person. A subtle change goes unnoticed. All you need do to link the new topic to the old is to repeat a word or phrase. Consider the following examples.

Josh has been talking about the difficulty of getting a refund of college tuition for his daughter, who got sick and dropped out of school the first week of the semester. He says, "I've written, called, e-mailed and just keep getting the *run-around*." You want to talk about a problem at work, so you bridge with, "I know what you mean about the *run-around*. That's what I feel like at work—particularly on this project that I'm working on now. We have this one supplier that's about to drive me crazy."

Your sister-in-law has been talking about a fund-raiser at the school. She says, "You wouldn't believe how hard it is to find volunteers. People tell you on the phone that they'll serve on committees. They sign up, but then they don't *show up* at the meetings to find out what needs to be done." You want to talk about your golf game, so you respond: "I know what you mean. People are irresponsible. They just don't *show up* and do what they say. Like last weekend. We had a foursome scheduled to tee off at 8:00, and one of the guys called at 7:00 saying he couldn't make it. That better not happen this weekend because . . . "

Savvy media guests are masters of this bridging technique when they show up with talking points and the talk-show host has other topics in mind.

Tip 264. Don't State the Obvious.

When you toss out a question, observation, or comment such as, "Times have changed, haven't they?" you'll probably get no response at all. It's not that the subject is too complex, but just the opposite. The topic is too mundane or monotonous to elicit a response.

Tip 265. Jump Over the Ho-Hum Screen.

Give people the "so what" up front. Tell them why they should care about a subject you introduce before they tune you out. Everybody needs an enticement to listen—even for fun.

Tip 266. Take No More and No Less Time Than a Subject Is Worth.

The difference between stimulating and dull comes down to pacing. Don't keep racing the engine when the conversation sputters. Keep a steady pace for as long as possible, with both of you sharing the driving duties. Unless you're discussing something that seems to be vitally important to the other person, change the subject every few minutes.

Tip 267. Add Fresh Information or Observations Rather Than Echoing What's Been Said.

When somebody makes an observation, even if you agree with it exactly, don't just nod or comment with a phrase like, "So true." Simply echoing what another person has said grates on people's nerves. Instead, add a new idea, a fresh fact, or an illustrative anecdote, or ask a question to elicit elaboration from someone else. Take your turn at dribbling the ball, even if you're standing still on the court.

Tip 268. Ask to Be Enlightened When the Conversation Is Over Your Head.

Everybody is ignorant, only on different subjects, according to Will Rogers. Your lack of knowledge will not necessarily be a hindrance to small talk; on the contrary, the more knowledgeable person will enjoy the solo attention that her expertise brings. Just don't try to fake it by throwing in tidbits that will sound awkward to others. Instead, invite others to educate you: "I'm afraid I know very little about the publishing industry. Tell me more about it." "I've had my head buried in six feet of paperwork for the past week and haven't the slightest idea what you're referring to. Give me a quick update, please."

Tip 269. Keep Your Mouth Shut if the Conversation Is Way Over Your Head.

On the other hand, if someone is talking about the latest developments in nuclear fission, you can't expect that person to give you a college course in 10 minutes. Either just listen and learn what you can, or excuse yourself. Don't make an entire group play catch-up while someone educates you with details that you don't really care to know.

Tip 270. To Share the Topic, Change the Pace.

To introduce surprise or arouse curiosity, change the pace of the discussion in one of three ways: louder or softer volume, faster or slower speech, or more or less emotion. If the group is winding down on a topic in a leisurely way, rush in with a fast line that shows upset at what happened to you the day before. If the group is moving along at a good clip, overlapping each other's lines, and running away with it, take a deep breath and make a drawn-out, slow-paced, intense, provocative statement. If the group is intensely serious, toss out a one-liner to generate a laugh. Any change of delivery gets attention.

Tip 271. Add Description as Elaboration.

Consider facts the skeleton of your conversation. Put flesh on the bones with elaboration. Set the scene. Paint pictures. Explain why. Don't just say, "Stephen is a funny character." Why is he interesting? When? Doing what? Saying what? Deciding what? Let us see Stephen in motion and come to our own conclusion. Don't just say, "The project is going to open new doors for us." Where? When? Why? How? With whom?

Tip 272. Make It Your Aim to Entertain.

By entertain, I don't necessarily mean a song-and-dance routine, or even amusing stories or witty one-liners. Entertaining has a broader meaning—making people enjoy themselves. Entertainment includes enlightening people on a subject of interest, letting them enlighten you on a subject, giving new information, exchanging different views on an issue, or meeting new people with unusual experiences and opinions. Entertainment rarely includes a lecture or a debate; both tend to make people increasingly uncomfortable.

Tip 273. Work on Witty Remarks.

You can have a stock of ready-made remarks for various occasions, or you can develop them on the spot. The trouble with those developed on the spot is that they lose their effect if they're irrelevant. And if they're spontaneous, you can't prescreen them. The downside of a witty remark at someone else's expense can be long-lasting and devastating. When you do come up with original remarks spontaneously, save them for a repeat performance.

Tip 274. Tell Great Stories.

You can make a great story of just about anything. A conversation overheard in the hair salon. The traffic jam on the way to work. The dropped call with your client. The aggressive language in the tweet stream of the morning. The town hall meeting last weekend. The ineptness of the exterminator who came to spray your apartment. These can all serve as story fodder.

Stories make a point memorable, clarify your message, engage others, inspire change, or simply entertain people. Your story doesn't have to be funny; it can arouse empathy, create surprise or shock, inspire pride, or anger people so that they take action.

Embellish your story as much as you like as long as the primary outline of what happened and why is true. Know when to add detail and when to omit it. Know when to use a preface with your story and when such a filler is irrelevant. Use dialogue. Create the scene. Know when to pause and when to interrupt yourself. Know when to slow down or speed up. Know when to throw in a bumper-sticker line before moving on to the end. Create suspense just before the punch line. In short, dramatize your delivery and end with a wallop.

Tip 275. Relate Your Stories to the Subject at Hand.

Although this is not always necessary, your story will have a bigger bang if it illuminates or further illustrates the point of the current conversation. Look for at least a narrow bridge from a key word in what has been said so that the story seems to fit. "Carl, your comment on your daughter's attitude about her grades reminds me of a friend back in college. This guy walked into my dorm room one Saturday night and . . ." Because this is not a speech or a sermon, the whole gist of the story doesn't have to be "on the point," but there should be some trigger word or thought that generates it.

Of course, if you're looking for a new subject, let your story be the lead-in. Build a bridge after the story and hand the subject to someone else: "So somebody tell me I'm not alone in feeling that X. Anybody been in a similar situation?" The idea is not to tell a story that leaves people with the reaction, "So . . . ?"

Tip 276. Make Someone Else the Hero or Heroine of Your Anecdotes.

When you toss out anecdotes of recent incidents, you don't always have to be the hero or heroine who saves the day. Tell something amusing, enlightening, or strange that happened to a friend, coworker, family member, acquaintance, or neighbor. People will enjoy your conversation without getting the feeling that you're self-centered.

Tip 277. Respond With a "Saver" if Your Remarks Fall Flat.

After a ho-hum response or stark silence, a friend of mine picks up the slack with, "Not of grave importance, but it killed a minute," which always brings a chuckle or a smile. Try others: "Not a front-page news story, but interesting nevertheless," or, "Maybe not something that will pull you out of a national crisis, but it could save the cat," or, "So I can tell you are big X fans here," or, "Funny, my mother loved the story."

If a flippant comeback seems inappropriate, you can pretend that you were serious and intended the remark as a conclusion to the subject under discussion. Allow a brief pause and then take up a new topic.

Tip 278. Do Frequent Reality Checks.

To test for a follow-on story, toss out a come-on and see whether the other person invites you to elaborate: "The same thing happened to me on vacation last year," or, "That sounds like my boss—he got into a similar scrape last week." The silence should tell you something. Or ask an unexpected question. If the other person can't answer, take that as a good indication that she hasn't been listening. Either change the subject, relinquish the floor, or move on.

Tip 279. Give Your Listener a Chance to Leave if He's Bored.

On occasion, you and another person may find yourself like two fish washed up on a dry beach. You can't get back into the conversational swim, and you're not sure how motivated the other person is to flop toward the water. Try, "Well, I know you have several people you want to say hello to, so I'll let you go," or, "I won't keep you—there are so many people here that it's hard to find time to chat with everyone."

Tip 280. When You're Caught Not Listening, Give a Keep-Talking Nudge.

If you let your mind wander and the other person discovers that you're not listening, you will offend. When you suddenly notice that the other person has stopped talking and is waiting for your response, give the person a nudge until you can get reoriented: "I'm sorry—I didn't understand what you were asking," or, "I missed your point, I'm sorry." Often people will continue talking and give you a clue where they were.

If that doesn't work, try the straightforward approach. "I'm sorry, I missed your last comment," or, "It's so noisy in here that I'm having a hard time hearing you," or, "I'm sorry, you lost me. I'm still thinking about what you said a minute ago when you mentioned . . . " or "I'm lost; something you said a moment ago made me think of . . . "

Tip 281. Avoid Stock Fillers.

Avoid peppering your talk with stock fillers such as, "Incredible," "Awesome," "Amazing!" "All right!" "Cool," "No kidding," "Bizarre," "Weird," "You don't say," or, "Thumbs up."

Tip 282. Unwind a Nonstop Speaker with a Pop Quiz.

When you want to stop someone's monologue, break in with two or three short-answer questions. You don't seem rude because you're asking the speaker to keep talking with questions that signal interest. But the idea is to take control. When the person stops the monologue to give one- or two-word answers to your specific questions on the subject, you have an opportunity to regain the floor and either redirect the conversation or end it.

Tip 283. Encourage People to Continue What They Were Saying Before Being Interrupted.

They'll love you for saying, "Please continue what you were telling me." "Please finish your story; you had me intrigued." "So back to what you were saying . . . " "Don't stop now; I'm just starting to understand your point." Such encouragement is an invitation few people can resist and that most remember forever.

Tip 284. When Someone "Pulls Your Leg," Release It.

Granted, I'm more gullible than the average person. When somebody with a quick wit or a penchant for gags takes me for a ride in conversation, I go right along, unaware to the very end. Living in Okinawa at the worldly age of 19, I often talked about my home state of Texas. One day my boss strolled into the office late, with this explanation: "We had to have the pest control people out to my house this morning. Last night I kept hearing this noise in the next room, like shoes scuffling across the floor. Sure enough, when I checked it out this morning, it was a big roach—the size they have in Texas—pushing my shoes around in the closet."

"Really? That's scary."

He became hysterical. And he repeated the story to everyone who would listen for the rest of the day.

When someone has obviously put one over on you, let it go. To get angry or "explain it away" ruins the moment. Just accept the fact that you're going to be the butt of the joke on occasion and enjoy the "fame" along with everybody else.

Tip 285. Cover Your Own and Others' Faux Pas with Past Ones.

That's right. If you've just stuck your foot in your mouth with your last comment, you can take the pressure off with an amusing anecdote from your own history. Say something like, "I've got a history here. Charm school I did not attend. In fact, last month . . . " Relate the past blunder along with your embarrassment, and the group will begin to empathize with you. Your entertainment value will displace the awkward humiliation of your latest blunder. People are gracious with those who admit their mistakes. Watch this phenomenon in a group, with each person starting to top the prior person's most embarrassing blunder.

With another person's gaffe, use the same maneuver to help alleviate their pain: "Hey, don't worry about it. I've done worse. Did I tell you about the time when . . . ?" The others in the group will admire your graciousness and "sacrifice" in lessening someone else's embarrassment. And the person you're covering for will love you forever.

Tip 286. Tactfully Reject Questions That Are Too Personal.

Often people seem to feel as put on the spot as they did in second grade when their teacher asked them what their dad did for a living. We grow up thinking that we have to answer all questions asked of us, or at least we feel uncomfortable not doing so. Instead, develop some gracious or witty deflectors: "I don't like to discuss that sort of thing on Tuesday evenings. Or Wednesday mornings. Or Saturday nights." "The only people I give that information to are my doctor and my analyst." "Even my hairdresser doesn't know for sure." Or be straightforward enough to suggest that the person withdraw the question: "Why would you ask that?" or "Why do you need that information?" or "I'm sorry, but that's personal with me."

Tip 287. Signal Before You're Offended.

If you have strong feelings about a particular subject, let the members of the group know before they offend you and embarrass themselves. For example: "I've gotta warn you—I have some pretty radical opinions about that. We'd better steer clear of that issue," or, "I'm getting a little uneasy with this topic. I'm on that project team, you know." Others will appreciate the warning.

Tip 288. Neutralize Before You Express an Opposing Viewpoint.

When someone expresses a very strong opinion with which you disagree, you can, of course, always remain silent to avoid a debate. However, if you're "bursting at the seams" to have someone hear the opposing viewpoint, walk across a neutral zone before you try to speak. Don't begin with, "Yes, but . . ." That sets up a debating tone for what is to follow.

Instead, make a neutralizing comment between the opposing viewpoint and yours to follow: "You've made some very good points. I have a different view for other reasons. From my perspective,...," or, "I don't think I've ever heard anyone express that view exactly. My own thoughts on the subject are quite different. I think that..., " or, "I understand what you're saying. I feel differently. I believe . . . "

Tip 289. Be Noncommittal if You Want to Avoid Debate.

After someone voices an opposing view, after someone makes a slur that you don't want to be associated with, or after the topic moves to one that you'd rather not discuss, try the most appropriate of these comments: "Other people, I'm sure, feel just as you do." "The workplace keeps you on your toes—that's for sure." "Life's full of surprises." "You've got a point." "You think so?" "Yes, I've heard people say that." "Hmmm." "Well, . . . we've about exhausted that subject." "Mind if I change the subject for a moment? I've been wanting to ask you about . . . "

Tip 290. Avoid Editorializing.

On controversial topics, avoid stating a dogmatic opinion if you don't know the other person well. Arousing someone's emotions on her pet peeve or cause is a good way to get burned.

Tip 291. Accept Specific Compliments with Sincerity.

If you're like most people, you feel a little uncomfortable when you receive a compliment. It's not that you don't appreciate the compliment; it's that you feel you've been put "on the spot" in front of others. There's elegance in a straightforward response: "Thank you very much. It's nice of you to call attention to that," or, "Thanks. I'm glad you noticed," or, "I appreciate your saying so," or, "You made my day. Thanks for commenting on that. I try very hard to X."

Tip 292. Prepare Self-Effacing Comebacks for Frequent, Vague, or Insincere Compliments.

Some compliments are immediately recognizable as "lines," or insincere flattery. Responding to them with sincerity makes you feel duped—as if you don't know the difference.

A more comfortable response is a light, even self-effacing comeback. Flattering comment: "May I tell you you're breathtakingly gorgeous—as well as the darn best VP we've ever had in charge of Marketing?" Response: "Thanks. I write comments like that in my journal every night. Then when I get angry at my husband, I just pull 'em out and consider my other options."

Tip 293. Gossip at Your Own Great Risk.

How to define gossip? People who say they don't gossip will admit talking about others' lives—either positively or negatively. Rare is the person who never passes on a fact or commendation about another person's achievements, work, family, attitude, or character.

Why are people fascinated by gossip? On the one hand, it's a way of cutting others down to size, of showing up hypocrisy in those who are in places of fame or great fortune. On the beneficial side, it's a way of sharing common values and affirming with the listener that we feel the same way about a situation. Gossip also keeps us up to date and protects us. What we don't know about a pending merger may hurt us. Others gossip just to fill the conversational lull or to gain attention for having the "inside scoop."

What makes gossip negative is its intention and tone—talking *against* rather than talking *about;* passing on negative information, or passing on neutral information with negative intentions. Avoid passing on hurtful information, information that you would not want passed on if you were in the other person's shoes. And remember that not all people may be as "open" as you are. Even if the gossip is "good" gossip, be sure it's truth, not rumor.

Tip 294. Stop Gossip Without Offending the Spreader.

The reply that cuts gossips short is, "Oh, I didn't know that. He always speaks so highly of you." How's a person to continue after that line? It's effective in stopping almost any negative comment, but it feels like a slap in the face to the person talking. Try a gentler approach like the following. *Gossip:* "I hear Bill Burgess really gave you guys in Audit a mouthful today." *Response:* "He was upset, yes. But we worked through it. So, what's new with you?" *Gossip:* "Did you hear that Tseuko didn't get the promotion?" *Response:* "No, I didn't. I guess I'll have to ask her the reasons myself. You know how rumors go." *Gossip:* "I hear their company is about to go under." *Response:* "Rumors run rampant, don't they? I guess we'll hear the real truth sooner or later."

Tip 295. Squelch Complaints.

Even if others happen to agree with you, they'll notice your poor taste in complaining about the room, the food, the guests, the entertainment, the lack of planning, or anything else about the circumstances or events. You'll appear to be ungrateful for being included.

Tip 296. Don't Hard-Sell When the Purpose Is Chitchat.

Don't take advantage of people who have come to relax and get to know others on a personal level by turning your time with them into a sales call. Yes, a brief overview as a teaser of what you do, maybe. But don't put them on the spot for a further commitment unless they open the door and very overtly invite you in.

Tip 297. Don't Pester a Professional for a Prescription.

In my circle of colleagues, literary agents say that they hesitate to show up at networking events for fear of being bombarded with book manuscripts from would-be authors wanting "a professional opinion." In other groups, doctors, lawyers, accountants, and hiring executives become the targets of those who want to talk turkey about their migraines, their divorce case, their child-support payments, or their core competencies and the perfect résumé.

People pay real money for such knowledge or skill. Why should they risk a liability suit to give it away for free at a party? Ask for their card, take two aspirin, and call them in the morning.

Tip 298. When You Meet Two VIPs at Once, Don't Focus on One and Ignore the Other.

Although one will be flattered by your obvious attention, he will have to be the one to bring his buddy into the conversation, and he will feel awkward in doing so. If you ignore either, both will feel uncomfortable.

Tip 299. Make a Graceful Exit.

When you're ready to end a conversation, wait until after *you've* just finished talking, not immediately after the other person has introduced a new topic or pauses in midcourse. You don't want anyone to wonder, "Is it something I said that made her want to move on?"

There's no particular rule about how much time to spend chatting with each individual at a networking event, but conversations typically last 5- to 15 minutes. To mix and mingle is the purpose.

Use closing comments such as these: "Excuse me. It's been nice talking with you." "Well, so much for my views on X. I think I'll get something else to drink." "Excuse me. I want to catch Bob before he leaves." "Excuse me for monopolizing your time. I'll let you visit with someone else now." "Thanks for taking the time to chat with me. It was great getting to hear about your experiences with the Calhoun group." "I'm going to step over and say hello to someone else. May I have your card before I go?" "Thank you for the great information about the ski slopes. I'll let you know how it was when we get back."

Tip 300. Screen Small-Talk Topics at Job Interviews with Care.

Certainly your ability to make small talk is an asset, and most hiring executives will be pleased to see that you can carry on a conversation on a variety of subjects with ease. Skilled interviewers also know how to listen well and read between the lines. "Did you have any problem finding our building?" the interviewer asks. You answer: "No, my husband dropped me off on his way to his office—just a few blocks from here." (The interviewer hears, "Married.") "May I get you some coffee?" You answer: "Yes, that would be great. I spilled mine in the car hassling to get the twins out at the daycare." (The interviewer hears, "Two toddlers.) "Did you have a nice weekend in this great weather?" You answer: "Actually, I'm afraid I didn't. My mom's battling cancer, and I've had to fly back and forth to Baltimore the last few weekends to check on her." (The interviewer hears, "Hmm. Maybe she couldn't start work right away")

Tip 301. Recognize the Importance of Small Talk.

If you're on the other end of the conversation when someone initiates small talk, recognize its value to him, if not to you personally. Conversation isn't simply for passing on useful information or getting a job done. More and more in our high-tech, impersonal workplace, people want emotional involvement and connection with others. Talking—about anything—helps establish, maintain, and adjust relationships to keep them in good order.

4

Winning People Over to Your Way of Thinking: Being Persuasive

Great communicators have an appreciation for positioning. They understand the people they're trying to reach and what they can and can't hear. They send their message in through an open door rather than trying to push it through a wall.

—John Kotter

Facts alone seldom persuade and rarely inspire.

—Boyd Clarke and Ron Crossland

People are usually more convinced by reasons they discovered themselves than by those found out by others.

—Blaise Pascal

When dealing with people, remember you are not dealing with creatures of logic, but with creatures of emotion, creatures bristling with prejudice, and motivated by pride and vanity.

—Dale Carnegie

The more you say, the less people remember.

—Anatole France

Things that I felt absolutely sure of but a few years ago, I do not believe now. This thought makes me see more clearly how foolish it would be to expect all men to agree with me.

—Jim Rohn

One of the best ways to persuade others is by listening to them.

—Dean Rusk

I would rather try to persuade a man to go along, because once I have persuaded him, he will stick. If I scare him, he will stay just as long as he is scared, and then he is gone.

—Dwight Eisenhower

If I had eight hours to chop down a tree I'd spend six sharpening my axe.

—Abraham Lincoln

People never outgrow their need to be persuasive. Salespeople have to persuade customers to buy. Customers have to persuade salespeople that the time they are investing in servicing their accounts will pay off over the years. The entry-level employee hopes to persuade the manager to approve a raise. The manager wants to persuade the CEO to look at new ideas and proposals. The CEO has to persuade employees to be loyal, customers to buy, and the public to invest.

Parents have to persuade their children to obey, do their best in school, and make wise decisions. Children try to persuade their parents to give them more gadgets, spend more time with them, and allow them more freedom.

The challenge of persuasion faces all of us. These guidelines will take you beyond the typical "hoping for the best" attitude to awareness of what works best and how to prepare for your biggest opportunities.

Tip 302. Convince Yourself Before You Approach Others.

"Whether you believe you can or you believe you can't, you're right," as Henry Ford observed years ago. Whether you're talking about deserving a raise, doubling your sales volume, or convincing someone to date you, the outcome begins in your head. Ask any successful business development person about his key criterion for changing jobs, and he'll tell you that it's not money—although by nature these are money-motivated individuals. He'll tell you that his number one criterion in accepting a job offer is, "How much do I believe in the service or product I'll be selling?" These people cannot sell something that they do not personally believe will benefit the customer.

You may not be in sales. Your interest in being persuasive may be to keep your 20-year-old in college, to get a plum assignment from your division director, or to solicit funds for your favorite charity. Whatever the value statement or cause, you need to convince yourself before you attempt to persuade others.

Tip 303. Establish Credibility.

People believe people they like, people who are similar to them, people who are trustworthy, and people who have demonstrated expertise. Work on one or all of these to build your credibility with any given group. (Use Chapter 1 in this book as your bible.) The higher your personal credibility, the greater the impact your value proposition will have.

Tip 304. Understand the Three Dynamics of Persuasion: Logic, Character, and Emotion.

Aristotle's three prongs of persuasion are these: "(1) to reason logically, (2) to understand human character and goodness in their various forms, and (3) to understand the emotions—that is, to name and describe them, to know their causes and the way in which they are excited."

In short, once your boss thinks you're trustworthy (character), you have to make her angry enough at the unfairness of "the system" to change it (emotion). And then you'll have to give proof of that unfairness (logic).

You'll have to excite the customer about the status he will enjoy with the new product (emotion), and then you'll have to convince that customer that it's the best of its kind on the market (logic). Finally, the buyer will need to believe that you're an honest salesperson who tells the complete truth (character).

You'll have to make donors feel compassion for the homeless (emotion), show them exactly where and how their money will help (logic), and then demonstrate your own integrity and concern in the process of your fund-raising (character).

Most people shun the label of an emotional decision maker, preferring to consider themselves "logical" decision makers. But in reality, you need all three prongs if you're to persuade people.

Tip 305. Identify the Appropriate Emotion for the Moment.

Which emotions do you need to tickle most frequently in the workplace? Anger, pride, envy, love, peace, comfort, belonging, surprise—the same ones most people feel whenever they come together.

The idea of rewarding an employee with a gold watch for 25 years of service has this principle as its foundation. The ceremony surrounding the presentation elicits the same emotion as high school or college graduation, a scouting award, or a Junior Achievement badge. It's the symbol and the emotion of the thing that count. When you want to persuade a manager to keep you in the job, appeal to the feelings of rejection encountered by that person when he was kicked off the starting lineup for one lousy foul.

When you want to persuade your parents to buy you a bicycle, remind them of the day their grandfather taught them to ride and the thrill of independence they felt in riding to the store for bread. When you want to persuade a CEO to spend extra money on a glitzy annual report, remind her of her pride in bringing home a straight A report card.

Even in business situations, specific, identifiable emotions may carry as much as or more weight than logic. Decide which emotional appeal to make depending on your task and the decision maker's personality.

Tip 306. Persuade People to Do Something Specific.

Stanford economist Paul Romer once observed, "A crisis is a terrible thing to waste." Disaster—whether it's a natural disaster or a personal one—strengthens character. Likewise, emotion is a terrible thing to waste. Emotion drives action.

If you've moved people emotionally with an appeal (a story about an unjust situation, a great need, or a wonderful opportunity), don't waste the passion stirred in them. Persuade them to do something specific. They need an emotional release or a sense of closure if they've come to a logical conclusion. Give them something specific to do, decide, approve, buy, or create.

A sales rep for a client organization once wrote a two-page e-mail to her executive team, telling about a sale she'd lost because of her customer's reaction to the company's credit terms and down payment requirements. Following company policy, the rep had asked for 30 percent cash up front; the prospective customer had countered with an offer of a 20 percent down payment. The sales rep's credit manager refused to approve the deal, and the sales rep lost the sale. After a long recitation of the story, the sales rep ended her e-mail with this recommendation to her own executive team: "We must make it easy for customers to do business with us. We need to wake up to the realities of today's marketplace."

As a senior vice president reading that e-mail, what exactly would you have delegated to an individual or committee to review, consider, or investigate? To increase your chances to get appropriate action, people need specifics. Persuade with a plan in mind.

Tip 307. Organize Your Ideas for Greatest Impact.

The simple approach calls for these steps:

1. Get attention.
2. Overview the conclusion, action, or decision you want, along with the key benefits.
3. Build your case in detail:
   - Create or confirm a need.
   - Show how your idea, plan, service, or product will meet that need.
   - Elaborate on the benefits overviewed earlier.
   - Discuss how your ideas, plan, product, or service will be implemented (the practical day-to-day how-to's).
4. Call for a specific action or decision.

In developing Step 3, you have a plethora of arrangements for specific points to choose from: move from problem to solution, point out the cause and the effect, move backward from the effect to the cause, compare and/or contrast two options, or compare options to the criteria. Just get a plan and stay with it.

A clearly organized presentation represents clear thinking and leads to a fast, favorable decision.

Tip 308. Understand That One Size Does Not Fit All.

Whether presenting benefits of holding your next conference offshore, benefits of increasing staff, or benefits to a client of buying your widget, tailor your presentation to your specific listeners.

Biased against. Begin by acknowledging their point of view, and find points of agreement—statistics, surveys, principles, goals. This attitude will disarm them. Refer to sources and experts they will respect to establish your open-mindedness and fairness in looking at the situation. Aim to present a "different" or "another" point of view. Let them know that your goal is not to "change" them but to expand their thinking. Make your goal to reduce their resistance.

Neutral. Start with the benefits of accepting your value statement. Give them your bottom-line message and the action you want. Provide supporting detail—about three to five strong reasons or examples to make your case. Put flesh around this skeleton to make your points memorable—stories, metaphors, analogies, or case studies. Finally, create a sense of urgency to make a decision and take action to move them out of their state of neutrality.

Biased in Favor. These people support your point of view already. State your value proposition, and spend your time on the implementation of your ideas. Aim to inspire them to follow through with what they already believe.

Mixed. State your value proposition. Then build your case around benefits that will appeal to each interest group. Be careful, however, that these "benefits" don't contradict each other. Note how toy manufacturers sell both to parents (safety, educational) and children (fun).

Tip 309. Use the Bad-News-First Approach.

You disarm people when you give them the downside of your proposal first. They're disappointed. Then you present the upside, and things seem brighter. By the time you finish with your presentation, they've gained enough momentum to feel that the bad news wasn't as much of a handicap as they first thought. Keep the momentum moving upward rather than downward.

Tip 310. Calculate the Minimum Gain You Would Need to Justify Investing Time or Money in Your Idea.

Many ideas languish on the table of indecision because we can't calculate "the hard dollars." If we invest in training our salespeople to write better proposals at a cost of $X, what will be the payoff? Do we keep track of how many more deals they close after the proposal-writing course? But what if the price of the product they're selling rises or a competitor changes the marketplace drastically? How do we pinpoint with certainty that better proposals alone will make the difference in their sales volume? We face such issues daily.

When it's difficult to quantify savings or gains in time or money from a new idea, consider what the minimum time or dollar savings would need to be to make the idea worthwhile. What if the training resulted in our improved proposal that won the $12 million contract with Universal, Inc.?

Getting people to agree on a minimum is easier than getting them to agree on a valid, "real" number.

Tip 311. Make a Conscious Decision About Whether to Present All Sides of an Issue or Only Yours.

Structure should be a conscious choice—not an afterthought. Consider this: When you present an idea to your boss, staff, colleagues, clients, or partners, should you present all sides of an issue or all options to solve a problem with total objectivity—or only your point of view?

If you expect a hostile audience, one biased against your plan from the beginning, present all sides and all options and the pros and cons of each alternative. When chances are great that the group will hear other options and arguments from other sources before they make a decision, you'll create the extra credibility of being thorough, open, and objective about all the facts and alternatives.

If the audience is either positive or neutral, present only your alternative—an overview or message, the action you want, and the details to take the action. Then do a quick test before you conclude. "Are you ready to decide, or would you like to hear other alternatives and why I'm suggesting that we reject those alternatives?"

If the group wants more options, you can provide them with a thorough analysis. If they don't want to hear other options and trust your judgment based on criteria they agreed with, then you won't be wasting their time on the "also-ran" alternatives.

Tip 312. Talk About Rewards and Incentives to Those People Who Think in Terms of Payoffs.

Some people wake up every morning looking for ways to make their life better: how to save time, how to save money, how to move ahead in their careers, how to be better managers, how to get their coworkers to like them, how to win the lottery, how to complete a crossword puzzle. If these people are the group you have to win over, highlight the personal and corporate benefits of acting on your ideas.

Tip 313. Talk About Facts and Statistics to Those Who Think Analytically.

Some people don't buy cereal without figuring out the cost per ounce. Even if they are persuaded by emotion, they'll ask for the supporting evidence so as not to be embarrassed should anyone ask the reason for their break-fast choices. They don't believe in "soft dollars," "soft skills," or "soft data." For these people, quantify everything.

Tip 314. Talk About the "Bandwagon" to Those Who Like to Jump On It.

Whether to save the effort of thinking for themselves or to meet their needs for belonging, these people pay a great deal of attention to what everyone else is doing. Passwords here include: "The trends show..." "Experts in the field seem to think..." "The leading-edge companies have imple-mented..." With these people, you need to provide testimonials of what others think of your ideas.

Tip 315. Talk About Obstacles to Be Overcome to Those Who Welcome Challenge and Change.

Some people wake up each morning ready to climb mountains. Tell them that they can't do something and they start circulating petitions. Routine bores them. Tell them the system doesn't work, tell them you can't afford something, tell them it's too late or too early for a change—and that's when they'll start to work. Motivate them to act on your ideas by presenting them as obstacles to be overcome. Negative circumstances merely challenge these people to climb mountains of opportunity.

Tip 316. Sell What People Want to Buy.

Don't limit your thinking to products and services here. I'm also talking about ideas, policies, concepts, and feelings. Think along two channels: what people *want to have, be,* or *feel* and what they *want to avoid.* Align your pitch with one of these benefits:

Want to Have

Money	Opportunity
Prestige/status	Good reputation
Fun	Time
Possessions	

Want to Be

Successful	Healthy
Unique	Smart

Liked	Loved
Rich	Stylish

Want to Feel

Happy	In control
Successful	Important
Comfortable	Competent
Safe	Free
Guilt-free	Dignified
Committed	Respected or admired
Sexy	

Want to Avoid

Wasting effort	Being criticized
Losing time	Feeling stupid
Being forgotten	Being in danger
Losing possessions or money	Worrying
Losing reputation	

Tip 317. Appeal to Self-Interest.

Yes, people do make decisions for the sake of motherhood, apple pie, and country. But they feel an even stronger tug when the decision has something in it for them personally. So, don't just tell the manager that the new technology will save the company more than $400,000 in maintenance support during the next five years. Show how it will speed up preparation of the department's audits and help get the task off the manager's own checklist. The more personal the benefits, the stronger the tug.

Tip 318. Create Immediacy.

If you are a single adult reading a news story about a teenager killed on a motorcycle because he wasn't wearing a safety helmet, you may feel sorry, shake your head, and continue reading. However, if you just bought *your* 18-year-old a motorcycle and had an argument with him about the importance of wearing a safety helmet, you'll probably tune in to the statistics a little more closely to find out how you can convince him to wear a helmet.

If IBM or General Motors announces pending layoffs of 10,000 people in the next quarter, you'll empathize with the families affected. But if *you're* an employee there, you'll start preparing your résumé and talking to friends about job possibilities.

If your managers understand the high unemployment rate, they will have a general awareness of the difficulty of getting work done with fewer and fewer employees. However, if you cite the 28 percent unemployment rate at *your* Detroit plant, adding that the company's retraining costs hit the half-million mark for the year, these managers will quickly see the urgency of the problem in keeping up with the workload.

Don't tell employees that if XYZ legislation passes, health-care costs will rise. Tell them that *their* deductible will increase from $1,000 to $5,000 next year and you'll have their attention.

To spark interest and action, the situation has to touch people's daily lives. Make the listener see, hear, touch, and feel the situation. Whether you're talking about money, management, or marital problems, appeal to your listeners' sense of urgency.

Tip 319. Maintain Exclusivity.

The late comedian Groucho Marx used to joke, "I wouldn't want to belong to any club that would accept me as a member." Subscription websites, frequent flyer programs, and various CEO service clubs today sustain their membership on this principle of exclusivity. Even popular social media sites today like Facebook and LinkedIn that built their brand on welcoming everyone to join for free now offer "exclusive" programs for a fee. You pay your fee, and the sponsor commits to keeping out the riffraff while you enjoy certain privileges of the elite. As part of the "brand," admission to the group never gets discounted, access requires rigorous requirements, and prestige remains part of the payoff. Persuade people that not everyone has access to what you're offering and watch the response.

Tip 320. Sell Scarcity.

If you have a limited supply of data, experience, or access to experts, promote this scarcity. If you can put a deadline on its availability, that's even better.

Tip 321. Use Associations from the Past.

Why does the president speak from the Oval Office when he needs extraordinary credibility for a difficult decision? Because the camera frames Old Glory standing in the background. That symbol subtly evokes patriotic moments in our history when the president took a stand in a major crisis and pulled the nation together in victory. To be persuasive, evoke associations with other people, other groups, and other successes to lead people to transfer that past confidence to the present situation.

This principle is at work when a decorated military general speaks in favor of a tax increase. The subtle message: Voting yes is the patriotic thing to do. The principle is at work when you see a toddler in an insurance commercial. The subtle message: Buying insurance is the moral thing to do—for the helpless.

This principle is at work when you see a mom buttoning the jacket of her six-year-old before the child leaves for school. The subtle message: Buying Brand X cough syrup is what your own loving mother would do.

How do you know your employees will enjoy a '90s party at their annual convention? Remind them of the success of their senior prom. Will the bond campaign for the community convention center win support? Most likely, if you can remind the voting crowd of the bond-funded theater they currently enjoy.

Tip 322. Ride With the Flow as Far as You Can Go.

"We've always done it that way" serves as the reason to continue for many people. They resist change of any kind. Many voters still hold the political beliefs learned as a child at home with their parents. They watch TV ads for things they've already bought. They read cartoon series they've followed for 10 years, and they watch TV reruns for a decade.

For you, that means it's easier to ride the flow of opinion as far as you can. Find out what people feel comfortable with currently, and then present your idea as "a slight modification" rather than a "new" idea altogether. Think how much easier it would sound to you if someone asks you to "revise your report to include X" as opposed to "rewrite your report." To "modify" sounds easier than to "redo."

To avoid resistance to a "new" policy or procedure, just "alter" the old one.

Tip 323. Use the Lesser-of-Two-Evils Approach.

If the decision you want from your listener is not particularly pleasant or desirable, consider creating fear about the other alternatives. Outline what will happen if he stays with the status quo, what will happen if he does X, and what will happen if his competitors or customers do Y. Your purpose is to get the listener to decide *against* the other options rather than necessarily deciding *for* your option. The American public makes a similar choice every year at election time.

Tip 324. Provide a Better as Well as a Best Option.

Should your decision maker not go for your best option, don't let the entire plan or idea fall flat. Determine a second, lesser objective that you can present as a "second best" option.

Tip 325. Encourage the Person to Make a Public Commitment.

You yourself understand the value of making yourself accountable to others if you've ever started a weight-loss program, an exercise program, or a professional development regimen to read a book a month. You have good intentions, but as long as people don't know those intentions, it's easy for you to slack off when there's a time crunch. But once you sign up for the weight-loss program and attend the classes, or make a date to meet your neighbor every evening at 8:00 for a three-mile walk, or join a monthly book club, it's more difficult to explain why you're not following through with your commitment.

So lead your listeners to commit to action in a staff meeting. Accountability helps keep people on track.

Tip 326. Encourage Others to Invest Their Time.

People never like to waste time following cold trails—whether they're hunting for cold-blooded killers of kidnapped victims or looking for a new financial advisor. So don't worry that you're causing someone time and effort to educate herself on what you have to offer. Send people the information they want. Ask them to visit your YouTube channel. Give them references to talk to about how you helped them solve problems. Suggest that they tour your place of business or visit sites where your product or service is used. The more time people invest in your value proposition, the more they will "want to make it work" for them. Otherwise, that investigative effort has gone into a sinkhole.

Tip 327. Use the Jelly Principle.

When I was sick as a child, my mother used to put cough syrup in a spoonful of jelly to camouflage the taste. The same principle comes in handy with bitter messages. You may have to wrap them in more pleasing ideas or get them across in more subtle ways.

Tip 328. Try the Tom Sawyer Approach.

Twain's Tom Sawyer let a group of his friends whitewash his fence for him—just because they happen to be his friends. Actually, Tom tells his friends that getting to whitewash that fence is a real privilege—a rare opportunity.

A furniture salesperson sets up the same situation. The shopper: "I guess I like the blue chair better than the green one." Salesperson: "I'm not sure if we have it in stock. I may have just sold the last one. That has been our most popular chair. People practically grab that chair off the floor at that price. Better give me a moment to check the computer before you get your hopes up." What happens? All of the sudden the shopper *must* have that blue chair.

What happens in the furniture store can also unfold around the conference table. You can create momentum for your idea if you let people understand that nothing is a sure thing, that the time is now (may be not later), that the money is available now (and maybe not later), that the XYZ department is willing to cooperate now (and maybe not later), or that the customer is ready to sign the deal now (and maybe not later). You get the picture. Put the pressure on the other foot. Your listener must act now or miss a rare opportunity.

Tip 329. Let the Decision Maker Hear from the Converted.

Secondhand testimonials are not nearly as effective as the words straight from the mouth of those already converted to your way of thinking. If possible, bring these satisfied users/buyers/believers/beneficiaries to the discussion with you—in person or by video or audio recorded endorsements on your social media sites, your website, or your webinar presentation. Have them write their endorsement on LinkedIn or tweet it or blast it out in any number of ways. Unscripted and in their own unique way, let them speak to the effectiveness or truth of what you say.

For example, the marketing team at Tri4Him captures comments from triathletes as they finish an Ironman race, asking about the coaching they received from the company. There are few things more powerful than hearing those athletes talk about how their individual training plan helped them get the most out of their training time while trying to balance life and career: Tri4Him simply lets them talk about achieving their personal best in their own words just after they cross the finish line—how they've improved their overall fitness, how strong they felt throughout the race, and how they reduced their time from the previous race.

Tip 330. Make People Feel Safe.

Have you ever walked through a fairground or amusement park where barkers were calling to you from every exhibit: "Step over here, little lady, and play the game!" "Step inside and see the big show!" "Buy your ticket right now—the show starts in two minutes!" As a passerby, your automatic reaction is to hold your hands and arms close to your sides, look straight ahead, and keep walking. You feel vulnerable.

People have to trust you before they will lower their defenses and actually open their mind to your message. Make sure your tone and manner build trust rather than suspicion. Sift through your promises to make sure that they're not "over the top." Take a lesson from Sears's promise of "satisfaction guaranteed or your money back." Create a safety net for decisions. How can people "undo" a decision or action if they have a change of heart?

Tip 331. Demonstrate Goodwill.

Find a way to convey to the listener that you want to help him achieve his goals. Once the other person understands that you have his welfare at heart, he tends to trust you and believe your message. So how do you convey goodwill? Here are several ways:

- Listen to the other person and demonstrate that you heard what he said.
- Offer suggestions to help him save money.
- Give free advice if he is open to it.
- Recommend the best option—not necessarily the most expensive.
- Stay in touch when you have nothing to gain.
- Show a personal interest in the person's life and career success.

Tip 332. Ask Disturbing Questions to Keep People Awake at Night.

A client approached me about coaching her sales and marketing team of five people on a specific presentation that they were to deliver to a customer who was arriving from outside the country. Because it was short notice, I told my client that I was booked already, but that I could send another consultant from my staff. She didn't warm up to the idea, and her first reaction was that she would just stick with the presentation they'd developed internally or work with an internal coach to do a little "tweaking."

"Okay, I understand," I told her. "Just let me give you a key question to consider: Will that internal coach be able to win instant credibility with your team? That's going to be essential if you have only Monday to work on this." She called back in two hours and booked one of our consultants.

Tip 333. Develop an Elevator Pitch for the Ground Floor.

Sales professionals define an elevator pitch as a 15- or 30-second teaser that lets people know what you do in such an intriguing way as to open a conversation that has as its end result their asking you to follow up later with a full-fledged sales call.

But you don't have to be in sales to develop such a teaser to open conversation about whatever your value proposition happens to entail. A successful elevator pitch includes these components:

- *A question that captures a problem*
- *Your solution to the problem*
- *A credibility builder*
- *A question to engage*

Here's an example that you might use in pitching your boss on approving the budget for you to attend an industry conference:

- *A question that captures a problem:* "You know how often this past year we've had managers ask us about the legal ramifications of disciplinary actions and how much that's cost us in legal fees to outside counsel?" (Your boss says, "Yeah, almost $80K last time I looked at my budget.")
- *Your solution to the problem:* "Well, what I'd like to do is attend the upcoming XYZ Conference in San Diego in August that focuses on those very HR issues. I've identified five specific concurrent sessions on compliance issues that would address exactly what we're dealing with here. And my total cost to attend would be under $3,000."

- *A credibility builder:* Both Tom Hart from Exxon Mobil and Sandy Graves from JPMorgan Chase attended last quarter and said that it was excellent information. Sandy, in fact, has already settled a lawsuit based on what she learned there.
- *A question to engage:* "What's the latest question or problem we've gotten from the group in Miami about the downsizing issues and threatened lawsuits there?"

The point of ending your elevator pitch with a question is to keep the person engaged, to keep the conversation going, and to keep the proposal open rather than to ask for a decision at this point. You're on the ground floor, and you can rise with the level of interest—immediately or on another day.

Tip 334. Play on the Power of Your Expertise.

We rarely question our CPA, our neurologist, or our air-conditioner repair person when he tells us the cause of our difficulty and recommends a solution. Why? There's power in the perception of specialized expertise. If you establish your credentials in a certain field early, people seldom question them. They'll give you the benefit of the doubt on your facts and conclusions more often than not.

Tip 335. Roll with the Realities Rather Than Hoping for Martyrs.

In a perfect world, perfectly good ideas would be implemented. But political realities of the workplace—pressures from colleagues, customers, and coworkers—may force others to veto your ideas and plans. Find ways to help people handle those realities rather than expect them to become martyrs for your sake. Can you go with them to meet with a higher-up? Can you extend a deadline? Can you speed up your typical process? Can you remove a penalty clause? Can you draft the clause for their RFP?

Tip 336. Engage as Many Senses as Possible.

Show people a visual. Give them a slogan. Let them touch, feel, test, or experience the benefit you're offering—or the product or service that will deliver that benefit. The more senses you engage, the stronger the impact and the longer their retention.

Tip 337. Choose Your Timing.

The time to sell roofs is right after a tornado. The time to sell investment expertise is after the stock market takes a drastic upturn or downturn. The time to sell a quality process in your organization is after you've been removed from the bidder's list because of the rising percentage of defects in your deliveries. The time to ask for a transfer is during a downturn, not during a peak period. Timing is crucial. Ask any politician.

Tip 338. Create a Favorable Atmosphere.

Meeting planners claim that registrants rate educational seminars higher when they're held in resort locations. Job applicants prefer jobs where they are interviewed in plush surroundings. Shoppers shop longer when music plays in the background. Diners linger longer over meals served in comfortable restaurants. So it stands to reason that the principle can work for you.

Tip 339. Call Out Champions and Sponsors.

One of the most valuable things we learn from successful nonprofits is their methods for fund-raising: They seek celebrities and high-visibility CEOs to serve on their boards, sign their letters appealing for funds, send out autographed photos in exchange for donations, and lend their names as ex officio committee members for fund-raising galas.

Follow their lead for your own efforts. Who are the movers and shakers you need to get behind your movement, recommendation, or proposition? Can you ask them to voice their approval by sending out an e-mail blast, endorsing you on LinkedIn, posting a video testimonial on your YouTube channel, providing an endorsement for your website or Facebook fan page, making an introduction to another key resource, or attending a meeting?

Tip 340. Stand Up if You Want People to Take You Seriously.

If your office culture is generally laid back, with people walking in and out to see the boss without appointments, with no-agenda meetings, with "your office or mine" casualness, you may want to draw attention to the seriousness or urgency of a problem by changing the atmosphere drastically. Be formal. A stand-up presentation adds to your authority. Put people on notice that your idea deserves unusual attention.

Tip 341. Change the Media and the Method.

Do something out of the ordinary. If you typically use a flipchart or white-board for your discussions, create a slideshow and set up your laptop to present your idea to the boss. Show a quick video clip to present the problem. Grab footage from the company's YouTube channel to make your point. Create and send a 60-second trailer like your favorite book or movie trailer. Any change of media and method says, "This is important. Take note."

Tip 342. Present Your Idea to Several Small Groups Rather Than One Large Group.

Groups take on a personality all their own. Any large group presents the problem of getting to know individual members. Their experience, attitudes, uses for what you have to say, biases, needs, and personal agendas vary, so that you're at a great disadvantage in making your ideas relevant and clear to all concerned.

In smaller groups, you can select the details of most concern to a smaller number of individuals and relate your facts to their experiences, fears, and hopes. A less formal presentation to a smaller group will usually generate more participation and questions that give you important feedback and allow you to rechart your course. And, of course, you can build rapport more quickly and easily because you seem more "approachable" to them.

Aside from the extra time involved, smaller is better.

Tip 343. When There's a Parade, Take Either the First or the Last Spot.

If you're one of several people who are trying to persuade your audience to choose among you, ask for either the first or the last time slot on their agenda. The rule of primacy and recency says that people remember best what they hear first; they remember second best what they hear last. What happens in the middle is least memorable. If you're in a lineup of briefers, grab the first spot. If that's not available, go for the last. By the time those in the middle finish with all their statistics, charts, and promises, the decision makers will have grown weary and forgetful. Your presentation will be the last on their mind.

Tip 344. Know the Criteria Before Pushing the Solution.

Gain agreement on a group's or boss's criteria and then work backward: What does the decision maker consider to be the most important issue?

A selling price under $5,000? A maintenance agreement with a four-hour response for problems? Delivery within 60 days? A vendor with a SAP program in place? Unless your criteria match theirs, you'll look like a solution waiting for a problem to happen.

Tip 345. Limit Your Objectives.

Rome wasn't built while they were working on Sicily. You can't accomplish everything at once. Determine your primary objective in presenting your case, and focus your efforts on accomplishing that one goal. If your chief concern is getting your boss to hire three extra people in your department, leave discussions about rearranging the workstations and the lobby until another day.

Tip 346. Point Out What You Know for a Fact and "What Seems to Make Sense."

Always separate facts from opinion. We are constantly taking in information about what happens around us and drawing conclusions based on that information. The problem is that information is rarely complete, so we "fill in the blanks" and then forget which part we filled in. Then when we're questioned on a particular piece of information that was an inference rather than a fact, we lose credibility for our factual information as well. Head off such situations by pointing out what you know for certain and what you have inferred from those facts.

Tip 347. Credit Other People for Their Sound Reasoning.

Position yourself as an ally of anyone who thinks clearly. When people bring up opposing views, question them about the basis of those views. Understand their reasoning, and let them know that you understand that reasoning. Only with "we're in this together" positioning will you overcome the feeling of "us" against "them."

Tip 348. Recognize That People Support What They Help Create.

Rally support for your ideas in a subtle way by asking people to contribute to them. Tell them what your goal is, then ask for their thinking on the subject before you put together your formal presentation of the idea to the entire group. What figures, resources, or anecdotes can they supply for you? If this plan meets with opposition, what do they think the focus of that disagreement is likely to be? If others react negatively, what would they suggest you try as second best?

The White House uses this strategy in building support for major legislation in Congress. It seeks the facts, the opposing views, and the supporting views *before* the vote, not during the vote.

Tip 349. Encourage Others to State Their Own Needs or Problems to Be Solved.

What's better than your overviewing the needs that your idea, product, or service can meet? Letting your listeners voice those needs themselves. People believe what they say themselves. Ask the group members to help you list problems that they're having on the job relative to X. Record their answers on your laptop and project it on the wall, or ask if you can record their comments and then work that audio clip into your final presentation and proposal to the decision-making team. Or grab a napkin at the lunch table and ask your boss to help you identify things that need improving "by whatever solution we come up with." Encourage others to speak up, stand up, question, or counter—just get them talking and moving. Then, rather than your having to convince others of a need, they will believe what they have just told you in their own words.

Tip 350. Invite Others to Try On Your Idea.

How many times have you heard the lament, "If I could just get the boss to try it, she'd like it"? That's why we get toothpaste, cereal, and soap in the mail. A parent says, "If I could just get Joseph to go with us for the summer, I know he'd like it and meet a really good group of kids." The professor says, "If I could just get the students to read poetry, I know they'd like it." The car salesperson says, "If I could just get people to come in for a test drive, I know they'd be sold."

The same is true with ideas. People can't try on new ideas over old ones. Have you ever tried on a new suit of clothes while wearing the old one? You have to persuade people to throw away the old policy, procedure, or equipment—at least for a time—so that they can give the new policy, procedure, or equipment a fair trial. To persuade others to try on the new idea, you have to let them play with it first—discuss what-ifs, who-withs, where-necessarys, whys, and how-tos. Only then will they really embrace the idea.

Tip 351. Be Careful About Opening with a Broad Question.

Wrong approach: "So tell me a little about your operations." First of all, the other person will be reluctant to answer because he doesn't know where the question is leading. Second, much of the answer would probably be irrelevant to the discussion at hand. Even with the consultative approach, people want to know where you're trying to lead them. If you start with a question, focus it and give the benefits or the point of knowing the answer.

Tip 352. Ask a Question That Showcases a Benefit.

"What are you spending now on dry cleaning the uniforms?" Follow-up: "This new fabric doesn't need to be dry-cleaned at all." Raise a question: "How much time do your engineers spend in preparing these charts each month?" Follow-up: "This software package can generate such a chart with fewer than six keystrokes." Raise a question: "Do your managers look forward to performance appraisal conferences?" Give a response: "Our external consultants can identify performance problems objectively with this survey before these problems lead to termination."

Tip 353. State Quantifiable Facts Rather Than Opinions.

Studies show that people give credence to people who take the time to back up what they're saying with hard facts and data. Yes, initial impressions count, but hard evidence counts most of all. For things that you find difficult to measure and quantify, come up with an estimate. But don't pick a number out of the air. Be prepared to share the logic behind the number. Be straightforward about your numbers being estimates and share the rationale behind them.

Notice the difference in impact and authority in these statements: "We spent $82,000 from February to October on temporary staff in the operations and accounting departments" versus "We've spent a lot of money on temporary staff this year" *or* "Hyram completed his project three months earlier than his deadline and $50,000 under budget. The customer gave him the highest satisfaction rating we've received in our six years' work with that company" versus "Hyram deserves a raise—he's dependable, and customers respect his work."

Tip 354. Cite Your Sources and Ask for Those of Others.

"They" has probably become the most vocal group in our society. "They" say this and "they" say that. When you have credible sources to support your information, cite them. When the other person tosses out objections based on what "they" say, ask specifically where those ideas, statistics, policies, or preventatives originated. Then, when you are given a credible source, ask how current the information is.

Tip 355. Turn Information, Facts, and Features into Benefits.

As you prepare, with every point that you plan to make, picture your listener asking, "So what is that supposed to mean to me, my department, or my company?"

> *Feature:* "This printer prints X characters a minute."

> *Benefit:* "This printer can turn out one of your 200-page proposals in X minutes. If your clerk prints out only 10 per day for these engineers, she'll be saving Y minutes."

> *Feature:* "Our shelter provides 100 adult beds and 50 youth beds."

> *Benefit:* "Your donation will provide temporary housing for 100 women who don't want to return to abusive husbands."

> *Feature:* "Your corporate sponsorship of the seminar will pay for the keynote speaker's travel and lodging."

> *Benefit:* "Your corporate sponsorship of the seminar will allow your site manager a five-minute introduction at the beginning of the program to overview your services."

Big difference.

Tip 356. Vary Your Intensity.

If you intend to build to a passionate appeal, you can't start out screaming. Consider how a singer begins with a timid croon, builds on the refrain, and then crescendos to a rousing finale. Do the same with your own delivery.

Tip 357. Increase Your Pace to Increase Comprehension— Up to a Point.

The typical listener thinks about six times faster than the average person speaks. So to keep others' attention, increase your speaking rate. Otherwise, they will take a mental recess. You don't, of course, want to speak so quickly that you don't articulate. Variety is the key. Slow down when giving complex technical information (if you can't skip it altogether), and speed up for the remainder of your persuasive points.

Tip 358. Personify Abstract Concepts or Inanimate Objects.

People have a difficult time dealing in abstractions. Because they are emotional beings, people respond to things that they can touch, feel, and understand. Give human characteristics to abstractions to arouse the listener's emotions. Examples: "This machine is temperamental; you have to make love to it before it responds to what you want." "This company is like an octopus; it has so many arms reaching out in the marketplace that one arm can get cut off without severe pain to the rest of the body." "This organization is sick; it's underfed; its energy is drained. We've simply got to find operating capital."

Tip 359. Speak Metaphorically.

Metaphors create powerful pictures. One metaphor can convey a lifetime of experience or a head full of logic. In one of my client workshops, a sales rep presented an analogy between relating data files to socks. Black dress socks that are worn to the office every day represent data files needed daily; dress socks go in the top drawer for easy access, just as data files that you retrieve often must be easy to access. White athletic socks worn for exercising only on the weekends represent data files that you need only monthly or quarterly; these white socks are stored in the middle bureau drawer for limited access, just like data files you don't need often. The rep's green plaid socks, worn only when Aunt Martha comes to visit, represent the data files needed only once a year. Those plaid socks are stored in the bottom bureau drawer for infrequent access, just like files you may never need again. His audience immediately understood his explanation about quick access to storage space.

We occasionally explain the various fee arrangements for our licensing of training programs to customers with this analogy: "As you determine which is the best fee arrangement for your organization, consider it like a mortgage." You can buy a house by paying all cash up front, or you can pay for it over time with interest. With our licensing fee, you can pay for the entire course and all master copies up front, or you can pay participant by participant over time. The last arrangement will cost you more over time, but you will have your money free to use for other things as you go along. Customers understand the concept: they can make an outright purchase, or they can take out a mortgage. Metaphors clarify what would take hours to explain in detail.

Tip 360. Use Anecdotes and Stories to Make Your Points.

Aesop did. Jesus Christ did. Norman Lear did. Steve Jobs did. People can digest only so much factual information. Anecdotes tie it all together—logic and emotion. Don't tell us what kinds of problems users can have if the system crashes. Tell us what happened to Joe Smithers when his system crashed in the middle of his budget preparation. Don't tell companies that they should have a disaster recovery plan in place. Tell them what happened to customer data within companies in Florida when the last hurricane hit. Don't tell people how the typical salesperson responds to incentive awards. Tell the sales manager that Gerry Wainwright won a trip to Hawaii and has tripled her sales as a result of the contest. Stories hit the heart and head.

Tip 361. Use Humor to Raise Receptivity.

Humor acts as a pleasant distracter, lessening tension so that people feel more comfortable examining the pros and cons of an idea. A humorous approach— we're not talking slapstick, just witty or light—keeps people's attention and drives away boredom. Laughter lowers defenses and raises receptivity.

Tip 362. Package Ideas Like Products.

Some people lapse into lazy thinking if you permit them to do so. Make your concept understandable by its packaging. Politicians, policies, and plays are packaged like soaps and phone services. For example, insurance rates, employee compensation, unemployment, and tax incentives can all be packaged as "health-care" issues in Washington. Think beginning, middle, and end (idea, action, and implementation), and tie them all together in one packaged concept.

Tip 363. Create Slogans.

Politicians package their ideas in sound bites. Charities create a poster goal. Conference planners display their theme on a banner across their home page and tweet it in 140 characters. If you can summarize your point in a pithy slogan, do so. Make it catchy and current.

Tip 364. Triple Things—Use Triads and Alliteration.

One of the first lessons in speechwriting is the use of triads (groupings of three). If you can add alliteration (repetition of the sound from word to word), so much the better. Our ears love the sound of

> Government of the people, by the people, for the people.
> Blood, sweat, and tears.
> Clearly, quickly, concisely.

Motivate, renovate, captivate.

Pray, prepare, proceed.

They want jobs, they want justice, they want respect.

Change the rhythm or omit one word or phrase in any of the above groupings and you lose the impact.

Tip 365. Don't Be Too Cute.

At least weekly, I see a direct-mail piece, e-mail, or website that catches my attention: It offers a funny cartoon, a glitzy color, a sly slogan, or a provocative question. My problem is determining what's being sold. I don't know exactly what the advertiser is asking me to buy, decide, or do. If you have to work for it, the point is not persuasive.

Tip 366. Select Selling Words.

Get people's attention with words like these: *new, updated, exciting, fashionable, fast-acting, cost-effective, low-cost, no-risk, easy to use, successful, prestigious, opportune time, select few.*

Tip 367. Prefer Powerful Phrasing.

"I would suggest" sounds as if you're not quite sure, that if you were in a position to make a suggestion and if it didn't fluster anyone, you might suggest that maybe... Use instead: "I suggest." Rid your language of weak phrases.

> *Not:* "I think we should attempt to get approval on this before it's too late."
>
> *But:* "Let's get immediate approval on this."
>
> *Not:* "It seems to me that..."
>
> *But:* "I believe..."
>
> *Not:* "I've been thinking lately that maybe someone could..."
>
> *But:* "After careful thought over the past two months, I've decided that..."
>
> *Not:* "This plan could work if we really push it."
>
> *But:* "With our support, this plan will work."

Can you hear the ring of positive thinking and authority?

Tip 368. Use Both Rounded and Exact Numbers.

Exact numbers sound more credible: "The number of employees dissatisfied with their paychecks was 51.4 percent" sounds exact, and therefore accurate. Rounded numbers, on the other hand, give the appearance of estimations. Yet "slightly over half" is easier to remember than "51.4 percent of the employees surveyed." So which do you use if you want the numbers to be both credible and memorable? Use the exact number first, and then round it off in later references.

Tip 369. Make Statistics Experiential.

People digest numbers with great difficulty. Yes, pie charts and bar graphs help. But try to make statistics both visual and experiential. For example, randomly survey the members of your audience by asking them to raise their hands, then relate those findings to the random survey you did previously. Or do as one manager did when he dramatically ripped a dollar bill in two to illustrate what the administration had done to his budget for the upcoming year. Yes, supporting statistics lend credibility to what you say. But do all you can to help your audience digest them.

Tip 370. Never Let Facts Speak for Themselves.

Facts need interpretation. According to Mark Twain, "There are three kinds of lies: lies, damned lies, and statistics." If you don't believe it, tune in to the next political campaign. People can make facts and numbers mean almost anything. Interpret yours.

Tip 371. Consider the Legitimacy of the Printed Word.

To some people, putting something on paper means that it's official. For this reason, even small-business owners print all their fee schedules, prices, and terms and conditions on "official" letterhead. Quoting them orally makes them seem subject to negotiation. When traveling in unfamiliar countries, you can determine which street vendors dicker and which don't by the absence or presence of price tags on their wares. The same principle works whether you're selling a concept or a vacation: put it in a memo, a manual, or a mural.

Tip 372. Provide Memory Aids.

Listening expert Dr. Lyman K. Steil estimates that the average knowledge worker listens at an effective rate of 25 percent. Other research shows that after a 10-minute presentation, a typical listener forgets 50 percent of the information heard. After two days, the recall level drops to 25 percent. After a week, the recall drops to about 10 percent. Therefore, you have to help the listener remember your points. Use metaphors to make concepts easy to recall. Suggest a mnemonic device for your key points (the three Ps of Universal Services: Prepare, Plan, Promote).

Give your listener a personal experience with the concept; that's the idea behind ropes training for team building in organizations. You can provide a demonstration model to let the customer get a "feel" for extending his memory. Whatever method you choose, work on increasing others' recall of your idea, opinion, service, or product.

Tip 373. Use Visuals as Aids, but Don't Let Them Dominate.

Studies by the University of Minnesota and the 3M Corporation, along with earlier research at the Wharton School, indicate that an audience is 43 percent more likely to be persuaded with visuals than with words alone. Consider a written report, handouts, graphics, or other visuals to aid clarity and recall. *A warning:* Anything that's overdone loses its effect. If you underline every word in a report, nothing stands out. If you hang a picture on every wall, no one notices the masterpiece 10 feet to the left of the doorway. Likewise, if you use a visual for every point, the visuals become the presentation—a serious error.

Tip 374. Don't Ever Read Your Key Points.

Reading your ideas, rather than telling them, destroys your credibility, sincerity, and enthusiasm. Rapport suffers. The listener toys with these thoughts: Who generated these ideas? Doesn't she care enough to learn them? Isn't he convinced enough to deliver them from the heart? Why is she afraid to look me in the eye? Does he doubt what he's saying? Aren't these facts important enough to remember?

Tip 375. Match the Visual, Auditory, and Kinesthetic Patterns.

Neurolinguists tell us that we perceive the world through different senses: visual, auditory, and kinesthetic (the other senses). How do you know your listeners' preferences? Listen to their language for cues:

> *Visual.* I see what you mean; I just don't see it; he'll take a dim view of that option; that's a shortsighted approach; in my mind's eye; paint me a picture; she's got tunnel vision.

Auditory. That doesn't ring a bell; I keep arguing with myself; out-spoken people; call a spade a spade; word for word; spit it out; coming through loud and clear.

Kinesthetic. Heated debate; makes me uncomfortable; hotheaded; he's so formal and stiff; she's out of touch; hassle-free plan; hang tough; hanging by a thread; nailed him on that point; gut reaction; walk arm in arm on that; lateral moves.

Once you understand your listener's needs, match them with your own language.

Tip 376. Repeat, Repeat, Repeat.

If nothing else works, try the broken-record technique. If you state your message often enough in a variety of ways, eventually somebody will listen. If you hear something often enough, it becomes part of the atmosphere, like humidity. Repetition forms the core of advertising.

Tip 377. Prefer Understatement to Overstatement.

When you overstate your case, the listener raises his guard. Everything becomes suspect. A gross overstatement begs a customer to knock the wind out of your sails/sales. With understatement, the other person often takes up your cause. Suppose you make the statement, "We can save a minimum of $10,000 annually." Supporters will often chime in: "And in our situation this year, we saved twice that amount." Your credibility has gone up, not down.

Reverse the comments, and your estimation loses credence. You say, "In your situation, you saved $20,000 this year." They're likely to respond, "But this was an unusual year. Ordinarily, it would save only half that much." So prefer understatement, and let your listener add the persuasive point for you.

Tip 378. Get Past Clichés, Platitudes, and Truisms.

"You can't teach an old dog new tricks." "You pay for what you get." "Haste makes waste." "Let sleeping dogs lie." "He who hesitates is lost." When you resort to summing up your argument with one of these axioms, you give up your most powerful tool. People resist ruts. They'll think you're simplifying a complex problem and falling back on lazy thinking. Come up with your own new slogans and truths.

Tip 379. Don't Beg the Question.

Begging the question means stating the obvious or stating an assumption in a way that sounds as though it doesn't need additional proof.

- "It's obvious that..." (This dares anyone to challenge the statement.)
- "If we continue to collect more information, we'll have more facts upon which to base our decision." (Will you ever have fewer facts if you continue to collect information?)
- "I suggest that users perform these tests quarterly because the results will give them further information." (Will the results give them less information?)
- "The consultants determined that we should reinforce the welded joints because this was the wisest preventive solution." (Would they ever suggest the dumbest solution?)
- "More testing may be useful because it may shed more light on the subject." (Would more testing ever shed less light on the subject?)

Persuasive language involves a logical presentation of facts and information, not a fanfare of fancy, overblown pronouncements that are trivially true.

Tip 380. Anticipate Questions.

If you were the decision maker, what would you want to know before giving your approval? Go through the five Ws as prompters: have you covered who, when, what, where, and why, and also how and how much about your answer? If not, prepare to do so.

Tip 381. Use Others' Questions to Make Your Own Points.

When someone raises a question, think of bridging. How can you answer and then bridge back to a key point that you want to make?

Question: "How long did you say delivery on the widgets would take?"

Answer: "Delivery will take about six weeks; that's why we need a decision this week."

Question: "How complex will installation be, and what kind of downtime will we have?"

Answer: "It's complex. And if it's not done right, downtime can be six to ten days. That's why I think the credentials of the vendors are critical to our decision. As I mentioned earlier, the technicians at Universal can guarantee..."

Tip 382. Notice Whether People Listen to Your Answers.

If you answer a question or objection and the person seemingly jumps to another issue without giving your answer much thought, pay attention to that behavior. That question is serving as a decoy to cover the real reluctance to go along with your proposed idea. When the question is for real, the other person listens and incorporates your response into her thinking.

Tip 383. Prepare for the Standard Objections.

Certain objections in the workplace are, unfortunately, standard: "We've never done it that way before." "We can't afford to." "We can't afford not to." "It's risky." "Let's let somebody else work out the bugs, and then we'll see." "We've got too much invested in the status quo." "We don't have the time to devote to it." "We don't have enough people." "We don't have the expertise." "That's somebody else's job." "I just don't think we can make it work." "Our people won't like it." Plan your response to the objections you know will arise in your discussions.

Tip 384. Recognize Resistance in All Its Forms.

Some people voice their resistance openly: "I'm not interested." "I don't think the idea will fly." "I can't give it my full attention until next year." Others gesture their resistance: clock watching, foot or finger tapping, playing with objects within reach, doodling on paper, or staring out the window or door. Others look for distractions to take them away: phone calls, texting, or fires to put out. Some try to make a game of it. They ask unrelated, distracting questions, nitpick your data, and toss out silly comments. Some are openly rude and grow irritable. Some withhold key information and observations so that you have to guess what they know. Others just sit patiently and wait for you to "get it over with" so that they can politely say no.

Recognize all these signs so that you know how far you are from your goal of agreement and can deal with people's concerns early—while there's still time to resolve those concerns and rally support.

How? Engage the other people early. Make the interaction a dialogue, not a monologue. People believe their *own* data. They decide things for *their* reasons—not yours. So what that means for you and me is when trying to persuade, we need to engage others in the conversation sooner rather than later.

Tip 385. Dig for Unspoken Reservations.

Don't stop at recognizing the signs of resistance. Get the reservations on the table. When people seem reluctant to accept your ideas, be persistent in uncovering the reason. You can't respond to an unasked question. You can't calm an unspoken fear. You can't compare options if you have no idea what the other options are. Encourage your decision maker to think aloud so that you can either confirm or correct your presentation along the way.

Try statements such as: "Why not?" "How do you think your people will like this?" "Do you think your own customers will welcome this change?" "If somebody comes up with an objection later in the process, what do you think that might be?" "What else would stand in the way?" "Is there anything else that would keep us from moving on this?" "What about other things that would make you reluctant?" "Are there related issues?" "What else stands in the way of an okay?"

Keep pushing until you get the resistance on the table. Silence does not necessarily mean consent; it may mean that the obstacles against what you say are looming so large that the listener doesn't see the point in even discussing the matter further. You have to see the hurdles to jump them.

Tip 386. Investigate the Standard Causes of Resistance.

If you're having difficulty getting people to accept your point, take the time to investigate their points. Your willingness to investigate and listen goes a long way in demonstrating your integrity and intelligence.

People resist change because it creates uncertainty. Maybe your idea will work, and maybe it won't. What if the group invests time and money in the new plan and the old one turns out to be better? That fence-sitting period of indecision creates discomfort.

A second reason for resistance is the not-invented-here insecurity: "Why did someone else, rather than I, think of that idea?" "This is my department; why are you trying to tell me how to run it?" "What's mine is mine." This insecurity is especially at play if the person with the new idea has less experience or time on the job.

Then there's competitiveness. In some situations, if your idea wins, mine loses. Fourth, there are personality issues: "I don't like you; therefore, I don't like your ideas" or "I'm a negative person—I don't like anything or anybody."

Only after you hear the unspoken concerns and identify their causes can you set about minimizing resistance.

Tip 387. Brace Yourself Through the Negatives.

Just because somebody is bent on bringing up all the cons to your point or detailing all the pitfalls if you're wrong, don't think that all is lost. You don't have to do a point-by-point rebuttal. Many decisions—maybe even most—are made in spite of all the negatives identified and discussed. Brace yourself and wait out the recitation. It's possible, even likely, to lose the small battles at several points and still win the war.

Tip 388. Guard Against Your Own Resistance to Others' Comments.

Do you tune out others while they're still talking and begin to prepare your rebuttal? Are you pouncing on other people's ideas immediately after they're stated? If so, you're not giving those ideas a fair hearing. Even if you've heard the ideas before and know where the person seems to be going with the comment, pouncing too soon conveys a closed mind and an unwillingness to hear others out carefully. Is the pace of the discussion getting faster and faster? If so, the other person, you, or both of you are resisting, not thinking.

Tip 389. Don't Censor Emotional Comments Out of Hand as Irrelevant.

Someone may raise a question that you don't believe is germane to the decision. Don't rush through the concern "to get back to the real issue." Some concerns may not be *logically* relevant, but they may be *emotionally* relevant. For example, the marketing people may bring up a gripe about the way the customer-service people handle angry callers. That issue may have little bearing on how the group monitors Twitter comments, but it may make a big difference in whether the customer-service people keep their jobs. What is relevant varies according to the purpose of all concerned.

Tip 390. Agree Before You Disagree.

To avoid the appearance of not listening to points that others raise, hear them out, pause, and then agree with at least something the other person has said: "That is a related issue, all right. The first thing, we need is . . . ," or "You have a point. Do you think that should be our primary criterion?" or "You're right about that. I wonder if . . . ," "I understand how frustrating that can be. We probably should set aside some time to deal with that issue in and of itself. The current problem is that..." Others will tag you as a reasonable, flexible person.

Tip 391. Use the Every-Cloud-Has-a-Silver-Lining Principle.

Example: Your project manager states that he is opposed to your idea of buying Brand X pens as gifts for all new hires because of the "exorbitant cost." You concede the point that the Brand X pens cost more than most brands, but you point out that the new hires will feel proud that the company has lavished such an expensive gift on them on their first day on the job. Reinterpret negatives as positives.

Tip 392. Ask for the Reasoning Behind Someone's Counterclaim.

Don't argue against the wind. Let's suppose you present a plan for providing computer maintenance service to a customer who says, "It's too expensive." You respond, "Not really, when you consider the X feature." The customer listens and then responds, "But it is much more than we wanted to pay." And you say, "That may be true, but..."

You get the picture—you're arguing over a vague assumption. What does the customer mean by expensive? What is her reasoning? How did the customer decide what she wanted to pay—what should be a reasonable price? When you get the answers to those questions, you'll have something specific to work with. If the comment "too expensive" is based on the customer's budget, you'll know that you need to spend your time figuring out how to help the person finance your service within that budget. If the comment is based on a comparison of your price to that of competitors, then you'll spend your time telling how your service differs from the competitors' offering.

Take another example. A boss says, "We can't change that policy because people would get angry." You can't deal with that unless you know why the boss thinks people will get angry.

Of course, be sure to ask for the other person's reasoning in a nondirective, nonchallenging way: "The way we set our price is to determine X, and then add 10 percent for Z. How did you set your budget figure for this service? Let's see if we're on the same wavelength, or if we're comparing apples to oranges here."

To argue without knowing the basis of assumptions is working blindfolded.

Tip 393. Check for Reasoning Errors.

Here are the most common reasoning faults:

Force fitting an analogy. Someone uses an analogy to explain how two things are alike—and then gets carried away. "A maintenance agreement on your copier is like an insurance policy on your automobile." Yes, there are similarities that would help someone understand the idea of a prepaid maintenance agreement, but it doesn't follow that the two arrangements are alike in all ways. Insisting that they are in order to make a point is faulty reasoning.

Generalizing from a single case. The sales manager in Tupelo feels uninformed by headquarters about the introduction of new products and ad campaigns; therefore, the manager reasons that all sales managers feel uninformed on important new developments.

Focusing on all or nothing. This reasoning insists on considering all ideas as a package deal. We have to accept all of it or none of it. This product will meet either all our needs or none of our needs. We have to reward everyone for perfect attendance or no one for perfect attendance.

Stating rather than proving. "That manager has been delinquent in dealing with safety issues." Where's the proof? What specific incidents have gone unresolved? "Ferdinand has no ambition to move up in the company." What specifics support this conclusion? Calling a process "primitive" or equipment "state of the art" doesn't make it so.

Confusing sequence with cause and effect. A demanding controller joins the company August 1 as head of Max's department. Max resigns on August 31; therefore, Max left because he had difficulty working with the new controller. In this case, chronology may have little or nothing to do with the result. Check for these gaps in logic before someone points them out to you in front of a group and damages your credibility.

Tip 394. Unravel the Rope of "Why" Strand by Strand.

When someone takes a position that's diametrically opposed to the available facts and opinion, rather than tackling the job of trying to open her mind all at once, go for one explanation at a time. Select one aspect of the opinion and ask why the person feels or thinks that way. After that explanation, pick out another part of the opinion and ask why. After that explanation, select another thread of the opinion and ask why. Make sure that your tone remains even, not accusatory. And allowing time between questions also works well. By spreading out the questions and unraveling the position strand by strand, you'll have a better chance of leading the person to discover weaknesses in her own thinking.

Tip 395. Paraphrase Trivial Objections.

When someone raises a trivial objection, listen carefully. Then, to show him that you've listened, paraphrase the objection aloud to him "for clarity's sake." Not only will the other person know that you've really listened, but he will hear how weak the objection sounds when it is stated independently. The response is often, "Well, never mind. I guess that's a minor concern at this point."

Tip 396. Change Yes-No Issues to Multiple-Choice.

Don't make accepting or rejecting your idea an all-or-nothing proposition. If you agree that some action is better than no action, help your listeners see other choices. If they can't purchase the equipment to do the printing now, are they willing to let you contract with freelancers to get the work done? If they can't give you two operators for the week, can they contribute funds to help you pay for a virtual assistant? If the management team insists that they can't afford to fly employees to the West Coast for a seminar, would they consider conducting the same training locally? Providing a personal coach? Hosting a webinar? Subscribing to tips sent to individuals' mobile phones?

Tip 397. Propose the Let's-Write-It-into-the-Contract Alternative.

Realtors have become masters of this technique. They walk through a vacant house with the prospective buyer, and the buyer says, "Do the drapes go with the house?" The Realtor replies, "We'll write it into the contract." Buyer: "How about the fireplace tools?" Realtor: "We'll write it into the contract."

Try the same approach when your group continues to bring up unlikely what-ifs. "If X happens, we'll stop payment on the check immediately." "If Y happens, we can always have them remove the new equipment and bring back the old." "We'll add a clause to the contract that says if Z happens, your intellectual property reverts to you." This approach minimizes wasted time on unlikely scenarios.

Tip 398. Develop a List of Picturesque "Saver" Lines for Recurring Snags.

Speakers have a pocketful of witticisms to cover common mishaps on the platform. When the microphone suddenly drops from the stand or makes weird noises, they say things like, "Sounds like mating season." "Funny. I brushed my teeth this morning." "Nothing like a live censor."

Likewise, when you anticipate getting bogged down in persuading a team, have some "saver" lines that call attention to a particular problem. Let's say your team always generates a lot of possible solutions but has trouble focusing on specific solutions. You might say, "The grocery store with the most items doesn't necessarily stock gourmet food. I think it's time to stop generating suggestions and start evaluating what we have."

If your group gets hung up on "who won't like it," try: "Not everyone voted for Abraham Lincoln. I think people who don't now support what we're doing will come around when they see X happen."

If the team argues all the pros and cons and never seems to come to a decision, try: "I'd rather buy a tight pair of shoes than hike the mountain barefoot. Maybe the decision isn't perfect, but let's move on something. We can always make adjustments down the road."

Recapping the problem in such a succinct, picturesque way makes a strong point.

Tip 399. Don't Aim to "Outargue" People.

As my mother used to say, even if you argue "until you're blue in the face," you will lose if you make the other person feel outdone. You can outtalk, outsmart, and outreason someone, but you still may fail to gain agreement if the other person doesn't feel good about the decision in the long run. Aim to present your point accurately, enthusiastically, and sincerely. Then listen. Know when to be flexible and offer a compromise. Don't go for the kill.

Tip 400. When Someone Pushes, Don't Push Back.

Opposition spawns opposition. If you don't believe it, ask a partner to stand face to face with you and align yourselves open palm to open palm. Push gently. You'll notice how your partner pushes back to maintain his balance. Push harder. You'll notice that your partner increases his pressure to equal yours.

The same principle is at play in persuasion. The harder you push, the harder someone else will push back. So, to neutralize an emotional exchange, as soon as you feel the other side becoming agitated, dial down the pressure. You can even come around to the other side of the table. "Okay, let me stop here and summarize where we are. If I understand you clearly, you think the decision is a bad one for three reasons. First, the proposal won't work because. . ." Once you stand on the other side of the table and take up the other person's viewpoint, that person becomes neutral again. The pushing stops. You may even want to ask the other side to summarize your key points "for clarity's sake."

The idea is to neutralize the emotional conflict long enough for logic to take its course—should logic be on your side.

Tip 401. Don't Make the Other Person Wrong for You to Be Right.

Ego blinds people to logic. Let the other person save face if she wants to agree with you: "Maybe you didn't have access to the data I just received," or "The situation has changed drastically since you were last briefed," or, "Despite what he told you, the customer has obviously changed his mind again. Here's his latest wish . . ."

Tip 402. Minimize Stress for the Other Person.

Putting the other person under psychological stress does not pressure that person to go along with you and "get it over with." Although as adults we might tend to believe differently, kids do attempt to wear us down with whining and complaining. But studies show that this is not the case in the workplace. If people feel pressured to decide something, they'll usually cling to the status quo rather than make a change.

Tip 403. Hold the Sarcasm; Avoid Detractors.

No matter how "outmoded," "primitive," "ridiculous," or "wasteful" you believe the current plan, procedure, or product to be, avoid labels and sarcasm. People identify closely with what goes on in their departments and within their areas of responsibility. The reaction is much the same as when you put down someone's hometown. *That person* can disparage his hometown all he wants to, but he won't permit an outsider to do so.

Tip 404. Avoid Frames as Power Plays.

Emphasizing that you're the celebrity engineer who holds the patent frames you in a more powerful position than your listeners. Reminding the employees in the warehouse that you write their paychecks will not go over well if you're using that position to persuade them to participate on the company softball team. People resent those who rattle their sabers.

Tip 405. Lower Others' Guard with Graciousness.

Alcoholics Anonymous and hundreds of other self-help groups can verify this truth: You cannot motivate people from the outside; their motivation has to be internal. People are more motivated to believe you, help you, or at least get out of your way if they like you. Avoid an adversarial relationship. Be gracious in your words, tone, attitude, and actions.

Tip 406. Dodge Zaps and Zingers to Get to Your Goal.

Should people not be gracious to you in your attempts to persuade them, keep your goal in mind. As best you can, dodge any personal attacks, any I-don't-like-you statements, or any performance deflators. If your goal is acceptance of an idea, approval of a plan, or purchase of a product, then try to put your ego aside.

Tip 407. Provide Opportunity for a Trial Run.

Cereal companies don't make us spend $4.89 on a box of new flakes, fruit, or nuts. Instead, they mail us a trial packet to taste before we have to plunk down our money in the supermarket. Create ways for people to give your idea a low-risk trial before making an irreversible commitment of time, money, or reputation. The lower the risk, the more likely it is that they'll take a step in your direction. Never be afraid of their asking, "What do I have to lose if I go along?"

Tip 408. Note the Difference Between Selling an Idea and Motivating People to Act.

In "selling" something, the focus is on the seller's success—what does the seller need to do? In "motivating," the focus is on the other person's attitude and benefit—what's does the buyer need and want? The subtle difference implies different methods, language, timing, and attitude.

Tip 409. Show Passion.

If you're not sold on your own idea—sold enough to find and organize the facts you need, to develop the strategy to suit your audience, to prepare the presentation, to energize your body, to select the perfect phrasing, and to anticipate and prepare for objections—then the decision makers never will be.

Boredom brings disaster. Enthusiasm drives interest. Energy connects inquiry with action.

5

Holding Your Own in Meetings, but Working as a Team

"Meetings… are rather like cocktail parties. You don't want to go but you're cross not to be asked."

—Jilly Cooper

People who enjoy meetings should not be in charge of anything.

—Thomas Sowell

A meeting is an event where minutes are taken and hours wasted.

—James T. Kirk

The ability to express an idea is well nigh as important as the idea itself.

—Bernard Baruch

Many a good idea has been smothered to death by words.

—No attribution

Sometimes I get the feeling that the two biggest problems in America today are making ends meet—and making meetings end.

—Robert Orben

Meetings can bring the world to peace—or kill 15 hours a week for even the best time manager. Communicating ideas and creating solutions as a team take the best of attention and skill. These guidelines will help you lead and participate in team discussions both to contribute and to evaluate ideas.

Tip 410. To Meet or Not to Meet—Study the Question.

How many times have you accepted an invitation to a lunch meeting, only to realize that you've spent an hour and a half on something that could have been done in a 10-minute phone call or a 5-minute e-mail? The higher you go, the busier you get. And the meetings you attend must count.

If you get a reputation for conducting useless meetings, the busiest and best people won't show up. If you're asked to attend someone else's typically unproductive meetings, defer with one of the following: "Is attendance mandatory?" "I'm unavailable. Is my attendance important enough to change my schedule?" "Could I send a representative?" "Would you mind if I offer my input in writing or in a follow-up phone call?" Others will generally surmise that you expect meeting time to be well spent.

Tip 411. Call a Meeting Only for the Right Reasons.

When you call a meeting, make it significant and be prepared. In a client situation, you may have been working for months on a deal that will either thrive or nosedive based on a single meeting. The higher you go in your own organization, the more expectations others have for your abilities to conduct yourself in a meeting—either as a participant or as a leader. Take things seriously. Call a meeting to

- Present information to a lot of people quickly without writing it.
- Get immediate input from others.
- Gain "buy-in" from the team and provide a setting in which some members can influence others positively.
- Motivate and energize the group about the idea.

Skip the meeting if

- You have nothing special to discuss.
- You don't need others' input.
- Your mind is already made up about what you plan to do.
- Getting others involved would only complicate your plan.

These are even worse reasons to meet: meeting as a substitute for work; rubber-stamping a decision; complaining; demonstrating the power to make everybody show up. Because joy and misery love company, sorting out true motivations may require some soul searching.

Tip 412. Set an Agenda.

Some people think that agendas lend too much structure to a meeting, that people can't be spontaneous when there is an agenda, or that the atmosphere will be too formal. Nonsense. That's like saying that if you plan for a vacation by packing the right clothes, arranging for transportation, and deciding on a destination, you can't relax and be spontaneous along the way.

Tip 413. Make Your Agenda Informative.

Use questions, not topics. Summarize the issue at hand in a succinct question. Examples: "Should we hold the convention in St. Louis or in Portland?" (Not: "Convention Location.") "What ideas do you have for our annual fund-raising drive?" (Not: "Annual Fund-raising Drive.") "Should we upgrade our equipment?" (Not: "Outdated Equipment.") "How can we use YouTube more effectively to engage prospects?" (Not: "Using Social Media Tools.") A question that is well formed reduces your meeting time by a margin of 50 percent.

Then let the group know what you expect on each issue—"for discussion only," "for their information only," "to collect your data," or "for decision." Whether you stay right with the agenda or take a few minutes' detour, having an agenda will give others a little peace of mind that the meeting is going somewhere—and that it will end.

Tip 414. Start with the Most Important Idea or Issue and Work Backward.

There's a great temptation to begin with the routine matters—the FYI items. But the all-too-frequent problem is that when you save the most controversial and important item until the last, you run out of time. Maybe a Freudian move?

Tip 415. Announce Odd Start and Stop Times.

An executive at a health-care organization expressed ongoing frustration that people routinely showed up at meetings between 5 and 15 minutes late. Because these meetings involved busy physicians, hospital administrators, and researchers who spent much of their week in meetings, the problem had become a huge drain on productivity that irritated all involved when they themselves "owned" the meeting.

After a little analysis, the problem became clear. The start and end times for all meetings were on the hour: 9:00–10:00, 10:00–11:00, 11:00–12:00, and so forth throughout the day. The locations of the meetings, however, were scattered across the hospital campus—some as far away as a 15-minute drive. The simple solution: all meetings for the system must end at the three-quarter-hour mark to give participants time to travel between meetings. End of problem.

If you want people to take your meeting time seriously and tune in while they're there, do four things:

- Set an odd start time so that they remember it: 10:10 or 11:15.
- Start at that exact time. Every time. No matter who's present. Reward those who come on time; don't punish them by disrespecting their time and making them wait for late arrivers.
- Don't waste others' time by "catching up" the late arrivers.
- End on time.

Tip 416. Select Attendees Carefully.

Use the following checklist: Who can provide necessary expert advice? Who will support your cause? Who will oppose your cause? Who will sabotage the project if he doesn't "get in on the ground floor"? Whose commitment do you need to "make it happen"? There's your guest list.

Tip 417. Own the Setting.

If you're planning a clandestine affair, go for a dark bar with soft music. If you want an energized group, go for a well-lit poolside table. If you want an informal chitchat session, try somebody's office. If you want an equal, on-target exchange, look for a conference table in neutral territory. If you want a no-nonsense atmosphere, schedule the boardroom. If you want to play host-and-guest, provide coffee or snacks in a parlor or suite. Whatever your choice and purpose, if you're in charge, "own" the surroundings to produce the best outcome.

Tip 418. Take a Cue from Your Kindergarten Teacher.

Consider short attention spans, and minimize distractions from the outside that are under your control. Familiarize yourself with the audiovisual equipment. What distractions will the windows create? Can you change the seating to minimize people walking by and waving to those in your meeting? What about volume from closed-circuit TVs mounted in the hallway? Are there plants that might block someone's view of a video clip that you plan to use?

Tip 419. Control the Dynamics by Controlling the Chairs.

Choose seating arrangements as carefully as you choose your meeting site. If you intend to flatten the hierarchy for the meeting, arrange the tables and chairs so that there's no "end of the table." Create a hollow square, a circle, or a U arrangement. Should you remove the lectern that signals "authority" and replace it with a stool or chair and a hand-held mic?

If you expect to be dealing with controversial topics, make sure that opposing parties don't sit on opposite sides of the table. If they do, they're physically setting themselves up for a face-off. When you think that may happen (as in the case of two departments coming together to "defend their turf" on key issues), then assign seats so that like-minded individuals can't line up on the same side of the conference table.

The bottom line: Seating arrangements may dictate the tone and outcome of the meeting.

Tip 420. Take Your Seat with Forethought.

Where you sit makes a great deal of difference in how you interact with others and how they interact with you. Studies show that people seated across the table from each other tend to communicate more than those seated to the left or the right. That across-the-table communication, however, may be adversarial rather than supportive. The head honcho typically sits at the end of the table. The power seat is to that person's right; thus, the person in that seat becomes the leader's "right-hand man" (or person).

Put yourself in the spot where you can be a positive contributor and a reconciler of those who disagree.

Tip 421. Take Your Body with You.

Even when you're in an informal meeting, appearances and posture count. Yes, rolled-up sleeves, an open collar, and stocking feet may be the attire for a "working meeting." But that's not always the attitude to convey. Someone who's "laid back" (meaning loose papers scattered, ruffled hair, sprawling in the chair, hands playing with trinkets and toys) conveys an informal look—and a disorganized mind and agenda. If you have something important to say, look like it. Sit erect (leaning slightly forward in your chair). Organize your props, paperwork, or gadgets. Look alert and thoughtful. Your body reflects your mind.

Tip 422. Stay Out in Front if You Intend to Lead.

Nothing frustrates meeting attendees more than having a supposed leader who doesn't lead. State your role at the beginning and what authority the group will have. Questions to ask yourself as you prepare: Do you intend simply to facilitate a discussion? Will you allow the attendees to set the process and the agenda? Do you intend to tell them how you will discuss each idea and come to a decision—consensus or vote? Do you intend to have the final say, or will the group have the authority to make the final decision? Are you going to keep the discussion moving or abdicate that responsibility to others randomly? Are you going to be a silent observer on each idea, or do you plan to put in your two cents' worth? Are you strong enough to stop a feeding frenzy should the stronger people begin to attack a weaker person's ideas?

When the group starts spinning its wheels, as a leader, you need to be there with a comment such as: "Where do we go from here?" "What's the solution?" "Which way do you want to go?" "Let's back up and redefine the problem." You don't have to have all the answers and make all the decisions, but you should be out in front. Either lead or delegate the responsibility to someone else and get out of the way.

Tip 423. Do an All-Clear Check Before You Begin.

Given today's typical hectic pace, attendees frequently want to check their cell phone "one more time" for the latest e-mail, dash off one more text message, or make one more call "while things are getting underway." Consequently, they gradually tune in one by one over the course of the first few minutes of a meeting.

To stop the habit of doing "just one more thing" and to gain people's prompt attention, ask for an all-clear to open: "Does anybody else have something to take care of before we begin?" Wait for response. Make eye contact. Use peer pressure to get agreement to turn off cell phones and focus for the allocated meeting time.

Tip 424. Encourage Participation from Others—If You Want It.

Some meetings serve only to inform. If that's your purpose, tell the audience what you're going to tell them and be done with it. But if your intention is to generate ideas, get feedback, or come to a decision, you may need to take a more active role in encouraging participation.

Try these techniques: Ask for a show of hands on an issue. Toss out an open-ended question and see who takes the ball. Toss out an open-ended question and suggest that you go around the circle and let everyone give her views individually. Present your question or issue in writing, give all members a copy, and ask them to jot down their responses quickly. Take up the responses and read them to the group for reactions. Text or e-mail your question or issue to the group prior to the meeting, and ask attendees to "reply all" with their initial thoughts before the meeting. Use the meeting to come to consensus. Invite nonparticipators by name: "Carl, we haven't heard from you—what do you think?"

Finally, you might assign two or three people a devil's-advocate role and ask them to toss out any objections they can think of. Participation takes effort, and some people are too preoccupied, uninterested, or tired to contribute without encouragement.

Tip 425. Don't Set People Up to Refute You.

If you've already made a decision and intend to simply present that decision at a meeting, say so. Or, if you still have doubts that your decision or planned course of action is the best and the purpose of the meeting is for feedback, say that as well. But choose your wording carefully. Avoid introducing the topic like this: "I've decided to do X—unless someone has a serious objection." Few will have the chutzpah to speak up.

If you want to get feedback whether or not you plan to change your mind, try something like this instead: "I've decided to do X. What do you think the fallout from our customers/employees/management will be?" Or: "I plan to proceed with Y; what positives and negatives do you think I might have to deal with?" In any case, don't announce your decision or plan in such a way that people have to "refute" or "oppose" you to give you feedback. If you want feedback and forewarning of the difficulties, make it easy for people to speak their minds.

Tip 426. Don't Use the Group as Camouflage.

Don't use a meeting as a way to make your point with someone else when you don't have the courage to make it directly. Meetings are not battlefields.

Tip 427. Discuss Taboo Issues Anonymously.

If you know that certain issues are hot topics politically dangerous to careers, you have to work hard at creating a safe environment. Consider doing an anonymous survey on the issues and simply "reporting the results" for discussion. Or, you can quote anonymous sources from the grapevine. Say: "Someone has expressed the concern that... How do you think we can handle that issue?" "Other people have stated that they don't intend to... What would make people feel that way? What suggestions do you have for convincing them otherwise?"

Tip 428. Don't Expect Participants to Pool Their Ignorance.

Some issues, problems, and decisions require information and expertise, not just untrained opinions. If your issue falls into that category, don't bring it up in a meeting format where participants are uninformed. If you do toss out the idea and they offer their ideas and opinions in a noble effort to help, and you find their "help" inadequate, you'll have put yourself into the position of having to ignore their input. And if they've wasted time and effort in the process, they're going to be angry. If you want to get input only from those with special expertise, either go to them privately or call for their input specifically by name. People feel much more comfortable discussing what they know rather than what they don't know.

Tip 429. Participate; Don't Pout.

Even if you didn't want to attend a meeting, when you're there, be there. Listen to what's going on rather than fidgeting with your gadgets, glancing at your watch, or rolling your eyes. Your body language speaks volumes to those who consider the meeting important and want your input.

Tip 430. Be Versatile in Playing Several Positions in the Process.

Good meetings require a process. The *traffic cop* makes sure that everybody gets a turn to speak, shuts up the monopolizers, and generally ensures that everybody receives fair treatment. The *coordinator* continually brings people up to date as the group concludes each item and then calls for the next step. The *compromiser* takes an active role in bringing people who disagree together on an agreed-upon next step. The *commentator* reads everyone's body language and verbal clues to give the group updates on the progress it's making toward its goals and points out where, when, and how the group is getting stalled. The *clown* throws out one-liners, either to get attention for an idea or to break tension in the group. On occasion, you'll need to learn to play each role.

Tip 431. Summarize Frequently.

Whether or not you see the summarizer or leader as your official role, if no one takes on that role, do so. To keep the discussion moving toward its target, somebody has to recap what's been said and point out the next topic for discussion.

Tip 432. Call for a Process Check Occasionally.

At times, the group process will stall. You'll be talking in circles, covering the same territory. You'll hear tempers flare. You'll see that people feel they are under personal attack. You'll notice that you are deciding, undeciding, and redeciding the same issues. Be the one who calls attention to such breakdowns: "We don't seem to be getting anywhere. Let's see where we got off track. We had started to brainstorm the Y issue. Does somebody have a more effective suggestion for moving us along?"

Tip 433. Remind Yourself and the Group That Not All Ideas Are Created Equal.

In the course of any specific discussion, team members may generate several suggestions for dealing with a problem. Don't fall into the trap of giving them all equal billing with something like: "Okay, we have five alternatives on the table. Let's discuss the pros and cons of each." In many situations, only two or three of the many ideas offered are serious contenders. Don't waste your time with all the details of the other, lesser ideas.

Tip 434. Use the "What a Baby!" Response.

Doctors, politicians, and pastors have perfected this technique. The proud father stands outside the hospital nursery looking through the glass at his red, wrinkled newborn. He nudges the doctor beside him, "Well, what do you think, doc?" To which the doctor replies, "What a baby!" When someone presents an idea that you don't approve of or one that seems inappropriate, don't feel that you have to accept it or take time discussing it. After the person finishes speaking, look at her for a moment and say something like: "That may be true." "That's another idea." "Interesting." "Some people seem to think so." "Possibly." "Hmmm." Then break eye contact and move on. That person will rarely know how to take the comeback.

Tip 435. Don't Digress, Ramble, or Sidetrack.

Determine that you won't be part of the biggest meeting problem of all: digressions. Stay on target. If you can't remember the issue, jot yourself a note as the group moves from agenda item to agenda item and refer to it often. Not only is the agenda topic important, but also you should keep track of where you are in the process of dealing with each topic. Are you into the overview? The analysis? The idea-generation phase? Brainstorming alternatives? Testing agreement on the proposed solutions? Don't make a habit of wandering along two or three steps behind everyone else.

Tip 436. Omit War Stories.

When they have an audience of admirers, some people yield to the temptation of telling war stories, sharing inside jokes, and recounting wonderful things they once did. Unless time is of no importance to the rest of the group, don't.

Tip 437. Support, Explain, or Reject Only One Idea at a Time.

Poorly facilitated meetings encourage people to dump everything once they finally get the floor. That is, because they have had to wait so long to get airtime, once it's granted, they dump their ideas about everything that has been said so far. Don't dump. Unload your thoughts on only one issue at a time, and then get off the court. If people learn to trust that you're not going to sidetrack them by dealing with several issues at once, they'll let you take the court more often.

Tip 438. Stop a Filibuster.

If one person continues to monopolize the discussion, use body language to cut that person off. Break eye contact. Lower your eyes to the paper in front of you. Turn your body away from the offender. If necessary, firmly but kindly say something like: "Lisa, I think I understand your viewpoint. Let's hear from somebody else."

Tip 439. Use a Prop to Tag the Motormouth.

Now that incentive awards have become increasing popular for team effort, you've probably seen the idea of the roving trophy or banner that moves from winning department to winning department. Try the same idea in a meeting to "subtly" remind motormouths that they're being repetitious and/or long-winded. A foghorn. A whistle. A bat. A balloon. A broken record. Whatever the object, place it in the center of the table. Then when someone bogs down the meeting, push the prop into that person's space at the table. At its best, it stops the offender; at the least, it generates a laugh and breaks the tension.

Tip 440. Set a Timer for Input.

Take this tip from Congress. Members get their allotted minutes and no more to state their case. Timed input works especially well for teleconferences and videoconferences, where you can't use body language to discourage a long-winded group member from holding the floor. You may physically set an alarm so that participants hear it when it goes off. Or you can start a timer on your computer screen so that it "runs down" to zero. Or, as meeting leader, you can simply ask at the outset that participants take no more than three minutes to give their view of a situation.

Tip 441. If You Don't Have Something to Say, Don't Say It.

Participating doesn't mean that you should necessarily feel obligated to comment on every issue. If someone hands you the baton and you have nothing to contribute, pass it on: "I think everybody has already expressed my views." "I don't have an opinion one way or the other." "I don't know a thing about that subject and don't want to confuse the issue." "Thanks, I'll pass." People will love you.

Tip 442. Don't Ask a Question Simply to Ask a Question.

Some team members become uncomfortable with silence. So when a colleague tosses out an idea that's met with silence, some people feel compelled "to get the ball rolling" by asking a question. Don't. If you really don't have a legitimate question and don't care about the issue one way or the other, don't add to the problem by opening your mouth. Hours have been lost by people chasing down answers to questions that should never have been asked and that bear little or no relevance to the decision or problem.

Tip 443. Avoid Answering Questions That Nobody Has Asked.

In presenting ideas, try to anticipate others' objections and questions and be prepared with answers. But that doesn't mean you should dump data without cause. Such thinking leads to talking in circles, digressing, and rambling on, with the same information being given four different ways. Make your point succinctly. Then pause. If you get questions, pull out your bag of tricks and answer them. If not, don't dump details that nobody wants or needs.

Tip 444. Don't Assume the Role of Translator.

Example: "I think what Garrett is trying to say is that his staff is..." Trying to "translate" for others conveys to them very loudly that you don't think they voiced their ideas well. It also irritates the group to have an echo effect in the room. Finally, you'll be embarrassed if Garrett responds that you did not translate correctly. Some people are inarticulate; learn to live with it.

Tip 445. Avoid Letting Others Put Words in Your Mouth.

If you've expressed an idea that someone feels the need to "interpret" for the group, don't let him misquote or misinterpret you. Example: "No, Bill, that isn't exactly what I meant. I meant..." "Wait a minute. I said it exactly as I intended to. I'm saying that..." "No, that's not what I meant. Maybe I was unclear. Let me put it like this..." Only you know what you mean to say. Say it directly without an interpreter.

Tip 446. Don't Set a Pattern of Expressing the "Downside."

Yes, you will disagree from time to time, and you can make a valuable contribution by expressing that differing viewpoint. But don't make the negative a pattern. Offer solutions and encouragement when the others get down, dumb, and defeated.

Tip 447. Know the Difference Between Being Realistic and Being Gloomy.

Have you ever known people who think their view is the only "realistic" one? Their comments begin: "Let's get real here about..." "You've gotta be realistic about..." "You need to do a reality check here if you think X."

"Let's use a more realistic number for..." "Come on, you people; you have to face the hard facts and quit this pie-in-the-sky rationalizing." The difference? Realism focuses on the facts; gloom adds attitude.

Tip 448. Apply the "You Break It, You Buy It" Principle.

Never be the one who tears up everybody else's ideas and then has none of your own to offer. If you criticize the best solutions that others have tossed out, you're obligating yourself to present substitutes. According to author Milo Frank, this idea originated with Larry Kitchen, retired chairman of Lockheed Martin Corporation. Based on the frequent sign in curio shops, "You break it, you buy it," Mr. Kitchen applied the principle to stop people who continually tossed cold water on others' ideas with their routine negativism.

Example: "Regina, since you have serious reservations about the proposal we're discussing, why don't you do a more thorough study of the ramifications of its implementation and bring us an alternative proposal next week." *Caution:* The idea is a poor one if your intention is to encourage openness and avoid "groupthink." So apply the principle only to those routinely negative people who run down every idea.

Tip 449. Disagree Without Being Disagreeable.

Never let yourself become a victim of groupthink, a condition in which group harmony becomes more important than results. If the purpose of a meeting is to generate ideas and get input, by all means speak up when you disagree. Just don't be disagreeable. The difference is attitude.

Tip 450. Strip Ownership from Views.

If you're functioning as a team, you will want to bring all contradictory facts and viewpoints into the open rather than pretend they don't exist. Try to strip away direct ownership and the associated ego to evaluate the ideas independently. "We have a proposal and two viewpoints on the table: one, that the plan will take too long; the other, that the cost takes away Marketing's veto power. Let's discuss the first objection. What support do we have for that?" Notice that all names have been removed from the suggestions and viewpoints. Treat conflicting ideas openly and objectively. People hold on most strongly to ideas that haven't been discussed, and especially to ones bearing their name.

Tip 451. Use Positive Questioning to Convey Your Reservations.

When people bring up issues that you don't agree with, your questioning can put them on the defensive. However, failing to ask questions and express reservations defeats the purpose of the discussion. To overcome the dilemma, make sure that your questioning can be taken only in a positive way. First, demonstrate that you have heard what the other person has said by paraphrasing it, and then lead the person through your confusion or reservations with positive questions.

"Jeanine, I understand your position. You want to use contractors because all the projects planned to date call for a specialized expertise that we don't have on board, right? Well, help me understand why your people who have the same degrees as the contractors you've mentioned don't have the expertise... Now, I'm still confused about where we could find experienced contractors on such short notice... Okay, what would you suggest we do about the up-front payment that most will require?"

This line of positively worded questions emphasizes your openness to answers while still expressing concerns. If the concerns can't be answered adequately, the owners of the ideas often conclude that they have defeated themselves because they didn't have the answers—or a good idea, whichever is the case.

Tip 452. Don't Invalidate Others' Feelings.

Examples: "Kabrielle, I don't know why you're so punchy about that." "Jennifer, there's no reason to get so defensive." "It'll be okay, Javier; really, it will." To say or imply that people don't have a right to their feelings makes them robots. People do not live by logic alone.

Tip 453. Legitimize Others' Feelings Without Agreeing.

When you present an idea and hear someone's emotional disagreement, you can legitimize that feeling and then move on. Legitimizing is not the same as agreeing with the comment. Example: "Yes, Keeley, I can understand how you might be concerned that X would come across hypocritically to your staff." The speaker hasn't agreed with Keeley, but has simply expressed a legitimate concern. Keeley will appreciate that acknowledgment and will usually quit pressing to make that point.

Tip 454. Lighten Up—The Point Doesn't Have to Be Perfect.

Not all platforms and purposes are created equal. Your career will not rise or fall based on the interactions in every meeting. If a particular meeting is not necessarily "yours," jump in and participate even though you may not have given it thorough preparation. Spontaneity still succeeds.

Tip 455. Don't Engage in a One-on-One Battle.

Avoid letting a discussion degenerate into dialogue with only one other person. Inevitably, others in the group become onlookers and begin to take sides. Then the opposing ideas become an ego issue, and the discussion has a winner and loser. This is bad for morale. When you realize that only you and one other person remain in the discussion, say something like: "Well, let's open it up again. Charles, you said . . . , and Eugenia, you mentioned that . . ." The idea is to leave the impression that all have contributed to the exchange and that you are conceding to the group opinion.

Tip 456. Don't Harpoon an Idea Because It's a Poor Swimmer.

Not all creative thinkers and technical wizards are effective communicators. Be careful that you don't ignore someone's input simply because she did not phrase her ideas well.

Tip 457. Use Another's Question as Your Platform.

An excellent way to get a message across without having to hog the floor is to look for someone's question that you can use as a platform—an invitation to speak up. Have your prepared message ready, and look for the opportunity to step in when someone raises an appropriate question. You'll be accomplishing your goals on someone else's airtime.

Tip 458. Be Flexible on the Issues.

We're not talking about flip-flops like the politicians make—whatever the polls support today, they "believe" tomorrow. Instead, be open to the facts and flexible in your feedback. The purpose of meetings—most staff meetings, anyway—is to exchange ideas. If someone presents facts and sways your opinion, don't hesitate to change your position. That's not weakness; it's democracy.

Tip 459. Listen to What's Going On.

Listening is more than the absence of talking. It requires active participation—only with your mind rather than your tongue. And listening increases in difficulty as the number of meeting participants grows from one person to a group of individuals, all of whom are competing for airtime. Listen and interpret so that you're not the one who's always asking for a repeat of issues already discussed and clarified.

Tip 460. Don't Derail Others' Proposals While They're Still on Track.

Follow what's going on before you propose something new. If you really want to upset a crowd, let a speaker propose an idea, with all the related facts and analysis, ask for discussion, and get just to the point of calling for a decision . . . and then interrupt with a proposal of your own. Your insertion of a proposal at the wrong time may derail the entire train of thought for the group. Pay attention to the logical process and avoid bringing up out-of-order issues and proposals. After you get past the idea stage and into the proposing stage, let the first proposal work its way through the group discussion and be accepted or rejected before you toss out your alternative for evaluation.

Tip 461. Remain Seated if You Want to Emphasize That You're Tossing Out Ideas "Off the Cuff."

Bringing up an idea while you're seated plays down your forethought and preparation. It conveys that the ideas are spontaneous and relevant to the issue at hand. Your physical position says that you're on an equal footing with the rest of the group and that you encourage give-and-take. As a result, you'll probably get feedback, pros and cons, agreement and disagreement.

Tip 462. Stand if You Want to Convey Authority and/or Underscore the Importance of an Issue.

When someone "rises to the occasion," the team generally settles back and lets him have the floor. The group dynamics change from an informal team discussion to a formal presentation. A formal presentation says three things: "I already have an opinion on this issue," "I am well prepared with supporting details," and "The issue is bigger and more important than the routine ones we deal with." From your physically elevated position, your words take on more authority; the group is likely to grant you control of the meeting, even if only temporarily.

As a result of all these dynamics, you probably will get less feedback on your idea. Those who support it will withhold their comments, thinking that you obviously sound authoritative and need no help in garnering others' opinions. Those who disagree with you may hate to buck authority before an audience; they often save their negative comments for the hallways. You can sometimes have it both ways by presenting your proposal standing up and then taking a seat for the follow-up discussion and turning over the facilitation to someone else.

Tip 463. Opt for a Stool if You Want to Stay on the Fence.

If you still can't decide whether to stand or sit, you may want to prop yourself on the edge of the conference room table or a desk or opt for a bar stool. This position is not as formal as standing, but you convey authority because of your physically elevated position. You give the "prepared and in charge" appearance while creating a relaxed attitude by sitting down. Whoever has the physical height advantage has the psychological advantage as well.

Tip: 463A: Create Voice Intensity if You're Meeting by Phone

When others can't see you physically, you'll need to create authority with your voice rather than physical stature. Speak up with energy and intensity. Make sure you enter the conversation with a strong voice, and make a statement long enough and strong enough to hold the floor. What can you say to pique others' interest and cause them to say, "Tell me more"?

Tip 464. Take the Stage; Don't Just "Drift In."

When you intend to present your own ideas, take the stage just as a performer does. None of this, "Just a minute, before we go on here..." "Maybe this has already come up in earlier meetings, and I missed it." "Don't want to get us off track, but it seems to me we should be looking at this a little differently." "I'm not saying I disagree with what we've already said, but just another, you know, thought about how we could approach it..." Instead, when you want attention, take it. Sit or stand purposefully. Project your voice. Use a confident tone. Spit it out.

Tip 465. Forget the Warm-Up Drill.

Ever since students first learned the five-paragraph essay format, teachers have required introductory paragraphs. Some business professionals remain in that rut. Forget a long introduction when you're offering informal comments. Start at the point of new information or the new idea. Then pause and take your cue from others. If they want elaboration, add it. If they have questions, answer them. If they nod agreement, you've made your point.

Tip 466. Try Being Obscure.

Try the direct-mail approach. Start with a provocative or intriguing statement to get people's attention and whet their appetites for the main course. "So maybe we should hire only those with no experience in this industry." "I've got an idea—let's beat them at their own game." When the point's "not all there," you'll grab people's attention for your elaboration to follow.

Tip 467. Set Yourself Up to Keep the Floor Until You Finish.

If you frequently meet with a group of strong personalities and routinely get interrupted, preface your input with something like the following: "After listening to what has been said, I have four observations to make about the X situation. First, . . . ," and then keep enumerating as you go along so that people understand that you're not finished when you take a breath.

Tip 468. Control Interrupters.

The only way to prevent some people from interrupting you is to insist on finishing. You can call attention to the interruption with other comments like these: "Paul, I didn't get to finish. What I was about to say was . . ." "Excuse me, but I got interrupted. I had one more item to mention . . ." "Please let me finish . . ."

Or you may choose to prevent an interruption with body language and voice. Raise your hand to the interrupter and continue to speak at the same or a louder volume. Keep talking until the interrupter realizes that you do not intend to relinquish the floor.

Tip 469. Be Conversational; Don't Move into "Meeting Mode."

Nobody said that formal ideas had to be presented in lecture format. Use your conversational voice, not your lecture tone. *Lecture tone:* "I want to inform you that..." *Conversational tone:* "I just want to let you know that..." *Lecture tone:* "Please voice your objections if I'm wrong, but..." *Conversational tone:* "Please say so if I'm wrong, but..." *Lecture tone:* "The research and development group, of which I've been appointed chair, effective May 1, has asked that you be notified that the team is receptive to your proposals about..." *Conversational tone:* "On May 1, R&D asked me to chair a team to come up with a solution. So, as part of that effort, we need your input about..."

Tip 470. Talk *with,* Not *to* the Group.

Consider yourself as being in a conversation with more than one person rather than "addressing a group." In most situations, that means that you'll pause to let others speak or ask questions if necessary for clarification as you move through your ideas. Use the inclusive pronouns "we" and "us" rather than "you" and "I." Use terms that others will understand rather than lapsing into jargon. Make eye contact with everyone around the table rather than reading from your notes or staring at the floor, the ceiling, or your favored ally.

Tip 471. Remember That People Are Most Interested in What's on Their Own Minds.

If you want to grab attention for your ideas, you have to start where people are and lead them to where you stand, not expect them to meet you halfway. What policy is bothering them? What do they fear might happen tomorrow? What frustrates them today? Start there and tie your idea into that concern or hope.

Tip 472. Make Abstractions "Hit the Gut."

Accept the fact that we don't make all our decisions based on logic. When people get emotional about an issue, accept that emotion, show that you understand it, and then, when they regain their composure, ask if they can share the reasons for those feelings. When it's in your interest to do so, play to others' emotions. Abstractions are difficult for people to rally around. Tie them to specifics so that people "feel" an issue. For example, if you want your team to provide input into designing your corporate policy concerning charitable contributions, don't deal with nameless agencies and noble causes. Talk about specific people who benefit from these contributions and specific agencies that will be receiving the money allocated by the policy your team helps draft. If you generate appropriate emotion, "dull" tasks can take on new life and importance.

Tip 473. Don't Plead with Puppy-Dog Eyes.

Your eyes can say that you're sincere, you're courageous, or you're confident, but don't let them cry for help. When you're presenting ideas for approval, don't let your eyes fall into a puppy-dog plea. Those who disagree with you will hop on that body language and drag you through the streets. Present your ideas confidently and then wait for response and approval. If approval isn't forthcoming, don't beg.

Tip 474. Don't Build Your Case—For or Against—on Secondhand Information.

On important issues, refuse to give secondhand information the same credence as you give firsthand information. When Helena says that Jack said that Lana thinks, stop right there. If the information is crucial to the decision, verify it. Make a phone call or postpone the discussion until the relayed information can be verified.

Tip 475. Present Your Proposal Only One Way, and Be Specific.

When you're courting several people with differing viewpoints, it's natural to think that the more general you can make your idea, the more "hooks" you're creating for people to latch onto. In that effort, you tend to explain your idea first one way and then another. You use this analogy and that. You think maybe this and maybe that would be part of the final product. Often, the intention of the elaboration is to offer something that will appeal to everybody.

A broad, generally expressed idea, however, usually has the opposite effect: everybody hears something that he disagrees with. And you wind up spending more time dealing with the minor details and "what you didn't mean to imply" than you do with the gist of the idea. The group has the sense that your proposal has been thrashed to death, when in reality only the chaff around it has been discarded. Prefer, instead, to propose the idea succinctly, in only one specific way. Let it stand there in all its glory until people force you to add details by their questions.

Tip 476. Listen to the Counters to Your Proposal Rather Than Planning Your Rebuttal.

Do you recall presidential debates in which candidates seemed to have gone to sleep while their opponent took a turn? The same thing happens in meetings. Don't get so carried away with preparing to defend your ideas when the next person quits talking that you miss what that person says *throughout* her full turn. If you do, you may find yourself focusing on an issue that the other person has just conceded, while failing to respond at all to the new issues raised. You can't take a time-out while the ball is in the other court. You have to stay alert while the other person serves.

Tip 477. Don't Withdraw Your Proposal Simply for the Sake of Harmony.

Encourage others to express either support or disagreement, but don't let people turn down an idea simply because "someone doesn't like it." Ask for supporting explanations, and be sure that everyone either accepts or rejects the idea for objective, logically sound reasons. If you're going to toss out an idea, support it until someone changes your mind.

Tip 478. If You Can't Manage a Touchdown, Try for a First Down.

If you can see that your idea will not be accepted in total, settle for measured success. Suggest that the team give you the go-ahead in a limited way. Ask for a "test run" at some phase of the project "before too much money is spent." All you may need is a little running room to prove that your idea or plan has merit. Don't give up simply because you don't make a touchdown with the first play.

Tip 479. End with Impact; Don't Just Fade Away.

If you're presenting an idea, don't limp away with a sputter. Don't simply drop your eyes, tune out with body language, or let others grab the floor and run away with it. Bring the discussion to closure. Summarize your idea, the pros and cons mentioned, and any decision made and suggest the next follow-up step. Also take responsibility for the fate of the entire meeting. Do your part to make it successful. If the meeting is unproductive and disruptive, decide on the corrective action you'll take next time to change the dynamics.

Tip 480. Don't Sound Like a Broken Record.

Present your idea and support it. After a fair hearing, if the group nixes it, move on. Bring that discussion to an end and meet the next agenda item head on. Nothing irritates others more than having someone continue to bring up a pet proposal or peeve and whine, whine, whine.

Tip 481. Build Support for Your Ideas Behind the Scenes.

Take your model from Congress and the White House on this technique. Just as the president calls individual representatives and senators to the Oval Office for a "briefing," rally support by giving others a preview of your ideas before you ever go into a meeting. You'll overcome the element of surprise that blocks some decisions simply because people don't want to "be rash" and make a decision "too soon." You'll also have the advantage of hearing opposing viewpoints so that you can prepare your counter before the formal presentation in the meeting. If you think that people might be hesitant to give you negative views one on one, encourage them with something like: "Help me see the other side of this issue if you don't agree." "If somebody were to object to this idea, what do you think that objection might be?" "What ideas do you have for responding to those who may be unhappy about this?" A behind-the-scenes briefing wins more friends than it creates enemies.

Tip 482. Don't Surprise Your Boss.

A husband and wife, Glenn and Nan, attended a community auction for a local charity. In a feverish round of good-natured bidding, where several CEOs present began to challenge each other to "dig a little deeper" for a good cause, Glenn popped up to say that he'd pay $20,000 for a canoe trip for six down the Mississippi River. Sitting beside him, Nan almost gasped aloud. They had agreed before the auction on how much they could afford to donate. Glenn's "surprise" angered her as much for his taking the liberty of not including her in the decision as for the large amount that she didn't think they could afford.

Bosses most often feel the same way. Generally, it's better to present the idea to them privately before springing it on a group and chancing a public embarrassment for them or a reprimand for yourself. The boss may suggest that you "wait on that idea until X happens" or tell you to go ahead and bring up the issue even though he doesn't fully agree. Either way, you've followed corporate protocol.

Tip 483. Ask for Input and Approval From Your Superiors.

Don't leave a meeting in which you've presented information or proposed a plan without having a clear mandate for the next step. If a response is slow to come, and you want input and honest reactions, ask the lower-ranking superiors for their feedback first. If you want a quick yes-no decision, go right to the top. Ask the senior person for questions, a response, or a go-ahead. After the highest-ranking person speaks, you'll get conformity from there on. There's no use being given "busywork" from the lower-ranking people if the answer from the top will eventually be no.

Tip 484. Withhold Your Ideas Until Last if You Want to Encourage Others' Input.

This strategy makes sense if you're in a position of power to make the final decision. If you state your views first, your team may lapse into groupthink and let the matter pass without expressing honest concerns or opposing views. When that's the case, toss out the issue, minus your opinion, and ask for others' reactions first.

Tip 485. To Shorten the Decision-Making Process, Call for a Vote.

Consensus feels good, and on occasions when motivation matters, it's a must. But that's not always the case. When time is short, democracy may rule. Call for a vote to bring the matter to closure.

Tip 486. To Shorten the Decision-Making Process, Abdicate Your Right to Make a Decision.

Another alternative to end frustration when the team can't seem to come to a decision is to call attention to that fact. "It seems that we just don't have enough information to make a thorough analysis. I suggest that we leave the decision to Matt and his department—that they finish their research and then make their decision based on that information." Nobody says you have to accept all the authority that's handed to you.

Tip 487. Call for a Q&A Session at the End.

Although people routinely allow questions and answers at the end of oral presentations, some do not think to do so at the end of meetings. Frequently, the questions will be about how to carry out actions or conclusions decided in the meeting. Never leave a meeting with fog still hanging in the air.

Tip 488. Thank Others for Their Contributions.

Even bad ideas have some merit. "Thanks, Joel, for bringing up the analogy of the tires. That provided a simple way to look at things." If the ideas were helpful, new, insightful, resourceful, supportive, convincing, relevant, or any combination of the above, say so. Commendations keep them coming.

Tip 489. Play Santa.

People work harder and more quickly for rewards. Figure out ways to reward yourself and your team members for contributing ideas and solutions. After you've made a quick, effective decision, suggest a reward: "We put that issue to bed in 10 minutes. Let's grant ourselves a 5-minute caffeine break." "Great. We have everybody on board and are feeling positive about this plan. Let's order pizza." "Well, we've just worked out the last detail to make this idea fly. I say we all take part in the presentation to the board. Everybody should share in the glory. What do you say?"

The reward doesn't have to be big—a shared bag of Jolly Ranchers, a long lunch break, recognition for individual contributions to the group, or a verbal pat on the back in front of the executive team. Santa says that it's the thought that counts, and he brings a new bag of tricks each year.

6

Listening Until You Really Hear

It's a toss-up as to which are finally the most exasperating—the dull people who never talk, or the bright people who never listen.

—Sydney Harris

The most important thing in communication is hearing what isn't said.

—Peter F. Drucker

Know how to listen, and you will profit even from those who talk badly.

—Plutarch

The road to the heart is the ear.

—Voltaire

Most people do not listen with the intent to understand; they listen with the intent to reply.

—Stephen Covey

A good listener is not only popular everywhere, but after a while he knows something.

—Wilson Mizner

Conversation in the United States is a competitive exercise in which the first person to draw a breath is declared the listener.

—Nathan Miller

No one ever listened himself out of a job.

—Calvin Coolidge

One advantage of talking to yourself is that you know at least somebody's listening.

—Anonymous

L istening makes the difference between passing or failing a test, making or losing a sale, getting or losing a job, motivating or discouraging a team, mending or destroying a relationship. But listening has gotten a bum reputation as a passive state. Not so. Listening is simply the precursor of successful activity.

Tip 490. Decide That You Want to Listen.

Many people listen poorly simply because they have no intention of listening well. They're preoccupied. They're too busy talking so that they can feel understood. They're focused on getting what they want done or heard; they have no time to be interrupted by someone talking to them.

Parents, teachers, and other authority figures confuse us with other poor listening habits and clues. These adults send us the wrong messages about listening with comments like, "Don't pay any attention to her." "Just look away and he'll leave you alone." "Just pretend you don't notice and he'll stop." "You can't believe everything you hear." "Don't let the bully know it bothers you." "Forget what she says; she didn't mean it—she's just angry." "He just talks a good fight and blows smoke. Nothing will come of it." "Tell her what happened. If she doesn't listen, that's her problem." No wonder kids doubt their ears and eyes and can't decide whether to listen or not.

Have you ever heard people say that they don't have time for something—golf, or walkathons, a charity event, or church, or dinner with a friend? Not true. We all have the same 24 hours each day; what they mean is that something isn't important enough to them to make time for it. The same is true of listening. We will find ourselves being poor listeners until we make up our minds that we want to become good listeners. Listening requires conscious effort and a willing mind. It's a decision to take an action, not just waiting your turn to talk.

Listening involves actively processing what the other person says to you: clarifying, asking questions, drawing out additional information, reading between the lines, giving feedback, verifying understanding, analyzing, and drawing conclusions about what you've heard.

What's the payoff? Listening keeps you informed, up to date, and out of trouble. It increases your impact when you do speak. It gives you a negotiating edge, power, and influence. It makes other people love you. Whether you're sitting around the conference table in a team meeting or around the dining table for your Thanksgiving meal, make a conscious effort to listen.

Listening is a gift to yourself and to other people. Give it on purpose—not just when you're forced to do so.

Tip 491. Listen with a Clean Slate.

Good listeners welcome new information and new ideas. Good listening does not require building a wall to screen out ideas and people that have as their purpose to change you or the things you believe. Rather, listening means standing on level ground, listening as though you were a doctor gathering new symptoms from a patient or a pilot in touch with the control tower during a storm. Excellent listeners expect to grant differences, grow their views and values, and gain insights.

Tip 492. Clean Your Listening Filter.

There are some announcements that we've trained ourselves *not* to hear. When the TV sports commentator says, "Let's pause now to let you hear from our sponsors," you take that as your cue to get something to eat. The digitized voice on the airport tram says, "Please stay clear of the doors; they are about to close." The mysterious voice on the parking lot of the rental car agency instructs: "Please leave your keys in the car and note your gas mileage. Before leaving your car, please check the car for your personal belongings." At times you do not hear these routine announcements at all.

We all have built-in filters to save us time in listening. The trick is to identify the ones that we should keep in place and the ones that we need to clean or remove. Executives may filter any advice given by an outside consultant. Bosses may filter any suggestions given by certain employees. Customers may filter any advertisements from a company that has disappointed them in the past. Some filters save time; others prevent opportunity and understanding. Continually upgrade your list to determine which are which.

Tip 493. Recognize That Listening Is Not Waiting Your Turn to Talk.

Salespeople are often surprised to find that listening is one of the key ingredients of the most successful performers and the downfall of the poor performers. For them, awareness is half the battle. The same can be said of listening by most other professionals. Once you become aware of the benefits of listening and the pitfalls of not listening, you've gone a long way toward making improvement. The absence of talk is not the same as listening.

Tip 494. Avoid "Listening" as a Retreat.

Those who are afraid to speak their mind on an issue, those who don't want to risk being wrong, those who are tired, and those who don't want to "get involved and make connections"—those people often pretend that they're listening. They may be looking at you, but they're not listening; they're just not talking. When you recognize this habit or attitude in yourself, be aware of the difference between that and real listening. Listening takes energy and requires reflective talking; retreating is a mental recess. People you're "listening" to and encouraging to continue with a slight nudge of a question every so often will not be fooled. They may continue to carry the conversational ball along for you, but afterward they will feel let down, if not resentful.

Tip 495. Listen with Compassion.

Some people listen with a superior tone, a critical spirit, or aloofness. In addition to speaking this way, they listen with the same attitude: eyebrows raised, scowling mouth, glaring eyes, folded arms, smirking lips. This behavior does not encourage people to open up and speak their mind. Nor does it free them to think reflectively about themselves and change the way they're acting or feeling.

Don't confuse compassionate listening, however, with simply giving verbal reassurances: "That's all right. You couldn't help reacting that way." "Well, don't worry about it. Things have a way of working out." "I know what you mean—bosses are all alike; you can't trust them to be fair." These responses are not helpful at all. They tend to brush the listener's feelings aside and imply that she isn't a good judge of what's worth worrying about or working on, what's a problem and what's not, or what action to take or not take. Compassionate listening provides something more than glib assurances. It empowers people because it enables them to lower their defenses, share themselves, and find their own solutions in an accepting atmosphere.

Tip 496. Listen for Feelings as Well as Facts.

Noted clinical psychologist Carl Rogers believed strongly that a patient's healing could be greatly speeded up by the simple act of having an analyst who really cared. "If I can listen to what he tells me, if I can understand how it seems to him, if I can sense the emotional flavor which it has for him, then I will be releasing potent forces of change within him." Far too many people pay an analyst for what friends should and could do if they practiced listening for emotions. Letting the other person know that you understand the emotion behind his words gives him the satisfying sense of *really* being understood.

Tip 497. Listen for the Context.

When we read a news story about a cousin who shoots an uncle over a card game, the incident shocks us because of the enormity of the deed relative to the provocation. When such incidents occur, we can be sure that the immediate act was not the whole of the situation. Words and feelings always have a context. A friend says to you: "There are so many rumors going around in my company that you never know from one day to the next if we're going to be merged, acquired, or just laid off. I'm not sure whether I'll be canned or not. So I can't decide about buying that house. We'd have to do some remodeling, for sure. The mortgage payments will really stretch us, and if Jill decides to switch careers, that'll affect our cash flow severely. I'm totally puzzled about the next step." With this comment, you have a broad context that lets you understand the whole situation: the rumors at work, the spouse's job uncertainty, and the necessary remodeling.

But what if the friend says only: "I can't decide about buying that house. We'd have to do some remodeling"? You might respond by talking about the pros and cons of the house—the location, the down payment, the interest rate, the condition of the inside. And you'd be way off base about the total meaning. Words do not mean much outside the context of someone's experience and situation. Probe for the context so that you can listen adequately and respond appropriately.

Tip 498. Listen for What Is Not Said.

Why did the talker decide not to tell you a particular fact? Why did the boss not mention the delay on the related projects? Why did the customer not mention volume discounts when she always buys on price? What's not said can be as revealing—and as important—as what appears in the headlines.

Tip 499. Paraphrase; Don't Parrot.

Reflective listening has often been misunderstood. When psychologists first introduced the concept, many people thought that it meant simply repeating to the talker what he had just said, as if it were an attempt to prove that you heard him. The purpose was lost. The idea of paraphrasing is to show talkers that you fully understand their meanings—not just hear their words.

The difference is enormous. By paraphrasing their views, you give talkers a chance to reflect on what they've just said, to make sure that what you heard was what they meant, or maybe even to change what they think or feel after hearing you repeat it.

Here are paraphrasing responses: "If I understand you correctly, you're saying..." "You really mean that..." "As you see it,..." "From your perspective,..." "Let me see if I get where you're coming from on that. You think that..." "What I hear you saying is..." "Am I hearing this right? You think..." "So to sum up, then, you feel..."

An Example of Reflective Listening/Paraphrasing

DAVID: I've told Angie a thousand times to get invoices out the same day that Accounting gets them done. And the summaries that I've given her to do are inaccurate again. I asked her for the raw numbers, and she spent two hours averaging them all. Then she doesn't know why she's got so much to do and complains that she can't get everything done!

JUAN: So you feel pretty exasperated with her performance, right? It's putting the whole department in a bind?

DAVID: That's an understatement. We have reports that don't go out. We have customer e-mails that don't get responses. We've had to spend money on temporaries twice this week because she's so far behind.

JUAN: You think that if Angie would follow instructions better, you wouldn't have had to hire temporary help?

DAVID: Well, I'm not saying that exactly. I don't know whether we do or don't need to hire anyone else. I can't tell if the job really is too much for one person or if Angie just can't handle it. If she followed instructions better and at least did things right, then I'd have a better handle on the real workload.

JUAN: You'd then know how much of the problem was due to rework caused by Angie and how much of the problem was that there's just too much to do.

DAVID: Exactly.

JUAN: So at this point, I guess you're feeling a lot of pressure from the customers who don't get answers or invoices and the rest of the guys around here that are complaining to you about Angie. And if Angie's complaining that she's overworked, you've got everybody unhappy.

DAVID: No, I don't think Angie really feels overworked. She just says that. I think she realizes that she's not performing up to standard. The workload issue is just an excuse.

You get the idea. Juan has paraphrased on three levels: the words, the feelings, and the implied words and feelings. Of course, paraphrasing is not called for on all occasions. Here are occasions that do call for such in-depth listening:

- When you or the other person is experiencing strong feelings and wants to talk things over
- When you or someone else has a conflict to resolve
- When someone needs new ideas or wants feedback on ideas
- When you're inclined to disagree with or ignore what someone wants you to accept

Not all conversations are created equal. Be choosy about which ones require the effort to paraphrase. Then give those important conversations all you've got. Paraphrasing helps the talker feel understood, think openly, hear and verify what she's really feeling and thinking, and reflect on what to do next. Paraphrasing electrifies both people involved.

Tip 500. Attend with Your Entire Body.

As part of an exercise in our communication workshops, we have a participant-speaker address the group. Then, while that speaker goes out of the room to prepare, we ask the group to help with a little demonstration that the speaker doesn't know he's a part of. We ask the audience to give the speaker a couple of minutes to warm up and then start to act uninterested. Some people lean forward with their head propped in their hand, resting on an elbow. Others lean back in their chairs, hands behind their heads. Some shuffle through their pocketbooks for a mysterious item. Others gaze out the window. Most break eye contact with the speaker. Nothing is overtly rude, just subtle.

In less than a couple of minutes, the speaker becomes flustered and even angry, totally unaware of what the audience has been instructed to do. When they begin to see the signs of inattention, some speakers will began to talk faster and louder. Others will stop, start again, stop, then lose their train of thought completely. Some will begin to pace around the room more feverishly and gesture more dynamically. They don't know exactly what has happened or why, but they understand that people are no longer listening. People want you to sit or stand in an alert position, lean toward them, stop rummaging through papers, and look at them when they talk to you. Your whole body has to listen. The experience dramatically illustrates for the group the importance of a listener's attentive body language.

Tip 501. Invite People to Talk by Commenting on Their Body Language.

Shy people may need encouragement to talk to you, particularly when they're unsure whether you'd be interested in what they have to say. A good way to communicate to them, "Hey, it's okay; I'm ready to listen" is to comment on their body language and then listen to their response: "You look puzzled." "You look excited; your eyes are flashing." "What a smile—what gives?" "Lost your best friend or your dog? You look down." Although the person may not take your cue, she has an open invitation to respond with meaningful conversation.

Tip 502. Play "What-If" to Encourage Reflection.

Have you ever had a coworker come into your work area and say, "Hey, I got a problem. I need some help." Then, as he starts telling you the problem, he suddenly says, "Wait a minute. That's an idea. Never mind," and dashes out. He has solved his own problem just by hearing himself talk about it. Having someone listen gives us an acceptable reason to talk to ourselves aloud. And talking about a problem as if you are explaining it to another person clarifies details, identifies issues, and raises possible solutions. On such occasions, help others think aloud by asking "what-if" questions. It's not that you have the answers—the other person does. Your helpfulness comes in listening to her and reflecting what she says to cause her to think differently.

Tip 503. Respond to the Feelings, Then the Facts—Not the Other Way Around.

"Calm down, calm down. Tell me what happened." Although it's a typical response, that's not the best approach when someone is angry, frightened, or frustrated. Uncork the emotion first, then ask for the facts. Customer-service reps understand the concept in dealing with irate customers, parents understand the concept in settling sibling battles, and ambassadors understand the concept at the negotiating table. Disregarding this concept can cost you a sale or a customer.

For example, a hotel guest calls down to the front desk and says, "There's a husband and wife next door having a knock-down, drag-out fight. They're yelling and screaming. Would you see what you can do about it? I'm trying to get some sleep."

The desk clerk says, "We can move you to another room, if you prefer."

Wrong move. That's an obvious solution. But the hotel clerk would have done better to respond to the feeling: "It's late, and I'm sure that's very disturbing. We'll call their room and take care of it." The "solution" response presumes a superior position, as if the other hotel guest hadn't thought of moving to another room. Not only does the response sound unfeeling, but it sounds like a put-down. Questions, comments, explanations, and observations come a lot more easily and clearly *after*, not before, the emotional release.

Tip 504. Be Careful About Attaching Any Labels to What You Hear.

People may experience the same situation and use different words to describe it. What one listener calls "worry," another calls "concern." What one calls "petulant," another calls "feisty." What one labels "angry," another calls "afraid." "Shyness" can be mistaken for "aloofness." Once you've labeled the feeling expressed to you, you tend to see everything else from that perspective. Be sure the labels don't take you off track.

Tip 505. Take Off-the-Subject Comments as the Subject.

In the middle of a conversation, when someone makes a remark that seems to be off the topic at hand, that comment is irrelevant. But that irrelevancy often provides a big clue to what's really on the person's mind. Consider dropping the topic at hand and taking up the new subject. You'll help the other person get the pressing problem "finished."

Tip 506. Overlook "Trigger" Words to Get to the Real Message.

When you hear emotional words, derogatory words, profanity, or politically motivated words, try to get past them to the real message: *bureaucrat, lazy, windbag, hustler, unfair, gross negligence*, and so forth. If you get hung up on the speaker's word choice, you may miss the primary message. Hear the person out. Then you can always go back and correct the word choice mentally.

Tip 507. Recognize "Stoppers" Before You Deliver Them.

When someone starts a serious conversation with you, your reaction will either encourage that person to keep talking or stop him cold. Stoppers include ordering, commanding, threatening, moralizing, advising, lecturing, criticizing, blaming, shaming, diagnosing, and interrogating. If you doubt that these tones and words will stop a conversation, recall the last 10 unpleasant interactions you've had.

Tip 508. Avoid Me-Too Interceptions.

"I don't know what I'm going to do with my teenager; he's totally irresponsible when it comes to money." Response: "Oh, do I ever identify with that! I've mentioned that my oldest is a junior at the university. Out in an apartment on his own. Well, the other day he calls me up and says..." Before you know it, the situation has been reversed. The person who introduced the subject and wanted to express her frustration is now the listener for the other person's saga. Yes, empathetic listening means that we share common experiences, but the key is timing. The first talker was cut off before she was able to tell about her situation and fully express her frustration. Take care not to intercept the conversational ball.

Tip 509. Use Silence to Encourage the Talker.

Recruiters understand this as their best tool to find out more about a job applicant. Silence makes some people uncomfortable, and they will do anything to fill it. Whether by making someone uncomfortable so that he will chatter on with revealing information or by inviting a friend to unload, silence encourages talk.

Tip 510. Probe With Open-Ended Questions.

Probe someone's comments with questions that begin with the five Ws: Why is that so? When is that true? Where is that true? With whom is that true? What is true? How is that true? How much is involved? Don't become an interrogator with yes-no questions; closed questions put you too much in the driver's seat. Instead, with open-ended probes, you encourage the listener to explore both feelings and facts for errors and insights.

Tip 511. Be Wary About Listening for What You Want to Hear.

My entrepreneurial son asked his stepfather if he could use part of his office building for teaching country-and-western dance lessons. His stepfather replied, "I have reservations about that, Jeff. I'm often working late at night, and having people here would be distracting. And the cleaning crew that comes in might not always clean up after them—I don't know exactly what time they make it to our building. And the tenants next door have a silent alarm that even our own employees set off when they walk through the lobby after hours—and they know it's there. Dancers in here would be setting it off, and the police would be coming out. Besides that, I wouldn't want people milling around through our workstations."

"But couldn't you move those wall dividers over into the big open area and keep people out of the workstations?" Jeff asked.

"Well, I don't know. I guess that's a possibility... What nights are you planning to give lessons—I'm up here working late just about every night but Wednesday."

"I haven't decided on a specific night yet," Jeff answered. End of conversation.

My son came home and told me that his stepfather said it was okay for him to have the dance lessons in the building—as long as they were on Wednesday nights and as long as he used the partitions to keep people out of the workstations. We hear what we wish to hear.

Tip 512. Be Wary About Not Listening for What You Don't Want to Hear.

A regional manager of a construction firm had a long talk with his vice president to express dissatisfaction with what he considered were misleading comments made to customers. "You tell customers that we're not just a contractor—that we have our own manufacturers for the cabinetry we install in the office buildings. But a warehouse with a table saw is not a manufacturer. I don't like misleading people." The vice president soothed the manager's concerns with promises that they had plans to get into the manufacturing side of the business shortly. As time went on, there were other such discussions. The regional manager told the vice president that he was upset about late commission checks and unnecessary requested travel. Each time the vice president responded to the manager's concerns with promises, agreed that things were not as they should be, and guaranteed improvements to come.

Six months later, when the regional manager offered his resignation, the vice president looked shocked. "You pull in more business than all the other regions put together. You can't leave. What will it take to make you change your mind? How much of a raise do you want?" Whatever the specific mindset—worry, upset, misguided, uninformed, or dumb—people don't hear what they don't want to hear.

Tip 513. Never Focus on the Exceptions.

When you hear *always* or *never*, set your brain to skip it. Otherwise, you'll be tempted to focus on the exceptions and miss the message—as in this case:

> MOE: You never tell me when you're taking a day off. So I'm caught off guard when you're out and clients call me about your projects.

> SANDERS: I don't know what you're talking about. I told you last Thursday when I had that dentist appointment.

> MOE: That's because you walked out of here like a zombie. Of course, I knew you were taking off then—everybody in the office knew about that toothache. But I'm talking about all the—

> SANDERS: How about on Memorial Day? I told you I was taking off that weekend.

MOE: Okay. You told me that weekend. But there have been count-less other—

SANDERS: And I told you that Marty Frazier might call...

Sanders is off to find the exceptions. Wrong move. Skip the exceptions and redirect your attention to the general message being communicated.

Tip 514. Avoid an In-and-Out Pattern.

Because we listen four to six times faster than someone talks, wandering ears become a temptation. We fade in and out just like channels on a TV. Become aware of this habit by forcing yourself to do something constructive with the extra listening time: Chunk the information and learn it as you hear it, make notes, or analyze comments. Just stay tuned.

Tip 515. Listen All the Way to the End; Don't Assume.

Doctors and their patients provide the best illustrations of this common weakness. After the doctor has seen three patients during the morning, all complaining about vomiting, headache, fever, and upper respiratory problems, the fourth patient gets half an ear. The doctor begins to write out the prescription before the patient finishes giving the symptoms. I would venture a guess that our health-care system pays for a great many unnecessary medical procedures and tests for exactly this reason. The one word *not* can make a whopping difference in someone's meaning. Listening costs less than testing.

Tip 516. Ask for Confirmation.

You ask for confirmations on your hotel reservations, airline reservations, online merchandise orders, and bank deposits. Make it a practice to ask others whether you yourself heard things right. Repeat back to the speaker any numbers, dates, technical terms, or names (along with the spelling), and ask her to verify that you've heard them correctly.

Tip 517. Decide When *Not* to Listen Reflectively.

If a speaker is so eager to get out his story that he doesn't stop to allow you to paraphrase, then doing so would be an interruption. If speakers are having difficulty expressing themselves, to paraphrase might interrupt their thoughts. They might even begin to let you "talk for them." If the speaker just wants to vent his emotions, you may choose not to listen and not to para-phrase abusive comments to you. If the speaker is simply passing along infor-mation, there's no reason to paraphrase unless you yourself want to verify what you heard for accuracy sake. And small talk certainly requires only a casual response—not the effort required by reflective listening.

Make reflective listening a conscious choice, depending on the cir-cumstances.

Tip 518. Eliminate Physical and Psychological Noise.

Taking calls while in my kitchen presents a number of challenges: The washer and dryer from the nearby laundry room. The dishwasher in mid-cycle. The TV in the adjoining family room. The music through the inter-com. And a conversation left in midsentence with a husband finishing in sign language. These background noises and concerns prevent my hearing accurately.

We've become so accustomed to some background noises that we're unaware that they affect our hearing. In the workplace, we have printer noise, music, coworkers' conversations, ringing phones, hallway laughter, and street traffic. We don't realize how much this noise affects our con-centration. If you want a comparison of what you can accomplish without all that noise, try staying after hours or arriving early, before the noise starts. Compare your concentration with that during peak noise hours.

Tip 519. Make Up for the Listening-Talking Differential.

I've already mentioned that we can listen about four to six times faster than we can talk. So, what to do with the "differential"? If the talker merits your attention, use the extra thinking speed to listen well. You have several choices: You can make notes. Or you can evaluate what you're hearing: Why is the person saying this? When is this true? Where is this true? Why is this true? How is this true? Why is this important to know? How can I use this information? How should I respond? That evaluation makes efficient use of your extra listening speed. Finally, you can use this extra time to fix what you're hearing into long-term memory. Chunk it into pieces, develop a mnemonic device, outline it with key words, or just repeat it to yourself—use any of these methods to fix the information in your mind so that it stays put.

Tip 520. Make Notes on What You Hear and Don't Be Afraid to Ask People to Repeat.

When angry customers call to tell you about a problem—or even when mild-mannered, happy customers call to tell you about a situation—don't be hesitant to ask them to repeat key facts or details. Say something like, "Would you repeat that attendant's name, please... Okay, now let me repeat these key facts to you to make sure I have everything correct. I want to make sure I have all the essential information so that we can get a quick resolution." The caller will want the account to be accurate as much as you do.

Tip 521. Don't Take Copious Notes.

If you have to err one way or the other, take fewer notes rather than too many. If you try to write down everything someone says, you'll invariably miss things. And not only will you miss words. With your eyes glued to the page or the screen and your mind intent on getting the words down, you'll miss pauses and nuances of meaning, voice inflection, and body language that will help you interpret the words. Less is more when it comes to note taking.

Tip 522. Ask for Clarification of Instructions.

Everybody needs feedback: presidents, priests, and parents. When the machinist gives the new hire instructions on how to operate the lathe and finishes with, "You understand?" the typical new hire will nod and respond, "Yes." Why is that? (1) People think they understand and don't know that they don't understand until they make a mistake. (2) People don't want to look stupid by admitting they don't understand. (3) People don't want to waste other people's time by having them repeat themselves. (4) People don't want to criticize the way the other person gave them the instructions or suggest the instructions were unclear.

Whatever your reason for the hesitancy, forget it. Ask. You're doing the instruction giver a favor by verifying that you understand and by asking clarifying questions if you do not. People will find it much easier to repeat the instructions, if necessary, than to repeat themselves later while they are trying to undo, redo, or make do.

Tip 523. Listen to Difficult, Complex Information as It Relates to You.

Seminars, symposiums, and staff meetings may all include information that you consider dull or complex. During these times, you may give your mind permission to go on recess. But is that in your best interest? If it is, be my guest. If not—if you really need to know the information, but you find listening to it a chore—practice discipline. We're used to "absorbing" information through entertainment without having to work for it. Listening to things that require concentration takes effort.

Try jotting down key points—not comprehensive note taking, but keyword or key-point note taking. It forces you to pay attention and look for the structure in the information you're receiving.

Also, look for personal applications in what you're hearing. If you were about to be sent up in a space rocket, you'd probably find it easier to listen to instructions on using the oxygen mask than if you intended to spend the weekend lounging in front of the TV. Always dig for the WIIFM (what's in it for me?). Why do I need to know this? How can I use this information? If you're a business development manager trying to learn new product specifications, visualize the paycheck resulting from your knowledgeable response to a customer's technical question. If you're hearing why management decided to set up a certain retirement plan, visualize yourself having to explain it to your spouse. Look for purpose. Whet your appetite.

Tip 524. Know When to Listen Analytically.

When someone dumps her feelings about a broken love affair, you'll want to listen reflectively to hear the feelings along with the facts. On the other hand, as a manager, you want to listen analytically. You may have to take the lead in helping the other person to sort fact from fiction, to discern hidden agendas, to develop creative alternatives to problems, and to evaluate those alternatives. Good management demands knowing when to listen and paraphrase versus when to listen and analyze.

Tip 525. Overcome Personal Bias to Evaluate Effectively.

Although difficult, recognizing the need for objectivity on occasion improves our reception of messages. Be aware of stereotypical thinking and negative thinking; otherwise, your reactions and the resulting situation become self-fulfilling prophecies.

Tip 526. Sift Out Propaganda Techniques as You Listen.

The *bandwagon* approach invites you to accept an idea or take an action just because everybody else is doing so: "This has been our most popular desk chair," or, "Here, listen to what Mr. Smoe says about this plan." The *all-or-nothing* persuader insists that you must either accept everything about an idea or reject it in total. Either you take the plan in its entirety, or forget it. Either you buy the product and all the related services, or it won't work at all. The *generalization* leads you to come to a conclusion based on a single or a few incidents or facts. "John Smith is an engineer who can't write well; therefore, no engineers write well."

The *like-one-like-'em-all* pitch links the new to the old, with the intent of giving your one idea a free ride. "You loved hearing Roland speak last year? Then you're really going to like Fred," or "You remember how well this process worked last year? Then we can set it up the same way this year." This next propaganda technique is more subtle: *I call 'em like I see 'em.* The persuader hopes to color your thinking simply by his word choice: he speaks of "this outdated system," and before long you find yourself thinking that the system is outdated. Or he talks of "this leading-edge technology," and soon you find yourself thinking of his company's technology as the wave of the future—all because the persuader labeled things that way.

The *card-stacking* persuader tells you only the facts that she wants you to hear, selectively omitting others that would give you both sides of the picture. And every argument seems right until you hear the other side.

Finally, the *evangelistic* persuader uses hot, emotion-evoking, descriptive words to stir people to action. "Are you going to let those tycoons sitting in their Manhattan high-rise with their $3,000 pin-striped suits kick you while you're down?" Think critically to avoid being taken in by these indirect tactics and inconclusive arguments.

Tip 527. Analyze the Persuasive Tone as You Listen.

When you're about to be "sold," your defenses go up. Why? It's not so much that people mind buying an idea as that they mind having someone think that they've been deceived by someone's tone or manner. Listen critically for the following attitudes:

> *Good ol' buddy.* This persuader makes you feel that because you're a long-lost friend, he's going to give you the real scoop—the inside story that he wouldn't tell just anybody.

You and I are different from those other folks. This persuader pushes to find things she has in common with you—we have the same hometown; we both have toddlers; we both like to drink at Grady's Bar. And it follows that if there's a strong identification, you'll buy what the persuader is saying. Why? Because you two fall into a different category from "average folks," so you'd better stick together.

You're so wonderful. This persuader loves your office, your kids, and your management philosophies. How could you not go along with someone who thinks you're wonderful, talented, and lovable?

Let me enlighten you. This persuader wants to educate you so that you can see the light and understand those complex things that he has mastered. The person shows such "patience" with you.

If any of these tones and attitudes come through, listen past them to the real message and action to make sure you're not being persuaded by the communication style or tone rather than by the ideas themselves.

Tip 528. Use a Checklist to Avoid "Morning-After" Remorse.

If you frequently find yourself with buyer's remorse—whether you're buying a product or an idea—hone your critical listening skills with a checklist. Before making a quick decision, ask yourself these questions:

- How credible is this persuader?
- What are her credentials?
- What does this persuader have to gain or lose?
- What is the major premise here?
- Is there supporting evidence?
- Is that evidence logical and conclusive?
- What is fact and what is opinion?
- What other information do I need before deciding?
- Why does this idea appeal to me logically?
- Why does this idea appeal to me or repel me emotionally?
- Why do I need to decide quickly?
- Why am I trying to delay this decision?

Listen critically to stay on the straight and narrow. Many a buyer and decision maker wishes "the morning after that he pulled out this checklist."

Tip 529. Summarize What You've Heard After Lengthy Sessions.

In addition to paraphrasing as a conversation unfolds, summarize at the end to make sure that you've understood the key points covered and any next action items. Writers add a summary paragraph or chapter at the end of their articles and books to make sure that they've hammered home their theses. Meeting leaders recap major conclusions at the close of formal meetings. Attorneys summarize their arguments to the jurors before they leave the courtroom to decide the fate of the accused. But for some reason, if people have talked one on one, face to face, they forget the need to do the same thing. Big mistake. Lost opportunity. Summaries provide one last chance for clarity. Grab it.

7

Asking the Right Questions Without Being Intrusive

Question everything.

—Ernest Gaines

Judge a man by his questions rather than by his answers.

—Voltaire

It is harder to ask a sensible question than to supply a sensible answer.

—Persian proverb

No man really becomes a fool until he stops asking questions.

—Charles P. Steinmetz

The man who is afraid of asking is ashamed of learning.

—Danish proverb

It's better to know some of the questions than all of the answers.

—James Thurber

Children ask better questions than adults. "May I have a cookie?" "Why is the sky blue?" and "What does a cow say?" are far more likely to elicit a cheerful response than "Where's your manuscript?" "Why haven't you called?" and "Who's your lawyer?"

—Fran Lebowitz

Children grow up asking questions. The better their questions, the more challenging and important the answers we give them. Questions embody a child's creativity, serve as an aid to learning, cause others to reflect on the meanings of things, irritate those who are cooped up with the child for long periods of time, and embarrass parents in front of friends and strangers.

As adults asking questions in the workplace, we run into the same concerns, issues, and irritants—for better or worse.

Tip 530. Know Your Purpose in Asking Questions.

With purpose comes organization. You can go from the broad and general to the narrow and specific. For example, if you're interviewing someone for a job, you may begin with a broad, general question: "Tell me a little about your last job—what you liked or disliked." As the applicant begins talking, you'll follow up with more specific questions generated from the earlier answers: "So why do you think you were so successful at selling the widgets when others couldn't meet quota?"

On the other hand, you might decide to go from the narrow and specific, easy-to-answer questions to the broad and general. "How long were you at your last job?" "What was your title there?" "Did other people work with you on those projects?" Then move to broader questions: "What are some of the difficulties you think arise in working in teams and being held accountable for results when others are involved?" "What steps do you take in preparing your project bids?"

On other occasions, you may want to ask unrelated questions in a random fashion, such as when surveying customers about price points or asking team members what projects they want to tackle next. Broad, general questions give the asker more latitude to explore and gather information that he didn't know to ask about. They also give listeners great latitude in leading where they want to go.

By contrast, specific, narrow questions give the asker more control, but sometimes provide less information. Specific, narrow questions can be either easy to answer or difficult to answer if the answer puts the listener on the spot. To choose which is best, know your purpose.

Tip 531. Decide Whether to Lead and When to Lead with Questions.

"Isn't it obvious that the MIS department needs these figures by the end of the week?" clearly says that you expect the listener to agree with you. As a result, the listener may feel pressured or trapped. In other situations, however, you may need to lead a customer to a quick decision that she would consider helpful: "You probably want a matte finish, don't you?" Here are other reasons to lead with questions:

- *Lead a customer to clarify.* "Can you elaborate on what you mean by inadequate turnaround time?"
- *Lead a customer who is digressing.* "Yes, you mentioned the filter earlier. You started to tell me something about the missing label, didn't you?"
- *Lead a customer who keeps going in circles.* "Okay, let me see if I have things straight to this point. You said that the delivery driver arrived at noon, that he didn't have the right tools to install the machine, and that he waited out on your deck for one hour until his backup driver arrived. Now, was there any other wasted time that you noted and want us to deduct from your repair bill?"
- *Lead a customer to generalize and get to the point.* "So your main concern is that the bill should not reflect time spent as a result of the driver's incompetence?"
- *Lead a customer to be specific.* "You said the driver was discourteous. Did he yell? Act sullen? Refuse to give you his name?"
- *Lead a customer to clarify seemingly conflicting facts or statements.* "Your colleague said he arrived at noon. I understood you to say that he arrived at 2 o'clock. Which time is correct, or did I misunderstand one of you?"
- *Lead a customer to give you feedback.* "Do you think you will go ahead with the February order if this repair is completed on time?" "What other concerns do you have before awarding the contract to us?"
- *Lead a customer to agreement.* "I've decided to delete all the service charges. Will that be acceptable to you?"

"Leading questions" are neither good nor bad within themselves. Simply realize their purpose.

Tip 532. Give Your Question a Context.

A manager asked his assistant how much small plastic trash cans cost. His assistant called three stores to put together a list of potential suppliers of trash containers, with the available sizes and prices for volume purchases. When she reported back to her boss with her list of suppliers, he commented that they were all too expensive for the one-time use he intended—to place them in the firm's three exhibitor booths for the upcoming trade show. When he amplified his purpose, the perturbed assistant explained that her next-door neighbor ran a janitorial service. This janitorial service supplied containers for a fee far less than the cost to purchase containers. Wasted effort. The manager hadn't given the assistant the bigger picture that prompted the question. Context makes a big difference. If people know why you're asking, they may be able to supply helpful information that you haven't even thought to ask.

Tip 533. Ask Closed Questions to Gain Agreement.

Closed questions call for a specific, limited answer, not an expansive one: a word, phrase, or simple sentence. Salespeople learn firsthand the hazards of giving customers too many choices, because they can't make up their mind. Instead of, "What color staplers do you want?" they ask, "Do you want those in black, gray, or putty?" When you're in a hurry to get agreement, try the same technique with your boss or coworkers: "I need to talk with you about the Compton project. Would Tuesday morning or Wednesday after 2 o'clock be better for you?" To a customer, try, "Would you prefer that we send you a refund check now, or credit your account next month?" Closed questions focus others' thinking and bring them to a decision quickly. When you want a specific answer, ask a pointed question.

Tip 534. Ask Open-Ended Questions to Gather Information.

Open-ended questions usually cannot be answered with a simple word or two. Such questions begin with *who, what, where, why, when*, or *how*. They give listeners a wide range of responses. Examples: "How do you think the client will react to this proposal?" "When do you think would be the best time to survey our employees?" "What things should we be wary of when we change suppliers?" "Where have you had the most success with this procedure?" "Who do you think could benefit from these new data?" Open-ended questions provide you with the most information.

Tip 535. Use a Question to Suggest a Topic to Draw Others Out.

Requesting a fact limits a person's thinking. He answers with that fact and grows silent again. If you want to have the person expand so that you can gather a wide range of information and impressions, use a question to suggest a topic: "Tell me what you think about how the president is handling the economy." "What do you know about nuclear energy—have you given it any thought for heating your home?" "How about employee morale around here?"

Tip 536. Avoid Cliché Questions.

Don't blame others for not being talkative if the only stimulating questions you ask are clichés. "How's it going?" usually elicits a response like, "Okay, I guess." The same is true for these unimaginative questions: "How are you?" "Is it morning?" "Did you have a nice weekend?" "Nice weather, huh?" "What's up?"

Tip 537. Ask Even if You Don't Expect an Answer.

Reporters and lawyers use this trick. My first experience with this technique was when a reporter called, introduced himself and the story he was working on, and then said, "I've just talked to Jim about this and thought it only fair to give you a chance to comment on your side of the conflict."

"Conflict? What conflict?" I asked. "Well, he seemed to think ... " The reporter paraphrased what my colleague Jim had supposedly said and ended with, "So is that the way you see it?" As an inexperienced young writer, I took the bait. "Well, that's not exactly what happened." I provided further comment. The reporter had his story. I've since learned my lesson.

Even if you don't expect an answer, ask a question just to see how the other person reacts. The attitude revealed may be as important as the information released. You can get information without getting a formal answer. This technique can be useful in negotiating and learning where the limits of information exchange fall.

Tip 538. Act as Though You Expect an Answer.

It's amazing how many people pose question after question in their conversations, as if those questions were rhetorical, and never pause for an answer. When you ask a question and then either rush ahead with an answer yourself or move to the next topic, the other person notices the pattern and decides that you don't intend to take any answer seriously. Nervousness also plays a big part in someone's talking right through where the pauses should go. Be aware of that habit; ask, pause, and wait.

Tip 539. Make Sure Your Body Language Encourages Answers.

Have you ever tossed out a question as though it were "busywork" while you attended to something more important, like finishing up an e-mail or text message to your friend? Your body language either supports or undermines the intention of your question.

Tip 540. Remember That Wording Makes a Great Deal of Difference in the Answer You Get.

Pollsters point out that the wording of questions often influences survey results. For example, multiple-choice questions that mention alternatives will elicit more responses from people who agree with the alternatives than questions that do not suggest alternatives at all. "Knowledge" questions get fewer responses than opinion questions.

Positively worded questions generate more positive responses than negatively worded questions. If the question you intend to ask is an important one, take great care in how you word it. If you don't have time to read body language and rephrase your question on the spot, write out important questions and practice them before you get an audience with someone who holds the key to your future.

Tip 541. Don't Give Overlapping Alternatives.

If you want to walk away with a clear understanding of expected action, avoid ambiguous questions with "and/or" or "both/and" implications. For example, in a staff meeting, a manager poses this question: "Do you think the team is moving along all right in drafting the new procedures, or do you think we should look into hiring a consultant for analyzing and drafting some of our processes?" It is entirely possible that some people in the staff meeting would answer, "The team is doing well, but yes, it would *also* be a good idea to hire an outside consultant for some of the processes."

Others may hear the question as an either-or choice: either the team is doing well enough alone or the team needs input from the consultant.

Another example: "Do you want to go to Hawaii for the sales meeting, or would you enjoy something closer in Canada?" The answer could be, "I'd love to go to Hawaii, but yes, I'd also enjoy a shorter trip to Canada." If the person answers, "Hawaii sounds great," that doesn't necessarily mean that Canada is an undesirable choice or even a second choice. Take care in structuring questions so that you know the difference between "either-or" and "both-and" responses.

Tip 542. Clarify Whether You Want Evidence or Opinion on Speculative Issues.

For example: "If we raise our prices on this item, what effect will it have on our customers?" Do you want the other person to give you evidence— comments from prospective customers about price, market trends in pricing, or rumors about the plans of competitors? Or do you want an opinion about the effect the other person thinks the price increase will have? Unless you clarify that opinions (even unsupported ones) are welcome, you're likely to get few answers about the future.

Tip 543. Ask Behavioral Questions to Predict the Future.

As my psychologist friend Paul Green, Ph.D., says in his video *Actions Speak* about interviewing job applicants, "Past actions are the best predictors of future performance." Instead of asking a candidate what she *would* do in any given situation, ask her what she *did* do: "What was the last safety hazard you identified at your past job, and what recommendations did you make to your boss to improve the situation?" "How many inactive customers did you discover in your territory when you took over that region last year, and how many of those have now placed orders with you?" "You mentioned being an excellent customer-service rep. What is an example of a time when you really went out of your way to resolve a difficult customer situation?"

To a client, you might ask these behavioral questions before deciding that you want to work with him: "You mentioned that 24/7 service was important to you. In what ways have you needed that kind of availability previously?" "Have you had other suppliers disappoint you? How did you handle that?" Listen carefully to these answers, because past behavior is the best predictor of... repeat it with me here.

Tip 544. Frame Off-the-Hook Questions When Asking for Favors.

If you don't want to impose on a friendship, phrase your questions in such a way that people know that it's okay to say no. "We need someone to pick up the gift for Rafael's retirement luncheon. Is everybody in a big hurry, or would someone have time to stop by the mall?" Such phrasing lets people off the hook without making a big deal of turning you down.

Tip 545. Don't Solicit Opinions Unless You Intend to Evaluate Them.

Asking doesn't guarantee listening. Listening doesn't guarantee use. But people will watch for a pattern when you ask for their opinions. Follow through by listening and evaluating what you hear. Just going through the motions of gathering opinions and ideas creates hostility.

Tip 546. Establish Rapport by Asking Questions.

When you ask another person's opinion or ask about her experiences or interests, you're complimenting her. That attention builds rapport.

Tip 547. Solicit Feedback by Asking Questions.

It's a mistake to think that because people give you no negative feedback, they agree with your decision, approach, philosophy, or action. People may feel intimidated by your position—especially if you can help or harm their career.

If you are a powerful person, when you want feedback, it's up to you to solicit it repeatedly: "What would you consider a creative incentive for achieving our quarterly goals?" "How do you think we performed on the last project?" Just because you ask questions doesn't mean that you'll get honest answers, or even *any* answers. But not asking almost always ensures that you will get none.

Tip 548. Encourage Buy-In Action by Asking Questions.

If you have colleagues who can't seem to meet deadlines, let them set their own. When you are faced with soliciting their cooperation or information on a new project, instead of stating the deadline, ask *them* to set the deadline. "Nicolas, please let me know what day I can expect the printout on the Carlton site." When people set their own deadlines, they are more likely to meet them. Here are other examples that encourage people to participate and buy into group action or decisions: "Do you think this plan will work?" "Can we count on your help?" "Does this approach make sense to you?" "Which of the two alternatives do you think we should try first?" "Are you willing to give this plan a try?"

Tip 549. Ask Questions to Lead Others to Analyze Their Own Suggestions.

An employee speaks up in a meeting with this suggestion: "Why don't we go ahead and print 100,000 copies of the brochure now, since we'll be doing more mailings later in the year?" Rather than snapping back with, "Because our test mailing will determine whether we need to change the copy," lead the employee to evaluate his own suggestion by asking, "Will later mailings go to the same prospective buyers? If so, will they respond to the same copy?" or "How much would we save by printing all 100,000 copies now, as opposed to the expense of two print runs?"

Questioning leads others to analyze their own suggestions without your intervention, giving them confidence in their abilities for later situations and leaving the impression that you're listening to their suggestions.

Tip 550. Analyze Your Own Ideas with the Five Ws Questions.

Set up the five Ws as a framework for analyzing new ideas: *Why* do it? *Where* would it work? *Who* should be involved? *When* would be the ideal time? *How* do we implement this? If your answers are unfavorable or discouraging, rephrase the questions before you give up: *Why* did the process not work for us? *What* could we improve to make things work better? *What* results did we want that we didn't achieve? *Who* else could benefit from joining us in the process? *How* should we modify the idea next time? *What* can we learn from this effort?

Tip 551. Stimulate Creative Thinking with What-If Questions.

Reflect on the unknowns of various events or circumstances by posing what-if questions: "What if we held congressional elections only once a decade rather than every two years?" "What if we cut out sales commissions altogether?" "What if we make this project a charitable contribution?" "What if we could get the customer to pay us up front?" Strangely enough, most of us don't put ourselves on the spot often enough to come up with creative solutions. Yet, when we are challenged with such questions, the result often provides insightful answers.

Tip 552. Plant Your Own Ideas with Questions.

"Has anybody given serious thought to bypassing the marketing department with this campaign?" "Is it realistic to think that people will not mind lengthening the workday by 10 minutes?" "How would it work if we combined the flyer and the catalog in one mailing?" "What would happen if you went back to your own supplier and suggested the change?" With such questions, you've planted the idea in a low-risk way. Others can take it or leave it without your having to defend the position or sell the idea actively.

Tip 553. Persuade People by Asking Questions.

"Do you think your career could benefit from exposure to this training?" "If you were to seek such a lateral move, what experience could you pick up along the way that might help you get to the next level when a spot opens up?" "How would a customer react to your offer to provide the service at no charge—do you think she might be more inclined to ask us to bid on other, more profitable projects?" All of these questions frame a benefit for the listener.

You may help persuade by helping others "suppose": "Let's suppose you accept this transfer; what other responsibilities might come your way?"

You may help others justify: "How could you justify the extra cost involved in the move if you didn't intend to refinance your mortgage anyway?" Help them to compare or contrast: "If you accept this job, will you be in a better or worse position to transfer to headquarters than if you stay here another 18 months?"

By the very phrasing of such questions, you are encouraging the other person to consider the merits or probability of a situation. The secret to being persuasive is posing the right questions.

Tip 554. Ask Questions to Uncover Resistance.

A silent prospect doesn't necessarily mean a ready buyer. When your internal proposal doesn't get a response from your executive team, ask questions. Uncover resistance to your proposals so that you can deal with it. Question a stall.

Tip 555. Move People From the Emotional Level to the Analytical Level (or Vice Versa) with Questions.

For example, suppose someone comments to you: "I'm really upset about the news report on the accident. Public opinion polls say that most people blame our company." You can respond with a statement or a question, depending on your intention. Empathetic statements: "Yes, I can see why." "It could be bad for stock prices." "It's going to be rough talking to neighbors and customers who call in." Any of these empathetic statements will encourage the other person to elaborate on his feelings.

On the other hand, you might respond with a question: "Why do you think reporters are trying to turn this accident into a controversy?" "Do you think they've investigated all the details about the accident at this point?" "Do you respond to customers face to face on this issue? How are your customers responding to the explanations the company has provided for you to pass along?"

With any of these questions, you're calling for a rational answer. You're asking the listener to move away from emotions and dig into the analytical realm for answers.

Tip 556. Resist Demands or Commands by Using Questions.

If you don't think you can be straightforward with authority figures, use questions to force them to rethink their demands or commands. Examples: "Are you aware that it will take me about three days to collect this data?" "Are you sure that the client really needs this report?" "Could you detail the parameters so that I understand fully what's involved before I begin?" Tone is all-important here so that your question is perceived not as a challenge to the person's authority, but rather as a second chance to rethink the objective and best approach.

Tip 557. Find Commonalities with Questions.

A large part of building rapport involves discovering things that you have in common. Questions move the process along—especially if they're broad enough to allow expansive answers, and thus connections: "What's your background in the industry?" "What part of the country do you like best?" "Do you feel as confused as I do about the new family-care policies and options they're offering us?"

Tip 558. Reduce Your Anxiety by Asking Questions.

When fear of the unknown grips you, pose that fear as a question to colleagues. On the surface, your questions seem to be gathering information; in reality, they are collecting others' reactions to the fearful situation. "When do you think our industry is going to stabilize?" "Are we the only people gullible enough to volunteer for this committee?" "Have any of you polled our customers to see how they're reacting to our price increases planned for next month?" In other words, asking if others share our fear has a calming effect. We find either the comfort to go along as planned or the courage to resist.

Tip 559. Use Questions to Stall.

You can almost always stall a decision by asking for more details, more data, more analysis, more options, more explanations, more benefits, more comparisons, or more testimonials. As long as people are chasing down answers, everyone is stalled in coming to conclusions.

Tip 560. Use Questions to Guide Conversation.

With questions, you redirect conversational traffic to a new topic. As long as you aren't demanding and insensitive and you don't sound like an interrogating district attorney, using questions to guide conversation can serve you well. Open-ended questions for this purpose give the responder some latitude to take off in several directions on the new topic.

Tip 561. Pose Questions as Fun.

Consider the people who bend over crossword puzzles daily or the popularity of quiz games on TV. Radio stations pose trivia questions as contests for their listening audiences. People like to use their minds constructively and answer questions "just for fun."

For fun and reflection, toss these out in your small circle at the next party: "Who remembers the number one pop hit of last year?" "How many CEOs running the Fortune 1000 companies would you guess are under 40 years old?" For a dinner party: "Opinion poll here: What star has had the biggest influence on the movie industry to date?"

Tip 562. Use Questions as a Display of Control.

We allow only those in the appropriate positions of power to impose questions. Talk-show hosts, emcees, panel moderators, reporters, bosses, politicians, lawyers, and judges rule the world. A friend has a sign on his desk that reads, "Who decides who decides is more important than who decides." Likewise, the person who asks the questions wields control.

Tip 563. Use *Why* Questions with Care.

Questions in a neutral tone that ask "why" certain *events* happened cause few problems: "Why is the floor tile on backorder?" But asking "why" questions about *people* puts others on the defensive, especially if they already have a tendency to be defensive. "Why did you miss the meeting?" can be a straightforward call for information from a person who is surprised that you missed the meeting and knows that you must have a reasonable explanation. On the other hand, "Why did you miss the meeting?" can also be a blaming statement meaning, "You shouldn't have missed the meeting—what do you have to say for yourself?" Most people resist "why" questions that evaluate and judge their reasons, motives, and intentions.

Tip 564. Avoid Trapping People with Questions.

A father comes home from the office and asks, "Johnny, how many times have I told you not to leave your bike in the driveway?" Does the father want a number? Hardly. His point is clearly that Johnny should have gotten the message by now. We've watched too many court trials in the movies not to feel the rush of adrenalin when the prosecutor is moving in for the kill. With the unwary witness on the stand, the lawyer lays the groundwork with "innocent" questions to which the witness gives false answers. Then the prosecutor comes through with the real zinger question, and the witness realizes that she has been caught in her lies.

In the office, such questions sound like this: "Have I not made it clear that these expense reports are due on the fifth of the month?" "Did you miss the staff meeting where we discussed that issue?" "Did you not know that the customer expected to have this merchandise arrive undamaged?" "Don't you feel any concern at all for the outcome?" "You do want to make the sale, don't you?" These questions are meant to either entrap the person or make him feel foolish however he answers.

Give people the freedom to express disagreement or to refuse to take the either-or choice. On occasion, you do already have the answer to a question and need to ask others to verify that you're correct. If that's the case, tell them what you're doing so that they won't feel that you're trying to trap them with game playing. For example: "Susan, why don't you tell me what happened out on the dock when the truck pulled up to unload? I already have a couple of witnesses who have told me what they saw, but I'd like your perspective on the incident."

Tip 565. Avoid Questions That Accuse.

A question like "What did you think would happen if you let this situation rock along without notifying me?" accuses the listener of ulterior motives—or stupidity. Other accusing questions: "Why did you not send an e-mail to begin with?" "How do you know that's true?" "When did you expect to complete that study?" "How did you think we could process that many orders in one day?" "Who did you think was going to pay for that kind of promise to the customer?"

It's far better simply to make a statement about what you think would have happened in any given situation or to ask neutrally for the other person's viewpoint: "Did you consider notifying me about the incident, or did you think that was unnecessary at the time?" "Do you think the customer will be willing to pay for this extra service that you promised?"

Tip 566. Don't Demand with Questions.

"When are you going to call that committee chair back and tell him that you don't have time to participate and also do your job here?" "How can you even consider taking vacation that week when we have such a short deadline?" "Where can you possibly think of finding a replacement at such a late date?" "Why can't you develop the proposal yourself with our boilerplate?" Such questions make demands rather than call for answers. Using them simply makes the other person wary of other questions on other occasions.

Tip 567. Don't Use a Question as a Dare.

"Well, when are you going to do something about it?" "What are you going to do to turn that situation around? I consider it a lost cause." "What do you mean by that kind of comment?" "Are you implying that I'm incompetent in my job?" Questions of this type dare the other person to be honest with a response. They "needle" the person to take action or risk the relationship or other consequences if she answers.

Tip 568. Don't Design Multiple-Choice Questions Where Both Choices Are Wrong.

"Are you so far behind that you thought it didn't matter that one more form was turned in late, or were you going to claim that my instructions to complete it were unclear? Of course, either alternative puts the other person in a bad light. People don't like multiple-choice questions when all the choices make them look wrong or incompetent.

Tip 569. Don't Use Show-Off Questions.

"Did I tell you about having lunch with the CEO last week at the sales meeting?" "After reading several of the most recently published articles about nuclear fission, I'm wondering what you think about Clarendon's theories?" Such questions are attempts to show off the asker's own connections or expertise—not true questions that gather input. Most people identify and resent such purposes.

Tip 570. Don't Overpower the Opposition with Questions.

To wrap up a discussion in a staff meeting, the manager says, "We're already half an hour later than I hoped we'd be in coming to a decision. If nobody has a serious objection to that campaign theme, we'll move on. Any more objections?" The effect of that question is much like a speaker announcing, "Well, it's time for a break—unless somebody has a question?" Who in his right mind will incite a group in serious need of caffeine and a bathroom break? In effect, such I-plan-to-do-this-unless-you-fail-to-follow-my-cue questions kill any honest feedback or alternative ideas.

Tip 571. Make Statements Rather Than Hide Opinions in Questions.

Instead of asking, "Isn't the IS group taking a long time to forward those documents?" state your opinion: "I think the IS group is taking a long time to forward those documents." With the question format, you might get a response, "No, not necessarily," and then you'll be put in the position of having to either drop the issue or argue with the person who responded with the opposite view. Instead of, "Do you like the way I set up these tables?" make a statement: "I hope you like the way I set up these tables." With a statement, people can choose to agree or remain silent rather than put you on the spot.

Tip 572. Use the Pregnant Pause to Replace a Question.

When you want to encourage another person to continue to elaborate but don't want to give the impression of "cross-examining" her with a follow-up question, try the pregnant pause. Many people feel uncomfortable with silence and will do just about anything to fill it. After the other person stops talking, pause for five seconds and allow her time to continue with other details.

Tip 573. Use the Echo Technique.

When you want to encourage people to continue talking, repeat the last word or phrase as a question. They'll take the lifted voice as a cue to elaborate. For example:

> SHARON: So I'm undecided on whether the transfer will do me any good.

BOB: Will do you any good?

SHARON: You know—whether it will count as technical experience should the Boston job open up later in the year.

BOB: Later in the year?

SHARON: Well, maybe by December. Or it could be January before it's open, but soon, anyway. I'm just afraid I don't have the patience.

BOB: Patience?

SHARON: To work with Brenda and Harry. They're both such perfectionists.

BOB: What do you mean by perfectionists?

SHARON: They just never sign off on a project. They've always got to modify just one more thing. They never make a development deadline.

You get the idea. The echo technique gets elaboration by default.

Tip 574. Remind Others That It's Okay Not to Have Answers.

Sometimes a question meant to provoke thought is taken as a serious question that must have an answer. When others mull over the issue and toss out answers that you refute or punch holes in, they begin to feel stupid, frustrated, angry, trapped, or wrong. Your question may put a damper on the entire meeting or party. When you see that happening, rush to reassure them that you don't expect a rock-solid answer—that you intended the question to generate ideas, nothing more.

Tip 575. Adopt the Ben Franklin Perspective.

Ben Franklin, a philosopher without formal training, demanded that people think. He questioned everyone about everything—scientists, community founders, medical professionals, public educators, and administrators. What-ifs made his world go around. In fact, if he were alive today, Franklin might have originated the "Really?" cliché.

If you want to challenge the status quo, charge up your staff meetings, or spark your social life, ask questions. You'll force people to justify or change their views, to think creatively, to gather new information, to have fun, and to expand their horizons.

8

Answering Questions so People Understand and Remember What You Say

Silence is golden when you can't think of a good answer.
—Muhammad Ali

It infuriates me to be wrong when I know I'm right.
—Molière

There are no embarrassing answers—just embarrassing questions.
—Carl Rowan

An educated man is one who has finally discovered that there are some questions to which nobody has the answers.
—No attribution

It's frustrating when you know all the answers—and nobody bothers to ask you the questions.
—No attribution

When somebody says, "That's a good question," you can be pretty sure it's a lot better than the answer you're going to get.
—Franklin P. Jones

I was gratified to be able to answer promptly. I said, "I don't know."
—Mark Twain

Answers to questions can take ideas from the proposal stage through successful implementation; they can soothe broken relationships; they can provide instruction and advice. But answering questions correctly, confidently, competently, completely, consistently, compassionately, and concisely is no easy task. With the proper structure, substance, and style, however, you can prevent your answers from becoming off-track ramblings.

Tip 576. Use The SEER Format® for Thinking on Your Feet.

Does this after-game interview between jock and reporter sound familiar? "What was your single biggest mistake in today's game?" the reporter asks. "Well, we had problems, that's for sure. Some difficulty running the ball, that's for sure. The other side was out there where we should have been. We made some mistakes all right. They cost us some points. Our passing was just so-so. And blocking was a problem. They just beat us—that's all there is to it. They outplayed us."

So what was the biggest mistake? Who knows? The same rambling occurs when politicians meet the press or bosses ask employees for project updates. To avoid having your listener walk away with a vague sense of "nothing said," try using The SEER Format®, a format we at Booher Consultants developed to help executives in our presentation workshops learn to think on their feet. The SEER Format® is an organizational structure for stating opinions or answers in a clear, concise, compelling, memorable manner:

S (Summary)	Give a one-sentence summary of your answer or opinion.
E (Elaboration)	Elaborate with appropriate details: who, when, where, why, how, how much.
E (Example)	Give a concrete example to make the ideas or information clear, usable, and memorable.
R (Restatement)	End with a one-sentence restatement of your answer or opinion.

Here's an example: let's say your prospective customer asks, "Does your company really care about the small customer?"

Summary. Yes, most definitely, we care about small customers. They keep us in business.

Elaboration. In fact, 70 percent of our volume comes from accounts that we've labeled "small business." We'd rather have 100 customers doing $75 to $100 a month with us than to have one customer doing half a million a month. That's our perspective. There's far less risk than if something happens to that one big customer. Also, we think we get a broader grasp of the industry by dealing with a large variety of small accounts. We even have a special website and login just for small businesses, showing products and services they specifically need. They have their own help desk for 24/7 support.

Example. Just last week, a VP of operations at Universal, Inc., one of our accounts, told me that because we had learned so much about Universal's business just by selling to it, the company had decided not to hire a permanent purchasing agent. Instead, it's contracted with us to place its orders for related products supplied by other vendors. It's a real partnership. We'd like to do that with all our customers.

Restatement. So, yes, we do care about our small customers.

When you structure your answers in this format, you'll find that others understand your main point and, more important, remember it.

Tip 577. Use the Genesis Technique.

If you're asked a question and no immediate answer comes to mind, you can always use the genesis technique: Start back at the beginning of time and talk until your mind focuses on a specific answer.

Question: "How did you arrive at the exact commission rates for the sales reps?" Answer: "When we began to set compensation policy for all our employees, we tried to look at the entire package—salary, bonuses, other incentive programs, and fringe benefits like company-car use. We tried to investigate which were most valuable to employees. When we surveyed our sales reps, we . . ." Eventually, the answer will hit you, and you can continue on target. Such a long-winded, roundabout answer may annoy people, but that may be preferable to drawing a blank on issues you're supposed to know as well as your own name.

Tip 578. Answer One Question at a Time; Avoid Multiples.

When someone asks you multiple questions in one large chunk, you have several choices: (1) Answer all of them. (2) Pick one or two to answer. (3) Lump them all together and give a general answer. Examples: "You've asked three good questions. For the sake of time, let me deal with only the last one." "Whoa—I don't know if I can remember all those. Let me pick

out a couple to respond to." "Your questions really all point to one concern, I think: Do we know how to Y? I can answer in a word—yes."

Tip 579. Remember That Few Answers Are Really "Off the Record."

When someone catches you in the hallway and asks for your "honest opinion, off the record," don't count on its being held in confidence. Even if
you respond to the question with a shrug or a nod, you might be surprised
to hear what you "agreed with" according to the next day's rumors. It's best
to take such questions on the record in front of a group so that you have
witnesses to your response.

For example, during the break at a staff meeting, George asks, "So,
do you think we'll really ever get management to respond to our suggestions?" Response: "I imagine that's on everybody's mind. When we recon-
vene, let me bring that issue up to answer for everybody." And do so.

If you really don't want the question to surface in front of the group,
ask George to bring it up himself in front of the group and hope that he
won't because he doesn't want his name attached to the question either.
Or try one of these responses: "That's a question I don't have the authority to answer. Why don't you write it down and I'll present it to my boss?"
or "I wouldn't want to speculate on that because I don't have all the facts,
and I could be wrong. I suggest that you ask someone else."

Tip 580. Probe for the Real Interest or Concern Behind Hypothetical Questions.

With a hypothetical question, you have three choices: (1) You can decline
to deal in speculations. "I'm sorry, but I don't want to get into what-if situations that we may never have to face," or "I think any speculation on this
issue would be meaningless." (2) You can speculate, waving a big red flag
identifying your answer as purely hypothetical. "I will give that question
a stab. Let me remind you that I think such a situation would never, never
happen under the plan we developed. However, in that highly unlikely situation, we'd try to . . ." (3) You can probe for the real issue behind the question and deal with that issue or concern.

Question: "If Samuel's diagnosis had been cancer, would we have
made an exception?" Answer: "Is your concern with that question that we
haven't fully thought through the new leave policy? If so, I can assure you

that we have considered the treatment of patients who might be off work indefinitely. In those cases, ..." You would simply refuse to deal with Samuel's individual case.

Always consider the danger of answering hypothetical questions. Even if you answer them satisfactorily, if the asker's intent is to trap you, she will continue to change the details of the hypothetical question until she backs you into a corner. If your first response is satisfactory, the asker will respond with, "Yes, but what if Samuel... ?" You answer again with the new details. Then the questioner comes back with, "Yeah, but what if then Samuel decides to...?" You can almost never win. If the asker intends to do so, with hypothetical questions as bait, she can reel you into the net or keep you on the hook forever.

Tip 581. Expand Your Options on Forced, Two-Option Questions.

Don't let others design your multiple-choice exam. Expand your options. Question: "Do you think we can win the bid if we come in under $50,000?" Answer: "I don't think price will be the deciding factor. The customer's impression of our credentials will be an equally important factor." Other examples: "The question is more complex than either a yes or no answer." "If you ask me, we have more options than either A or B. We might even consider C." Stay in control, and don't let others force you into a limited answer if the limited answer won't do justice to the issue.

Tip 582. Help a Questioner Who Is Bogged Down in a Rambling, Long-Winded Question.

Body language goes a long way in helping people spit out questions. If you start to back away from them, they'll subconsciously speed up and get to the point because they see you "leaving." Or if you slowly move toward them with outstretched hand and nodding head, they'll subconsciously speed up, seeing that you're "rushing" them. If body language doesn't work, help the person phrase the question by breaking in with one of the following: "Okay, I think I understand your question now. My answer is...," or, "So you want to know if X happens? Well, my answer is..." If the individual keeps talking without ever seeming to come to the question, you can call for the question directly: "I'm sorry. I didn't understand a question in what you said. What exactly is the question?" If someone starts a monologue, you can interrupt with a short question of your own to which the person can give a one-word or one-phrase answer. When he stops the monologue to answer your question, you regain the floor.

Tip 583. Interrupt Your Own Monologue.

Long-winded answers can irritate others as much as long-winded questions. If you intend to wax on about an issue, seek a group platform where the audience knows that you intend to give a speech and grants you the privilege. If your answer runs longer than 60 seconds or so, you're no longer in a dialogue; it's a monologue. If you feel you're going on too long, but you haven't finished what you intended to say, pace yourself by stopping to ask the other person for some reaction to what you've just said. Does she agree, disagree, not care, or have different information? Then, after you listen to her comments, deliver your next point on the earlier answer.

Tip 584. Assume That a "Dumb" Question Has a Connection That You Don't Yet Understand.

Probe for clarification. If you brush aside what sounds like a dumb question, and then someone points out its relevance, you'll look foolish yourself. If the question seems "out in left field," or irrelevant, clarify before answering: "I'm sorry, but I don't quite understand how X relates to Y. Would you explain the connection?" "I'm confused. What prompts the question?" "I missed the point. We are discussing Y, and I don't understand why Z would be an issue." If the person clarifies and the question is pertinent, you've saved yourself some embarrassment. If the person concedes that the question is off base, you've saved yourself some time. If the question is in fact irrelevant, answer it briefly if you can and circle back to the main issue without embarrassing the asker.

Tip 585. Unload "Loaded" Questions.

Identify the hot words—those with negative connotations—and restate the question in a neutral way before answering it. Or, if you don't choose to repeat the question, respond to the question minus the negative words. *Example:* "Why is management being so *stubborn* about lifting the ban?" *Answer:* "Are you asking why management has not set a definite deadline for lifting the ban? I think partly the executive team is concerned that..." *Example:* "Are you saying that we're too *stupid* to make that decision ourselves without going to a supervisor for approval?" *Answer:* "The reason we're asking you to go to a supervisor for approval is that this brief delay of even 15 seconds while you leave the customer alone at the counter allows time for..." Don't let the offensive, negative words hook you into responding negatively to an important issue. Neutralize, neutralize.

Tip 586. Turn a Negative Question into a Benefit Statement.

A customer asks, "Why do you have so much red tape associated with these service agreements?" Here's a "benefit" answer: "Why does having a list of all the company liaisons benefit you? Well, let's say Kathy in your department calls for service. Within seconds, we can check the file, verify her as an authorized contact, and answer her question while she's on the line—without waiting for a callback. Your doing the paperwork up front by providing us with the names of liaisons saves you time when you have a problem and need service immediately."

Tip 587. Challenge Questions Based on Misinformation or Invalid Assumptions.

Example question: "Given the huge sums of money we've spent on market and trend studies in recent years, why haven't our earnings matched those of other investors in local real estate?" That question contains four assumptions that may or may not be true: (1) The company has spent "huge" sums of money. (2) The market and trend studies contained accurate and helpful information. (3) The company's earnings did not match those of other investors. (4) The other investors presented accurate numbers, and those numbers were based only on local real estate investments.

With such a question, you can either accept, qualify, or reject any of the assumptions or facts, then answer the "leftover" question if you care to do so.

Answer: "First, I don't consider $4,000 'huge sums of money.' Second, those studies were based on old information and did not contain relevant industry data. Third, you're correct that our earnings were one percentage point lower than our competitors' earnings. And, finally, I'm not sure that their figures included only local real estate. Nevertheless, the question remains, 'Why were our investment returns less than we had hoped?' First,..."

Tip 588. Define Terms and Agree on Criteria Before You Give "Value-Based" Answers.

Two meeting planners spent an hour debating the best site for an upcoming annual sales and awards meeting. The first meeting planner argued that Orlando was the best choice because of the nearby attractions for families accompanying the salespeople. The second meeting planner insisted that Dallas was the best site because of its central location and airport. Neither stopped to define how he was defining the "best" site. What exactly did the criteria include? Cost, tourist attractions, weather, travel time required, local accommodations?

Had they been clear up front in defining and agreeing on criteria, answering the question concerning which site was "best" would have been much easier. Carefully come to an understanding on questions phrased like these: "What is the most favorable? Highest quality? Most prestigious? Honorable thing? Ethical? Profitable?" Define, then answer.

Tip 589. Help Questioners Meet Their Objectives with Their Showcase Questions.

When people ask questions simply to show off their own expertise, oblige them if you have the time. Question: "Tell me what differences you see in the quality principles set forth by the gurus Smith, Palan, and Sanchez." Answer: "Actually, I haven't made a study of the uniqueness of their individual programs. You seem well versed on the subject. What differences do you see?" She'll love you for the showcase opportunities, and you're off the hook.

Tip 590. Defuse Hostile Questions.

Myles Martel, in *Mastering the Art of Q and A,* has expressed this well: "Composure can speak as loudly—or more loudly—than content." You have only to ask people which political candidate "won" the various presidential debates to verify that truth. Hostility comes in three flavors: (1) questions that show hostility toward the person, (2) hostility reflected in the situation, or (3) the asker's personality.

If the hostility comes from the pressure of a situation or from a typically hostile person, defuse it by removing the "hot" words and then answering the concern in a straightforward manner. If the attack is personal, try to put your ego aside, omit the negative comments or words, and answer with facts as you see them. Example: "Don't tell me that with *your limited expertise* in the field, you're going to handle our account yourself?" Answer: "You are correct that my academic training has been in psychology rather than in finance; however, I have been managing financial portfolios for large clients for the past 20 years. The performance of these funds has matched or surpassed the results of all our other investors. If your concern is my experience in global funds, I can give you the statistics on those accounts specifically. And I can assure you that should I ever find myself in a quandary over a decision, I would not hesitate to bring the issue up in our daily staff meetings, which are set up just for that purpose for all our representatives."

Give a straightforward answer dealing with the facts. If you meet hostility with hostility, you lose. If you match hostility with graciousness, you win in the mind of most observers.

Tip 591. Bridge from the Questioner's Agenda to Yours.

If you don't want to answer the question you're asked, bridge to your own points with one of the following: "I appreciate your question, but more to the point in our organization, I think, is the issue of X. The X issue involves . . . or, "A more fundamental issue than that in your question is . . . ," or, "The larger question than the one you raise is . . ." Chase your own rabbits.

Tip 592. Change Intensity by Switching from the Abstract to the Specific or from the Specific to the Abstract.

You can change the pace and tenor of a discussion by increasing or decreasing the intensity of your answers to questions. For example, if the person asks you a broad, general opinion question, supply a specific, factual answer. Question: "So what do you think about the president's new tax plans?" Answer: "Well, I know I don't like paying 5 cents a gallon more every time I pull into the gas station."

Or you can reverse the situation: supply a broad, general opinion answer to a specific question: "Why do you think employees have not been more responsive in signing up to participate in the tutoring programs we're sponsoring in the community?" Answer: "Volunteerism in the United States isn't what it used to be."

Tip 593. Use Cliché Answers with Care.

Suppose someone approaches you in the company cafeteria and asks, "So how is the Fullerton deal moving along?" You answer: "Pretty good." Similar answers to similar questions follow these lines: "Same song, second verse." "So-so." "It's still on target." "Fair to partly cloudy." "We're hanging in there." All such clichés create distance. If the other person has asked the question as a show of interest or wants straightforward information, he will be put off. If you routinely deflect honest questions with pat answers, people will stop asking about your concerns, feelings, and opinions. They'll decide that you do not want to communicate sincerely with them.

Tip 594. Know When Flippant Answers Are Out of Line.

Having a sense of humor is an advantage in any situation, but flippant answers about serious issues or during a time crunch frustrate people. Some people find themselves reverting to humor when they can't face difficult issues squarely. Try to identify those times when you're using humor as an avoidance technique. Recognize that even humor, however generally welcome and refreshing, has a time and place.

Tip 595. Don't Drop a Bomb When a BB Gun Will Do.

Some people get a reputation for overanswering when they're asked a simple question. Nine-year-old Matthew, sitting in front of the TV one night, asked his father: "What does centrifugal force mean?"

Dad answers, "Go ask your mother; I'm busy."

"That's okay. I don't think I want to know that much about it."

Why do people respond to a question with a bomb when a BB gun would do? Some talk until they come up with an acceptable answer. Others react to their ego need to show off their vast knowledge on the subject. Others aren't sure that their answer is clear, so they keep explaining until they get some feedback that shows understanding. Others give a lengthy answer because they fear that a brief answer would sound curt. Some people feel defensive or consider their answers inadequate, so they keep attempting to justify their positions. Still others don't fully understand the question, so they talk all around the issue, hoping to say something that's pertinent and helpful. Whatever your reason for overanswering, use the BB gun on the first attempt. Leave it to your listener to ask for a more in-depth answer.

Tip 596. Don't Ignore Questions to Avoid Confrontation.

When people ask questions on controversial issues or make statements that you disagree with, it might be easier to ignore them and the issues rather than risk a confrontation. But no response at all feels like rejection to the other person. Instead, state your disagreement generally and then change the subject if you want to avoid the issue. Example: "Roberto's comments were really out of line in the meeting this morning, don't you think?" Answer: "Actually, I thought what he said was appropriate. But I haven't given it much thought since the meeting. I've been really involved in that project due tomorrow."

Tip 597. Give Multiple Answers Without Claiming Any as Your Own.

If someone asks you the best way to solve a problem, and you prefer to remain noncommittal, you can toss out several possible solutions without stating your preference. Example: "How do you think we can guarantee to the customer that we'll not miss any interim deadlines on this multiyear project?" Answer: "One way might be to co-train a backup crew. Or we might want to use a subcontractor during certain phases and run the work in tandem. Or we might ask the customer to supply liaisons at crucial decision points. We have several options."

Tip 598. Fog the Issue with an Irrelevant Point.

If you don't intend to give a clear, straightforward answer, you can sidestep the issue by bringing up an irrelevant point with a statement or question of your own. Example: "Why does this community refuse to approve a sales tax increase that would support the kind of parks and recreational facilities the citizens seem to want?" Answer: "Some people cannot understand the need to plan for the future—they don't even have their own retirement savings plans. How can you expect them to plan for the city?" Example: "Do you think our virtual environment and the ability to work from anywhere has been a big morale booster for the staff?" Answer: "The snarled traffic still doesn't make it easy to get from one customer location to the next if you have to make a trip to a customer site."

Tip 599. If You Intend to Be Clear, Ask for Explicit Confirmation and Feedback.

Simply because you give an answer doesn't mean that the answer was understood, even if you conclude it with something like, "Is that clear?" or "Do you understand?" Most people will nod and answer affirmatively. To say otherwise would be tantamount to saying, "No, I'm stupid—I don't get it," or, equally insulting to you, "No, your answer wasn't clear." Instead, ask for more explicit feedback to make sure the person understands: "Based on the information I just outlined, what do you think would be your first two or three steps in implementing this policy in your department?" "What kind of reaction do you think we might get from our customers on this new policy?"

The answers will confirm whether your original comments have been understood. On some occasions, such as when speaking before a group, you may not want to answer a question at all. Routinely asking, "Did I answer your question?" or, "Is that clear?" may get a response such as, "Not really," or, "No." The impression created will be that you gave a wrong or incomplete answer.

Tip 600. Forget Feedback if You Want to Show Confidence in Your Answer.

In situations with your boss, ending a question with, "Did I answer your question?" or, "Did I cover what you wanted to know?" makes you appear insecure and lacking confidence in your ability to answer. Give the best answer you can and wait for a response. If the question is rephrased, make a second attempt to answer it by providing more in-depth elaboration—not just rephrasing what you said previously.

Tip 601. Frame a Piggybacking Answer Tactfully.

For example, in a meeting, your human resources director has answered a question about compensation packages, but she has omitted an important point. You feel the need to add her answer. Here's a no-no: "Elaine left out an important point that I want to mention." Better: "I want to add a point to what Elaine explained." Best: "Elaine's answer brings up another consideration—what we plan to do about X. Let me mention that briefly..." Your piggyback answer should not make the previous answer seem inadequate or wrong.

Tip 602. Set Boundaries for Questions—and Stick to Them.

A physician sets limits on his expertise with a difficult-to-diagnose case. "If the tests show that the problem is X, I can help you with medication. But if the X-rays indicate Y, I'm going to have to send you to a specialist for more testing." You don't respect the doctor any less for setting the boundaries. If anything, you're glad that he's honest about the limits of his expertise rather than experimenting.

You may have similar limits, either because of a lack of expertise or simply because you prefer not to answer. Say so. "In this meeting, I'd rather not go into issues of costs. I'm here to respond to technical questions about how the system works." And if a question about cost surfaces later, stick to your limits: "As I mentioned earlier, I am not prepared to discuss costs." People will respect your boundaries if you yourself do.

Tip 603. Consider the Risks and Opportunities Before Answering.

When your answer may be crucial to your future, run through a mental checklist: What is prompting this question? Do I fully understand the question? What does the body language of the asker communicate? What am I risking with an answer? How clear do I want to be? What information would it be best to withhold? How will my tone affect the response? What do I want to communicate with my body language? Which is the most important in this response—style or substance? What opportunities does answering this question present for me? All of these questions should flash through your mind as you pause and prepare to answer. That brief pause can be the difference between results and regrets.

Tip 604. Use Verbal Stalls with Care.

As an instructor or frequent presenter, you may have learned to reinforce questioners or give yourself thinking time with comments such as, "That's a good question," or, "I'm glad you brought up that point." But when you're talking one on one in conversation, these comments may sound patronizing. And comments such as, "As I mentioned earlier today in the teleconference," can sound like a verbal slap on the hand and a reprimand for not listening. They destroy rapport. Be silent with a reflective gaze rather than stalling with judgmental phrases that sound as though you're about to hedge, make something up, or respond with reluctance.

Tip 605. Remind Yourself That You Don't Have to Answer Every Question.

Growing up, kids in school know that they're expected to answer a teacher's questions, and that feeling of "must" still hangs on as adults. When facing a reporter or an audience, people often feel trapped when they get a question that's better left unanswered. To deflect a question that you don't want to answer, consider these responses:

- "If I understand your question correctly, you're really asking if...," and give your own interpretation of the question—a question that'd prefer to answer.
- "Your question prompts me to ask you something first. Is...?"
- "I think the real question is not X but Y... And I can certainly respond to that..."
- "Let me phrase your question a little differently before I answer it."
- "I'm sorry—that information is confidential. What I can tell you is this:..."
- "I'd rather not answer that question, if you don't mind."
- "I don't think that question has an answer."
- "The answer to that question would be purely speculative."

If you're unsure whether the questioner has manipulative intentions, you can always ask the reason for the question or explain your reluctance in a straightforward way. The delivery of the following lines should be confident, deliberate, and with direct eye contact.

- "I'm curious. Why do you ask that question?"
- "What do *you* think about the situation?"
- "As you might imagine, that question is difficult to answer. If I say X, you may think Y; and if I say Z, I'll look uncaring. I don't think I could win with any answer to that question."
- "Under the circumstances, I don't think I want to answer that question."
- "Such a question makes me a little uncomfortable. I'm not in a position to know all the related facts."
- "I don't know how to answer that, Charlie."
- "I'd have to think about that."
- "I'd have to give that more thought."

- "That's difficult to say—given all the moving parts and changing scenarios."

If the question is personal or confidential, you may choose to be flippant or coy:

- "What a question—do you want to get me fired?"
- "Don't we all wish we had the answer to that one—I'd settle for even half an answer."
- "Asking the questions is the easy part; answering them makes me break out in a cold sweat."
- "You must have spent all night phrasing that question; give me a couple of weeks to come up with an answer, will you?"
- "I can't remember the last time I checked."
- "Don't know. Maybe I should ask my hairdresser to see if she knows."
- "Care to guess? We could place bets."
- "It's all relative."
- "That depends. Depends on which day of the week and who's asking."
- "I try not to think about that—at least when I'm sober."
- "I try not to think about that—at least when I'm awake or asleep."
- "You want to call my analyst? I have him on speed dial here."

Tip 606. Know When to Make Your Answers Universal.

As a speaker, webinar presenter, or panelist, you often have to deal with participants who ask questions that pertain only to their individual situations. Your challenge is to turn the question to a universal application. Otherwise, audience members quickly lose interest. Example question: "I'm new to the job. Hired six months ago. But I can already tell that there seems to be a distance between me and my boss—even though he's the one that hired me. We went to a trade show last week; he didn't mention going out to dinner in the evenings. Several things like that. He's very friendly with the other guy they hired at the same time. But not much critique on my work. Should I say something about this sudden distance, or wait until he does?" Response: "So the question is, How do you get feedback from a boss who seems reluctant to give it? Let me address it this way..."

Tip 607. Remember That the Whole Performance Counts.

When it comes to questions, style is equal to substance. Your competence can be communicated in the clarity and conciseness of the content; in your delivery of the answer—with courtesy, confidence, composure, and concern; and finally, in the results you achieve with your answer.

Substance plus style equals success.

9

Saying No and Giving Other Bad News Without Damaging the Relationship

Learn to say "no" to the good so you can say "yes" to the best.

—John Maxwell

The worse the news, the more effort should go into communicating it.

—Andrew S. Grove

I will not take "but" for an answer.

—Langston Hughes

"No" is always an easier stand than "Yes."

—Rosabeth Moss Kanter

Many a manager has planned a trip across country for a week simply to delay giving his staff bad news. Saying no to an idea, a proposition, or a request from a customer, salesperson, partner, or parent creates knots in the stomach and costs hours of sleep. And the damage done by the delivery can be far worse than the answer itself or the discomfort of the person giving the message. Saying no will seldom be easy. But with the following tips, you may find the task less painful and more productive than you imagined.

Tip 608. Be Clear About Your Own Priorities.

Some priorities stay on your front burner; you know you don't want to be a part of this, and you know you do want to be a part of that. Your values constitute your basis for saying yes or no to every request for your help or your time. And for the bigger issues, you can ask the age-old question,

"If I had only six months to live, would I take on this project?" That thinking will help you focus on the important, time-consuming, life-changing commitments. Unfortunately, everything else falls in between the definite yeses and the definite noes. If your most distressing indecisions about time and money come at work, take some time every few months to focus on your own career and personal goals. Write them down. That list will help you focus and weed out the requests that deserve a "no" response.

Tip 609. Choose Consciously Among the Three Ways to Say No.

You can say no with an uncaring attitude: "No way will I let you borrow my car. Go rent one yourself." You can say no passively, hiding behind an excuse rather than a real reason. "I can't. My manager has me so involved in another project that I can't look up." Or you can *say* yes and *do* no. That is, you can agree to do something and then not come through at the last moment. The last way is the easiest—at the time. But in the long run, you disappoint the person more deeply and often cause more severe problems than you would with an honest, earlier no.

Tip 610. Ask for Time to Think.

Don't say yes simply because you've been caught off guard and you can't phrase the negative in a tactful, acceptable way. It's perfectly acceptable to ask for time to think about your response—even if you know that you plan to say no: "Let me think about that and get back to you." Noes rarely have to be immediate.

Tip 611. Forewarn People When You Have Devastating News.

When you're delivering an unexpected bad-news message that will certainly be a shock to someone's emotional system, warn that person by simply saying the words, "I'm going to have to give you some bad news." Such an outright statement lets people prepare physically and emotionally for the upset. During this adjustment time, their bodies make the necessary preparation for handling the shock.

Tip 612. When Writing, Be Positive or Neutral in Introducing the Bad News.

When you find it necessary to write your "no" message, you do not have the benefit of the rapport established by personal contact—a warm smile and a firm handshake. When writing, begin by trying to establish that rapport by simply bringing up the topic in a neutral or positive way. If you're going to have to tell a subordinate that you have decided not to grant him a transfer, you may begin with a neutral opening: "Bill, I'm responding to your request that we consider you for the opening in the La Jolla office." This neutral opening of the topic sets the stage and a matter-of-fact tone.

Tip 613. State the Reasons or Your Criteria for the No if You Are in a More Powerful Position Than the Other Person.

If you want to help others understand your decision, give your reasons or criteria before you state the no. By the time they've heard your explanation, they'll have already "read between the lines" to know that your no is coming at the end. But this arrangement softens the tone of your no and allows the other person to retain her composure and save face in making an appropriate, accepting response.

Example: "In any transfer decision, we consider several things: tenure in their current position, performance in previous jobs, costs of relocation, and trained replacements. In your case, the cost of relocation has been of major concern." By the time, you get to the no, the listener will probably have guessed the message that's coming. But the decision will not sound so arbitrary and cold; the criteria explanation provides a cushion.

Tip 614. Remember That a No Doesn't Require a Reason.

An explanation is not the same as an excuse. An excuse involves making up something that sounds logical but is not the real reason. An explanation includes your own choice and control about what the other person has asked. "Yes, we do have money in the budget for a few year-end bonuses. But I've allocated the money for additional training on our new equipment." With this explanation, you haven't shunned responsibility for the decision; you've just explained your refusal.

People have a right to ask you to do almost anything—and you have a right to say no without explanation. Examples: "I'm sorry that I can't explain my decision, but the answer is no." "Under normal circumstances I'd be happy to help you, but this is a bad time for me." "I can't participate." "I regret that I can't help." "I've decided that the trip would not be in my best interest." "After careful thought, I've decided not to participate myself, but I wish you the best in the undertaking."

Tip 615. Phrase Your No Positively When You Can.

Wording a positive no requires tact. Positive wording to minimize the damage to someone's self-esteem takes the most tact of all. Examples: *Not,* "We don't have time to include you on the program," *but,* "I regret that we're not going to be able to take advantage of your expertise on this program." *Not,* "We're not going to be able to do business with you because your price is just too high," *but,* "I wish we could have found a way to do business together. I'm sorry price had to be our major consideration on this contract."

Tip 616. Be Firm, Fair, and Nonjudgmental in Your Response.

If you're saying no because you do not approve ethically or morally of something the other person has asked you to do, it's usually best to be nonjudgmental and succinct in your response: "No, I'd rather not participate." "No, I don't feel comfortable supporting that position." "I've decided not to attend for personal reasons." "After careful thought, my answer has to be negative. And I'd rather not share my reasons, if you don't mind." "No. Thank you for your consideration in asking me to join you, but I've decided not to."

Tip 617. Thank People for the Honor of Saying No.

Many "no" situations involve someone asking you to accept a voluntary task or project. When you are overloaded, you want to decline, but you hate to disappoint a colleague or a friend. As a result, you find yourself either taking on the assignment and doing less than your best, taking on the assignment and resenting the requester for asking, or accepting the assignment but not following through.

All these weak choices tempt us when we can't find a gracious way to phrase a "no" response to a friend or colleague.

Instead, express appreciation that your colleague "considered" you or "thought" of you for the project: "I feel honored that you even considered me to speak to your group on such an important occasion," or, "I'm so pleased that you considered me capable of serving on this committee; I know this work is critical to the overall success of the event. Unfortunately, however, my schedule just won't allow it."

The implication of your phrasing is that your friend has honored you by asking. When you thank him for that honor—but are firm in your turndown—he typically understands your sincere regret that you cannot take on the assignment.

Tip 618. Learn to Say "Yes, and" Rather Than "No, but."

I once asked a systems analyst if his company typically assumed any and all liability for the performance of the computers it installed and the service it performed. His answer was, "Yes, we'll do *anything* the client wants at a price. Believe me, clients will pay for our assuming that risk. If they insist—and pay for it—we'll find a way to say yes."

When you'd like to be in a position to say yes, check the limits to see what's negotiable. "Yes, we can do it, and here's what it will mean. We'll have to have temporary help, leave X undone, or forget about doing the usual Y." With your boss's requests, bump against the requirements of the job to find ways to say yes: "Are you absolutely certain that the project has to be finished on July 15?" "Can we use our best guess if we can't locate the actual numbers by then?" "Can you find someone else to cover for me in California if I make the meeting for you in Beijing?" Yes makes everybody smile. "Yes, and here are the details to make that work."

Tip 619. Be Dramatic with Your No.

Sometimes you can celebrate your no as a major decision in life. Be dramatic with theatrics and props, if necessary, to make the point that you have "won a personal victory" by the careful process of coming to no.

Example: "Ta-da, you're looking at the new West Coast regional director. After three pepperoni pizzas and two bottles of No-Doz this weekend, I forced myself to make a list and check it twice to find out who's naughty and nice. I've decided that the regional director's job is it. That's where I want to hitch my star. Unfortunately, that means I have to say no to *your* offer here. At first, I was torn between the choices, but now I feel good about the decision. I was feeling so stressed trying to make up my mind. But now that's settled and the stress is gone. A direction at last. Please understand my decision."

With such fanfare, the requester often feels as though she should celebrate with you for having come to a difficult turndown decision. At the least, she will know that the "no" answer is definite.

Tip 620. Use the Broken-Record Technique.

If someone refuses to accept your no and continues to harangue you, give thought to phrasing a one-sentence "no" statement and using only that sentence over and over. Don't get sidetracked if the person brings up other benefits, mentions other issues, or makes other concessions. Say your one sentence again and again in a matter-of-fact tone. Example: "Would you trade weekends off and work for me May 15 and 16?" Answer: "I'm sorry, but I can't. I'm planning to attend a family reunion then." Requester: "But I traded weekends with you the last time you asked." Answer: "I know. I'm sorry. But I'm planning to attend a family reunion that weekend." Requester: "I'd pay you double time." Answer: "I can't. I'm attending a family reunion that weekend." Be firm, calm, and courteous. It will end.

Tip 621. Use the Sandwich Technique.

Begin your no with a positive or neutral statement about what the other person has asked you to do. That shows the person that you have listened well. Make the second statement the "no" part of your message. End with a neutral or positive statement about the request or situation to show that you have no hard feelings because you were asked and that you feel no guilt about saying no. Example: "I understand why an early copy of my report could be useful to you in tomorrow's decision. However, I can't release the sales numbers until the close of business today. I do hope the meeting goes well because that decision will have a big impact on both your division—and ours."

Tip 622. Give the Rain-Check No.

When you want to make sure the other person knows that you have a legitimate reason for saying no rather than an excuse, and when you want to encourage further requests, offer a rain check: "What an opportunity for on-the-job training! If it were any other week, I'd love to accompany you on the tour. Please put my name at the top of the list the next time you have an opening."

Tip 623. Offer Alternatives.

If you can't offer to help the other person with his request, suggest alternatives. Consider the results the requester wants and think of other ways to meet those needs or criteria. "I can't attend, but maybe you'd like to have my assistant attend and offer insights on the project." "We can't do the project in-house to meet your deadline, but I can give you the name of an excellent freelancer who might be able to work your project in on short notice." "We can't get our delivery truck out there today, but I could ship the items overnight so that you'd have them before your 10 o'clock meeting with your boss."

"If this price is a little higher than what you expected, you can always find them a little cheaper if you order online." Any such offers convey concern over the situation.

Tip 624. Mention Any Conditions Under Which You Might Change Your Mind.

If your answer is not definite and irrevocable, let the other person know that; it softens the message. Example: "If you decide that you don't need the work completed until next week, let me know and maybe I can reschedule my tasks at the end of the month." "If you can get by without CAD drawings, I'd certainly take on the project for you." "If you decide to change your terms, please talk to us again about your products because I like what I see online."

Tip 625. Let the Facts Speak for Themselves; Show Rather Than Tell.

When delivering bad news about a situation, speak up in the meeting with the numbers and results in black and white. Show them rather than tell them. This tactic distances you from the situation. If an individual or the group doubts your bad news, welcome any comments from group members about their doing their own investigation. In fact, express the hope that the group is right and you are wrong; if your information comes into question, encourage people to seek other expert opinions.

Tip 626. Find One Kernel of Good in the Bad.

Emphasize any positive twist at all. Point out that it is better for the company to "find out the truth now rather than lose another $50,000 down the road." Mention that at this point, people have spent "only two weeks on the project—it could have been two months." Maybe they will "take comfort in the fact that your division is one of the first to know and will not be caught by surprise like competitors." Suggest that all has not been lost—there may be information or insights that can be salvaged from the experience. Look hard for the grain of good.

Tip 627. Sit on the Other Side of the Table.

Identify yourself psychologically with the group hearing the bad news. Position yourself as one of them so that you will not be beheaded as the bearer of bad news. "I am as disappointed with the situation as you are." "I had hoped that the figures would be different." "I'm just as puzzled as you are about where we go from here." Use "we" phrases to show that you are looking at the bad news from their point of view: "We could always revamp the survey in the second quarter to see if the results change." "Our suppliers may be waiting for us to make the first move in this alliance." Refuse to be the scapegoat in a bad-news scenario that you did not create.

Tip 628. Deliver the Worst News Personally.

Don't hide behind the media—text messages, e-mails, intranet posts, committee announcements, press releases, or rumors. The worse the news, the more important it is that you deliver it in person—whether that be face to face, by teleconference, by videoconference, or by satellite. Not only will the individual or group be disappointed at the bad news, but they'll resent your lack of courage in failing to deliver the message personally. Courage shows up most in the midst of adversity.

10

Apologizing (and Accepting Apologies) Without Groveling or Grit

No persons are more frequently wrong than those who will not admit they are wrong.

—François, Duc de La Rochefoucauld

It is very easy to forgive others their mistakes; it takes more grit to forgive them for having witnessed your own.

—Jessamyn West

Sorry is the Kool-Aid of human emotions. It's what you say when you spill a cup of coffee or throw a gutterball when you're bowling with the girls in the league. True sorrow is as rare as true love.

—Stephen King

A good apology is like antibiotic, a bad apology is like rubbing salt in the wound.

—Randy Pausch

Apologies only account for the evil which they cannot alter.

—Benjamin Disraeli

The three most difficult words to speak are, "I was mistaken."

—No attribution

Where apologies are concerned, most people would rather receive them than give them. The biggest rebuff of all comes when an apology is shunned and tossed to the wind. Yet, apologies can have great effect. An apology can be the glue that keeps teams together, makes people productive after problems, and enables leaders to regain credibility after mistakes. Apologies keep relationships in good repair.

Tip 629. Decide What Apologizing Means to You.

In one of our communication workshops for a corporate client, a participant made this comment: "We never apologize in this company. The company lawyers adamantly refuse to allow any individual representative to write an apology to a customer without having the legal department review the document. From this company's perspective, apologizing means accepting liability."

To others, on the other hand, apologizing means simply saying, "I'm sorry for the situation." They apologize profusely only to avoid more serious difficulties or to win favor. According to the dictionary, apologizing means expressing regret for some fault, failure, insult, injury, or outcome—but it does *not* mean accepting *responsibility* for an outcome or failure.

So bottom line: you can attach either significance to any particular apology situation, from *expressing* liability to *avoiding* it. It's your choice. Your wording. Your opportunity.

Tip 630. Determine Your Priority—The Point or the Person.

To get yourself in the right frame of mind for an apology, decide which you want to win: the point or the relationship. That is, do you want to make your point in an argument or build your case at all costs? Or is keeping the relationship intact your highest priority? Once you make that decision, deciding when and how to apologize comes much more easily.

The power of apology doesn't lie in an admission of guilt or wrongdoing; its power lies in your intention to restore a relationship. Success comes from moving the feeling between you and another person from anger, stress, disapproval, sadness, resentment, or distance to calm, approval, acceptance, joy, friendship, or love.

Tip 631. Consider Whether You Want to Give or Ask.

Is an apology something that you give? Or is forgiveness something that you ask for? The difference is huge.

"I'm sorry" is an apology, something that you give. You are in control.

"Will you forgive me?" is a request—something that you ask for that puts the other person in control. And that's a humbling experience. If you don't believe it, the next time a relationship is in need of repair, ask for forgiveness and wait for an answer.

Tip 632. Apologize Specifically.

The most frequent cliché in apologies is the blanket statement: "I'm sorry for any inconvenience this may have caused you." That comment only makes angry people angrier. "For *any* inconvenience" implies that the speaker hasn't given any thought to how the person might have been inconvenienced. The choice of the word *inconvenience* implies that whatever happened was "no big deal." "This *may* have caused you" implies that the situation may have caused no problems at all. In other words, you can translate the sentence this way: "I don't know or care how my actions could have inconvenienced you, but if they did, here's a blanket apology."

Instead of vague wording, be specific. Let the person know that you understand either the difficulty of the situation or the hurt caused by your actions or words. "I'm sorry for the delay in responding to your call; I know you were in a hurry for the proper operating instructions." "I'm sorry the shipment didn't arrive until Friday. I know we had promised that you'd have it by Tuesday, and because of our late shipment, your own customer orders have been delayed." "I failed to notify you of the additional charge. You're right, I should have done so. I apologize for that." "You were expecting a complete report today, and without it, you'll be delayed in making the final committee decision. I'm sorry the information is still incomplete."

Such statements may or may not accept responsibility, but they do let the other person know that you are aware of and concerned about the outcome.

Tip 633. State Any Corrective Action That You Plan to Take or Have Taken Rather Than Reminding Someone of the Problem or Issue.

Start with the "punch line," the most important concern, to let someone know that he no longer has to protest to get his problem addressed. Once the issue is settled to the other person's satisfaction, there is less will to continue to discuss the details or disagree over whose fault something is. The other person's primary concern is resolution.

Tip 634. Explain the Reasoning Behind Corrective Actions.

Giving an explanation of how a mistake happened adds credibility to your corrective action. Let's say you have car trouble, and you take the car into the repair shop. When you return to pick up the car, you ask the mechanic what he found wrong with it. He responds, "Well, we thought it might be the starter, so we put a new one on. But that didn't seem to be the problem. Then we checked the spark plugs—but they were okay. We never did pinpoint exactly what was causing the problem, but the car seems to be running all right now." Do you feel confident about driving that car out of the repair shop? Of course not. If the mechanic can't tell you what was wrong with the car, you're not sure he has repaired it.

On the other hand, this explanation sounds reasonable: "I checked with our shipping about why your package did not reach you on time. And Terry said that unless packages have an 'express' tag on them, they may remain in the warehouse for two to three days when they're understaffed and can't find time to box them. Therefore, I've made the following changes in procedures so that you will receive future shipments promptly..."

If you can't state how something happened or can't explain your reasoning when you made an error in judgment, other people cannot be sure that you'll handle future situations any differently. An explanation lets them know that you cared enough to investigate and that you've gained insight from your investigation or reevaluation of the situation. Your explanation adds credibility for the future.

Tip 635. Never Make Excuses if the Mistake Was Caused by Your Carelessness or Insensitivity.

There is no excuse for obvious carelessness or insensitivity, and an explanation doesn't help. Your excuse will only elicit new accusations about the problem and escalate the whole affair. Own up to the insensitivity or the behavior: "You're right. I have logged in to the meetings late for the last several weeks. Everybody is busy, and everybody has crises on their hands. I simply didn't plan well. I kept you waiting, and that was wrong. I'm sorry." Or: "That tweet was insensitive. I certainly could have and should have phrased things differently." Or: "The humor was totally out of line. In fact, I don't think too many people found my text funny at all. I know it was hurtful. I really regret that I made light of what could have been a really serious situation."

Tip 636. Express Regret for the Problems That an Inadvertent Mistake Caused.

We were training three new employees in our office, and I had worked out a complex training schedule for each, noting certain classes they were to attend on a master schedule. Then I e-mailed a copy of the master training calendar to each employee. On several occasions, when a question arose about when one of our employees was to be out of the office, I reminded the administrative assistant that information was on the training calendar. "Didn't you see the training calendar?" I asked, to which she answered yes each time.

On the third such mix-up, we discovered the miscommunication. I was referring to the *employee* training calendar; she was referring to the client workshop calendar! A classic, inadvertent mistake. Even though an error or misjudgment may have been unintentional, the repercussions for the other person may be just as severe as if the mistake were a direct affront.

Even if you could not have foreseen the problem that your actions caused, you can express regret for the results: "I changed the meeting room at the last moment to escape the outside noise from the renovation crew. I'm sorry you were unable to find where we had moved and missed the meeting. I never thought of leaving a message with the lobby receptionist because I didn't know you planned to attend. You must be frustrated, however, to miss the meeting after driving an hour to get here." Such a statement doesn't admit blame, only regret at the situation.

Tip 637. Leave Others Out of the Picture.

It's often tempting to lift ourselves out of the mire by mentioning other people who've fallen into the ditch with us—those who think like we do, who turn in late reports, who've said insensitive things, who... fill in the blank. An objective observer might decide that the apology sounds like a teenager tattling on a sibling who should be grounded as well.

Above all, the temptation is to make the other person at fault along with us: "I know that you too have often had difficulty with blah, blah, blah. I was only reacting to what you said earlier. But I apologize for my part in the mix-up."

Consider it no apology at all if you're pulling more people into the picture and piling the responsibility for the problem on them.

Tip 638. Be Sincere.

Apologies from some people sound like a cease-and-desist order. "Look, I said I'm sorry. What else do you want me to do?" To be effective, an apology has to be more than an attempt to demand that the other person "forget it" and move on. Apologizing implies regret and an intention not to repeat the performance that led to the problem.

Sincerity comes through in tone, body language, and word choice. For example, suppose your team leader stands with his hands on his hips facing you with a grimace: "Look, I'm sorry I didn't tell you the due date was tomorrow. I've got 15 irons in the fire, okay? Complaining about working late isn't going to get it done any faster." Sincerity sounds like this: Your team leader is standing beside you with dejected, downcast eyes. "I should have told you the due date was tomorrow. Ivan told me, and I failed to pass it on. I'm sorry. What can I do to help you get it done?"

Tip 639. Reestablish Rapport on a Neutral Subject.

Like lovers who kiss and make up, coworkers or friends need to "sign off" on the difficulty and move ahead. A good way to do that is to make an additional comment or two on a neutral subject before ending the conversation. That final effort to establish a new topic, or at least an unrelated detail of the current topic, serves as the final handshake and brings the relationship back to normal. This closure helps to prevent any awkwardness at the next encounter.

Tip 640. Avoid Apologizing to Gain Sympathy.

The too-frequent apologizer is a second cousin to the person with low self-esteem who continually delivers self-effacing put-downs, hoping that the other person will counter them with a compliment. Bleed according to the pain you caused. If your actions or words caused severe problems, apologize profusely. If your actions or words caused only an understandable inconvenience, a brief apology will do.

Tip 641. Consider Apologies an Important Way to Build Rapport.

Research suggests that women tend to apologize more often than men. Why? Because women enhance their self-esteem through their relationships. When relationships are broken, women feel the impact strongly. Men, on the other hand, may apologize in a more matter-of-fact, take-it-or-leave-it manner. They consider it a ritual more than a relationship necessity. Others may resist apologizing because they think it puts them in a less powerful position. They may think that others will lose respect for them or that they'll have to "jump through hoops" if they own up to an error. But that's seldom the case. Apologies restore and revitalize damaged relationships.

Tip 642. Accept Apologies Graciously.

Although an apology may not be enough to soothe wounded pride or to make up for a catastrophe, accept whatever is offered. "Your apology is accepted." "Thank you for mentioning the incident." "I accept your apology." "All right. Let's forget it." "Okay. Accepted." "I appreciate your talking to me about it." Any of these comments acknowledges the other's efforts to rebuild the relationship and confirms your willingness to move ahead to better days.

Matching the apology with your own restores balance also: "Forget it. I also should have double-checked the status," Or: "Accepted. And I apologize for not notifying you of the trip earlier."

Even if you don't match the apology offered because doing so would seem inadequate or insincere, accept the apology attempt, however feeble, graciously. You'll help the other person save face and eliminate a stumbling block should your paths cross in the future. And in our global, virtual environment chances are good to great that you will meet again in the future.

11

Giving Feedback and Criticizing Without Crippling

There are people who take the heart out of you, and there are people who put it back.

—Elizabeth David

He has a right to criticize who has a heart to help.

—Abraham Lincoln

A smile in giving honest criticism can make the difference between resentment and reform.

—Philip Steinmetz

There has never been a statue erected to honor a critic.

—Zig Ziglar

Tact is the art of making a point without making an enemy.

—Howard W. Newton

When I complain, I do it because "it's good to get things off my chest"; when you complain, I remind you that "griping doesn't help anything."

—Sydney Harris

The art of managing people is stepping on their toes without messing up their shine.

—Anonymous

It is a sad thing when men have neither the wit to speak well, nor judgment to hold their tongues.

—Jean de La Bruyère

nlike apologies, criticism rolls off the tongue rather easily. The difficulty surfaces when we intend to give *constructive* criticism rather than
destructive criticism. The true measure of giving successful criticism, however, is not intentions but results. The person hearing the comments can't
see the intentions; she hears only the words.

Today more than ever, people consider it a status symbol to have a
personal coach. In fact, the field of executive coaching is booming. People
hire a coach for help in running a marathon, building their business, or
learning to invest in the real estate market. They gladly pay for feedback—
what they're doing right, what they're doing wrong, what they could do
better, and accountability for future action plans.

So why do these same people resist feedback from a spouse or significant other when he or she comments on their cooking, their weight loss
program, or their parenting skills? Or why do they resent feedback from a
boss about their presentations, their proposals, or their personal presence?

Someone has said, "The difference between coaching and criticism
is your attitude." I'll add to that observation two things: your timeline and
your relationship. Coaching involves a long-term, agreed-upon commitment to help another person improve and meet a specific goal. Criticism
or feedback involves one-time input about a specific task, event, action, or
attitude. The receiver may or may not want the feedback.

Now back to your relationship: it's the desired norm and expectation
for a professional coach to offer positive and negative comments about your
efforts to create a personal brand for your entrepreneurial business. But it's
not the desired expectation for your spouse or significant other to criticize
your skiing. It's the desired norm and expectation for a mentor to "coach"
you toward long-term career advancement by pointing out positives and
negatives in your decisions and goals. But it's *not* the desired outcome for
your boss to offer negative comments about a project that you just completed. Instead, you want the *immediate* feedback to be all positive.

As you can see, the concepts of coaching, feedback, and criticism
are inextricably linked—but they are not exactly the same. Feedback takes
many forms, depending on the relationship, attitude, and time commitment
involved. For the most part, the following tips apply to situations where
no formal coaching process exists. Instead, consider boss-employee scenarios, peer-to-peer relationships, friendships, and situations involving
family members.

Intentions count—but methods and results matter most.

Tip 643. Identify Your Motive for Negative Feedback.

Positive reasons for criticizing include a commitment to and concern for another person and a sense of responsibility for things done "right." Negative reasons for criticizing include poor self-esteem and a resulting attempt to build yourself up at someone else's expense or as a defense or excuse for your own failures. If those two statements can't help you sort out your motives, try the following, more detailed checklist:

- ☑ Will you enjoy or do you dread giving this feedback?
- ☑ Do you want to demoralize the other person?
- ☑ Do you want to condemn or guide the other person?
- ☑ Do you want resolution or more conflict?
- ☑ Is the issue a personal matter with you?
- ☑ Do you criticize habitually?
- ☑ Are you open or manipulative in your comments?
- ☑ Do you feel negative or critical simply because you're in a bad mood or feeling depressed?
- ☑ Are you the best one to give this feedback?
- ☑ Are you giving this feedback to appease some third party?

If you don't like the answers to any of these questions, consider waiting to give the feedback until your motives are clear.

Tip 644. Check for Feedback Preferences.

When you're beginning a long-term relationship—either as a family member or as a boss and employee—have a frank discussion. Ask if the other person anticipates making any mistakes over the next few months or years. Most people, of course, will admit to that probability, usually with levity. Ask the other person, then, how he'd like you to handle the feedback. Would he prefer that you be direct, or would he prefer that you use a softer, less-direct approach? Would he prefer that you wait until the end of the day or talk early in the morning? Would he prefer that you talk on site or talk away from the office or home? Or would he prefer to have the feedback in an informal e-mail or phone call rather than in person? In addition to the obvious benefit of knowing the other person's preferences, when such discussions become inevitable, you can remind him of this earlier conversation and point out that you've tried to comply with his preferences. That in itself sets forth a caring, but matter-of-fact, situation.

Tip 645. Realize the Stress of Hearing, "I'd Like a Word with You."

Do anything you can to reduce the stress for the person about to receive negative feedback, not create more. Keep your tone as matter-of-fact as possible, without the high school principal effect. At the beginning of the conversation, preface your remarks to let the person know the severity of the discussion. If your discussion is going to end in a formal reprimand, you don't want to start off with chitchat.

However, if the criticism is a one-issue agenda and is of a more routine nature, say so at the beginning. "Kate, I'd like to take about 20 minutes to talk to you about the way we're shuffling projects between departments. I want to share my perspectives with you and get yours and see if we can come up with a better process." In other words, lay out an overview of the parameters of the discussion, the time involved, and the hoped-for outcome. Take the pressure off about the unknown so that the person can concentrate on the major problem and resolution without the anxiety.

Tip 646. Watch the Red-Pencil Mentality.

This term, used by Sidney Simon in *Negative Criticism,* refers to what some perceive as their mission on earth—to point out others' errors for all the world to see. This attitude becomes a compulsion, like a housekeeper who can't pass a picture frame without straightening it. Before you're tempted to red-pencil somebody, try to recall the sense of pride with which you turned in an English composition with precision footers, proper punctuation, and required bibliography. Do you remember the disappointment when the professor returned your graded paper with all your comma errors marked in red? Why do that to people? Is the feedback really worth voicing?

Tip 647. Separate Fact from Opinion as You Gather Your Thoughts and Information.

"Jill, you're lazy" is opinion. "Jill, you have processed only 28 applications today; your quota is 48" is fact. Particularly if the "facts" are coming from another department, make sure that you probe enough to distinguish which is which. Did the customer actually *say* that Stan hung up on her, or did the customer say that Stan was rude? Did Bill actually *say* that the report was too late to do any good, or did he say that the report was submitted three days late? Know which is which—fact or opinion— and be ready to point out the difference. The receiver of criticism will seldom dispute facts, but will often ask for support of opinion. In either case, you want to be able to cite the appropriate information.

Tip 648. Make Sure You Know What You're Talking About.

Ask yourself if you have all the facts, figures, and circumstances of a situation before you bumble into a hornet's nest to offer criticism. You'll back out of such a discussion with a big sting if you haven't done the preliminary investigation. Even then, double-check. It's too easy to put three facts together and come to the wrong conclusion.

Tip 649. Screen Yourself Before "Being Frank" and "Telling the Truth."

The "truth" will not necessarily change the world—or another person. Remember that "truth" is often subjective, and "frankness" may be a code word for insult. Examine your motives for criticizing. Determine the intentions of the person who "needs the truth." Then consider discretion. What are your ultimate goals for your relationship with this person? Preserving that relationship may be a higher priority than preventing a recurrence of some minor incident.

Tip 650. Consider the Positive Results of the Exchange: Improved Mental Outlook, an Improved Relationship, New Insight, Possibility of Effecting a Change.

Before you decide to offer criticism, think about the positives of the situation. Will people feel better about improving themselves, a process, or a plan? Do they generally seem to want feedback and make an effort at self-improvement? Will your offering this criticism actually improve your relationship with them? What new insights might you both gain from a frank discussion? What are the possibilities for improvements in how you both interact and accomplish your work goals? In other words, focus on the positive aspects of an open discussion. These incentives will give you confidence to begin what you would otherwise consider an uncomfortable dialogue.

Tip 651. Consider the Negative Results of the Exchange: Mental and Emotional Outlook, Time Involved to Help with the Change, Probability of Effecting a Change, a Severed Relationship.

Forget about trying to change people who are manipulative and maliciously destructive, those with a conflict in values, those without the mental capacity to master a task, those who are addicted to drugs, and those with mental problems and low self-esteem. These mental and emotional problems indicate that the time spent in providing negative feedback will be fruitless. These people either can't or won't change.

A second concern is time: Do you want to spend the time it will take someone to change? Finally, will your help produce the change? Ask yourself how many times this person has probably heard the same feedback. Has she done anything about it? The answers to these questions will tell you whether your time and effort will pay off. If not, withhold the criticism and figure out either how you can minimize contact with this individual or how you can get your work done without this person at all.

Tip 652. Consider Whether You Could Foster the Same Change with Praise Rather Than Criticism.

After you've identified positive reasons to go through with the criticism, use one last screen: Could you get the same result with praise? Without setting up a phony situation, could you entice the person to do a particular thing differently by rewarding the desired behavior rather than criticizing the less-than-desirable behavior?

Tip 653. Make Sure You're Not Doing the Same Things You're Criticizing.

We tend to react to attitudes, weaknesses, or traits in others that we dislike in ourselves. And the receiver of any criticism will be the first to point out any inconsistencies.

Tip 654. Rehearse Your Criticism.

Take the time to plan what you're going to say. Decide how to begin. Practice the proper wording and tone. Decide where and when you're going to have the conversation. Remind yourself that the reason for giving the criticism is not to hurt someone, but to help correct a situation. Focus on the fact that after the discussion, both you and the other person will be better off for having made the improvement. As with any other difficult task, preparation boosts your confidence and your effectiveness.

Tip 655. Select the Appropriate Emotional Timing.

Both giving and accepting feedback take emotional strength; find the peak time. Make sure that neither you nor the receiver is angry, irritated, or impatient. The receiver needs self-confidence, control, and motivation to accept your comments. Your emotional state is equally important for success. If you give criticism when you're angry, the receiver is likely to slough it off with, "When he calms down, it'll blow over," or, "She's blowing this all out of proportion. I'll just lie low until she gets over it."

Tip 656. Select the Proper "Real Time."

Giving criticism at the end of the day, just before employees go home, allows them time to regain their composure overnight and minimizes the time lost for productive work after the discussion when they're upset over the criticism. On the other hand, giving the criticism earlier in the day sometimes allows people the opportunity to see and feel from your back-to-the-routine manner afterward that your relationship has not been altered substantially. They must move on with their day's tasks and function around other people. In other words, they won't have time to brood.

Know your audience and the potential impact of your comments on the person's recovery rate. The most crucial aspect of "real time" is that your feedback comes promptly enough to prevent another mistake.

Tip 657. Criticize in Private.

Praise in public; criticize in private. Consider the need to keep not only the actual discussion away from others' ears, but also the surrounding circumstances and appearances that create rumors. "Get hold of Keith and tell him I want to see him in my office before he goes home today," said in an angry tone to your assistant, may be a broadcast to the world. At the least, Keith will probably know that the assistant knows and will fear that others have overheard the edict also. The humiliation of being confronted in front of peers or customers will shut down any and all lines of communication.

Tip 658. Avoid Beginning with a Trapping Question.

Do you remember a parent asking you, "Son, how many times have I told you not to leave your backpack in the middle of the hallway?" Did she really want to know how many times? Of course not. And even if you smarted off by saying, "2,349 times," that wasn't the point anyway. Workplace versions of childhood trapping questions sound like these: "Do you think this product is going to sell itself?" or, "How many times have we discussed in staff meetings the importance of correct invoices?" or, "Do you recall my warning you earlier that you need to watch the tax consequences of these revenues each month?" A trapping question produces only a defensive stance. And more important, you'll be discussing the answer to that question rather than the real issue and solution.

Tip 659. Don't Play "Trivial Pursuit."

If you already have in mind the way you want a problem corrected or a situation handled, don't force the other person to guess. That becomes some form of the TV game-show question, "Guess what's behind door number 1?" Indeed, your discussion will become a trivial pursuit as the listener tries to read your mind. Simply fill in the blanks for the other person and move on.

Tip 660. Ask First; Suggest Second.

After you've made someone aware of the negative consequences of his action or inaction, lead him to analyze the situation rather than jumping in with your solutions. Ask questions first: What options does he see to prevent future occurrences? What precautions can he take? Should there be a check-back plan or point? For the strongest buy-in, make your suggestions only after he's done his own thinking.

Tip 661. Remove Threats from the Feedback.

A threat sets up a condition for continuing the relationship or creates fear about consequences and future work. When a person is frightened, she freezes. No one performs best when she's fearful. Her thinking becomes muddled. Her timing becomes questionable. Tempers flare.

Tip 662. Avoid an I-Told-You-So Tone.

Remind yourself of the implication: A superior tone confirms the correctness of your own position rather than focusing on change in another's behavior. It says: "I was right all along." A more productive focus is: "I'd like you to be right in the future, and in order to do that, you need to change X." Granted, you are not necessarily going to create a pleasant, happy atmosphere; criticism delivered in that tone would be perceived as phony. But you can be straightforward, businesslike, and direct.

Tip 663. Criticize Specifically, Not Generally.

General criticism cannot be substantiated or corrected, so most often it's ignored. But the words hang there, festering. When you identify the specific things you want to correct in someone's behavior, you improve your effectiveness in several ways. First, you gain credibility. When the receiver calls your hand on a sweeping generalization about his behavior and you can't offer immediate specifics to back up what you say, your feedback loses validity. Often the person dismisses what you say as untrue.

Second, with specific feedback, you both automatically focus on concrete actions to improve the situation. Third, with specifics, you can be sure that the criticized person will define the issue or problem the same way you do.

For example, with generalized criticism, you might say: "Heidi, you just don't seem to care about your work anymore." (You mean that Heidi is frequently late, takes long lunch breaks, and never stays late to finish projects.) But Heidi may respond: "What do you mean I don't care? I even called in on my vacation last week to see if Jason had any questions." (Her interpretation of "care" differs.)

Specific criticism (1) forces the receiver to define acceptable behavior and performance the same way you do, (2) focuses on concrete corrective action, and (3) adds credibility to what you say.

Tip 664. Criticize the Viewpoint or the Behavior, Not the Person.

Try, "I asked you to let me know if your blog would be late, and you didn't notify me," not, "You're simply undependable when it comes to doing what you say you will." Try, "I think you mishandled that customer situation. You didn't try to reschedule the appointment, and you didn't offer to deduct the shipping charges. You failed to offer either option, and both are within your power," not, "You seem preoccupied. You don't think." Try, "You didn't let me know that the equipment wasn't working properly and that you needed it repaired by next week," not, "You're uncooperative when it comes to supporting our department's projects."

People can discuss viewpoints or behavior and verify facts; they can even verify interpretation of those facts. But they'll rarely agree to personal labels, much less agree to make a change. How, specifically, does someone become "less preoccupied" or "more cooperative"? Can she do that by next Friday?

Tip 665. Focus on Observable Behavior, Not Conclusions About That Behavior.

Discuss what you saw or heard before you label it. After the person criticized verifies that your observations are correct, then you may agree to label the behavior or attitude as "right," "wrong," "rude," "incompetent," "in poor taste," or "offensive." But even after you label that behavior, express such labels as your opinions, not facts. Those labels often lead the other person to explain his intentions and "compare conclusions" with you.

Try wording like this: "I can appreciate why you felt it necessary to do X, but here's what I expected," or, "I can understand your reasons; my viewpoint is different," or, "I agree with some of what you said, but I still have concerns about Y," or, "That's true; here's another consequence of that action, however." In other words, in a meeting of the minds, state the criticism as subjective and under consideration. The result will be a more constructive dialogue rather than a conflict of emotions.

Tip 666. Don't Turn Comments About Work Problems into Major Character Flaws.

If you're talking to people with low self-esteem, they often have a way of turning even the slightest correction of their work into poor-me pitter-pat. "Rosalinda, you've missed several meetings, and I'm concerned that you're not going to be up to date enough on these projects to anticipate our staffing needs. One week you're upbeat and excited, and the next week, you seem discouraged." Rosalinda's response: "So are you trying to tell me that I'm manic-depressive? Or that I intentionally sabotage your projects because I'm envious—is that what you're implying?"

Don't let that happen. Tell others to discuss any such personal issues with their analyst at $200 an hour. Instead, stay focused on the work problem.

Tip 667. Bring the Criticism Forward.

Don't talk about what people *did* in the past; instead, highlight what they *are doing* now. The difference is enormous. What someone did in the past sounds irrevocable, unchangeable, and damning. What someone is doing now emphasizes transience rather than permanence. If he can change or improve it, there's a hopeful attitude. Yes, of course, you have to mention past behavior, but link that behavior to the big-picture trait, habit, or process that can be changed.

Tip 668. Don't Ask Why.

"What" questions focus on someone's values, intentions, and results. Granted, a "why" question may lead to insight and understanding to resolve a problem. But more often than not, it leads to a defensive discussion of motives. Will you handle the situation differently if you can identify who's to blame? If not, asking why will be fruitless. You may or may not agree with someone's motives, but in any case, you'll almost always be off track in terms of changing the observable behavior. Instead, ask, "What happened?" This question removes personalities and fault and focuses on causes and resolution.

Tip 669. Use "I Need/Want/Expect" Phrasing When Possible.

Thomas Gordon of the Parent Effectiveness Training program first suggested these three steps: (1) Say clearly how you feel, what you want, or what you expect. (2) Describe the observable problem or behavior. (3) Explain the consequences or results of the behavior. Here's an example: (1) "I feel rushed when I'm given four or five proposals in a one-week period for which I'm supposed to plan graphics." (2) "When I have to 'beef up' that many documents, I find myself just grabbing graphics from our ready-reference file and not really giving the concepts much creative thought." (3) "Then the proposals go out to clients half-baked. They're just not up to the standards we've set."

With this three-part statement, the focus is on the action and consequences rather than on who's doing what. Not, "You need to be doing these faster," but, "I need these proposals done faster." Not, "You should make appointments ahead of time with the clients rather than trying to catch them when you're in the building," but, "I expect our service people to make appointments with clients ahead of time because our clients can't set their work schedules around us when we cold-call them to do routine maintenance. As a result of our not making definite service appointments, we've lost two accounts this month." Phrasing determines the difference in many reactions.

Tip 670. Don't Substitute "You Need to" Phrases for Feedback.

These comments don't count as feedback; they're merely commands: "Christopher, you need to be at the Security Desk by 7:00 a.m. when the front lobby opens." "Sarita, you need to send out the e-mail blast to a larger group of prospects before the Denver trade show." Such directives fail to give the person any feedback about what went wrong. What happens when Christopher's not at the front desk exactly at 7:00? What hardship does that cause? Why was the number of e-mails Sarita sent insufficient? How did you measure this? How can Sarita know in the future what will be a sufficient number?

Directives do not necessarily provide feedback that improves future performance.

Tip 671. Don't Compare People.

Adults in the workplace hate comparisons as much as siblings do. If you supervise others, compare their behavior to your expectations, compare it to their own stated goals, compare it to the standards set to earn rewards, or compare it to mutually set objectives. But don't compare one individual's work to another's work—past, present, or sainted. "When Leanne was in this job, she always sent us managers an annual needs-assessment survey. I think that was a more precise way to collect the necessary information." Such comments don't win friends—or motivate changes.

Tip 672. Include Credit with Your Criticism.

Try to keep balance in your observations. What is the person doing right? What do you admire? What positive changes has this person made? People tend to do more of what they're doing right than they tend to do less of what they're doing wrong. In what order does one give the praise and criticisms? There are two schools of thought: giving the credits first or giving the criticisms first. The problem with giving the positives first is that the person doesn't really enjoy them because of her anxiety in waiting for the negatives.

The drawback to giving the criticism first is that if the negative discussion gets out of hand, neither of you may be in a frame of mind to share and enjoy the positives. Although you'll be ending on an "upbeat note," the receiver may be so hung up on the criticism that he can't hear the positives at the end.

A third structure is to focus only on action—ways in which you'd like to see the person improve and then what she is already doing right. People would much rather work on "self-improvement goals" than on "problems to be resolved." This arrangement also ends on positive affirmation.

A fourth alternative is to give both praise and criticism in balanced proportions—but at different times. For some people, you can give 99 compliments and one criticism, and the criticism will outweigh the 99 positive comments. Choose one five-minute period in the morning and offer your praise. The next day, offer your criticism. They're balanced, but not in the same setting.

Which structure should you choose? Let the subject of your criticism and the receiver's anticipated reaction determine the format. *Criticism* originally meant to give an objective appraisal of ideas, plans, or work. Book or movie critics discuss both the merits and the demerits of a manuscript or play. In the workplace, however, the term *criticism* has somehow taken on the negative meaning only.

When you give criticism, why not change that perception with a balanced discussion? Communicate your observations in such a way that the person benefits and can use your comments for long-term improvement for all concerned. Both all-stars and substitutes have good days and bad.

Tip 673. Avoid Giving Mixed Messages

However you structure any positive and negative feedback, make sure that the other person receives a clear message. For example, after overhearing a heated phone discussion between one of your staff members and a client, you give this feedback to your staffer: "Sounds like Mr. Bradley was quite upset. And you got a little huffy with him, didn't you? Be careful to watch your sharp tone in the future. We can't afford to lose that contract." You wag your head, give a half smile, and walk on down the hall. One employee may interpret this feedback as disapproval, while another will interpret it as, "No big deal."

The words communicated disapproval; the body language communicated "no worries."

Tip 674. Lead the Person to Do a Self-Critique.

When we train participants in our presentations skills workshops, we like
to lead them through the process of self-critique: What did you think went
well in your presentation? What didn't go as well as planned? If you could
present this information a second time, what would you do differently?
Finally, what would you like me (as coach) to watch for and offer more
critique on during your next performance?

It always amazes me how accurate self-critiques are. And what's
more, people believe their own feedback more strongly than they believe
comments from others. Try using the same principle by leading your
employees to critique their own performance on particular projects. Lead
your kids to critique their own attitudes; they may surprise you.

Tip 675. Wait for the "I-Dunno" Shrugger to Bounce Back.

Not everyone is willing to do a self-assessment. No matter how negative
the feedback, some people prefer to let you do their thinking for them. They
respond to your reflective questions ("What do you think would be the best
approach next time?") with the limp, "I dunno."

If you're as impatient as I am, you're tempted to tell them and move
on. But don't. Wait. Persist—that is, if your goal is to help them grow. Say
something like, "Okay, I understand that you don't know for sure. But what
do you *think*? I know you haven't written a job aid or anything on this situation. But think for a moment and then tell me: what do you *guess*?"

Typically, they'll come up with choices and suggestions—which is
your goal. If you don't like those ideas, then you can lead them to analyze
further: "What's your thinking about that option?" "Okay, let's consider
the pros and cons of that plan. What would be the upside? How about the
downside? Do any better alternatives come to mind?"

Forcing feedback in this way can be an ideal option for the reluctant
staffer or student. Nobody claimed that giving feedback was fast or fun.

Tip 676. Assume Some of the Blame Yourself.

If you can do so honestly and if you have the ego strength to meet the other
person more than halfway, this approach will certainly generate a welcome
response. "I certainly can share in any blame for the vendor-selection
process; I know I've been traveling a lot lately and probably was not around
enough to give you the opportunity to bounce ideas off me on issues that

affected both our departments," or, "Maybe I was too fuzzy in the last webinar about exactly what I planned to do with those projections. In any case, they're not set up in a usable format." Let the receivers of criticism save face by your sharing any blame that needs to be assessed. It takes the pressure off them to defend themselves and make excuses.

Tip 677. Substitute "Problem Solving" for Feedback When Possible.

Offering to approach the situation as if it is a problem that merits cooperation shows a positive attitude. Confirm that you have mutual goals, and spend your time developing alternatives to get what you both want. Your conversations will probably end up with transitions like these: "So what are the alternatives?" "What suggestions do you have for...?" "I'm open to suggestions."

Tip 678. Focus the Feedback on Resources.

Many negative situations have gotten that way because someone failed to take advantage of the resources available to her. Point people toward online repositories, databases, or tutorials; experts; or mentors. Turn an underperformer into a resourceful star with a nudge in the right direction.

Tip 679. Couch Your Feedback as a Request for Help.

This approach works most effectively with bosses or peers. Point out the consequences that a certain behavior is having for you, and ask for suggestions for handling the situation.

Tip 680. Criticize Only One Thing at a Time.

People rarely do a complete makeover. None of us has the luxury of deleting all the files or scrubbing all the database and starting over. But we can handle one improvement at a time—say, contact all the inactive client files in a six-month period. Let people focus on one improvement until they master that area. Then offer another goal—and another carrot.

Tip 681. Relate Your Feedback to the Other Person's Goal.

Try to point out how the observed behavior thwarts a mutually shared goal. People put more effort into correcting things that have a positive benefit for themselves. And that benefit doesn't have to be intrinsic. Correcting problem X doesn't have to make the person healthier, happier, or sexier immediately and directly. The benefit of correcting the behavior may simply be to get a higher performance rating, resulting in a bigger raise later. The resulting raise may bring the direct benefit—health and happiness, depending on how he spends it.

Tip 682. Criticize to Some End.

Feedback on things that people can't change only frustrates and demoralizes them. For example, they can't change their height, their family, or their past. Hearing negative comments on such things makes them feel powerless, confused, and hopeless. At best, they'll simply shrug their shoulders at the silliness of someone expecting them to change the unchangeable and ignore the criticism altogether. When you offer negative feedback, end with a specific goal for the other person to take action on.

Tip 683. Describe the Change or Action You Want Others to Take.

If you tell employees that you want them to deliver better customer service, what does that look like? Answering the telephone on the first ring rather than the third? Double-checking the spelling of the customer's name in e-mails? Making home deliveries? Responding to service calls within two hours? Smiling more often? Posting a blog daily rather than weekly? Mentoring at least two interns per year rather than only one?

Here are the kinds of vague improvements that frustrate people and defy change: "Demonstrate a better attitude." "Do something about the morale around here." "Get better control on the use of social media by your staffers." "Eliminate these miscommunications between departments." Instead of the vague "goals" alone, *describe* the "better attitude" that you expect. *Describe* the "morale" improvement. Identify the controls you expect or the problems or risks you've noted in the staffers' use of social media. *Name* the "miscommunications" that you want eliminated. If you can't describe the corrective action or improvement that you want, the chances are reasonably high that you won't get it.

Tip 684. Monitor the Pace of the Feedback.

If you're apprehensive about giving criticism, you tend to talk faster and faster. That rapid feedback often leaves the receiver feeling run over, dumbfounded, overpowered, and unable to respond. When the receiver can't respond, you have no idea whether she acknowledges the problem and intends to correct it. So to slow your pace and relax your delivery, take deep breaths. Break eye contact. Fiddle with a prop, such as your eyeglasses, your soft drink, your computer, or phone. Pause for questions. Slow yourself down long enough to give the other person the opportunity to absorb and respond to your comments.

Tip 685. Play Coach Rather Than Cop.

Check your demeanor. An angry or condescending demeanor shuts down communication. If the receiver rejects you as a person, he will dismiss your feedback as invalid. The goal in giving criticism is to have others respond and make a change.

Tip 686. Summarize Key Points and Actions for Correction.

If the discussion has been lengthy, help the person attach the right importance to what you've discussed. The receiver may have overreacted to parts of your message and missed other key points altogether. It's helpful to recap at the end and outline the action steps: "So we've discussed the problems in the lab when the power goes off without warning, the difficulty with getting the machines repaired, and the safety concerns with contractors just walking through the lab at will. You've agreed to talk to the temporary people about wearing hard hats. And I have volunteered to write an e-mail to the facilities people about the outages." The summary puts everything in perspective.

Tip 687. Don't Ask Whether the Person "Understands" the Feedback.

Doing so communicates a parent-child, patronizing tone. If you want to verify what the receiver understands, ask for "confirmation" of the key points and ask about her ideas and timelines for making changes.

Tip 688. Recognize When Enough Is Enough.

After you've made your point, illustrated your point, and asked for confirmation of your point, stop. There is nothing but resentment to be gained by repeating yourself.

Tip 689. Decide Who Should and Shouldn't Know What.

Decide how you will put the situation behind you and continue with the relationship. Will you need to explain changes to other people? Who will or will not be told details of the discussion?

Tip 690. End Feedback with Encouragement for the Future.

Stress cooperation and mutual goals rather than conflict, blame, and defeat. Communicate your confidence that the person can change or improve his behavior. Even movie moguls have bad rehearsals and occasionally get unfavorable reviews. Your goal with feedback is to create a box-office bonanza.

12

Taking the Sting Out of Negative Feedback or Criticism Leveled at You

People ask you for criticism but they only want praise.

—Somerset Maugham

A remark generally hurts in proportion to its truth.

—Will Rogers

One of the surest marks of good character is a man's ability to accept personal criticism without feeling malice toward the one who gives it.

—O. A. Battista

It is the peculiar quality of a fool to perceive the faults of others, and to forget his own.

—Cicero

Adverse criticism from a wise man is more to be desired than the enthusiastic approval of a fool.

—American salesman

Most people would rather defend to the death your right to say it than listen to it.

—Robert Brault

Men occasionally stumble over the truth but most of them pick themselves up and hurry off as if nothing had happened.

—Winston Churchill

One way to avoid criticism is to do nothing and be a nobody. The world will then not bother you.

—Napoleon Hill

Whether from a boss, a peer, a friend, or a family member, negative feedback or criticism smarts, no doubt about it. So how do you respond to it emotionally, evaluate it objectively, use it constructively, or discard it appropriately? The following tips may smooth the rough spots.

Tip 691. Consider the Value of Criticism.

Criticism has been given a bum rap in our society, possibly because there are so many different kinds of criticism that can come our way. Actually, to give criticism means to point out both the positive and the negative. But in our day-to-day world, criticism typically focuses on the negative.

You may be criticized for something that was not your fault; for something that you have no control over; for being smarter or performing better than someone else and making that person jealous; for deliberately doing something wrong; for unintentionally doing something inappropriate; for something that is true; for something that is untrue; or for your intentions, actions, results, appearance, attitude, personality, or job performance. It's difficult to lump all these kinds of criticism together. But consider the value of criticism: It is a form of communication (although a negative one). Sometimes negative communication from someone is better than no communication at all. As a source of information, it can be your best plan for self-improvement. You can either disregard it or benefit from it. Think of the person who offered the negative comments as a coach, and you'll be less resentful. If that person's intention is to help you improve, try to forget the framework for the comments and latch on to the benefit.

Tip 692. Remember That Even the Best Get Criticized.

If you're among those criticized, you're in good company. Heads of state receive criticism, even though a majority of voters consider them worthy of high office. Religious leaders receive criticism, even if they're living on bread and water to feed the poor. Celebrity athletes get booed when they don't live up to their previous feats and track records. Movie stars are forgotten if their latest performance flops at the box office. CEOs receive criticism if the company's profits drop during the most recent quarter. No one is immune; criticism is our national pastime.

Tip 693. Think Twice Before You Invite Criticism by Habit or Attitude.

Few people go through life with such thick skins that they don't care whether others approve or disapprove of what they do. Not that they live their life with approval as a guiding force, but most mentally healthy people notice and care when others are displeased with their behavior.

Here are several surefire ways to invite criticism on the job and at home: being unprepared, being poorly organized, failing to do what you promised, putting other people down, running over the rights of others, always demanding your own way, being confrontational in tone or manner, failing to be clear about your expectations of others, being inconsistent, doing sloppy work, disregarding or being oblivious to what is going on around you, or disregarding the social or work norms for behavior, speech, or dress.

If you're unaware of any of these expectations or averse to going along with them, you may as well get used to criticism. Understand that criticism will be a fact of your life and learn to shrug it off.

Tip 694. Determine Whether Criticism Is Intended to Be Constructive or Destructive.

You can often tell whether a person intends to destroy you with a comment or intends just to bring about some change. Pay attention to the person's word choice, emotion, and body language, and the specifics of the comments. Did the person say that you were always late, or did he call you lazy? Did the criticizer sound as though he had planned the comments in a logical and thoughtful way, or did he just blurt them out in an emotional rage? Did his body language show control or indicate an uncontrolled outburst? Did the criticizer back up what he said with specifics and have suggestions in mind, or did he seem foggy about changes?

What could be the criticizer's agenda? To score points at your expense? To build or protect her own self-esteem? To impress onlookers? To vent her anger at you because she is afraid to show anger at the person causing the trouble? To hurt you?

Finally, ask yourself about the subject of the criticism. Are the comments about your personality, lifestyle, or appearance an attempt to control you or make you feel guilty? Or is the feedback about a mistake, something regarding a problem that needs to be solved?

The answers to these questions will tell you whether the criticizer's primary intention is to hurt you or to improve a situation. If you're still in doubt, try asking the person directly about his intentions: "Did you simply want me to know how you felt about me personally? Or did you want us to try to work out the problem?"

One caution: Some people are inept at offering criticism. They will choose the wrong words, become emotional, and focus on the problem rather than the solution only because they are incompetent. You'll have to use your best judgment in determining their intentions. Don't attribute to them ill will when their problem is incompetence.

Tip 695. Invite People to Criticize You Only if You Mean It.

If you routinely ask for criticism, don't be surprised if you get it. When you ask for feedback, people rarely point out what you're doing *right*. Instead, they feel compelled to tell you what you could do better, quicker, faster, easier, or smarter. So if you don't really want criticism or suggestions, don't give others a license to dump them on you.

Tip 696. Consider the Setting Before You Decide How to Respond.

If you're in a large group when someone offers a critical comment, you may decide to let the remark pass rather than make a scene and prolong the attention directed toward the issue. If you're in a situation where the outcome could be crucial to your future (such as in a staff meeting), correct a false impression politely and briefly. If, however, you're one on one with someone and you have time and privacy, discuss the criticism thoroughly. Make your response a conscious choice—not an off-the-cuff comeback.

Tip 697. Arrange to Have Criticism Leveled on Your Own Turf.

If you know that there's a problem when the boss or a coworker says that she wants to "talk to you about something," suggest your own office. You can control the timing and the privacy. And unlike the feeling of punishment we had when as children we were called to the principal's office, there's something about familiar surroundings that gives you a sense of control and dignity.

Tip 698. Stifle an Immediate Denial.

Denial by adults is just as normal as that of children in these chants: "You did." "I did not." "Did too." "Did not." When someone levels a criticism, stifle the urge to close the person down with such responses as, "You don't know what you're talking about," or, "You're wrong and I don't want to talk about it anymore," or, "That's none of your business," or, "You're just jealous." Counter your instinct. Ask for elaboration.

Tip 699. Squelch the Urge to Counterattack.

Counterattack comes naturally. When the criticizer offers comments, you return the heat. Criticism: "This manual was done much too hurriedly. You've left out some of the most important procedures." Counterattack: "Well, you're not such a polished writer yourself. That e-mail you sent out yesterday confused the heck out of everybody." When the pattern is to "top" the criticizer, the original issue becomes blurred in the process.

Tip 700. Stifle the Urge to Rationalize.

Rationalizing involves providing a perfectly logical excuse for your actions—but not the real reason. For example, someone criticizes you for being late to client meetings downtown. You know that you lose time because you sleep later than you should, but you claim that it's the heavy traffic and unexpected accidents on the freeway that prevent you from arriving on time. Such rationalizing is usually acceptable to the other person, but it's untrue. Rationalizing becomes a habit—and never solves a problem.

Tip 701. Don't Project the Blame onto Someone or Something Else.

Here's how such projections go: If you write a weak report, you claim that it was the fault of the manager who didn't give you enough information. If you take poor photographs, you decide that it was because of poor lighting or because you had the wrong kind of camera. If the proposal is late, it's because you had a computer crash. The lead-in to most of these projections is, "Yeah, but..." Listen to kids; they're experts at "yeah, but he/she/they..."

Tip 702. Avoid Superficial Acceptance.

Some people toss aside criticism, giving little real thought to change or prevention. "Sorry 'bout that!" "Uh-oh. I blew it." "Can't win 'em all." "Better luck next time." "If that's the biggest mistake of my life, I'll be sainted someday." Such a pop-off may get others off their back for the moment, but it doesn't resolve a recurring problem.

Tip 703. Don't Pretend It's "No Big Deal."

Do you remember back in high school when a friend didn't win the student council election? His response may have been, "It doesn't matter. I really don't think I would have had time to do all the committee stuff anyway." Trying to avoid hurt by pretending indifference allows someone to save face, but it doesn't change the criticism or the situation. Withdrawal or passive acceptance can become a habit-forming response to all of life.

Tip 704. Don't Go Home and Yell at the Dog.

Psychologists call this reaction "displacement." That is, you're angry with a customer who says you're not servicing her account properly and threatens to take her business elsewhere. Instead of dealing with the comment, you go home and yell at your spouse, your kids, or your neighbors to vent your frustration.

Tip 705. Guard Against Overreaction on Your Sore Spots.

Know your own hot buttons. If you know you're always late and you hate being late, chances are that when somebody criticizes you for being late, you're going to overreact. You're going to either fly into a rage, yell, scream, deny, or counterattack by accusing the criticizer of something else. Why? Because she hit a sore spot—something that you yourself don't like about your own behavior or attitude. The totally unreasonable reaction represents rage directed at yourself. Instead, breathe deeply and wait for control.

Tip 706. Maintain Your Emotional Equilibrium.

When criticism is unexpected, it feels like a punch in the gut. Humiliated, we don't speak up to defend ourselves or state an opposing view because we're embarrassed to find ourselves in the situation at all. Particularly if our integrity is questioned, we're hurt or angry that someone has even brought up the issue. Tears may well up. You may yell or curse, throw things, slam doors, slap desks, slam down phones, or stalk out of meetings.

Or you may do the opposite: You may turn inward with undeserved self-blame and become depressed or resign yourself to the fact that you have to "put up with" the situation. All such responses are inappropriate as either short-term or long-term reactions. Instead, take the time to calm down. Breathe deeply or play with a prop like your eyeglasses, your smartphone, your keys, or your laptop. Take a brisk walk, hit a golf ball, or otherwise change your surroundings. Do whatever it takes to regain your emotional balance so that you can think clearly and act deliberately.

Tip 707. Be Willing to Accept Responsibility Without Accepting Blame.

The higher you go in an organization, the more frequently you'll receive criticism for things that you did not have direct involvement in. To a customer, *you* are the company. Have some of these stock phrases ready when you must take responsibility without taking blame:

- "I'll check into that situation, determine what happened, and correct the problem."
- "I'm not sure who handled that project, but I'll see that your concern is addressed."
- "You're correct. Such a situation should never have happened."
- "This result is disappointing. There must be a solution—I'll do my best to find it."
- "I agree that we have to change things to improve X."

To assume a position of power requires broad shoulders. Can you imagine the CEO of a billion-dollar corporation responding to criticism about the poor performance of the company with a comment like, "Well, it's not my fault; *they* did it"?

Tip 708. Avoid Taking All Criticism as "Absolute Truth."

Many criticisms are subjective: "You don't respond enthusiastically when your team's ideas are accepted for an award. Aren't you a team player?" or, "You haven't taken any initiative for your own career growth." Only you know if such opinions ring true. If someone doesn't offer convincing evidence of his position, don't feel compelled to take his assessment as gospel truth. Even if he's in a position of authority, that position does not give him a corner on absolute truth about your motivations or attitudes. Some things are not observable or measurable by others. Don't let attempts to label those feelings or motivations devastate you.

Tip 709. Separate Opinions from Descriptions.

Opinions about what you're doing are subjective; descriptions are factual comments about what you said or did. When someone gives you opinions, ask for supporting details to determine whether their opinions are accurate. If someone says you're "lazy," that you "don't care about your job," or that you "have a bad attitude," then you need to know specific actions and behaviors that create such an impression. Ask for examples. If necessary, guess what the person may be referring to and ask for confirmation.

Example of criticism: "You seldom follow instructions. Sometimes I wonder where your focus is. You seem preoccupied half the time. What's bothering you?"

> *Ask for specifics.* "What instructions are you referring to? Which projects are affected?"
> *Offer specifics and ask for confirmation.* "Are you talking about the travel arrangements for the last two conventions?"
> *Ask for more elaboration of any kind.* "Do you think we could have found a cheaper fare? Is that your concern? Do you notice specific situations where you think I'm more or less capable of following your instructions? Do you think we have more confusion when the task is a hurried one? Or, do you mean even on daily projects?"

With specifics, you can correct someone's assumptions about those situations or change those actions. But it's next to impossible to respond appropriately to a subjective opinion without collecting the person's supporting detail.

Tip 710. Listen to Someone's Feedback Without Interruption.

If you interrupt someone, the exchange quickly escalates into a full-blown argument. Instead, let the other person finish completely what she intends to say. Then ask questions, collect details about opinion statements, and finally present your own interpretation of the facts or your own position.

Tip 711. Consider the Source.

After you've identified someone's intentions—destructive or constructive?—then consider the source of the criticism in more detail. Is this person qualified to judge your actions, attitude, or performance? Does he have the appropriate academic or job training, the experience in similar situations, and the opportunity to compare your actions with those of others? Is she basing her comments on an isolated incident, or has she observed you over a long period of time? This assessment should tell you how valid the comments are.

When the source of the criticism is vague, probe further. People who don't like confrontation often couch their own comments in claims such as, "I've heard others say that...," or, "Rumors around here are that...," or, "People are upset because..." Probe for the true source: "It would be helpful to know how much credence I can put in that comment. Exactly who is saying that?" "I could figure out the basis of that feedback if I knew where those comments were coming from." "Without knowing who has actually said what specifically, I can't really take any corrective action. I need specifics."

When the person identifies the source, then you can evaluate the comment appropriately.

Tip 712. Consider the Emotional Climate.

When others criticize you, evaluate the sincerity and validity of their comments by gauging their emotional condition at the moment. Are they angry at someone else? Are they afraid of the consequences of a particular action? Are they upset because of a missed deadline? Do they fear they'll look bad because of your action? If any of these extra pressures are part of the climate, let them cool off and handle the immediate situation before taking their criticism at face value.

Tip 713. Ask Yourself if Others Have Made the Same Observations.

Before you disregard someone's criticism as unfounded, consider whether you've heard the same comments from other sources. If your boss has commented on your "procrastinating with your projects," has your spouse also complained that you've been promising to clean out the garage since last summer? Have your kids complained that you keep saying you'll take them to the ballpark but never find time? Has the United Way chairperson called several times to ask for the list of names on your subcommittees? Do you have late charges assessed for overdue bills? Have colleagues moved ahead on their own while waiting for you "to get back to them"? Take a hint.

Tip 714. Agree with the Criticism.

If we're honest, most of us will have to admit from time to time that some negative feedback is accurate. For example, the boss says, "You're late with your status report again." Kelly responds: "You're right. It was due last Friday. I always seem to try to make a few more appointments on Friday than I can realistically handle and then wind up with insufficient time to do the report at the end of the day." Chances are, the conversation will end there. The other person often just wants acknowledgment that there is a problem and that you accept responsibility for it.

However, if Kelly responds: "Yeah, it was late, but I was just trying to make a few more calls. You want us to meet quota on the calls, don't you?" the boss would probably respond, "Yes, but this report has nothing to do with meeting quota. We've got to have the report for planning purposes. Other people manage to get theirs in on time." And the conversation will escalate from there.

What could be simpler? Agree with the essence of the feedback (even if you don't agree with the comments in their entirety). Then state what you will do differently. The pressure is off immediately. The other person doesn't feel compelled to keep pointing out the problem, and you don't feel compelled to keep refuting it and losing credibility.

A second way to agree is to state that you understand what the other person is saying. This doesn't mean that you agree with *what* that person has said; it means that you have listened well. Example: "Okay, I think I know where you're coming from. You've seen me reprimand two or three of my telemarketers for forgetting to mention this month's special, and you think I don't give enough praise because you've never heard me comment on what they do well. Is that what you're telling me?" Get the person's confirmation that you have correctly interpreted his comments.

Then state your own view of the situation, which may or may not be the same. For example, "I don't see my behavior in that light. I know there can be different perceptions in situations like this. Here's my view of what happened...," or, "I think we probably have a fundamental difference of opinion about how those situations should be handled. I'll keep your comments in mind next time." In either case, you have accepted—not interrupted or argued with—the criticizer's comments.

What if the other person's perceptions are blatantly wrong? You have a third option for agreeing: Agree with the person's right to an opinion. State something like this: "I understand that you think my strategy with this client is wrong. You want me to try to submit a proposal for the equipment, and you think I've been dragging my feet. I disagree that a formal proposal is the best way to handle this account, and I've given you my reasons. But I accept your opinion. Which way would you like me to handle it—your way or mine?"

Finally, you can agree in principle. That is, maybe the other person has compared your performance to an abstract ideal that no one could meet. You can agree in principle on the goals or the desirability of certain actions or performance in a perfect world. For example, someone has criticized how you've handled an irate customer. You might respond: "Well, I agree that with signs posted about these policies, our customers would be more likely to accept our position about needing a deposit," or, "Well, I agree we shouldn't let a customer leave angry," or, "You're right. It would have been better if I had thought to remind the customer that her company had paid these deposits in the past."

Agreeing with the other person's criticism or agreeing that the other person has a right to express a critical or opposing opinion is a powerful response.

Tip 715. Ask for Thinking Time.

If you're unsure whether you agree or disagree with someone's criticism, ask for time to think: "I understand what you've said, but I'm not sure I agree with your interpretation of the facts. I'd like some time to think over what you've said. Could we talk again later this afternoon?" This reflection time will allow you to present your own position in a much more thoughtful, logical way. It adds credibility to your response because it's not a "gut reaction," but rather one that you've considered fully. Such a discussion also minimizes the chance for escalation.

Tip 716. Express Regret About the Results of a Situation.

Even though you may not be the cause of something the criticizer mentions, you can always express regret for the situation. "I know you were expecting the shipment on Friday. I'm sorry you were delayed in finishing the project." With this comment, you did not say you were responsible—only that you understand the other person's frustration over being delayed. "I understand the client may cancel the contract over this issue. I hate that. They've spent thousands of dollars with us. It's too bad he insists on that kind of volume discount." With this comment, you did not say that you mishandled the account—only that you regret the client is threatening to cancel. There's a big difference. Empathy with a situation costs nothing and paints you as a reasonable, understanding person.

Tip 717. Limit the Criticism to Your Goals While Discarding the Unusable.

Changing takes time, energy, and attention. If someone has criticized you for something other than a simple mistake—such as your lifestyle, your attitude, or your personality—then change will take considerable effort. Evaluate the payoff before you decide to tackle monumental change. What are your personal goals? For example, if the criticizer has said that you're a selfish person, do you care? Do you want to become a more generous person? If that's not a personal goal, forget the criticism and save your energy. If the criticizer says that you're disorganized, and having a messy, disorganized desk doesn't bother you, forget the comment. Accept her opinion, state that your disorganization is not causing you or others any problem in life, and then forget the comment.

Tip 718. Thank the Criticizer for Helpful Comments.

When you know that someone has your best interests at heart or when he is criticizing you for a simple mistake, accept the comment graciously. Yes, maybe the person could offer the comment in a more positive way, and yes, maybe the person has failed to acknowledge her own part in a difficulty, but if the comments have benefited you in some way, say so.

"Thank you for letting me know that this was a problem rather than just taking it to my boss. I appreciate your coming to me first." "I appreciate your perspective on how the situation should have been handled. I'll give it more thought in the future." "Your points are well taken." "I can see how that situation might cause real grief with a bigger customer. I'll be more careful." "I know this discussion was difficult for you, too. I appreciate your caring enough to mention the issue to me." That's class!

Tip 719. Ask How the Other Person Would Have Handled the Situation.

In a matter-of-fact, not belligerent, tone, ask a boss or peers who criticize you how they would have handled a similar situation. Then listen. If your purpose is to argue with their answer, you'll only escalate the situation. But if your purpose is to learn from their comments, you'll present yourself as a reasonable, self-assured, open individual. And, at the least, if the criticizer can't respond with concrete suggestions, your asking and his reflection may change his perception about your competence in the situation.

Tip 720. Change the Mistakes That You Alone Control.

If the feedback concerns a mistake, simply go about finding ways to solve the problem. Everybody is entitled to honest mistakes, and everybody is obligated to correct them when they're pointed out. Move into a problem-solving mode rather than wallowing in self-pity: "But nobody told me." "But the situation changed." "Yeah, but I didn't mean to." "How was I supposed to know that X would happen?" "Your instructions were unclear." "You couldn't have done any better yourself." "Life isn't fair." "Nobody appreciates what I do around here."

Tip 721. Rechannel Your Emotions to Concentrate on Your Mission.

What are your goals concerning the project, the job, or the position? The anger caused by an unjustified criticism can be put to good use with positive action. Psychologists offer the same advice to those suffering from a tragedy. The parent whose child is murdered by a drunk driver works through her grief by serving on the citywide campaign to enforce drunk-driving laws or organizing an escort taxi service for New Year's Eve parties. The same principle can work for you with criticism. Put that emotional energy into improving your skill, attitude, or behavior.

Tip 722. Agree on a Plan for Change and Set Timelines.

If the person who has offered the criticism is an authority figure whom you must please (your boss, a team leader, or the chairperson of a committee), then after your exchange of viewpoints or positions, agree to a new course of action. Ask for or offer specifics. Gain agreement, and set timelines.

Tip 723. Eliminate Bitterness as an Alternative.

If someone suggests that because you haven't had broad managerial experience, you're unable to supervise a new unit, you're going to find it difficult to reconstruct your work history. Instead of growing bitter at someone's bias, choose another alternative. Either change your goal, change his opinion, or decide that this person's assessment doesn't count. Bitterness over things that you can't change creeps into the crevices like a cancer until it colors all your interactions with others.

Tip 724. Keep Yourself Physically and Spiritually Strong.

Our emotional stability for dealing with negative feedback is closely related to our physical and spiritual condition at the time. If you're feeling lousy with a sinus infection, irritable because you haven't gotten a good night's sleep in a week, or depressed because of your lack of worthwhile personal goals, criticisms will cut deeper than normal. Guard your outlook on life and your physical ability to meet challenges.

Tip 725. Recall Your List of Strengths.

If you're not a great supervisor, remind yourself that you're a great father. If you can't learn to sell, then remind yourself how well you manage projects. If you can't speak well before large groups, recall how well you give advice one on one. If necessary, write out a list of your strengths and post it where you can refer to it quickly in moments of high emotional crisis. Focus on your strengths if you lose your equilibrium. Strive for balance.

Tip 726. Don't Take Yourself Too Seriously.

Do you really expect to go through life without having anyone differ with you or express a negative opinion of you or your work? Whatever the matter, is it a life-or-death issue? Will it make a good story to tell your family and friends? What difference will it make a year from now? Play the worst-case scenario. If you can live with that worst case, forget it. Have a good laugh at your own expense.

13

Giving Advice or Coaching That Someone Can Really Use

Men give away nothing so liberally as their advice.
—François Duc de La Rochefoucauld

A word to the wise ain't necessary—it's the stupid ones that need the advice.

—Bill Cosby

Nothing is more confusing than the fellow who gives good advice but sets a bad example.

—No attribution

A mentor is someone who allows you to see the hope inside yourself.

—Oprah Winfrey

Be careful when you give advice—somebody might take it.

—No attribution

Advice is seldom welcome, and those who need it most like it least.

—Samuel Johnson

Advice after injury is like medicine after death.

—Danish proverb

Unlike giving criticism, most people enjoy giving advice. Heartfelt advice about issues of vital concern oozes out like so much salve from a tightly compressed tube. The difficulty comes in determining whether the person wants to be healed, anointing the right sore spot, making sure the medication is appropriate to the problem, and recapping the lid after the initial diagnosis and treatment.

Tip 727. Know Your Own Motives for Offering Advice.

People like to give advice and solicited feedback for any number of reasons: to bolster their own egos; to show off their knowledge or wisdom; to control others; to "prove" something; to "get back at" others who're excluded and won't have access to their privileged advice; to help; to lessen another's pain or speed the learning curve; or to show empathy and support. Some of these reasons are praiseworthy; others are not. Knowing your own motivations helps you "cap the flow" when tempted to spew off advice too frequently.

Tip 728. Don't Sneak Advice into Informational Statements.

Why isn't advice always welcome? It often makes others feel wrong, dumb, or inadequate, and thus defensive. *Advice:* "I think you should go ahead and start the meeting." *Information:* "It's twenty past seven." *Advice:* "Don't you realize that if you're going to get a summer intern in your department, you'll have to put in a request by February?" *Information:* "Most summer interns are placed by February." *Advice:* "I'd think twice before asking Gerald to head that campaign." *Information:* "Gerald headed our campaign three years ago, and he resigned right in the middle of it without even giving us an explanation."

Other unwelcome forms of advice can creep into your conversations when you may think you're actually comforting someone: For example: "Just take it easy and relax. There's no reason to worry." Although the intention is noble, the result can be that the friend thinks you're not taking his situation seriously. If such impromptu advice drips from your lips, try to catch yourself in midsentence and retract it.

Tip 729. Nudge People to Ask for Advice, but Be Willing to Wait.

You may edge into advice if you see that another person has a problem or difficulty: "I noticed that the phone call from your boss upset you. Do you want to talk about it?" "It seems that you've had to redo these reports for several months now. Do you want to brainstorm ways that we might improve the layout before you submit them?" "Hey, if you want to talk about the issue, let me know. I can be all ears this afternoon." Such nudges let people know that you're available to offer feedback. If they don't take you up on your offer, squelch the urge to speak up anyway.

Tip 730. Identify What Kind of Advice the Other Person Wants.

If you can't tell what the other person wants by how she introduces a subject or asks a question, ask a few questions yourself. Does the person want to know how you did something? What you've observed others do well with good results? Key information and facts? Suggested options of which she is unaware? Your opinion? Help with brainstorming alternatives? A double-check on her reasoning? Asking specifically what the other person wants will both save you time and produce better results.

Tip 731. Remember the Purpose of Advice or Feedback.

Your most important function may be to stimulate the other person's thinking and help him formulate options. You provide a sounding board by listening for gaps in logic, missing information, tangent trails, or dangers lurking out of sight along paths that a person has decided to take. Being a good coach or advisor is often like being a good journalist—you listen for and investigate the what, who, when, where, why, how, and how much.

If the advice seeker has provided all these answers, then your job may be to expand the answers, rethink the answers, or consider more suitable answers. Often, you as coach play the part of a professor guiding graduate students in their doctoral research, asking questions that will lead the students down new paths of investigation rather than answering questions and closing doors in their face. Be careful to keep the other person's motives and goals (not your own) in mind. Otherwise, the feedback will be useless to him.

Tip 732. Stifle the Urge to Give Premature Advice.

When others delve into their psyches or souls to access and pass on information to you as a basis for your advice, they reflect on what they're saying. That reflection itself can be helpful in leading them to their own answers. Don't stifle their thinking by jumping straight to "the answer" to their dilemma.

Tip 733. Continue to Test the Water as You Go Along.

If the first advice you offer makes the other person defensive, wade no further. Let the other person give you more information about her situation and goal. Then stick your toe in to test again: "Is what I'm saying helpful?" "Does any of this make sense to you?" "Is this line of questioning keeping us on target?" "Let me know if I'm off base in my reasoning here." You don't want to plunge into the rapids and leave your friend standing on the beach.

Tip 734. Ask Provocative Questions.

Since people believe their own data and trust their own instincts far more readily, lead them through the proper analysis of a situation by asking provocative questions:

- "How is what you're doing working for you?"
- "Is this where you want to be?"
- "What are the real facts in this situation—honestly?"
- "What assumptions are you making? Are those really valid?"
- "What issues are you avoiding?"
- "Would every objective observer in the situation agree with you about what you've just told me?"
- "What options do you see for the situation?"
- "What are your choices for each option? What are the advantages of each option?"
- "How can you manage the downside of each option?"

Knowing the right questions can be far more powerful than offering the right answers.

Tip 735. Call Attention to Past Successes.

Has the friend, colleague, client, or family member dealt with similar challenges in the past? If so, call attention to the relevant details of those situations to help him analyze the current issue or problem and draw parallels. You can toss in your insights about what made him successful in the past and what parallels you see as encouragement for the current situation. Often, what worked well in the past deserves a repeat performance. The person has simply forgotten his lines. As a trusted advisor, simply call out the cues from offstage.

Tip 736. Ask What Would Nido Do.

When I was a young author, speaking invitations began to come my way from major corporations. Although I'd started a successful training business as a result of my published books, I knew little about the professional speaking industry. So when I attended the first few conventions of the National Speakers Association, one particular name kept popping up—a guy by the name of Nido. He needed no last name. Through the years, Nido Qubein, chairman of Great Harvest Bread Company and president of High Point University, became a good friend and an informal mentor. When I've been puzzled about some business decision in the past two decades, I've often caught myself asking, "What would Nido do?"

When you're advising a perplexed colleague, sometimes it helps to remove her from the fray by suggesting that she imagine what someone else would do in her shoes. That "someone else" might be the former person in her position, her boss, her grandfather, her competitor, her hero, or Superwoman. Force her to think creatively about how a star performer would react in a similar situation.

Tip 737. Ask for Clarification on Points You Don't Understand.

You don't want to give the impression of judging the other person. However, before you offer advice, you have to understand his situation. If you don't see the cause, the logic, or the meaning of something, ask in a nonthreatening tone: "Explain to me again why you think that..." "I don't understand what X has to do with Y." "Help me understand the difference between option 1 and option 3." "I think I'm missing something here. Larry said X, and now you said Y. That seems to be a contradiction."

Tip 738. Feel Free to Offer the Opposing View.

If people want only agreement with and affirmation of what they intend to do or what they believe, oblige them. If, on the other hand, you think they sincerely want advice, feel free to give an honest opinion—with tact, of course: "That alternative just doesn't seem to stand up." "Your analysis doesn't feel right to me." "I'm afraid I don't see it that way." "I think you ought to reconsider one more time."

Tip 739. Use the Appropriate Tone.

Offer your feedback as suggestions, ideas, recommendations, considerations, or opinions. Avoid stating opinions as facts, ultimatums, solutions, directives, or musts.

Tip 740. Lead the Other Person Through a Self-Critique.

If the other person's goals and yours match, you can play the part of coach with the right language. Your most successful gambit will be leading the other person through an insightful self-critique to self-motivation. My graduate professor used this approach in my student-teaching days. After each session, she'd pose these three questions: "What did you like about how the session went?" "If you did it over, what would you do differently?" "What information, help, or direction do you need from me?"

Try variations of these questions in other situations where you're responsible for another person's results: "Do you see a problem or difficulty?" "Are you getting the results you want?" "Can you describe the problem, difficulty, and result as you see it?" "What makes the problem worse?" "What helps the situation?" "What needs to change, improve, or happen differently? "What kind of help do you need from me?" "What action do you plan to take?"

Tip 741. Make War Stories Realistic.

War stories are usually welcome. If you're successful, rich, and happy, others often want "this-is-how-I-did-it" stories. But they want realistic, not simplistic, ones. Don't look back from your lofty perch and throw out tidbits of encouragement and how-to's—just enough to tempt other people. They want practical approaches, successful strategies, and usable information. If you want raving fans, be straightforward and honest, not glib and condescending.

Tip 742. Go Around the "Friend-of-Mine" Framing.

Sometimes people hesitate to present their own quandaries, and instead frame them as if they belong to a friend: "I've got a friend over in Accounting who just can't seem to keep her mind on her work. She's having some health problems and marital problems, and she thinks her boss won't be flexible about her hours. What do you think . . . ?" If you go along with the ploy and try to give secondhand advice to the person in need, your advice will typically be off base.

Why? Because you have to make too many assumptions without being free to ask questions and probe. If all indications say that you're talking to the "friend" herself, blow her cover and get to the heart of the matter. "Madison, you can be frank with me. Are we talking about you or someone else?" Such a probe lets others know it's okay to be straight—that you accept them rather than judge them.

Tip 743. Share "I Once Did/Thought/Had" Stories with Those Who Need Advice but Won't Ask for It.

For example, "You know, I once had the same difficulty with a client in the oil-and-gas industry. For some reason, they considered the delivery terms unacceptable. So I offered to do X if they would do Y. That arrangement seemed to address their concerns, so they moved ahead with the deal. Now whenever any client brings that up, I make the X offer again." Such stories have a testimonial ring, show others explicitly how you accomplished the good result, and take the pressure off them to actually follow the advice. Such advice comes across as helpful, not pushy.

Tip 744. Use Turn-Over-the-Keys Phrasing with Your Suggestions.

If you do give explicit advice, give ownership as well. That is, along with any concrete ideas and suggestions that you provide, make sure that your phrasing clarifies that the responsibility for accepting—or not accepting—the advice rests with the new owner. Give him accountability for results and success.

- "If I were going to make this decision, I would probably do . . . But the final choice has to be yours."
- "You may want to consider X when you make this decision."
- "In the end, of course, this has to be your decision."
- "You have to live with this decision day in and day out, so it has to feel right to you."
- "Whatever you decide, I'll support you in it."
- "It's a tough decision, I know. But I'm confident that you'll make the best choice."

Tip 745. Avoid Pushy Language and a Pushy Attitude.

Don't say, "I think you should...," "You simply have to...," or, "That'll never work. What you ought to do is..." Instead, try, "Here's an idea...," "What do you think about...?" "Here's an approach that could work...," or, "Well, here's what I think..." Remember that it's the other person's decision, career, pain, joy, life.

Tip 746. Don't Offer a Money-Back Guarantee.

Not even the most qualified professional advisors guarantee results. Trainers never promise their athletes that if they train eight hours a day, they'll win an Olympic medal. Stockbrokers issue disclaimers with their investment advice. Pharmaceutical companies advertise that their medications may cause serious side effects and warn patients to stop taking them immediately if reactions appear. Guard against letting someone take your advice as a sure thing and bank all she has, emotionally, physically, or spiritually, on the hoped-for results. Life offers few guarantees. If you're smart, neither will you.

14

Getting Advice or Coaching That's Helpful

Many receive advice; few profit by it.

—Publilius Syrus

Advice is what we ask for when we already know the answer but wish we didn't.

—Erica Jong

No one wants advice—only corroboration.

—John Steinbeck

Advice is like mushrooms. The wrong kind can prove fatal.

—No attribution

Asking for advice is how some people trap you into expressing an opinion they can disagree with.

—Franklin P. Jones

Always listen to the advice of others—it won't do you any harm, and it will make them feel better.

—No attribution

Three cases where supply exceeds demand are taxes, trouble, and advice.

—No attribution

Listen to advice and accept instruction, that you may gain wisdom for the future.

—Old Testament, Proverbs 19:20

We don't have difficulty finding people who want to offer advice; the problem comes in finding the right people with advice that's profitable. When you're on the receiving end, the trick is to guide your advisors down the paths you want to travel with the appropriate questions, the right details, and a correct analysis. These guidelines should help you decide how to profit from—or reject—the advice you receive.

Tip 747. Develop a Feedback Obsession.

When you look into your lover's eyes and whisper, "I love you," what do you expect to hear in return? Silence? If that happens often, your relationship's in trouble. Yet every day that awkward silence can be "heard" when you say to your boss, "It's done," and you hear silence in response.

So if that's happening to you and you're serious about getting feedback in your new job or advice on that next big assignment, take matters into your own hands. Make it easy for others to offer advice and feedback—even if it's negative—by asking key questions, either periodically or after you complete key projects:

- "What ideas do you have for making this project even more successful next time?"
- "What would you change if you were handling this account?"
- "I'm always interested in self-improvement. What skills would you suggest I add to my developmental list for the next 12 months?"

Take the information you gather during such conversations and create your personal action plan. Without feedback in marriage, lovers drift toward divorce. Without feedback between friends, they become only acquaintances. Without feedback at work, employees disengage.

Tip 748. Don't Wait for the *Big* Issue.

Solicit advice on any reasonable issue. If you've elected to become part of a formal mentoring program, you may hesitate to schedule time with your coach, mentor, or friend because you don't have an important, looming challenge facing you. That's a mistake. Advice comes in preventive doses as well as cures. Select a topic for discussion that you'd like to learn more about: finances, legal issues, governmental compliance in your industry, cross-functional responsibilities, life balance, productivity tips, strategic communication.

Put together a couple of questions for your advice giver: "Could you give me a five-minute overview of how X relates to my job?" "What are the five most important things I should know about Y?" "What are three pitfalls I should be aware of regarding Z?" "Can you give me your three best lessons learned about X?" "Can you point me to the three best books or other online resources to get up to speed on Z?"

Tip 749. Be Firm When You Don't Want Advice; Don't Give Mixed Signals.

If you don't want advice, say so firmly, but gently. "Thank you for sharing that experience with me. I'll keep that in mind as I investigate my options." "Thanks for letting me know how you feel. I do think that I'm going to have to follow my own gut on this one, however."

Don't ask for advice when what you really want is affirmation. When you state a position in a wistful, hesitant tone or express reservations about a course of action, people often interpret that wavering or hesitancy as indecision. They then offer "help." If you're giving ambiguous messages and then resent interference, be firm: "I've already made my decision. I'd rather not discuss it any longer," Or, "I have the information I need, and I'll be making my decision next week." Those who care may fear that you've made the wrong choice; assure them tactfully that you'll handle the consequences.

Tip 750. Don't Signal the Answer You Want.

Most people will do their best to tell you what they think you want to hear. That's why it's important to give the other person permission to disagree with you, to give you "upsetting" facts, or to offer "contradictory" opinions. If you want unbiased feedback, ask your question or pose your position objectively. "I've just quit my job to set up my own consulting practice. Do you think I can make a go of computer troubleshooting as a consultant in this area?" If the listener has a heart at all, she'll offer encouragement and reaffirm the decision. On the other hand, if you, as an advice seeker, want a real opinion, try this phrasing: "In this area of the city, how much need do you think there is for a consultant with my speciality doing troubleshooting?"

Tip 751. Ask Specifically for the Kind of Advice You Need.

Do you want ideas? Insights? Data? Instruction? Reactions? Affirmations? Personal experience? If you include that information when you ask for feedback, you'll save yourself and the other person much time and often hurt feelings—yours and his. If you want someone to ask probing questions and double-check your thinking, say so. If you just want moral support for a decision you've already made, say so.

Tip 752. Ask for Comparisons Based on Criteria You Understand.

Your "excellent" may be someone else's "good." When you ask the hotel concierge to recommend a "good" restaurant, do you mean one with good *food*? A nice *atmosphere*? Reasonable *prices*? Or *quiet enough for business discussions*? If you've ever been vague, then you know the results can be disastrous.

Ask the advisor to make comparisons on specific terms. Not, "Do you think Cary Martin would work well with the other people on this project?" but, "Do you think Cary Martin or Cheryl Glass would work better with the others on this team?" Not, "I'm in charge of refreshments, and I was wondering if you expect a good attendance at this conference," but, "I'm in charge of the refreshments, and I was wondering how many you expect to attend the conference. We had about 200 last year. Do you expect more or fewer than that?"

Tip 753. Avoid Giving So Much Information That You "Freeze" Your Advisor.

If you give people too much "background" information, you may discourage them from even trying to understand enough to attempt to advise you. A greater danger in overloading the other person is passing on so many biased statements, invalid assumptions, and unsupported claims that she can't get a new perspective on the issue—she sees the same things you do. If you push the same raw vegetables through the blender, you're likely to get the same kind of vegetable juice when you finish.

Tip 754. Don't State Your Opinion or Position and Then Argue if the Other Person Disagrees.

Arguing with the answer or position offered doesn't mean that you want to win; it doesn't even mean that you disagree. Unfortunately, however, people often think it does. Sometimes any hint of disagreement translates to displeasure and often shuts the advisor down. To counter this tendency, you have to tread lightly at the beginning. Let the other person get the position stated, and then carefully point out—or simply ask about—gaps in logic.

Tip 755. Stifle Objections and Use Accepting Phrases.

Even though you may not have asked for conclusions, you'll probably get them. If you begin to raise too many objections at the beginning, you'll stall your advisor. You can't be choosy about advice after it starts to flow. Use accepting phrases and let it come: "That's a new approach." "I don't think that option had occurred to me." "That's a different way to look at it." "I'm not sure I understand your point, but keep going." "Can you be more specific about why you think my approach was illogical?"

Tip 756. Lead Your Advisor to Argue Both Sides.

On the other hand, for best results, you do want to hear and consider both sides of an issue. Rather than arguing against an advisor's perspective, simply ask for opposing views and let him argue both sides: "Would anybody with your same expertise disagree with what you've said?" "Would everybody in the industry agree with that position?" "Do you yourself have any concerns at all that this approach won't work?" "Do you think I should look out for anything along the way?" "Do you have any cautions for me if I do exactly as you say?" "Are there any extenuating circumstances that might alter your opinion?" "What's the downside?" Let the advisor play devil's advocate so that you hear both sides without seeming to be rude or ungrateful for his best opinion.

Tip 757. Don't Overlook Good Advice Because of Its Packaging.

Some people ignore advice simply because they've heard it before (a big clue that it might be on target!), find it "to be expected," consider it too complex, or think it too simple. But the repetitious can be true. The "expected" may be reality staring you in the face. The complex can be worth the effort. The simple may be profound.

Tip 758. Ask the Right Source.

This sounds obvious, but actually few people are so methodical in their quest for advice that they choose work and play advisors with much forethought.

Many people ask advice from whoever happens to be available and willing to listen. If the situation has grave consequences, choose career advisors as carefully as you choose doctors. The pain can turn out to be similar and the result as grave.

Tip 759. Consider Multiple Advisors Rather Than One "Perfect" Advisor.

Rarely does one person have the full scoop on anything. And even if she did, finding that perfect advisor could be extremely difficult. You need someone who is interested but not necessarily biased in the situation. You need someone who shows concern but does not become too emotionally invested. You need someone who is knowledgeable but not overbearing. You need someone with specialized expertise, but who can understand the big picture as well.

If you can't find one person who suits the situation on all counts, ask for advice from several sources. Pay particular attention to points where they agree and disagree. Then analyze their areas of disagreement in light of their history, educational training, career success, personal biases, and knowledge of your personal goals.

Tip 760. Evaluate the Credibility of Your Source.

Some people get sidetracked by personality instead of credibility. They tend to value and accept advice from those they like and discard advice from those they don't like. You may want to accept a *date* based on personality, but where your career or your future is concerned, make credibility the stronger criterion.

A particular client organization of mine has a staff psychologist who from time to time spends a few weeks shadowing key executives to observe their management styles and offer advice for their professional development. He has the prerequisite academic credentials, understands management's objectives, and knows each of the executives personally. When most people greet each other, they say, "Hi. How are you doing?" With Ed, they say, "Hi, Ed. How am I doing?" When Ed speaks, they listen. He has earned credibility.

Is your coach or advisor in a position to know? Is she successful at doing what you want to learn? Does she have access to facts that you think are relevant?

Tip 761. Look for a Match in Philosophy and Values.

Very little advice—other than facts or observations of a situation—can be separated from one's values and perspectives on life in general. For example, which weighs more on the decision concerning a job change: Possibility of increasing responsibilities? Better salary? Job security? Or a spouse's reluctance to move across the country? Don't expect your advisor to be able to give you the final tally on all the issues involved. He can only help you *view* the items, not *score* them.

Tip 762. Tell People You're Shopping Around.

If—and only if—your advisor will ultimately know that you did or did not take her advice, state that subtly up front. Some people think that advice given should be advice taken. When they discover that you disregarded their advice, they feel rejected and upset. If you fear that may be the case, when you solicit advice, say something like: "I'm shopping for personal experience about how supervising at-home employees has worked for various managers. What's your opinion on that arrangement?" Or, "I'm undecided about how to approach a client. I've asked several of our field reps how they handle the problem of X. I'm also interested in your expertise. If you were in my place, how do you think you'd handle the situation?" Then later, if you don't follow their advice, they assume that someone else was more persuasive, that the details somehow changed, that theirs was a minority opinion, or that you weren't particularly committed to following anyone's advice.

Tip 763. Thank People for Their Solicited Advice.

Be specific; tell them exactly what information or insights will be most helpful to you. Specific thanks sounds more sincere than general comments. Even if you didn't find the advice particularly helpful or insightful, thank people for their time and the effort involved. After all, they could have been eating, sleeping, playing, or chatting online with their friends.

15

Negotiating so Everyone Feels Like a Winner

Let us never negotiate out of fear. But let us never fear to negotiate.

—John F. Kennedy

Compromise may be man's best friend.

—George Will

Nothing astonishes men so much as common sense and plain dealing.

—Ralph Waldo Emerson

The man who says he is willing to meet you halfway is usually a poor judge of distance.

—Laurence J. Peter

Know how to ask. There is nothing more difficult for some people. Nor for others, easier.

—Baltasar Gracian

Nothing gives one person so much advantage over another as to remain cool and unruffled under all circumstances.

—Thomas Jefferson

Negotiations play a major part in our everyday work experience. We negotiate with coworkers, colleagues, and customers in accepting ideas and proposals, in winning jobs, in buying and selling products or services, and in resolving conflicts. Yet repetition of the task hasn't made it any easier. For centuries, negotiating in a formal setting has instilled fear in the hearts of people: the fear of intimidation and the fear of losing. Only recently have negotiators embraced the idea that all parties can walk away from a discussion as winners. And language plays a big part in setting the tone, shaping how people think and feel about working together, and dictating the final outcome.

Certainly, the economic meltdown and recession of 2008–2010 turned executives in the financial, auto, and housing industries into negotiators—whether they welcomed the role or not.

But former President George Herbert Walker Bush and his secretary of state, James Baker, probably did more to shape thinking about successful negotiations than any other pair of negotiators in modern history. Bush reasserted our security role in Panama, built the best relationship with Mexico in U.S. history, negotiated and signed the North American Free Trade Agreement, stood close to center stage in unifying Germany, remained resolute with regard to reshaping policies in South Africa, and held a careful balance on the sidelines during the collapse of the USSR. His finest hour was Desert Storm, when he assembled the largest coalition of nations in the history of the world to stand firm against Iraq's invasion of Kuwait. Although looking back two decades later at the ongoing Middle East unrest, critics might say that the negotiated peace in Iraq did not last, but that does not detract from his efforts to stop the invasion of Kuwait.

How did this pair triumph on so many negotiating fronts involving so many cultures and economies? The following tips will shed some light on this formidable process.

Tip 764. Avoid the Term *Negotiate* Whenever Possible.

The word *negotiate* implies a winner and a loser, or at best a compromise between two dissatisfied parties. Instead of "negotiating," use phrasing such as "come to an agreement," "work out a plan," or "arrive at a workable arrangement." Wording goes a long way in establishing a friendly atmosphere in which everybody feels like a winner.

Tip 765. Consider Several Kinds of Goals Before You Begin a Discussion.

To make sure you don't get sidetracked in talking, identify your primary goal, your immediate goals, your long-term goals, your "nice-to-haves," and your safeguards. Within each of these frameworks, set ranges. What is the "best" you can expect, and what is the "worst" position you can accept? Keep all of this in mind as you work toward agreement.

Tip 766. Research Your Position and the Situation.

Take the time and make the effort to support your position or requests. Read. Gather statistics. Talk to experts. Survey others for majority opinions. When you get ready to talk, you'll have adequate facts and opinions to support what you want. The more you know, the better the position you're in to negotiate a win for everybody involved.

Tip 767. Refuse to Negotiate with a Missing Person.

This technique has been perfected in car dealerships around the world. The rep who shows you the car always has to trot to the back room to see if the head honcho "will okay the deal you've cut." A more familiar version: An employee walks into your office and asks you to consider "sharing" an administrative assistant, proposing that the assistant work 40 percent of the time in your department and 60 percent of the time in his department. You discuss the division of labor and percentages back and forth and finally state "your best deal" for sharing salary and benefits.

Then the employee announces that everything you've negotiated is subject to approval by the boss. In effect, that means that your "best deal" now becomes the starting point for the next round of discussions after you learn "what the boss said." To avoid putting yourself in this one-down situation, don't begin to negotiate until you are talking to the person who has authority to make a final decision.

Tip 768. Use Tact in Finding the Real Decision Maker.

When you're unsure whether you're talking with the actual decision maker, check out the situation with comments and questions such as these:

- "If you and I come to some understanding, can we move ahead with the first step?"
- "If you and I can agree on the X issue, will anyone else have to okay the terms?"
- "Will you be making the decision alone, or is there someone else we should get input from?"

- "Do you deal with a committee or a team on matters like this?"
- "How exactly do things work in your organization—do individuals such as yourself make these decisions, or must they all go through a project team?"
- "Who else do we need to consult about the specifications on this project before we can come to final terms?"
- "I'm sure you'll be advising other people about your plans here—do you mind if I sit in on those talks?"
- "I'd be happy to provide backup information by sitting in on other meetings that may be necessary in your coming to a final decision."

Just be careful not to force the other person to admit to having no power.

Tip 769. Set Up a Cooperative Atmosphere.

When the other person feels like a loser in your discussions, you'll worsen your own position. Yes, work to get what you need, but also work to get the other person what he needs. Body language, tone, and word choice go a long way in establishing cooperation rather than competition.

Tip 770. Give Something at the Very Beginning.

When you start a discussion, be gracious enough to offer something for the good of the others involved: give them a small gift, buy them dinner, spend extra time with them, retweet their slogans online, post an endorsement online, give attention to their hobby or family, or concede a point. Thoughtfulness in any of these ways returns dividends. Giving something makes the other person feel as though she should reciprocate.

Tip 771. Ask Questions to Set the Tone for Mutual Advantage.

Some people fear being in a negotiating situation because they fear confrontation. So it's important to set the tone of a mutually rewarding discussion. Try questions like these:

- "What would you like to have as an outcome today?"
- "What things do you need from me?"
- "How can we help you in this situation?"
- "What are your goals?"
- "What things do you think we already have in common?"

- "What more can I tell you about my situation?"
- "What else can you tell me about your situation that would help me understand your perspective and your needs?"
- "What ideas do you have for generating a more workable solution?"

How do you know if you've come to a good, cooperative agreement? Everybody involved will think that the agreement is the best possible one. No one will feel worse off than before the agreement. Both people continue to have respect for the other and may even feel better about the other person. And finally, this agreement may result in even greater benefits than either of you thought possible.

Tip 772. Know How to Phrase Your Probing Questions.

Consider the difference in each of these pairs of questions:

"Do you mind if I come in an hour early every day next month so that I can leave early enough to take my son to soccer practice in the afternoons?"

versus

"Do you mind if I come in an hour early every day next month so that I can work without interruptions? I'd hate to leave things unfinished when I take off early to take my son to soccer practice."

"Can I wait to deliver his contract until I'm out for lunch?"

versus

"Would you like me to deliver this contract while I'm out for lunch?"

"Are you the only one who can make these kinds of decisions on bulk orders?"

versus

"Do all the decisions on bulk orders fall on your desk?"

Phrasing determines emphasis, and emphasis determines response.

Tip 773. Postpone Any Discussions When You're Surprised by a "Bomb Scare."

Here's the situation: You're trying to sell uniforms for servers at a large restaurant chain, along with your laundry service for the uniforms. Just as you've gathered around the conference table to discuss your prices, product, and service, the buyer-manager walks in and drops an e-mail on the table, saying that headquarters has just announced a new policy: uniforms are no longer mandatory at each restaurant. Individual managers of each restaurant can make the "uniform" decision for themselves.

In such a situation, what's the typical response to this sudden bombshell? The seller begins to make all kinds of offers to entice the other person and "save the deal." Beware. When you're suddenly surprised before negotiations are to begin, consider postponing your discussion until you have a chance to rethink your position and your plans. Take time to investigate the truth of the bombshell and its implications. A new situation warrants a new set of plans.

Tip 774. Send Up Trial Balloons Before "Getting Serious."

If you have something in mind that those on the other side may consider bizarre, you can always pose that idea or solution as an offhand suggestion and get a reaction. Try: "Well, you know we could always just...," or, "Frankly, the best way around all these issues would be to..." If the other person chokes, you'll be glad you didn't pose the solution as a "real" consideration. If the other person picks up the idea and plays with it, you can treat it seriously.

Tip 775. State Your Needs Up Front and Ask the Other Person to Do the Same.

You can both investigate invalid assumptions and find common areas of agreement before you tackle more difficult issues. Often people are surprised—pleasantly—that people's wants and needs are easier to satisfy than they had first assumed.

Tip 776. Mention *Everything* You Want Sooner Rather Than Later.

If you delay mentioning a key issue until later in the discussion, chances are that the other person will consider your doing so as an attempt to be deceptive. To avoid casting doubt on your intentions, start with all the issues on the table.

Tip 777. Focus on the Other Person's Needs First.

As you begin the discussion, ask what the other person wants and needs before you state your own goals. By demonstrating that you don't intend to run roughshod over the other person to get what you want, you'll build trust. Listen to what he says, ask questions about his needs and goals, and show respect. Once you've figured out how to get what he wants, he'll often be more helpful in getting you what you want.

Tip 778. Appreciate the Value of What You Have to Bargain.

Sometimes people undervalue what they have to trade. Don't forget the intangibles. Attach value to everything before you begin your discussions. For example, as an employee, you may own your own transportation to work, and so you can work early or late hours on special projects when asked without undue hardship. If that flexibility happens to be important to an employer, consider it a bargaining chip. Other assets of value include dependability, ethical behavior, responsiveness, contacts and networking opportunities, and emotional ownership—not to mention any number of other skills or attitudes. Take a fresh look at what you have to offer in any situation.

Tip 779. Dilute Your Weaknesses by Listing Them.

This principle works like an apology. If you apologize profusely for an error, chances are the other person will accept your apology graciously. At a minimum, the other person will stop ranting and raving about how you goofed and move on to the solution.

The same thing happens in negotiations. You lay your vulnerabilities on the line so that the other person doesn't have to recount them to you. Then the discussion moves on to focus on what you do bring to the table. For example, in interviewing for a job, the conversation might go like this: "I know I don't have the five years' sales experience you wanted, but I do speak three languages, and I think that fluency in building rapport will more than compensate for...," or, "What I have gained in lieu of sales experience is years of..."

Tip 780. Watch Others' Body Language When They Toss Out "Unimportant" Comments.

When people seem to throw "by the way" comments into the conversation ("Oh, I almost forgot...," "I forgot to tell you that...," "By the way, does it matter that..."), watch for hidden meanings. People will usually become stiff, nervous, and apprehensive about your response. Those subtle body changes should cue you that the comment may not be so insignificant after all. Investigate.

Tip 781. Bring Success Stories to the Table.

As you begin discussions about conflicts or needs, suggest that both of you relate ways in which you've seen other people solve the same problem or conflict you're facing. Tossing out these stories as alternatives offers a starting point for your own situation in a "safe" way—sharing them reminds both people that success is possible in a similar situation.

Tip 782. Draw a Definite Distinction Between Wanting to Agree and Having to Agree.

Make it clear to the other person—and then remind yourself frequently—that you *want* to come to an agreement, but never that you *must* come to an agreement. Any time you feel (or signal the other person) that you absolutely must make a deal, you'll obviously be at a disadvantage. In fact, you may start a rock slide.

Tip 783. Be the Caller When You're Negotiating by Phone.

As the initiator of a discussion, you have the edge—you have your notes in front of you, forethought, and control of timing. The person who is called has to play catch-up, and if she's not good "on her feet," she'll often fumble when she's caught off guard by a phone call.

Tip 784. Negotiate as a Team, Not as Individuals Working on a Team.

Another negotiating team may try to divide your team by addressing remarks to individuals separately—usually the ones who seem less knowledgeable and capable. In other words, a member of the other team will make eye contact with one individual and ask for a concession; that person will respond by agreeing with what the other team wants. Then the team will select another individual and ask for a concession, to which that person also agrees. The strategy is to negotiate with people as individuals rather than negotiating with the team as a group through the spokesperson, who is usually the most articulate, knowledgeable, and skilled of the group.

Don't let this divide-and-conquer routine work. If your team is negotiating on any matter, appoint a spokesperson to do the talking. When other team members want to contribute to the discussion, they can text the spokesperson, write notes, give hand signals, or take breaks to discuss the issues among the group.

Tip 785. Take Notes.

If you think you may not be able to recall key information, don't hesitate to make notes as you go along. Don't worry that note taking may slow you down in your discussions, because it has several advantages. It ensures accuracy, it gives you time to think about and react to what has just been said, and it forces the other person to notice that you have recorded certain information (should that person decide to "forget" what was promised or planned).

Tip 786. Make Good Eye Contact as You Negotiate.

If you avoid eye contact or look at the other person only briefly as you talk, that person may interpret your lack of contact as evasiveness, dishonesty, incompetence, or lack of conviction. To demonstrate honesty and openness, look at people directly.

Tip 787. Start on the Less Important Issues and Work Toward the More Difficult.

You'll gain momentum toward agreement, and you'll have more time invested in finding a resolution. The more success you have in turning each minor point to mutual advantage, the more emotional strength you'll gain to work on more complex issues.

Tip 788. Get Others to Invest in Agreement.

The more time, money, or effort people have spent in negotiating, the more likely they will continue trying to come to agreement. They will hate to think all that work, money, frustration, or delay has amounted to nothing. The more time they spend working with you to hammer out an agreement, the more committed they will be to working out any problems that crop up along the way.

Tip 789. Be Willing to Jump Ship.

If you find yourself on the opposite side of the situation mentioned in the last tip, learn when enough is enough. I've seen a Realtor friend of mine spend days showing property to buyers who couldn't make up their minds about which house to buy or whether they wanted to buy a new house at all. Why did the Realtor keep spending weekends showing them property? Because she'd already spent so much time showing them property!

Don't keep pouring more time, money, brainpower, and effort into a worsening situation just because you've already committed so much. The temptation to do so is great. It's the same phenomenon that causes people to keep their money in sinking stocks, hoping that the price will recover and their investment will recoup its value. The reasoning goes like this: "I've already invested so much time and energy that I should stay with it and see if I can rescue that investment from becoming a total loss." That reasoning has kept the United States in third-world countries and in ill-conceived social programs. It also keeps individuals in damaging relationships and poor business deals.

Tip 790. Start with Goals, Then Move to Solutions.

If you start with solutions to a problem and one or both of you can't accept the stated solutions, you may remain at odds forever. If, on the other hand, you state only your goals or motivations, then you can either accept or reject solutions as necessary and still come to an agreement that allows both of you to meet your goals.

Tip 791. Adopt a Brainstorming Technique to Generate Solutions.

Once you've stated goals or motivations, generate possible solutions together as a team rather than as adversaries. After you have a list of possible solutions, select the two or three best solutions and focus on those. Finally, work out the details of each of those solutions and select the best.

Tip 792. Present Fewer, Not More, Choices When Things Stall.

Having too many choices paralyzes people in decision making. Analysis paralysis can set in with even the smallest decisions. You walk into the local convenience store that has only Milk Duds and Hershey bars, and you can make a choice in two seconds or less. But drift into a candy store that has 28 different candies and the decision will probably take you five minutes. The same thing happens in setting appointments. Invite a colleague to lunch "sometime this month" and you'll have a devil of a time getting together; invite the colleague to lunch either Tuesday or Friday and you'll get a quicker commitment. When people seem puzzled and indecisive, don't take that as an impetus to brainstorm more options. Instead, narrow the choices. Lead them to focus on the two or three best contenders and forget the rest.

Tip 793. Remember That Others' Perceptions Govern What's "Fair."

Have you noticed how a young woman who has just graduated from college thinks that "all the good jobs" go to people who've been around longer? Then, as that young woman ages into her fifties, she thinks that "all the good jobs" go to the young people because management can hire them more cheaply? Have you noticed how the poor couple thinks that the tax burden should fall on the middle class? Then, when that couple has worked and earned its way into the middle class, they think the social programs for the poor are mismanaged, ineffective, and unnecessary? Everybody's overworked and underpaid. If you don't think so, ask them. What's "fair" will always be determined by each person's own situation, viewpoint, and values.

One administrative assistant who had left a job where he had a private office complained about his new job, where he had to work in a small cubicle. Another newly hired administrative assistant "inherited" the same workstation and said, "Great—my own cubicle and workstation! In my former job, there were two of us sharing a space this same size. I had only one drawer that was totally mine."

The matter of perspective knows no organizational bounds. The president of a client organization related a similar incident with seven senior managers during a layoff, when he downsized from three floors to two in the building to reduce his overhead. When the managers began to complain about having to "double up" in their offices, he reminded them that they had another alternative to help him reduce costs. Perspective determines the meaning of "fairness" on any issue. The bottom line is, if you have occasion to have a committee vote on your salary, make sure that everybody on that committee earns more than the salary you want.

Tip 794. Substitute "We" for "You and I."

Let language imply your intention to work out an agreement that is to everyone's advantage. Examples: "What would we have to do to get X to happen?" "What if we changed our criteria for hiring to include only five years' experience?" "How can we design this schedule so that your people don't have to work overtime and so that our people can meet the customer's deadline?" "What can we work out so that I don't have a large cash outlay up front, and you will still feel that you're not walking into a high-risk situation?"

Tip 795. Reset Expectations.

Let people know when they're being outrageous without telling them so. As parents or sweethearts, you may want your loved ones to think that you "hung the moon," but as negotiators, not so. When expectations about what you can offer, pay, do, approve, or provide are too high, the other person will always walk away feeling disappointed after you come to terms—as if getting a bad deal.

Before you get too far into discussions, reset expectations: "I hope you're not going to be disappointed that this year's order can't match the unusual one we placed last year." "I wish I controlled all the purse strings on this deal, but I don't." "With so many people who have to be pleased on these services, you're going to have to spend more time with us than you probably planned." "My budget isn't anywhere near what you're asking." "I don't think the price you quoted is competitive in this area." "The services you seem to be wanting us to provide are just not offered by companies like ours—at least, not at the low fees we charge." "The changes you need may be way beyond the scope of what we plan in this remodeling project." The idea is to make the other person's starting point realistic.

Tip 796. Take the Other Person into Your Confidence About Your Own Constraints.

If you have special considerations or constraints, say so. You may have legitimate issues that bind you with regard to pricing, scheduling, shipping, staffing, deciding, or any number of things. Then reverse the situation; ask the other person to level with you: "Do you have an especially tough time frame?" "Will it be difficult to get your team to agree?" "What is the mood around your organization just now?" "Are you used to having to sell your ideas to the IS department?" "Is there any other special need or consideration that I should know about here?" By sharing those restraints, you create trust. Reset expectations, and genuinely help the other person see how to meet your needs.

Tip 797. Don't State Your Position Unilaterally.

Be careful that neither your words nor your tone sounds like "take it or leave it." Once you've stated your position as unchangeable, the discussion may go downhill fast. Why? You've backed yourself into a corner. Unless losing face is of no consequence to you, you'll resist changing your mind.

If one side has to "give in," the other may feel embarrassed, defeated, or resentful. If nobody "gives in," you're at a stalemate. The best approach is for both people to start walking toward their goal and gradually fall in step.

Tip 798. Tag the Other Person's Unalterable Positions.

As you brainstorm solutions and test the details, tag unalterable positions that the other person mentions or implies. Determine the difference between "won'ts" and "can'ts." Once you tag the unalterables, you'll know how much leeway you really have in coming to agreement.

Tip 799. Test the Details Before Making or Asking for Full Commitment.

Make it clear that you're not agreeing or committing to anything yet. Then sort out details to see which are acceptable and which are unacceptable in meeting the other person's needs. Try comments such as: "If we were able to get delivery in 30 days, would that work for you?" "If Laura could come in an hour earlier for a month, would she be able to finish the task within your time frame?" If the idea is unacceptable, discard it immediately. If the idea is a possibility, keep it in mind, but remember that it is not a commitment until all the details are worked out.

Tip 800. Listen for Loopholes.

Nowhere is listening more crucial than when coming to an agreement in which everyone wins. Listen for the needs and wants of the other person. Which are must-haves and which are nice-to-haves? Does the other person have to win on a certain point—or simply not lose? Does the other person have to have X, or does he simply want a guarantee that Y won't happen? Listen for words that indicate which of the other person's points are negotiable. Listen for inconsistencies in "facts," wants, and values. Listening your way into agreements often pays bigger dividends than talking.

Tip 801. Make Your No Authoritative.

If an issue is nonnegotiable, say so. And be specific about what parts of the issue are unacceptable. "No, I definitely can't agree to the up-front payment, but I might be able to give you some room on the delivery date." If the other person refuses to accept your no, repeat it. Then repeat it. Then repeat it. If the broken-record technique doesn't seem to make the point, check your own body language and voice quality for inconsistency. Are your words saying no while your tone is saying maybe? Make sure that both your body language and your behavior match your words.

Tip 802. Get the Other Side to Go First.

As far as possible, try to get the other person to state what she has in mind first. With this information, you can alter what you have in mind before you commit to it. Try these comments: "What did you have in mind when you requested 'changes' for your office?" "You mentioned discounts earlier. What percentage are you accustomed to receiving?" "Can you give me some ideas about your budget?" When you must go first, state a range that allows you to ad lib as details about the possibilities and specifics become clearer.

Tip 803. Find Out Both Ends of the Range.

Try to discover the limits of other people's positions. What's the lowest price he'll accept, and what's the best price he expects? What's the most time she'll donate, and what are the fewest hours she expects to donate? On each issue, what's the other person's range of responses? No information is more important to you. On the other hand, when someone is trying to find out the limits of your position and you want to signal that you're reaching your upward limit, increase your resistance to the ideas he's presenting and reduce the concessions that you're granting.

Tip 804. Ask for More Than You Expect.

First, you might be surprised and get everything you want. Additionally, you allow yourself room to move—trading coupons for other issues that you want to buy during the discussion. Finally, you have some spare coupons to give to the other person to make her feel like a winner also.

Tip 805. Circle the Target.

When you're haggling over price, this principle often comes down to "let's split the difference." You ask $12,000 for the car; the buyer offers $11,000; and you settle on $11,500. Salespeople circle the target when they present product lines to their customers by showing them "top-of-the-line" refrigerators, "good" refrigerators, and "value-priced" refrigerators. Having set the upper and lower boundaries, they're expecting you to shoot for the middle.

Expand this principle into issues other than money. "I've asked you for four weeks' vacation, and you've said two weeks is standard. How about if we settle for three weeks?" Another example: "I need a full-time assistant for this project. You've offered no budget at all for an assistant. What about authorizing 20 hours a week for a virtual assistant?"

Tip 806. Be Prepared to Add or Subtract.

Before you go into a meeting to make some agreement, list your must-haves and your nice-to-haves. As your discussions move along, be prepared to offer concessions to "sweeten the deal" for the other person by adding on things that you can do. If the other person demands that you give in on certain things, know what items you can remove from the gift bag and take back home with you. All the add-ons and subtractions protect the heart of your agreement so that when you walk away, both sides feel as though they've shaped the final agreement.

Tip 807. Don't Counter an Outrageous Demand or Offer.

The term *lowballing* means that someone makes a preposterously low first offer and then edges up only by small steps. If you let this extremely low offer, on price, for example, become the bottom range of your negotiations, then the logical and fair price that you had in mind before you began the negotiations becomes the "high" figure. To respond in such a situation, simply refuse to start serious talks until the beginning offer becomes reasonable. Likewise with a demand. If you take someone's demands seriously enough to respond, he'll consider that outrageous demand his starting point. Simply keep silent or respond with humor to let the other person know that you do not consider him to be seriously interested in coming to agreement.

Tip 808. Be Prepared to Add or Subtract Only Upon Request.

Pay particular attention to this principle when it comes to price. If you've ever traded used cars, you've probably run into the individual who stated his price this way: "I want $18,000 for the car. Or, somewhere close. It's in good shape. Of course, it could use new tires—I could knock off $1,000 for that. I guess $15,000 would be a good price." People start stuttering and stair-stepping like this when they feel insecure or worried about the outcome—that the other person will walk away from the deal without even a salute. Never start making concessions until the other person asks you to do so. State your position on an issue and wait. Both of you may be in total agreement from the first step.

Tip 809. Add or Subtract in Small Increments.

You don't want to offer $400 for an item and then make your next offer $800, or to ask for a new company car and then immediately concede that you'll settle for being authorized to use a company credit card for gas. If you make such sudden, drastic movements away from your first position, you'll lose credibility about what you want or need and sound uncommitted or unknowledgeable about the whole issue.

Tip 810. Ask for the Other Person's Reasons Behind a Particular Offer or Demand.

Rather than simply challenging a demand or refusing a request, ask the other person to explain her reasoning. Even if the other person unexpectedly makes a concession or an offer, ask the reasoning behind it. This information can give you valuable insights into the other person's values and goals. Your asking for the basis of the offer or demand also identifies you as a reasonable person who wants to understand the situation and arrive at the best possible outcome.

Tip 811. Reverse the Other Person's Logic.

People tend to use logic in presenting their side of an issue—but their logic is apparent from only one point of view. Your goal is to help them see the reasoning from both angles. An example: An employee approaches you for a raise, saying that because the company plans to move its headquarters farther out into the suburbs, he will have to travel farther to work. Reverse his logic: would he be willing to accept a pay cut if you decided to move the company headquarters closer to his house? Another example: The employee wants a raise because the company has had a profitable year. Would she be willing to sign an agreement for a decrease in pay if the company does poorly the next year?

Tip 812. Forget the Matching Exercise.

Don't feel as though you have to give up something every time the other person makes a concession. For example, on price, if the other person raises his offer by $200 to come closer to your asking price, don't feel as though you must lower the asking price by $200 as a move in good faith. Or, consider a discussion with your boss about new flextime hours:

YOU: I'd like to come in later in the mornings to allow more time to take care of my elderly mother, who's living with me. I'd prefer to work 10 to 6, with no lunch hour.

BOSS: Well, I could give you some leeway from the set 8 to 5 schedule. How about coming in at 8:30?

YOU: Well, that's still a rush—I have to prepare my mother's meals for the day. I really need to have a 10 o'clock start time.

Don't feel obligated to give something or change something just because the other person has done so. Your request or position may have been closer to an equitable arrangement than the other person's at the beginning of the discussion.

Tip 813. Leave the Other Person Room to Back Down and Save Face.

Many a discussion has been lost when both parties wanted the same thing. Manager Karen states that she has given careful consideration to restructuring the business and has decided to transfer Matthew to Chicago. Matthew responds angrily, saying that under no circumstances will he transfer to Chicago and threatening to leave the company if he is forced to do so. He may then follow up his emotional outburst with logical reasons about why it would be in the interest of the company not to force him to transfer. Karen may agree with his reasoning and wish she could change her mind.

But she won't. Why? She'll be embarrassed that her earlier decision seems now to have been a poor one. Or, as a worse loss of face, she'll fear that a flip-flop on the decision would lead Matthew to believe that none of her decisions is final. Both may want to forget about the transfer, but Matthew's attempt to push her into a corner and make her feel that he is one up by threatening a resignation will keep him from getting what he wants. If you want people to concede a point, give them room to change their minds without embarrassment.

Tip 814. Avoid an Adversarial Tone of Voice and Word Choice.

Which of the following two people would you prefer to work with?

Person A	Person B
"I want $30,000 up front."	"I need $30,000 up front."
"You'll need to come up with..."	"Could you come up with...?"
"This is what we want:..."	"What could you say to...?"
"That shouldn't be a problem."	"Will X be a problem?"
"The logical solution is..."	"Does that make sense to you?"
"You'll have to..."	"We'd appreciate it if you'd..."
"Take it or leave it."	"I'm afraid that's as high as I can go."
"Your position is ridiculous."	"I know my position may sound extreme, but here's my situation:..."
"That offer is an insult."	"That's not what I had in mind."
"You're crazy."	"Possibly I have been unclear about why..."
"You should know better than to say something like that."	"I don't agree. Here's why..."

Attitude may be the wedge that drives people apart.

Tip 815. Don't Lose Your Composure.

When you get emotionally upset, you lose respect, trust, logic, and momentum. That's costly.

Tip 816. When Someone Makes a Threat, Don't Respond.

In the typical situation, threats elicit counterthreats. Then both parties lose because they begin moving into extreme positions and change the dynamics to "every person out to crush the competitor." To avoid this danger, don't respond to emotional outbursts or threats at all. Simply hear them, pause, and call for the other person to continue to elaborate. The point is to let that person spend her emotion and come back to a more reasonable position. When you counter the threat, solutions begin to disintegrate and the compromise position fades. The danger: You will either win big—or lose everything.

Tip 817. Treat Silence as Golden—or Yellow or Amber.

As an accessory to negotiations, silence changes colors as you need it. Silence is golden when you use it for reflection to avoid popping off without forethought. On other occasions, it may be yellow or amber; it may be taken as agreement or disagreement. When you don't want to commit yourself, simply listen and think about what the other person is saying.

Tip 818. Don't Let Silence Intimidate You.

Because many people are uncomfortable with silence, they talk... and talk... and talk. The more the other party remains silent in a discussion, the more uncomfortable they feel. As they feel more uncomfortable, they fear that something has gone wrong in the discussion, so they begin to offer concessions. "Well, you know, I guess I really could afford to let you...," or, "Frankly, I'm willing to..." If others simply sit silently rather than react to what you say, sit silently with them. Don't begin promising the moon just because they seem to have lost interest in discussing a matter.

Tip 819. Ask the Other Person How to Overcome Her Own Objection.

If the other person has refused to accept any of your concessions or alternatives, put the monkey on her back. "Okay, I've run out of ideas; how do *you* think we can work out this issue/overcome this objection/diffuse this concern?" The other person often has a suggestion in mind that is workable. And on other occasions, she may concede that the issue is unsolvable and, as a result, drop it as a criterion for coming to agreement.

Tip 820. Reduce Resistance to "Precedent Setting."

Sometimes people are afraid to give you what you want simply because they don't want to set a precedent for other people or for later dealings with you. You hear comments like these: "But if I do this for you, everybody will expect me to do it for them." "If I sell this one to you for X dollars, then you're going to want to buy all of them at X dollars." "But if I don't require *you* to do X, *nobody* will want to do X." To reduce this pressure on other people, you'll need to find a way to help them justify in their own minds how the current situation differs from others that may arise later. That difference becomes the crucial difference.

Tip 821. Borrow Someone's Library, One Book at a Time.

If you ask the other person for everything you want and that everything is a lot, your requests will be taken seriously. However, if you're asking to borrow only one book at a time, the person may not even take the trouble to padlock the library. In negotiating for added job responsibilities, the principle might work like this: Instead of asking to move into a new job when someone resigns from the company, you might ask to add one of his job responsibilities to your current job. Six months later, you may ask for another responsibility from that original job. Before you know it, you may have borrowed someone's entire job, one task at a time. Then you ask for the salary to match the new job responsibilities you're handling.

Tip 822. Apply the Rule of Supply and Demand.

Have you ever shopped in a department store and expressed interest in a clock, only to have the salesperson respond with, "Those may be all gone; let me check the stock on that." Then she returns with, "You're in luck— we have two left." The tactic: if you want it, we'd better write up the order quickly before someone else beats you to it. The principle doesn't have to be used as trickery, however. If what you offer has a limitation, say so. Let the other person know that if he waits, the choices may be limited, the quality may decrease, the offer may be withdrawn, the process may get more complex, or the price may change.

Tip 823. Win Instant Credibility by Association.

When presenting a new idea, process, or approach, introduce your point by relating it to a more renowned or credible source. Example: "Last week I read in *Fortune* magazine that more than half of the top 50 companies encourage X, so I was thinking that we too might consider...," or, "Our legal department has always encouraged us to do X, so I thought you would have no problem if I added this clause into the contract I intend to offer," Or, "My approach parallels one used by our CEO in the strategic planning meeting she facilitated. It calls for..."

Tip 824. Do It and Then Tell Them You've Done It.

This principle is second cousin to the "it's better to ask forgiveness than permission" rule. On occasion, you'll do better to take an action, then tell others what action you've taken and see if they let that action stand or try to counter it. For example, a vendor sends you a contract for signature containing a clause promising delivery in 90 days. Rather than phone the vendor to express your reservations and work out the complete deal before signature, you delete the 90-day clause, ink in 50-day delivery, and sign and return the contract. The vendor may decide to let the deletion stand to avoid reopening the negotiation and unraveling the whole deal. Even in simple situations, this principle works well: Your spouse moves all the furniture in the house and then asks you how you like it.

Tip 825. Don't Accept the Printed Word as Holy Writ.

A store sign saying "WE DO NOT GIVE REFUNDS" carries a lot more weight with customers than a clerk at the register making the same pronouncement. To most people, printed policies, proposals, prices, and plans sound more persuasive and authoritative than oral ones. However, even though they may sound more "official," they may not be unalterable. Written words can be rewritten.

Tip 826. Set Deadlines with Care.

If you say to a vendor, "We'll give you until Friday noon to make up your mind about whether you can give us the volume discounts," what happens if the vendor isn't ready to make a decision by Friday noon? What if the company is still waiting for bids from its own suppliers? If you really want to work with this company and you have the leeway to wait longer for a decision about the volume discounts, you've put yourself in a bad position. Either you lose face by admitting that you really didn't have such a deadline after all, or you back yourself into the corner of having to go to your second-choice vendor. Deadlines can cut both ways. Set them carefully.

Tip 827. Don't Let Your Clock Tick So Loudly.

You may have deadlines. Subscriptions run out. Contracts expire. People resign. Prices go up. But avoid making your deadline sound like an ultimatum to the other person. Pay particular attention to tactful, factual wording: *Not:* "You'll need to give me an answer by tomorrow; otherwise, I'll go ahead and list the property on the open market." *But:* "I'm going to be forced to list the property with a Realtor by the first of the month. If you want to make an offer, I hope you can make a decision before that time." *Not:* "If you don't have an answer for me by tomorrow at noon about whether you can customize the seats, I'm going to give the order to your competitor." *But:* "I hope you can have an answer about the customizing right away. I've promised myself that I'll make a decision by noon tomorrow." Word choice conveys attitude, and the proper attitude solicits a favorable response.

Tip 828. Don't Let Others' Calendars and Clocks Wear You Down.

The attitude "let's get it done" often wreaks havoc. Give yourself time to generate the best option and agreement. When the other person offers a concession or asks for a concession, wait, consider, and ponder. This simple concept may be your saving virtue. The devil is in the details. Yes, deadlines represent reality. But think back about decisions you've made up to now in your life and decide how pleased you are with the ones that you made "because you had to do something fast." When someone says to you, "I want an answer by five today," before you rush into a decision, ask yourself if you would decide to do X even if there were no deadline involved. If not, wait.

Tip 829. Don't Agree Too Quickly.

Even when you like a deal, be careful not to grab it and run. The other person will invariably think that she made a bad deal after all and "left something on the table." When you fall into a favorable situation, walk away with it—don't run.

Tip 830. Keep Quiet Until Things Are Final.

As you make progress in coming to an agreement, you'll be tempted to talk about it to others. Don't. Letting outsiders know about what's going on can add unnecessary pressure—either positive or negative—on the other person involved. For example, let's say you're negotiating with manager Victor about allowing your staff to use his department's equipment one day a week. He promises to think it over.

In the meantime, you mention to a mutual friend, Evan, what you've asked of Victor. Evan may decide that you're on to a good idea and that he'd like that same treatment. So Evan goes to Victor with the same request about using the equipment for his staff. Victor may decide to turn you down because he doesn't want to give special treatment to Evan's group as well. Had you kept the situation quiet, you'd have had a sweet deal instead of no deal.

Tip 831. Practice Your Response to the Nibbler.

After you come to a complete agreement, the nibbler wanders back into your office with "Just one more little thing" or, "By the way, I forgot to make sure that it would be all right if..." This person wants to get every last crumb on the table. Be prepared with your response if this should happen to you: "I feel good about what we agreed to yesterday. I'd rather just stay with that arrangement," or, "Actually, where we left things last week would be my preference. I really don't want to get into negotiating all those issues again." Shut the nibbler down by implying that all negotiations will have to begin again if anything changes.

Tip 832. Be Persistent.

Few things of value have been gained on the first try. Research says that most salespeople give up somewhere between the third and fifth attempt, and yet most buyers don't even remember your name until after the sixth impression. Persistence pays off in getting a customer's attention, in persuading peers to cooperate, and in winning a boss's approval of an idea.

Tip 833. Develop Trust.

To resolve a conflict, both people have to want to resolve it. When both people in a negotiating situation trust each other, they have a natural inclination to want to come to consensus and resolve any differences. When they distrust each other, one person may decide that he doesn't care if they ever come to an agreement. And typically, they won't.

Tip 834. Negotiate by "the Golden Rule."

Treat others with the same respect for their best interests as you would like to have shown for your own best interest. This rule should set the stage and raise and lower the curtain on any successful discussion.

16

Resolving Your Conflicts Without Punching Someone Out

Conflict cannot survive without your participation.

—Wayne Dyer

Speak when you are angry—and you'll make the best speech you'll ever regret.

—Laurence J. Peter

Only the weak are cruel. Gentleness can only be expected from the strong.

—Leo Buscaglia

We judge others on their actions and results and want them to judge us on our intentions.

—No attribution

A soft answer turns away wrath.

—Old Testament, Proverbs 15:1

Never, for the sake of peace and quiet, deny your own experience or convictions.

—Dag Hammarskjold

My idea of an agreeable person is one who agrees with me.

—Samuel Johnson

A person who has no conflict either on the job or at home should be mounted and sold by Neiman Marcus in its one-of-a-kind gift catalog. Conflict can result from excellent work or poor work, from good intentions or from evil intentions, from appropriate behavior or from inappropriate behavior, from praise or from insult. When the inevitable conflict surfaces, you need to know how to identify and deal with it so that it doesn't drain your energy, infect your whole life, and sabotage your effectiveness.

Tip 835. Pull the Plug on "Little Discussions" Before They Mushroom.

Something that starts out as a minor issue can become a major issue fast. A glance, a smirk, a mutter, a shrug, or an "Is that all you found wrong with it?" can take on an ominous appearance as quickly as rolling thunderclouds. When others seem to be on edge, back off. Give them maneuvering room.

Tip 836. Deal with Conflict Promptly.

Like hot coals, angry words or bad situations tend to grow hotter when they're allowed to smolder. Friends of mine, a married couple, have a long-time rule in their household (two mothers-in-law and a father-in-law, plus the husband and wife): They must deal with any conflict within an hour. If they decide that they're too emotional to discuss something immediately after it happens, they call for a one-hour cooldown, then resume their conversation about the problem. Things unattended fester. Hearsay happens. Intentions become suspect. Hurt humiliates. The faster you broach the subject, the less infected the wounds become.

Tip 837. Determine the Nature of the Conflict.

For the most part, conflicts can be divided into five categories: conflicts over personalities, conflicts over goals, conflicts over circumstances, conflicts over facts, and conflicts over values.

> *Conflicts over facts* fade easily. Facts can be verified or refuted. When both people become clear on the facts, their conflict goes away.
>
> *Conflicts over circumstances* are easier to handle than most other types. Creative thinking will usually generate new limits, new details, or new choices that can alter the bad situation.
>
> *Conflicts over personalities* can be solved by pinpointing traits that annoy you or work patterns that irritate you and by accommodating the other person's trait or style. Because personalities are difficult

to change, the best coping strategy may be to overlook the habit or trait or to limit contact with this person.

Conflicts over goals can be best handled by compromise. Creative alternatives allow both people to get their needs met. If both people can't reach their goals, they can always modify their goals.

Conflicts over values cannot be resolved. The difference between attitudes and values is generally time. Attitudes change; values have taken root in a person's life over a long period of time. Values form the basis for how people look at other people, at their work, at ideas, and at life in general. If you consider a situation or action immoral or offensive, that judgment is based on values, and you are not likely to be satisfied with a compromise.

Once you have categorized the kind of conflict staring you in the face, you'll have a clear understanding of the effort involved in resolving it and the potential for a successful resolution. Some conflicts will be resolved quickly; some will be never-ending. Plan your future actions and reactions accordingly.

Tip 838. Bring Masked Hostility to the Surface.

Recognize passive-aggressive behavior when you see it and develop a strategy for dealing with it. The term *passive-aggressive* originated with Army psychiatrist Colonel William Menninger during World War II. Now it's tossed into the workplace as frequently as tweets. This term refers to hostility in disguise. The passive-aggressive person promises to represent you at a board meeting, then shows up unprepared and with the wrong slides. The passive-aggressive person tosses out little barbs meant "as a joke." The passive-aggressive person agrees to work late one evening to get out the last-minute orders, but then has a headache and has to go home. The passive-aggressive person "misunderstands" your directions about the proposal that she "doesn't think the client needs anyway."

All of these are attempts to buck authority when the person doesn't have the courage to do so openly. Only when you identify the recurring behavior can you deal with it effectively. Once you understand that it is the person's attitude—not the "reasons" and excuses given in various situations—that is the problem, then you can cope with it just as you cope with any other confrontation about attitude. Unfortunate "mishaps" surrounding the events are only symptoms, not the problem.

Tip 839. Examine the Payoffs from Continuing Conflict.

Psychologists have counseled parents for years that sometimes children misbehave because negative attention is better than no attention. The same can be said of adult conflict. Ask yourself what you or the other person has to gain from refusing to end a running conflict. Does a continual uproar in the department create excitement for the group? Does the conflict feed someone's ego? Does the conflict serve as someone's excuse for not getting a task done or done well? Once you know what the payoff is, you can decide whether you can meet the need—ego gratification, excitement, entertainment, or success—in a less emotionally draining or disruptive way.

Tip 840. Assume a Resolution.

To a large extent, life is a self-fulfilling prophecy. We get what we expect. Expect that the problem or issue is solvable, and attack it with that mindset.

Tip 841. Determine the Most Productive Behavior: Either Swallow or Spit Out Conflict.

When conflict and the associated emotional upset surface, you have two choices: either you can suppress your frustration, or you can initiate a feedback session to bring the issues out into the open. Some people can swallow their pride, their feelings, and their goals and continue to work together successfully. If a situation is temporary, is of little importance in the big scheme of life, or is risky to their future, they may decide to avoid the conflict—to swallow it. Other people may choke on such an option. Determine which option is most productive for you at the very beginning. Don't wait until you're ready to explode before moving to the second option of feedback and resolution. Know yourself. Act accordingly.

Tip 842. If You Decide to Resolve a Conflict, Make a Conscious Choice Whether You Will Accommodate, Compromise, Overpower, or Collaborate.

Accommodate others in the following situations:

- When the issue is important to them and relatively unimportant to you
- When you cannot win or are wrong
- When you want to bank a favor for later recall

- When you want to shift responsibility for the outcome to the other person
- When harmony is more important than the issue

Compromise with the other person's wants and plans:

- When the issue is important to both of you, but is not worth fighting over to the bitter end
- When the situation is temporary and will lead to a quick fix for the immediate problem
- When you don't have time to haggle, but you need to meet some of your goals

Overpower others to get your way:

- When the situation is an emergency and you have to act quickly
- When you have to play the part of "statesman" and enforce unpopular principles or take unpopular actions

Collaborate to resolve issues:

- When the relationship is long-term and the situation will be recurring
- When both goals are too important to compromise
- When you need buy-in from other people on the outcome

Don't let conflict set you out to sea without knowing the kind of boat you need if you are to get back to shore. Make a conscious choice about how to come to terms with the conflict. Even if you decide to accommodate the other person, you'll do so with a better frame of mind if you realize that you have a choice and understand the trade-offs.

Tip 843. Don't Forgive Prematurely.

To err is human; to forgive, divine. Just don't confuse forced suppression with forgiveness. Some people dread open conflict so strongly that they'll do anything to avoid it—including trying to convince themselves that the matter is "no big deal." They smile, accept another person's apology, or even tell themselves that no apology is necessary. But the problem keeps gnawing at them. They can't forget it. Their hurt or anger continues to show up in different ways: by sabotaging the success of the other person's project, by talking behind that person's back, by withdrawing their approval from that person, by isolating that person. If you can't forget, don't forgive. Be willing to talk the problem through and get to a real resolution.

Tip 844. Set Clear Expectations.

Many conflicts are simply a result of unclear expectations. Managers set standards for their employees, but don't tell them what those standards are. Employees draw up a wish list for their bosses, but don't tell their bosses what would make them happy. Customers take their business elsewhere without giving the seller a chance to change or improve service.

When you discover that unstated expectations are at the heart of a conflict, you can empathize with the other person's viewpoint: "I know I never explicitly told you to do X, so I know you must feel that you have been taken by surprise." "I know we never had a formal agreement for you to do Y." "I clearly understand your confusion now, because the policy was never circulated to your department." Once you acknowledge those unstated expectations, the other person can save face, and so can you. Outline the expectations relating to any relationship—formal or social. It's difficult to live up to expectations that you don't know about, and it's easy to be disappointed when others fail to meet yours.

Tip 845. Establish the Relationship Rule.

Manager Melissa says to her counterpart in the next department, "Would you make sure that these printouts are sorted properly before they come to our department for processing?" Manager Kevin snaps, "No, I don't see that that's necessary. Our people don't have any more time to shuffle paperwork than yours do." This is not a conflict over printouts; it's a conflict over relationships.

Does Melissa have the authority to demand that Kevin do things in a way that suits her? That's the real issue. If she can tell him to sort the printouts, she can tell him how to run other areas of his department that affect her. His impulsive comeback is a reaction to a rule of the relationship that he doesn't agree to. Melissa would have done better to remember up front that she had no right to impose her ideas or to make assumptions about the relationship.

Until both people agree on the rules of their relationship—what can be expected, what is an imposition, what should be a request, and what can be demanded—they will continue to clash on various issues.

Tip 846. Confront Privately on Private Issues.

Discussing someone's shortcomings has no place in a staff meeting, in the hallway, or in front of a colleague or customer at any location. When there's an audience, people begin to play to the galleries. Ego takes over. Pride rears its head. What would normally have elicited a simple, "Oh, I'm sorry; my fault; I should have caught that" will turn into a battle of pride and put-downs when the issue is mentioned in public.

Tip 847. Move from "Study" to "Act."

When you don't know all the facts affecting a specific conflict, you may need to dwell on the problem: When does the problem occur? What's causing the problem? Why is A or B a problem at all? How is the problem affecting others? How much is the problem costing in time, effort, and money?

But once all the information has been brought to the forefront, move to a solution-centered discussion. Devise alternatives. Identify methods. Make comparisons and contrasts. Evaluate the efforts or costs. Propose solutions. Avoid analysis paralysis.

Tip 848. Focus on the Goal Rather Than the Obstacle.

When conflict creeps in, both sides tend to lose sight of what they have in common—the desire to maintain a relationship, the profitability of the business, the success of a project, the cohesiveness of the team, the winning of an award, or the welfare of their family or friends. Take time out to remind yourself of the goal.

Tip 849. Adopt the Doolittle Philosophy.

In the play *Pygmalion* by George Bernard Shaw, the main character, Eliza Doolittle, sums up her situation this way: "The difference between a lady and a flower girl is not how she behaves, but how she's treated. I shall always be a flower girl to Professor Higgins, because he always treats me as a flower girl, and always will; but I know I can be a lady to you, because you always treat me as a lady, and always will."

At work, the concept goes like this: "You get what you expect," or, "You get what you reward." To resolve a conflict, expect resolution. Assume that the other person intends to be reasonable.

Tip 850. Put the Issue of "Winning" or "Losing" Aside.

Conflict is not a competitive sport. Focus on meaningful decisions. Ask yourself: Do I want to compromise to get some of my needs met? Do I want to help all of those involved get some of their needs met? The only competition should be within yourself—to control your words and actions in such a way that you get what you need. The other person does not have to lose for you to win.

Tip 851. Turn the Sails to Catch the Wind When You're Wrong.

When you are dead wrong and you know it, don't stonewall. Don't persist in resisting. Instead of sailing directly into a fierce windstorm, turn the sails. Surprise the other person by simply agreeing.

1. Agree with the accusation or judgment against you.
2. Pause.
3. Give your rationale for what you did (but make sure it doesn't sound like an excuse). If there is no rationale for your behavior, or if the words would be inappropriate, comment on your "lessons learned."
4. Let the other person have the final say.

Example:

> *Repeat and agree with the accusation or judgment against you.* "You're right. I haven't been coming to staff meetings regularly—even when I was in town and even when I've had no schedule conflict."
>
> *Pause.* (Silence for 5 seconds.)
>
> *Give your rationale or lessons learned.* "My thought was that what I did in my region really didn't affect anybody else. But after talking to Joseph, I think I've had the wrong idea. Now I really understand that part of my responsibility here is to provide input to the whole organization. Even if things are going fine in my region, as a regional director, I'm expected to come to those staff meetings to offer input on problems and situations in other regions. I see that now."
>
> *Let the other person have the final say.* (Listen. Listen. Listen. But for the most part, you will have said it all for the other person, and the conflict will have disappeared with your agreement.)

Tip 852. Create Alternatives.

Define together what success will look like to all the people involved. Then work backward. Can we change the deadline? Can we get more help? Can we expand or cut the budget? Can we change the specifications? Can we alter the process? Can we break things into more "doable" chunks? Can we get more people involved? Can we get fewer people involved? Can we reverse the steps required? Can we redefine the problem altogether? Can we use different criteria to judge the resolution?

Try brainstorming. Put everybody involved into a big room and withhold food until you come up with a resolution. Generate ideas as fast as possible. Piggyback on one another's ideas. No evaluation. No questioning the ideas for clarification. No holds barred. Just think and record what's said.

After you've generated all the ideas that time will allow, go back and evaluate them one by one. Cross off the ones that don't meet your criteria and prioritize those that are left. Start with the alternative that looks the most promising and work your way down the list. The secret of conflict resolution is creativity. If you aren't good at thinking creatively, consider turning the problem over to someone who is.

Tip 853. Determine What Happened, What You Have Concluded About What Happened, and What You Feel About What Happened.

If people start giving you facts, ask them to interpret those facts. What conclusions have they come to based on those facts? If people start giving you opinions, ask for the basis of those opinions. If people have difficulty articulating the facts and opinions, ask them for feelings. How do they *feel* about what has happened or about the situation? When people express strong feelings, paraphrase those feelings back to them to verify that you have understood and that those are their true feelings. Then ask them for the events or facts underlying those feelings.

The idea is to help yourself and others distinguish between what actually happened, what they have concluded about what happened, and what they feel about what happened. In the process, you'll often uncover hidden invalid assumptions, wrong interpretations, and inaccurate information. You'll get closer and closer to seeing what needs to be changed or corrected.

Tip 854. Challenge a Power Play with Inattention.

Inattention is the least expensive, easiest to use, and fastest weapon available to control a power play. If you don't believe it, watch a waitress at the local restaurant or a flight attendant on your next airplane trip handle an obnoxious customer that way. Simply ignore a person's request or demands.

Tip 855. Work with People's "Want Tos" Along with Their "Do Its."

Bad attitudes. We recognize them when we see them, but they're hard to define. That's why a problem that has been resolved does not always *feel* like a problem that has been resolved. Only the action has changed, not the person's attitude. A little girl tottered and weaved as she tiptoed along a ledge high above a canyon ravine. Her father asked her to get down, but she continued her effort to walk the narrow ledge. Finally, her father reached up, physically pulled her off the dangerous ledge, and set her back on the picnic bench beside him. She screwed her face into a pout and said, "In my heart, I'm still standing up there."

On the job, it goes like this: Vonda misses several staff meetings, and Barry, her boss, tells her how important it is that she be there regularly and participate in decisions. Vonda starts coming to the meetings, but she arrives late, leaves early, and sits in silence. Barry would do well to express disappointment in both her "do it" and her "want to."

An elderly patient in the dentist's office wisely pinpointed the same problem with the receptionist. The patient paused briefly at the receptionist's window and handed her the charge slip. "Would you please file this on my insurance as usual," she said and started to walk away.

"We don't normally file on insurance," the receptionist answered rather haughtily.

"Yes, ma'am, you've always filed on my insurance."

"We don't normally do it. It's just a courtesy if we do it. We're not set up to do it."

"Well, I'd like you to do it again, please."

"I don't have your policy number."

"It surely is in my file because no one has asked me for it before. You must have a record somewhere."

"Do you know how much your deductible is?"

"No, I don't. But that's probably in my file also."

"I can't file on your insurance unless you bring in proof of having met your deductible and your policy number. We don't normally file. It's not our policy to do so."

"Yes, but I'd like you to do it, as always."

"That's not normally our policy."

After another two or three rounds of this repetition, the elderly patient finally cut to the heart of the matter. "Let me understand this. You said that you'd file it, but that it wasn't your policy to do so. I'm getting the message that you don't *want* to file it, but that if I *push* you really hard and insist, you will."

The receptionist blushed and took the charge slip. The problem was the "want to," not the "do it." When you understand that, you can choose an appropriate coping technique. Such problems will not be resolved until the attitude behind the action or inaction changes. Plan to deal with both in any conflict.

Tip 856. Stand on the Sidelines of Territorial Conflict.

If you're having difficulties with people because they feel territorial, respect their boundaries. If they own the turf, get off it immediately. Take your cue from lines like these: "We don't report to Mr. Big." "That's my decision, and I'll make it." "Those requests have to come through me." "You're talking about *my* budget." "Those are our accounts to maintain." Yes, territorial people are petty, and they generate a lot of laughs from those watching them, but they do have the final say. Grant their wishes and meet their ego needs. Stand aside and ask "permission."

Tip 857. Identify Who Is Playing Defense.

In the English language, tone and inflection can be subtle, but they can pack a walloping difference. Take these examples: "What proof do you have?" can be either a straightforward request for a further explanation or a challenge, suggesting that you're making unfounded allegations. "I don't know what you're talking about" can mean "That's nonsense" or "I'm puzzled." "Earlier you said X . . . ; now you're saying Y" can mean "I think you're lying" or "I'm confused; please sort out the seeming contradiction so that I can follow."

Such lines can escalate a conversation into arguments that go like this: "Why did you get so upset? All I said was blah, blah, blah."

"Yes, but what you meant was really blah, blah, blah."

"No, I didn't. All I said was blah, blah, blah, and that's exactly what I meant: blah, blah, blah." Somebody is hiding behind the words as if the tone didn't matter. Tone, mood, and attitude all convey meaning. The difficulty is deciding who is being defensive. Who is "reading something into" the conversation? If you're the one on the defensive, you're likely to hear double meanings in straightforward requests and statements. If the other person is on the defensive, he will let the defensive tone creep in and then deny it when challenged.

Instead of sorting out the problem by starting with the words, start with the attitude. Decide who has the defensive attitude, and then determine the meaning of the words. It's a remarkably reliable system.

Tip 858. Avoid Others' Vulnerabilities.

We all have sore spots. Ask yourself where you feel the most insecure, where you see a weakness in yourself, what track record you want to keep hidden from the world. Those are the bruises that you want others to stay away from. Others have similar bruises, and punching those sore spots unleashes emotions that can prevent the resolution of a problem altogether. For example, "Neal, I think this is just another example of a situation where that college degree you didn't finish would have helped you." If you make one of those comments, you'll be dealing with explosives from the past as well as those from the future.

Tip 859. Discard the Old Chant, "Sticks and Stones..."

Ever since we were children, we've heard the axiom, "Sticks and stones may break my bones, but names will never hurt me." Our parents taught us the chant as a defense mechanism, to be used when some neighborhood bully overpowered us with words. It might have worked when we were children, but it doesn't work for us as adults. Words do damage relationships forever. The most painful memories many of us have involve what someone said to us.

"I lost control" is no excuse. The tongue, a tweet, or a Facebook post as a weapon can destroy a reputation, a career, or a life. News stories of cyberbullying provide plenty of suicide examples that illustrate the power of words to destroy.

Tip 860. Prefer Statements to Questions During Conflict.

By the time you decide to discuss a conflict openly, trust has usually fallen and tensions have risen. Questions from either side will be suspect. Why? Because most will contain accusations. "Why didn't you tell me that you wanted these by Friday?" "How did you think we could spend that kind of money on this engineering project?" Granted, these may be informational questions—but they won't sound like it when there's tension and resentment in the air.

Prefer to make statements about what you feel or think. "I would have appreciated advance notice that these items were needed by Friday." "I think we can get this project done on a lot smaller budget." Ask questions only when you really are trying to gather information: "Is the deadline Thursday or Friday?" "Do you know if we have budget to use outside help?" A statement usually generates a response—either agreement or disagreement. An accusing question usually generates an argument.

Tip 861. Use the Three Ds to Structure Your Resolution.

Describe. Discuss. Decide. Describe what's happening. Discuss the feelings or other ramifications of what's happening. Decide what to do about it.

Describe. "Documents are going out of this department with typos and grammatical errors."

Discuss. "As a result, our communication is creating a poor impression with our clients. If we're careless in our writing, clients may think that we're careless in our analysis of their needs. Some of the grammatical errors even lead to clarity problems. It's embarrassing to me when a customer calls to point out careless errors like our misspelling a name."

Decide. "I think we need to make it a rule that at least two people proofread everything that goes outside the company. Do you have other or better suggestions?"

Describe. Discuss. Decide. That format focuses on the issues and a resolution without allowing room for sidetracking.

Tip 862. Use Thomas Gordon's Formula: "When You . . . , I Feel . . . , Because . . . "

Thomas Gordon, writing back in the late 1970s, introduced the concept of sending "I" messages. Example: "I feel angry when you forget to call or text when you're going to be late because I worry and can't get to sleep." He set up this formula: "When you X, I feel Y, because Z." This pattern includes all the variables—real and verifiable. X has to be an observable behavior. Y has to be a feeling, not an opinion. Z has to be an observable consequence.

Here's an improperly phrased statement that will bring argument: "When you act like a prima donna, I feel that you don't care whether this company turns a profit or not because you'll get your commission no matter what the profit margin is on what you told the customer that we'd do."

Such a comment won't work. "Acting like a prima donna" is a subjective statement. "I feel that you don't care" is an opinion—a judgment, not a real feeling. The listener sees no consequences from his behavior. That is, what's the negative impact on the company?

Here's the same sentiment expressed in a way that both parties can deal with: "When you fail to ask me about special discounts that you want to offer customers, I feel angry because we lose money on anything that's sold more than 20 percent below the retail price." That's a specific behavior, a true feeling, and a verifiable consequence.

Another example: "When you bring up my mistakes during a staff meeting, other people begin to blame me for things I have no control over, and I feel helpless to defend myself or explain. As a result, they disregard my authority on the shop floor."

Another example: "When you miss your deadline with the numbers on Friday, I can't close out my books and forward the final reports to Denver. And when they don't get the report by Monday morning, they can't issue checks to our suppliers, who add an interest charge on late payments. I feel really angry that I get grief from the Denver people for a delay that you caused."

Such a structure (1) describes the action, not labels it, (2) lets the other person know the consequences of the action, and (3) brings the related emotion out into the open. The resulting discussion will most likely, then, focus on the issue rather than on personalities.

Tip 863. Describe; Don't Label.

People can respond to statements like, "Your status reports are missing key information." They can confirm or deny that fact. They can't respond to a statement like, "You're evasive." How so?

> *Descriptive.* "You've taken off three Mondays in a row during a crucial project."
>
> *Labeling.* "You are inconsiderate of your coworkers."

Specific information can be verified or refuted; labels and value judgments cannot be.

Tip 864. Don't Use the Phrases "You'll Have to...," "You Must...," "You Should..., " and "You Ought to..."

People don't like to be told that they *must* do something. Think how perturbed you become when you hear one of these: "You'll have to check out at the next register." "You'll have to complete the XYZ form before we can help you." "You'll have to get approval from Joe." "You'll have to move that file." Try instead, "Would you please..." The same is true of *must, ought to,* and *should.* Eliminate these phrases from conflict discussions.

Tip 865. Offer the Other Person Face-Saving Comments.

Examples: "Your mistake is understandable. The map is confusing. Several people have gotten lost at that point." "The details are complex. Most people don't realize how overwhelming it can be to sort through so much information. I think you've made excellent progress so far." "Well, I can understand how you'd be upset. It's irritating when people don't let you know what's going on." If you expect the other person to take your side and come to an agreement, make it easy on her pride.

Tip 866. Let the Other Person Exercise Options.

People like to maintain some sense of power. That power may come from strong self-esteem, from freedom of choice about how and when a job gets done, from control over the success or failure of a project, or from freedom to interact with others. Be careful not to take away all the other person's choices. Otherwise, people will figure out a way to sabotage your project or will end the relationship altogether.

Tip 867. Shun Sarcasm.

Sarcasm humiliates people. "Thanks a lot. That was a big help to have these figures two days after the report has been turned in." "I appreciate your ordering lunch for me while I was in the meeting. My wife makes all the decisions at home; why shouldn't you take over the responsibility here?" Nasty no-nos.

Tip 868. Leave Exaggerations for TV Sitcoms.

When you exaggerate, the other person will always ignore the bigger issue and focus on proving your exaggeration incorrect. You'll wind up arguing about the misstatement rather than the issue. Examples: "They never let us know when they're going to take the computers down." "These overnight-express shipping charges are putting us in the poorhouse." "You always find fault with every suggestion." These statements will generate responses like: "Yes, they do notify us. They sent an e-mail last Tuesday telling us that we'd be down for two hours." "I don't think 68 dollars a month for shipping is putting us in the poorhouse." "Wrong. I don't find fault. I liked your suggestion about the flextime." When you make statements like these, you'll find yourself off the subject and onto defending the exaggeration.

Tip 869. Don't Act Incredulous.

The incredulous person greets the other person with a quizzical look of disbelief and shock at the "stupidity" of what has happened. Examples: "And you thought a phone call would solve the problem?" "So you left the car in the middle of the driveway so that everybody would have to either pull around it or hit it?" "Why in the world would you believe that?" "What makes you think that would work?" Most people can tolerate disagreement when they have to, but most snap when it comes to humiliation. The amused grin, the outright laughter, the mocking raised eyebrows cut a person to the quick—even those who have right on their side.

Tip 870. Don't Dismiss People.

A dismissal can be conveyed through words, gestures, or body language. We all know it when we see it. This mood pervades an atmosphere of conflict when one person makes it clear that talk will no longer help—that the details "no longer matter" and "won't change things," that the "mess" has gone too far for you to bother correcting it, or that what you're asking is "totally out of the question."

Tip 871. Forget the Condescending Phrasing.

A superior, patronizing attitude comes across in phrases like these, which sound as though they come from an all-knowing being on high:

- "That's a thought. I don't see how it relates here, however."
- "That would be an excellent idea—except for one small hitch: we can't afford it, and there's no way on God's green earth that the executives would approve such a thing."
- "That idea came up a month ago—and was dismissed quickly as totally unreasonable."

Tip 872. Don't Question Someone's Integrity.

People can handle a comment like, "You should have submitted the report last week with the information available to you at the time." They can't handle a comment like "Were you trying to put one over on us? Is that why you withheld the accident report? Did you think you could get away with that indefinitely?" A stab at people's integrity brings a torrent of anger.

Tip 873. Avoid Reruns.

TV reruns can serve as a rainy Saturday afternoon's entertainment, but stay with current issues during bouts of conflict. Granted, the past colors what happens in the future, but discussing all the details from previous run-ins gets you nowhere. Memories are fallible. The context of earlier problems also becomes muddled. Stay current.

Tip 874. Keep to One Issue.

Don't dump a decade's gripes into one discussion or you'll never get to the bottom of the current issue. Past details and experiences, while possibly relevant to why one person or the other feels or believes a certain way, will only confuse the current issue. Response is next to impossible. You simply can't remember and process all that's being said. One discussion, one issue.

Tip 875. Avoid "Hot" Words.

Just like radioactive material that triggers a nuclear explosion, some words set off an instantaneous upset: anger, defensiveness, denial, or blame. And any or all of these can be displayed by profanity, yelling, tears, pouting, withdrawal, or total silence. Every culture, conflict, and relationship is different, but here are a few typical "hot" words: *fair, unfair, reasonable, unreasonable, secretive, intentional, haphazard,* and *unconcerned.*

Before you send an e-mail, text message, or tweet, check for words that can set off an explosion. As you prepare for a sensitive discussion, plan your phrasing to eliminate hot words and select neutral ones.

Tip 876. Forget Verbal Ultimatums.

Communicating to understand differs from communicating to control. Ultimatums hinge on manipulation and control. "If I do not hear from you by two o'clock this afternoon, I will cancel the extension on the contract." When someone communicates with an intention to control, threaten, hurt, or produce guilt in the other person, he has missed the purpose of communication. He may succeed in controlling the other person, but he will fail in building understanding and repairing the relationship. Resentment will override any good that may come from the resolution.

Tip 877. Ask for What You Want from the People Who Can Give It.

People complain to coworkers, "I wish my boss would let us have an occasional party around here." "I wish my husband would get this car repaired." "I wish that receptionist would get my name right." "I wish the people who use this refrigerator for their lunches would clean it out occasionally." But they never get around to telling the person who can do something about the situation.

Years ago, when I worked on a military base in Okinawa, I reported to a GS–16 civilian boss who enjoyed having his comrades drop by to visit. During these social chats, he would frequently leave the door between our offices open while he and his friends swapped stories and escapades. Embarrassed at overhearing these conversations, I continued to complain—at home, not to the boss. Finally, my husband called the boss, calmly explained that these conversations embarrassed me, and asked the boss to close the door during these visits. Expecting rather cool treatment the next morning and angry at my husband for taking such "confrontational" action without telling me, I had a surprise waiting.

The boss stepped into my office, apologized for the offensive language and stories, and began to close the door during these visits. No grudges, no repercussions, no problem. And all just for the asking.

People complain, but they seldom state what they want to the person involved. They talk behind her back, pout, threaten, hint, and hope. But they don't ask. Try stating exactly how you feel about a situation directly to the person or people involved and asking them to make a change. You might be surprised at how easy it is to get what you want.

Tip 878. Don't Assume the Other Person Understands Your Point of View.

Even if you think the issues and repercussions of someone's action are obvious, state them. What is obvious to you is not necessarily obvious to the other person.

Tip 879. Listen Until You Experience the Other Side of an Issue.

At a Boulder, Colorado, church, one of the women had the most irritable dispositions I'd ever encountered. In addition to having a long face and sad eyes, she complained about the kids "making noise" in the nursery, about the money "wasted on the youth programs," about the time the pastor spent on marital counseling that could be "better spent on the needy."

Then one day she mentioned a past tragedy in her life: The day she was born, her mother had died. As a result, she had projected onto other parents and children all of her bitterness about her own mother's death. Her complaining became understandable to me.

Recently, we called a technician to take a look at an air conditioner at home. When I came in from work that evening, I saw a mess. Rusty-looking splatters of water covered the kitchen cabinets, appliances, and floor. Obviously, I decided, the technician hadn't cleaned up after himself.

I was perturbed as I scrubbed up the rusty splashes. But when he returned the next day to finish the repair job on the air conditioner, he explained, "Sorry I left such a mess yesterday. Just as I was about to leave, I noticed that you had a leak from some busted plumbing. The spillovers in the attic were just about to overflow and come down through your kitchen ceiling. So I rummaged around and found a bucket and tried to empty as much water off as I could. Saved your ceiling at least." My anger melted.

Listen to understand and experience the other side of an issue.

Tip 880. Argue Like Abe.

As a lawyer, one of Abraham Lincoln's most frequent and successful tactics in court was to argue the opposition's case first. He knew that those on the other side would present certain facts and theories, and he liked to beat them to the punch. That technique had several effects. It established his sense of integrity, fairness, and search for the truth. And it also lowered the resistance of the judge and jurors to what they expected to be a "hard sell" of only one side of the situation.

When you adopt this same approach in a conflict with a colleague, client, boss, or family member, you're saying, "I understand your viewpoint. We're both reasonable people here, and I see where you're coming from on this issue. I understand that you need X, and I know about Y, and I can see how Z might be a problem for you. Now let me explain my dilemma in this situation."

You've earned your right to be heard because you've argued the other person's point of view first and fairly.

Tip 881. State the Real Reasons or Effects, Not Just Logical Ones.

People sometimes find themselves off base in a discussion because they give a less-than-honest reason for and consequence of a problem. Such was the case with an acquaintance of mine, Tom, who assumed a new position as training director for a large organization. He immediately found himself embroiled in a conflict with the vice president of operations, who had asked for a leadership course for his staff.

The VP kept asking Tom when he intended to contact the outside vendor used for such classes and get a commitment on the date. Tom explained that he had been hesitant to set the date because the vendor had increased its prices and was now "too expensive." The VP insisted that he'd been pleased with other classes conducted by that vendor and wanted to move ahead. Tom countered that he didn't want to spend more money in his budget than was necessary for a high-quality course. The VP reluctantly agreed to wait a little longer while Tom solicited bids. But when the bids came in, the VP and Tom could not agree on their criteria for decision.

Tom's real reason for dragging his feet finally surfaced: He felt competitive with the earlier successful vendor and wanted to develop the class himself. When he instead cited reasons such as "increased prices" and "wasted budget," he and the VP found that their discussions had gone off track. In desperation, they compromised on a new outside vendor. And in the process, they created extra work for themselves, and neither felt that his decision was the best—all because Tom substituted a "good" reason (the budget) for the real reason (his desire to develop the course himself). Had he simply told the VP up front that he wanted to develop and teach the course himself, the VP might have agreed to give him a shot. In either case, they both could have saved a lot of unnecessary time if the real reason had been on the table.

Tip 882. Let the Other Person Vent Her Emotions Before You Try to Come to a Resolution.

Suggestions or concessions offered when someone is yelling sound less attractive than those offered when the person becomes quiet and rational again. People cannot resolve anything when one or both of them are crying, cursing, or shouting. Give the other person time to get the emotions out. Total silence will help. Whether you're on the phone or standing face to face, keep your face neutral and be silent. Eventually, the other person will run down and ask, "Are you still there?" (if you're on the phone) or, "Do you understand what I'm saying?" (if you're face to face). When she stops her tirade, you can begin the discussion again.

Tip 883. Own Your Own Feelings.

Accusations frequently begin with, "You make me feel..." Fill in the blank: *angry, inadequate, dumb, useless, ridiculous.* Think about the meaning of such a line: One individual is saying that the other person has control over his emotions. The other person will then usually counter with, "It's not my fault that you feel..." The conversation then degenerates into a discussion of whose fault it is.

Prefer to make statements that show that you have control and choice in the matter, and that center on the problem rather than on who's to blame. Example: "I feel stupid when you remind me over and over of a deadline.

I'd prefer that you state the deadline once and then drop it." Only you can decide how you feel. Choose differently. Better yet: "I feel uncomfortable when you remind me over and over of deadlines. Once is sufficient."

Tip 884. Make Sure Your Own Emotions Are Genuine and Appropriate.

Some people have learned to manipulate others by crying, yelling, or cursing. When they explode, people jump. It's a learned behavior that can be unlearned. Use the following checklist to take your own emotional temperature:

- How often do you "blow up"?
- When you get upset, can you pinpoint the cause, or do you just feel irritated at the world?
- Do you react in proportion to the problem?
- Who receives the brunt of your emotion—the person causing the problem, a scapegoat, or the person nearest to you at the time of impact?
- Do you let your emotion "blow over" quickly, or do you pout or hold a grudge?
- Do you rant privately or publicly?
- Do you humiliate other people and generate animosity for yourself?
- Do you think before you react, or do you react and then think?

The answers to these questions should give you a good handle on whether you control your emotions or whether your emotions control you. More important, the answers may pinpoint the root of ongoing conflicts.

Tip 885. Define the Areas of Agreement or Disagreement.

Good negotiators understand what contributes to their success: They start with the easy issues and then move on to the more difficult points. Likewise, when discussing a conflict, begin by confirming the areas of agreement. That might mean confirming undisputed facts or shared goals for the outcome. Finding that you do agree on some issues gives momentum to take you through the harder issues.

Example: "Mandy, as I see it, we both think the employee survey is a good idea. And we agree that the wording of each question is important and will drastically affect the way our people will answer the questions.

And we're together in wanting the results tabulated by December 1, correct? Okay, then our main differences involve whether we should pay a psychologist to help construct the survey and how long the survey should be." The sum total is three down, two to go. Encouraging.

Tip 886. Beware of Braggadocio-Generated Conflict.

If you're talking loudly every day in the cafeteria about your weekend trips with "men of your dreams," don't be surprised that you get more than your share of invitations from colleagues. If you're bragging that you had Thanksgiving dinner with your cousin Warren Buffett, don't be put off when your cube-mate expects you to arrange a meeting to ask for venture capital for his new idea. If you're announcing in weekly staff meetings that you're 30 percent over your sales quota, you can expect your colleagues to start to infringe on your time, wanting to know what you're doing differently from them.

Like spending the day at the beach with no sunscreen, some conflict is self-inflicted.

Tip 887. Get Confirmation on Unvoiced Expectations.

"Your wish is my command" makes a great line between lovers and even friends—but it's a lousy thing to try to enforce or demand. That's especially true when that wish has been assumed but not mentioned, and is off the radar until a critical moment. If you have certain expectations about how a job will be completed, what you want in an ongoing relationship, or what something will cost, bring that expectation to the surface and ask for confirmation from the other person. It's better to know sooner rather than later that there's another mismatch of expectations to be resolved.

Tip 888. Don't Interrupt the Other Person, and Don't Let the Other Person Interrupt You.

Some people think they're saving time by interrupting you in a recitation of the conflict details when they already know them. Don't permit such interruptions: "Margie, I want to finish explaining what I consider to be the problem." Say it in a matter-of-fact tone and keep talking. This assertiveness establishes you as a person with a right to be heard. And if you're the person doing the interrupting, remember that the issue is not time, or even "your version." The goal is to hear both versions of an event or situation, to piece the truth together, and to sort out the feelings.

Tip 889. Take Turns for Airtime.

For all the griping and complaining from drivers ensnarled in traffic or those people taking mass transit, most would agree that travel time is their own—at least mentally. It is uninterrupted time for listening to music or self-help advice, reading, talking, or thinking. When you are involved in a conflict, try the same principle. Give each other uninterrupted time to talk, say five minutes, and then take turns explaining your viewpoint. You'll have the best results if one person agrees to paraphrase what the other has said to show that she has listened. Only after the first person "signs off" that the other person has heard correctly does the second person get a turn to talk.

The process has four benefits: (1) It eliminates petty arguments because the other person loses immediacy—he can't interrupt impulsively with a counterattack or denial. (2) The other person has to listen. (3) The plan builds in cooling-off periods for emotions. (4) It helps people summarize and focus on the most important comments and issues because they can't remember the entire five-minute talk verbatim.

Tip 890. Discuss a Problem Sitting Down.

When both people are seated, they'll be less likely to use intimidating body language. Neither person can "tower" over the other person, invade the other person's space, stomp across the room flailing arms, or make a dramatic exit.

Tip 891. Eliminate Argumentative Words and Phrases.

Good communication includes the ability to keep flaring tempers to a minimum. A stressful business meeting involving strategies or budgets—or a "family meeting" taking place around your kitchen table—can turn heated with just a turn of a phrase.

Here are some examples of argumentative phrases:

- "That's not true."
- "You're wrong."
- "You're confused."
- "You don't know what you're talking about."

Commands are equally abrasive:

- "Stop interrupting me."
- "Hold on a minute."
- "Leave it alone."
- "Just drop it."

Any of these sentiments can be expressed in a more acceptable, less abrasive way:

- "My information doesn't agree with yours."
- "What I was told differs from what you just said."
- "I disagree."
- "There's some confusion here."
- "There are some issues you may not be aware of."
- "Please let me finish what I started to say."
- "Let's wait a moment."
- "I'd rather handle this myself."

Avoid "fighting" words unless you want to fight.

Tip 892. Do Something Physical to Break the Spell.

If your discussions grow too tense, agree that both of you will take a cooling-off break. Take a walk, shuffle through your notes, get a drink of water, or glance out the window. Just don't use the movement to rant and rave. Instead, do something to break the emotional contact and give yourself and the other person time to identify better coping techniques.

Tip 893. Don't Use Silence to Provoke.

Think of silence as a stabilizer, not a weapon. Don't use it as a provocative action. If the other person begins to comment on your silence, it's time to speak. Lead into a meaningful discussion with something like, "I was trying to make sure I caught everything you were saying." If the other person has not been yelling or abusive and if you have simply withdrawn into silence to think, say so: "Yes, I have been quiet the last couple of days. I'm trying to figure out how to solve our differences." If you have used silence appropriately, it will calm people, not punish or provoke them. Silence doesn't settle conflict; it stalls all attempts to resolve it.

Tip 894. Remember That Only the Dead Keep Confidences.

Keep in mind that whatever happens during your conflict resolution, others will eventually know of it. People talk, and what they say will be their version of the truth. If they have a character weakness, they will control the way others interpret "the facts" by which details they choose to tell and which they omit. Face the frustration that two versions of "what happened" will circulate.

Tip 895. Realize That Two Sides Can Both Be Right.

People bring different backgrounds, values, roles, experiences, and goals to the workplace. Not all differences can be reconciled. Policy A may be bad for Joe and good for Manuel. Alan may define success as plenty of time off the job, while Katherine may define success as a fat paycheck. Neither opinion—or goal—is necessarily wrong. Both may be very right. It's a fact of life that's difficult to accept, but accepting it is necessary to one's sanity.

Tip 896. Pick Your Fights.

You can't take on the world.

Decide which conflicts are worth the effort to resolve. You are known by the opponents you have and the friends you win.

17

Mediating Others' Conflicts Without Getting Caught in the Line of Fire

Unless someone like you cares a whole awful lot, nothing is going to get better. It's not.

—Dr. Seuss (Theodor Seuss Geisel)

Ego, not content, causes the most communication standoffs. Contrary to what is commonly believed, most disagreements are caused not by conflict over what people need but how they actually talk and act about those needs.

—Carmine De La Rosa

Hear the other side.

—Latin proverb

In a heated argument we are apt to lose sight of the truth.

—Latin proverb

The difference between discussing and arguing is whether the participants are using facts or opinions.

—Philip B. Crosby

Nothing makes an argument so one-sided as telling about it.

—No attribution

Effective cooperation between the parties is all but impossible if each plays to the gallery.

—Roger Fisher and William Ury

He knew the precise psychological moment when to say nothing.

—Oscar Wilde

You cannot sit on the fence and overlook the battleground without getting mud splashed on you from time to time. Those around you will have a conflict of goals, needs, values, or personalities. When you have some connection or responsibility to both, you'll feel the need to intervene and do your part to mend relationships between coworkers or friends. If you handle the chore with skill, you can contain the conflict. If you handle it poorly, the situation may escalate to such an extent that you yourself become the enemy of both. The following guidelines will help keep you from falling off the fence.

Tip 897. Intervene Only When Asked; Proceed with Caution.

And even then, think twice. Most conflicts are best handled by the two people involved unless their difficulty affects the atmosphere or the productivity of others. When you intervene needlessly, you may find yourself in the thankless position of giving it your best shot and ending up with both people angry with you.

Tip 898. Avoid "Taking Sides" and Talking the Opposition Over to the Other Viewpoint.

Work with both individuals from the very beginning. You may decide to meet with both people together or separately. If you decide to meet with each person separately, be sure that both people understand that what they share with you will *not* necessarily be withheld from the other person. You will have to use information from one person to verify and clarify with the other. If you don't warn the two people of this up front, they may lose confidence in your impartiality and think that you are breaking their confidences.

Tip 899. Ask Each Party for His Version of the Issues.

In separate conversations, ask each person in the conflict how he views the situation. Rather than having each person give you a once-upon-a-time version, have him start with a one-sentence summary of the conflict as he sees it. That one sentence will help you quickly clarify whether the two people have a true conflict or a simple misunderstanding. If it's a simple misunderstanding, then provide missing information, define common language, or clarify expectations. The problem will disappear.

If there's a true conflict, then dig deeper by asking for details with a few follow-up questions: "What do you think contributes to that problem?"

"What do you think is the best solution for everyone concerned?" "How do you think we could achieve that outcome?" "Is there anything you could do specifically that could improve the situation?"

Tip 900. Play the Role of Reporter; Go for the Five Ws.

Try to discover all the facts in a situation. Ask who, what, where, why, when, how, and how much. You can begin to make sense of someone else's conflict only when you're armed with an unbiased version of events and circumstances. An even better approach than asking the two people involved is to unobtrusively investigate the issues among "innocent bystanders" without their knowing why you're asking. Be careful, of course, that you don't just collect information that was passed on to the bystanders by the people directly involved. Probe for what they know or have observed firsthand. Identify facts, assumptions, assertions, and feelings. They all count.

Tip 901. Listen to Each Person's Criticism of the Other.

Why? Because each pile of criticism contains at least a grain of truth. Even if the criticism as a whole misses the mark, you'll gain insights that you can follow up and examine more closely. When you're listening to the complaints of each person, however, make sure that you remain neutral and do not let your body language convey that you agree with any of the criticisms. If you give so much as a nod, you may be surprised later to discover that one or the other of the two people "claims" you as her ally for having "agreed" with her recounting and her charges.

Tip 902. Pass Along Complimentary Things That Each Person Has Said or Believed About the Other in the Past and Express Your Confidence in Their Willingness to Come to a Resolution.

If you can pass on complimentary remarks made during the current discussions with each person, do so. If not, you may have to dig into the past to find these gems. "Jill, Martin does respect your work. If you recall, last summer he asked to be assigned to your team on the soft-drink campaign for the radio ads." Or: "Gloria agrees that you've always been fair in your dealings with her, that you've never tried to force her to travel on projects that she felt another staff member could handle. She appreciates your sensitivity on that issue."

The purpose of passing on such comments is to help people recall their past good relationship, if there has been one. Sharing positive remarks adds credence to other things the person says. If someone is honest and is willing to admit or confirm the good, chances are that he's honest—as he sees it—about the problem.

Tip 903. Restate Common Goals—Again and Again.

Focus on the two people's common goals. For example, "Joel and Marie, both of you want to see this client go to the proposal stage. You both have creative ideas to contribute about how we might analyze the client's financial systems. Both of you want to protect the client's privacy, and both of you want to make the sale," or, "Doug, you're concerned with cutting costs this quarter. Santiago, you have the same interest." They need constant reminders of where they're going—the finish line.

Tip 904. Point Out Where You Believe Both Have Miscommunicated in the Past.

You may decide to call both people together at this point, if you haven't already done so. After all your searching and probing into the problem, share your conclusions. Be straightforward and honest. Point out invalid assumptions, conversations with double meanings, and perceived intentions, along with your judgments and labels on those intentions. This will be the toughest part of your task as mediator.

Tip 905. Ask Both People to Reverse Roles.

If you're not sure that both people fully understand and appreciate the other's viewpoints and feelings, lead them to reverse roles. Paint the picture for each from the other person's point of view and ask her to explain how she would feel in a similar situation. If either person "doesn't get it," you may actually ask her to role-play the events with you. Repeat earlier conversations of the conflict and ask the other person to respond in the opposition's shoes. At the least, ask each person to paraphrase to you how she thinks the other person views things and how she feels about those events or circumstances.

Tip 906. Suggest That Each Profile the Other Person.

Many conflicts come down to style of communication. In other words, what starts out as a conflict of issues and viewpoints deteriorates into a clash of personalities and words. To clear the air, one or both sides would do well to step back and study his "opponent's" style.

My colleague Tony Alessandra, Ph.D., has made famous the Platinum Rule® (akin to the Golden Rule), which suggests that we treat people the way *they* want to be treated—not the way *we* want to be treated. He runs an online assessment center (www.AssessmentsBusinessCenter.com) that provides tools to help people determine their personal style. Pointing out such style and personality differences can be extremely helpful to people who routinely butt heads over insignificant matters. You may want to suggest that the two people go there, where they can download and take a personality profile (www.AssessmentsBusinessCenter.com/reports/Platinum RuleSampleReport.pdf) for insight into how to minimize such clashes.

Tip 907. Mention the Consequences of a Stalemate.

Call attention to the ramifications of an unresolved conflict. At the least, that may be a broken relationship and loneliness, the disrespect of coworkers or other family members, or a reprimand. At the worst, a continuing conflict may mean being passed over for promotion, losing one's job, financial penalties, or a legal battle.

Tip 908. Advocate "No-Fault" Resolution.

When a third party, such as yourself, is involved, the people who are in conflict have an added investment in maintaining their self-esteem. It's bad enough to admit error or fault to one person; it's doubly difficult to admit it to two people. Therefore, take every precaution to downplay any effort to affix blame.

Say it loudly, clearly, and frequently: "Conflict is inevitable. No one has to be at fault. Conflict just is. Let's focus on working things out." And then make sure your phrasing supports that premise. Avoid questions like, "Then what caused/made you think that...," "So you were only responding to her comment about...," or, "So if John hadn't done X, then Mary wouldn't have done Y." Forget cause and effect for purposes of mediation.

Tip 909. Summarize the Needs and Goals of Both.

This step is particularly important if the mediation has taken several days or even weeks. Make sure that both people know without a doubt what both of them want out of the situation or relationship.

Tip 910. Ask Those Involved to Suggest Resolutions.

If you suggest a compromise or resolution, it will be perceived as yours, not theirs. After clarifying the facts, identifying the misunderstandings, summarizing each person's needs, and reminding both of their goals, ask them for suggestions to resolve their differences. If necessary, reiterate their mutual criteria for coming to a resolution. When suggestions meet those criteria, accept them, record them, and ask for reaction from the other person. Accept. Check for agreement. Accept. Check for agreement.

Tip 911. Lead Them to Select the Solution That Best Meets the Needs of Both.

Your presence ensures that one person does not overpower the other. Your job as an impartial mediator who cares about both individuals is to see that the solution is acceptable to both—not a "win" for one and a "withdrawal" for the other.

Tip 912. Help Both to Keep the Lines of Communication Open.

Look over their shoulders occasionally to make sure that they are still interacting from day to day. Create conversations with them. Pass on "good news" from one to the other. If you've been successful in helping them through the crisis, they'll rely on you again and again. And you'll have the satisfaction of knowing that you've deactivated a potentially explosive situation, resolved a productivity problem, and kept one more relationship intact.

18

Responding to Insults, Boasting, Insensitivity, Gossip, and Other Goofs Hurled at You

How people treat you is their karma; how you react is yours.

—Wayne Dyer

Satire is traditionally the weapon of the powerless against the powerful.

—Molly Ivins

Answer them [critics] with silence and indifference. It works better, I assure you, than anger and argument.

—Gioacchino Rossini

The only graceful way to accept an insult is to ignore it; if you can't ignore it, top it; if you can't top it, laugh at it; if you can't laugh at it, it's probably deserved.

—Russell Lynes

There are times when silence has the loudest voice.

—Leroy Brownlow

Wit should be used as a shield for defense rather than as a sword to wound others.

—Thomas Fuller

No matter how limited your vocabulary is, it's big enough to let you say something you'll later regret.

—No attribution

Words can make a deeper scar than silence can ever heal.

—No attribution

Some people habitually let anything that flows through their mind roll out of their mouth. Others insult and offend with more forethought. Whichever we are dealing with, having an appropriate deflecting wit can shield us from some of the pain. But what happens when wit won't turn off the flow from those in the workplace? Try some of the following techniques for insulating yourself from the hurt or humiliation.

Tip 913. Avoid People Who Exhibit a "Put-Down" Demeanor and Manner.

An acquaintance of mine who is a professor has an air about him that causes people to slink away from him at cocktail parties as though they'd been slapped. Joe wears an amused grin, a slightly raised eyebrow, and a bored expression. Correspondingly, he uses a put-down tone when he speaks, offers silence when a response is expected, and gets sarcastic when straightforwardness would be appropriate. He sits on a condescending perch when equality would more accurately describe his relationship to those around him: In short, Joe's not a warm guy. If at all possible, minimize your contact with those people who put others down by both their demeanor and their manner.

Tip 914. Pinpoint Others' Motivations for a Put-Down.

Some people have grown up in such a hostile environment that they don't realize that they have an irritable, hostile disposition. Their background was chock-full of daily fights: "Get out of the bathroom, will you?" "Turn down that TV, you idiot!" "Even someone as dim-witted as you should be able to add." This hostility and the resulting self-protective thinking follow them into adulthood. Others put people down because they're miserable and want everybody else to join them in their sad state. We even have a saying about them: Misery loves company.

Some people pounce on traits or weaknesses in those around them because they're aware of the same weaknesses in their own performance or life. For example, they hate disorganization in themselves, so they notice it and gripe about it when they see it in other people. Still others put people down in an effort to build up their own egos. If you can make a game of guessing the motivation behind those who habitually insult you, you may be able to take their barbs with less difficulty.

Tip 915. Identify Put-Downs Meant as a Test of Ego Strength.

Some people make disparaging remarks in the workplace as a test of their coworkers' ability to "take it." If the other person can top the put-down, or at least laugh at the one hurled at him, he passes the test. The coworker's ability to laugh at his own expense conveys a healthy self-esteem, so others respect him also.

With these people, you lose if you play the part of victim. If others observe that verbal barbs offered in "good-natured" fun ruffle your feathers, they smell blood. They begin to see you as a victim, and victims soon fall prey to others' attacks. At best, the victim just gets dropped from the game. People ignore victims. If you're new to the group, identify yourself with the power players rather than with victims. If you want to pass the newcomer test and be admitted to the club, demonstrate that you're able to laugh at your own foibles.

Tip 916. Buy Thinking Time When You're Insulted.
[For lessons, watch TV westerns: The insulted cowboy slowly glances up from the card table, plays his ace, then slowly pushes away from his comrades and strolls up to the bar where the bad guy who insulted him sits. The move could take a good 30 seconds.]

To buy thinking time for yourself, take a deep breath and a long glance around the room. Playing with props is always good for another five seconds—taking off or putting on your glasses, finishing your drink, turning the laptop off, answering a text message, restacking your paperwork and pushing it aside. Just a few seconds is all you need to double-check the words, the tone, and the intention, and choose how you want to respond.

Tip 917. Ignore "Baiting" Comments.

Recognize these comments for what they are and refuse to get hooked. With a look or in a matter-of-fact tone, state your refusal to respond and your determination to remain calm: "I won't stoop to responding in kind." "I don't get involved in shouting matches." "Your outbursts will not change my decision." "That's your opinion." "You're entitled to your feelings." "That may be your perception." "We certainly don't agree. But then that's not a must, thank goodness." "I really don't have time to get into it with you." "I have my view, and you have yours." "Those are the facts as you see them, I guess." "You must be having a bad day." "Hmmm." Whatever you do, don't bite. You are letting them get away with it only when you succumb to letting other people make you lose control. When you don't bite, they *don't* "get away with it."

Tip 918. Tell the Other Person That the "Insult Tactic" Doesn't Work with You.

When you think someone is yelling, cursing, or otherwise abusing you simply to get you to change your mind about something, say so. "Geoffrey, yelling and exploding at me won't work. I understand you're angry that you have to wait another couple of days, but those tactics don't work with me."

Tip 919. Use Body Language to End the Insulting Conversation.

Look bored. Yawn. Wave the person away with a flip of your hand. Continue your work or make an exit. Break eye contact. Your body should say, "I don't have time for such nonsense. Stop it."

Tip 920. Change the Subject.

When the conversation grows uncomfortable, simply change the subject. No explanation or transition is necessary.

Tip 921. Clarify Rather Than Counterattack.

A friendly competitor phoned me one day to say that she felt the need to write and publish a book to establish her authority as a consultant. She wanted to ask my advice about taking the steps involved. After I'd spent several minutes with her on the phone giving her the information she requested, she asked me about literary agents.

"You really need agents," I said. "They can save you a lot of time in selling your manuscript. I work with two different agents, in fact, because they specialize."

"Would you mind sharing the name and phone number of one of them with me?" she asked.

I gave her the name of the agent who places my business books, and then said, "The other agent may not be interested in your book idea because they primarily handle TV and movie stars and other celebrity types, so—"

"So which are you?" she cut me off.

Taken aback by the sarcasm, I continued my interrupted sentence, "so if you're a business-book author, as I am, you don't get as much attention as the movie stars or the politicians-turned-authors."

I could tell that she regretted her insult immediately; obviously, she was no longer in a position to ask for additional information from me— nor was I in the mood to give it to her.

But I had clarified rather than counterattacked. As a result of her insulting retort, she left the encounter looking rather foolish. In fact, for years after that phone call, she ducked her head in embarrassment when our paths crossed.

Tip 922. Wear the Remark.

Try going along with the other person's comment. Such a response drains all the fun out of it.

> INSULTER: You took about twice as long as most people to do this report. Were you aware of that?

> YOU: It's really closer to three times as long.

> INSULTER: So did you realize that we were all waiting for the information?

> YOU: Yes, I knew it.

> INSULTER: So what are you going to do to speed up the process next month?

> YOU: I don't think I'll change a thing. It worked out just fine for me this way. I think I'll just try to see if I can set a new record for delivery time, since I'm already so close.

Tip 923. Create Inside Humor.

A shared joke or amusement builds intimacy. Try to find something that both of you have in common and develop a running joke about it—your lengthy staff meetings, the cafeteria pizza, customer Brown's absent-mindedness. Try anything that can give you a shared laugh. It's the same phenomenon as "our song" between lovers.

Tip 924. Use Self-Disparaging Humor.

A telemarketer at a major credit card company recently received an insult when she called to verify a prospect's receipt of his card. The prospect responded, "I do *not* want the card. What do I have to do to make that clear—tattoo it on your butt?"

The telemarketer started to laugh.
The prospect yelled, "What's so funny?"
She said, "Sir, if you only knew how big my butt is . . . it'd take all day."
The guy burst out laughing with her.

Various studies show that those who are credible and competent actually enhance their images with others when they use self-deprecating comments. Often, the most successful comedians are those who poke fun at themselves: the bald-headed man who tells "hairless" jokes; the obese lady who relates her tendency to eat the whole pie; the Jewish mother who talks about forcing the mail carrier to eat her chicken soup. To others around them, these coworkers appear to be witty, generous, and likable. If you have a strong ego and are generally competent in your job, laugh at yourself and invite others to join you.

Tip 925. Write Down the Insult or Hostile Remark.

Borrow the idea from your customer-service hassles. When hotel employees are discourteous or make poor judgment calls, you can always ask their names. They'll know that you intend to write a letter to their supervisor. You can use the same idea with colleagues. When they make derogatory remarks, make a point of writing down those remarks in their presence— even asking them to repeat the remarks so that you can record them correctly. If they ask why, make some flippant comment like: "They're a new chapter in my book." "I keep score." "I'm going to send them off for a contest." Whatever the remark, the person will immediately begin to see visions of HR people swarming around his work space. People think hard before "going on record" with insults.

Tip 926. Respond Only to the Surface Meaning and Words.

Pretend you didn't even "get it." Ignore the tone and respond only to the words.

Insult: "You're such an innocent. How do you think we win these contracts—by saying 'pretty please'?"

Response: "I don't know for sure what customers would attribute our winning to—low price or quality products, I'd guess."

Insult: "You act like this is your second month at work—where was your head during the last staff meeting when this was discussed?"

Response: "That was probably brought up when I had to take that extended phone call."

Insult: "My gosh—did you call every restaurant in the Yellow Pages to find a place this dumpy for Sam's retirement luncheon?"

Response: "Actually, I called only three."

Insult: "You're not the only person in this office who eats in this cafeteria, you know."

Response: "Really? I didn't know. How many do you think come in here on a daily basis?"

Tip 927. Twist the Assumptions.

That is, when the insult implies an assumption for its zinger, exchange the assumption for one of your own.

Insult: "At this rate, the project is going to take all day."

Response: "Did you intend to work even more slowly?

Insult: "I can't read these confusing reports."

Response: "Should I help you with the terminology—which acronyms don't you understand?"

Insult: "Do you think we can go back to management and get more money just 'cuz Simon says?"

Response: "I never thought of that. Do you really want to try to play games with them?"

Tip 928. Prepare a Comeback.

The comeback can be serious, humorous, or insulting. The choice is yours, depending on what you want as an outcome. If you want to keep the relationship intact and you want the barbs to end, be serious in your response. If you want to prove that you can take it and ruffle some feathers yourself, try light humor. If you want to kill the adversary and embroil yourself in an ongoing battle, go for the brutal barb.

Timing and tone may make the difference in each case. Examples: "Do you treat everybody like this, or am I just a favorite?" "I know what's bothering you—but your secret is safe with me." "You go for the kill, don't you?" "You're charming." "Everybody can't afford to go to finishing school." "Bad hair day, huh?" "I bet you go home and kick your dog, too."

Tip 929. Level About How the Insult Makes You Feel.

Tell the other person that the constant sarcasm, jokes, or grumbling has gotten out of hand. Be as direct as you can: "That remark is insulting." "Why do you enjoy hurting my feelings?" "Remarks like that embarrass me in front of customers; it sounds as though you think I'm incompetent at my job." "I feel very angry when you make jokes about X." "Did you mean to insult me? Are you aware that you did?"

Tip 930. Blow the Other Person's Cover and Ask for Serious Feedback Point-Blank.

Some people bury their barbs in humor, in double meanings, in sarcasm, or in innuendo. When you recognize an intent to hurt, identify it and confront the person directly. Examples: "Ramiro, although you laughed when you said X, I sensed an underlying message. Do you think my work is off target?" "I note a repeated theme in your comments about the X project. Do you have real objections to my plans?" "Your words are teasing, but I detect something more in your tone. Are you angry for some reason?" "Do you have a complaint about my work? Your comments seem to have double meanings." "I want to make sure I understood what you just said. I took the comment as a negative statement about my organizational abilities. Is that what you meant?" If you ask such a direct question, be prepared for a denial. Never mind; that's not the point. Your purpose is to call the other person's hand. Such comments force the hostility and/or work problem into the open so that you can deal with it.

Tip 931. Create a Sense of Obligation.

Feed other people's beliefs that they must depend on you—either because of your job function, because of expertise that you have and they need, or because of someone you know who can help or hurt their careers. People who realize that they are dependent on you will learn to cooperate with a much-improved attitude.

Tip 932. Prepare Gossip Stoppers.

If the shared gossip insults someone else and you don't want to play a role in it, stop the conversation with one of these lines; vary your tone with your purpose: "I'm surprised to hear you say that—Janice always has such nice things to say about you." "Frankly, I'm puzzled. I've never known you to pass on rumors that haven't been checked out." "I really don't pay much attention to the grapevine—things get so twisted. Don't you agree?" "That story has probably gone through so many tellings that I bet half the details are missing." "Really? I think I'll mention that to Cindy so that she'll know she needs to set the record straight."

Tip 933. Play the Reverse Gossip Game.

My colleague Bob Burg, in his e-book *Winning Without Intimidation*, suggests this game of solitaire—I say solitaire, even though it involves three people, because the challenge is all yours as a quick thinker. In a nutshell, the Reverse Gossip Game goes like this: you pass on the good things that people say about others rather than the bad. Here's an example.

SAM: Debi's always a little spacey, if you know what I mean.

YOU: Never noticed that. But very creative, wouldn't you say?

SAM: Well, I guess you could say that.

At lunch you see Debi and say,

YOU: Sam and I were talking about you earlier—about how creative you are.

DEBI: Really? I always thought he was arrogant. I didn't even think he knew who I was—much less gave me credit for knowing the time of day.

YOU: Hmmm. No, I've never noticed that. He's really committed to this project, don't you think? He's been putting in the hours like you wouldn't believe.

DEBI: You're right about that, for sure.

A couple of days later, you're talking to Sam again:

YOU: Debi and I were talking yesterday about how committed you've been to this project—what long hours you've been putting in.

SAM: Hmmm. I didn't think anybody noticed—or cared.

Result: The next time these two people are together, they're likely to feel differently about each other.

Tip 934. Show a Blank to the Braggart.

Braggarts have any number of reasons for blowing their own horn about their accomplishments, possessions, or connections: a form of intimidation, narcissism, insecurity, or simply ignorance. Whatever the reason, you can stop them with a bland response: "Oh." "Interesting." "Hmmm." "I didn't know that." "Nice." "Good." Pause and then change the subject. The message is: I'm not impressed.

Tip 935. Sidestep Invasive Questions.

Some people lack the social graces to separate appropriate topics from the inappropriate. Others like the challenge of seeing people squirm when they ask an insulting or highly personal question. Select your response based on what you perceive the other person's intentions to be—from silence and a mere shrug to a more direct response:

- "So why would you ask that?"
- "And why do you need that information?"
- "I don't feel comfortable in answering that, Jason."
- "That's personal information, Tina."

Or, if you prefer, try humor:

- "Are you writing a book? Then leave that chapter out." (My all-time favorite, used by a longtime friend when he doesn't want to answer me about something.)
- "I'll forgive you for asking—if you'll forgive me for not answering."
- "We have a long history of forgetfulness in our family."
- "And you want my job, Mike?"
- "OK, where's the camera? Where's the mic? This is going on YouTube, right?"

Tip 936. Minimize the Contact.

If you cannot get your message across because the other person refuses to hear it, do whatever it takes to minimize contact with that person. Ask that she be transferred to another job. Resign from the committee. Time your errands so that you do not pass that person. Write, rather than speak, any messages. Use go-betweens for any necessary interaction.

Tip 937. Don't Collect Injustices.

After once being hurt, some people keep a defensive mindset forever. For example, you walk into the office on Monday morning and someone asks, "How was your weekend?" You answer, "Lousy. I planned to go skiing and it rained." He responds, "Well, don't blame me!" After a conflict has finally erupted and then has been settled temporarily, be willing to let the tension fade. Choose to let it go.

19

Praising (and Accepting Praise) so Your Comments Carry Weight

They say such nice things about people at their funerals that it makes me sad to realize I'm going to miss mine by just a few days.
—Garrison Keillor

The deepest principle in human nature is the craving to be appreciated.
—William James

I've learned that people will forget what you said, people will forget what you did, but people will never forget how you made them feel.
—Maya Angelou

Kind words do not cost much ... Yet they accomplish much.
—Blaise Pascal

The greatest efforts of the human race have been directly traceable to the love of praise.
—John Ruskin

I can live for two months on a good compliment.
—Mark Twain

As the Greek said, many men know how to flatter; few know how to praise.
—Wendell Phillips

Some pay a compliment as if they expected a receipt.
—Frank McKinney Hubbard

Giving praise is much like giving love. The giver is usually the most
benefited. He casts bread upon the waters and often gets back cake.
                                                    —Irving Feldman

J ust because praising others comes easily, don't be lulled into thinking
that all commendations and congratulations are effective and welcomed. Praise, just like constructive criticism, takes skillful delivery. And
there's a big difference between flattery and praise. For some people,
accepting praise can be as difficult as accepting a gift. If you wouldn't consider insulting people who have given you a gift, you don't want to insult
them by not accepting their praise. These tips will provide perspective on
both giving and receiving compliments.

Tip 938. Distinguish Between Praise and Flattery.

Flattering comments focus on things that someone has no control over and
did nothing to earn. Praise, on the other hand, focuses on a person's commendable character, performance, or behavior.

> *Flattery.* "You're so tall. You strike an imposing figure as a leader."
> *Praise.* "You have analyzed our situation well and come up with a
> unique strategy to build market share. Your plan is highly creative."

Phyllis McGinley puts it this way: "Praise is warming and desirable.
But it is an earned thing. It has to be deserved, like an honorary degree or
a hug from a child." Flattery, on the other hand, can leave people feeling
as though they've been patted on the head like a cocker spaniel.

Tip 939. Notice Opportunities to Praise.

People withhold praise for many reasons. Some people feel that others
never come up to their standard of performance. Some people are naturally
impersonal and distant around others. Some managers hold the philosophy
that punishment works better than praise. Still others think they're too busy
to comment on "little things." And finally, some people's failure to praise
others can be attributed to the fact that they're too hard on themselves. They
see even stellar performance from themselves as routine. They do good
work, they get a paycheck, and they expect no verbal pats on the back. So
they take it for granted that others operate on that same principle.

You've probably heard the story about the husband who had been married for 40 years and never told his wife he loved her. When she complained, he replied, "I told you I loved you the day we got married; if I change my mind, I'll let you know." Some bosses and coworkers operate under the same philosophy: "You're still working here, aren't you? If you make a mistake, I'll let you know."

For better relationships, take notice of praiseworthy effort, performance, or results. Something's bound to surface that deserves a compliment. If it doesn't, remind yourself to look harder.

Tip 940. Consider Emotional "Behavior" as Being Worthy of Praise.

For a customer service rep to keep her cool under pressure when dealing with an irate customer can take as much presence of mind as designing an ad campaign. And it can be as important, as well. When it comes to praise, don't limit your thinking to action or performance. Examples: "I appreciate your admitting the error. Many people would have pretended they did not know what had happened to the machine." "Thank you for being honest about the situation and your misjudgment." "Your reaction to the criticism in the staff meeting this morning was commendable. You zeroed in on the issues and discarded the guff without defensiveness." "I admire the way you stood firm in your position yesterday, but did not become aggressive with the customer. That takes finesse and patience that many people don't have."

Tip 941. Follow the Military's Lead in Giving Medals.

Soldiers earn medals for everything from grooming themselves well to doing an assigned task well to saving a life. The benefits that soldiers receive from medals include recognition of personal effort, security concerning their job, approval by others, a sense of belonging and camaraderie, and the satisfaction of personal development. The list closely resembles Maslow's list of basic human needs, doesn't it? In the civilian world, praise can be as meaningful as medals.

Tip 942. Award Praise to Your Superiors.

Bosses usually dish out the praise to their staff members, but that doesn't mean that they would not benefit from and appreciate kind, sincere words from others. Recently, a two-star general in the U.S. Army arrived at a post to conduct the promotion ceremony for several lower-ranking officers. Afterward, most people were awed by the general's presence, and few people moved in his direction. Finally one colonel who was most impressed with the ceremony approached the general and commented, "Sir, may I give you a little feedback?"

The general cleared his throat and nodded. The colonel continued, "As you can imagine, I've seen hundreds of these ceremonies, and most of them are routine. But this one was not. You personalized your comments to each of the officers, and you remarked on what they had done to deserve the promotion. That took time and preparation. I could tell that it was a meaningful ceremony for the officers involved and their families."

The general smiled broadly. "Thanks for saying that. That'll make my day." He paused. "In fact, that's good enough to make my year." Superiors seldom hear praise. If you mean it, say it.

Tip 943. Watch Out for One-Up Praise.

A person who offers praise may appear to be placing himself in a one-up position. For example, consider this comment delivered to a speaker after a presentation: "I enjoyed your presentation. You did a nice job in comparing one investment to another. I think you mentioned all the relevant tax laws most people need to concern themselves with." That compliment implies that the giver is in a position to judge the thoroughness or accuracy of the material that the speaker presented. In a similar situation, take care not to word your compliment in such a way that you are elevating your own expertise. A better phrasing of the previous compliment might have been: "I enjoyed your presentation. Your comparison of investments was intriguing, and your insights on the tax laws were some I've never heard shared before today."

Tip 944. Establish Your Credibility as a Praise *Giver.*

Not all praise is equal. You can destroy the value of the praise you give if the receiver doesn't respect you or if she doesn't consider you to be in a position to judge. Other ways to damage your ability to praise include giving it lavishly, in the wrong place, at the wrong time, for the wrong purpose, with the wrong wording. Praise in and of itself is not *automatically* a motivator.

Tip 945. Be Aware That the Absence of Praise Can Mean Criticism.

If the boss customarily reinforces jobs well done with compliments and suddenly has nothing specifically positive to say, a staffer may fill in the blanks. "He didn't say anything about the new website design. He must not have liked it."

Tip 946. Praise People When You Don't Want Anything.

Offering praise should not be a prelude to more work. "I really like the way this report is organized. Do you have a few minutes to show me how to put the same kinds of graphics in mine?" is likely to bring a frown rather than a smile. Make praise an end in and of itself, not a transitional thought.

Tip 947. Praise Individuals Rather Than Groups.

Group praise leaves individuals feeling anonymous. Groups don't do work; individuals do. People feel better about their contribution when you recognize them individually by calling their names. *Not:* "I want to thank your group for its contribution on the project that turned out so well." *But:* "The project was finished ahead of time within a very tight window and with a lean budget—to the client's total satisfaction—thanks to the creative thinking of Luis, Andrea, Harvey, and Misong. I appreciate the contributions each of you makes."

Tip 948. Be Specific in Your Praise.

Specific praise sounds more sincere than vague generalizations. Let other people know that you understand what they had to do to get the good rating. *Not:* "Miguel, you handle irate customers with finesse." *But:* "Miguel, I observed how you handled that last customer. When he started yelling, it took a bit of restraint on your part to keep your cool. Heather said you even offered to deliver the customer's merchandise yourself on the way home. That's going to eat into your personal time. I appreciate that extra effort."

Tip 949. Create a Scene.

Typically, people go through life thinking, "Don't make a scene." When the coffee at the local diner arrives cold, you just move along and don't make a scene. When your toddler acts up in the supermarket, you think, "If I can just get her home and not make a scene."

But when someone's due for praise, that's another story. He needs time to enjoy the comments. If you don't believe it, recall praising comments from your past: a positive performance appraisal; a client testimonial; a thank-you e-mail or letter for work on a neighborhood committee; recommendations on LinkedIn. How many times did you read the comments? How many times did you replay the conversation in your head?

People deserve time to bask in the limelight. Create a scene. Elaborate on what they did to get the good rating. Make your comments last for a few moments.

Tip 950. Comment on the Deed Rather Than the Person When the Issue Is Performance.

When you compliment people by labeling them, they don't necessarily know what they did to get the good rating. As a result, they may feel that the praise is insincere. And if they enjoyed the praise, they will lack direction regarding what they did well and how to get a repeat performance.

Not: "Connie, you're so thoughtful."

But: "Connie, stopping to pick up lunch for us was thoughtful. That'll save a great deal of time that I desperately need to spend on that white paper. I'm glad you thought of that while you were out."

Not: "Leonard, you do good work!"

But: "Leonard, the proposal you submitted to Frank Hathaway was excellent. The benefit statements were well written and unique to that customer situation. Looks like you put a lot of effort into customizing it."

In the second statements, Connie and Leonard will feel deserving of the sincere, specific compliments on their actions.

Tip 951. Credit the Person Rather Than the Deed When the Issue Is Character or Personality.

At times, you want to compliment people on their good judgment, their ethics, their supportive attitude, or their disposition: "Max, you're a really solid employee." "Denise, I wish all our supervisors had your good judgment." If your observations are based on several situations over a long period of time, the comments will not come across as insincere flattery. Just be sure to mention a few of the specific situations that have led you to the praising conclusion.

Tip 952. Personalize Your Comments with "You."

Large corporations use the "you" approach in referring to individual customers by name: "Thank you, Ms. Harris, for shopping with us." Likewise, make your praise more affirming by including the "you." "You do a good job in maintaining this equipment" sounds more personal than, "Good job on the maintenance." "Great idea" isn't as meaningful as, "You came up with a great idea—thanks." "You put in a lot of extra time over the weekend" sounds more personal than, "This took a lot of weekend time, I'm sure."

Tip 953. Point Out the Positive Effects of the Behavior or Performance.

When you're at a loss for words about how to be specific with a compliment, simply comment on the positive results from a person's work or behavior. "Sidney, your survey at the customer's site certainly gave us a good starting point for proposing the new equipment and training. They had been sitting on the fence about whether to fund the project, and your survey pushed them over the edge. It was a smart idea that paid off."

Tip 954. Ignore Any Negative Outcomes.

Even a slight mention of a negative result will taint your compliment about the person's positive effort. If you're praising Joanne for doing an excellent job in drafting a contract, leave unsaid that the customer negotiated a better price in the final go-around. If you're complimenting the audiovisual manager on his lavish stage decorations and lights, don't lament the fact that attendance at the convention was disappointingly low. Even though the low attendance was no reflection on the meeting planner, that negative thought puts a damper on the praise and the overall feeling of accomplishment.

Tip 955. Toss Out a Few Criticisms Occasionally to Add Credibility.

Few people have the distinction of being upbeat and positive about everything that happens around them. If you're so lucky as to have that kind of disposition and the wisdom to keep your mouth shut when you don't have good things to say, you'll have to alter your style slightly when you praise people. If you're always positive, people may not give much credence to your praise. Consider occasionally saying what you don't like so that people believe you when you tell them what you do like about their work, their behavior, or their actions.

Tip 956. Avoid Praising One Person to Criticize Another.

A subtle way to criticize someone is to praise another person in her presence. Bert returns from vacation to hear: "Dru certainly did a thorough job of tying up the loose ends on all her projects before she left for vacation. It would have been nice if everyone had taken the time to do so." Parents make similar remarks about the obedient child to the "delinquent" child. The result? Resentment.

Tip 957. Follow Awkwardly Accepted Praise with a Question.

To lessen the awkward moment when your compliments might make shy people stammer and stutter, simply follow your compliment with a question. The other person can focus on answering your question without having to handle a response to the praise. Examples: "You did a nice job in handling that customer. Has he been in the office before?" Or: "I like your menu selections for all the convention meals—most people just take whatever's offered and don't put in the time you invested in making sure we had such a variety. Do you plan all of the sales meetings?" The shy person simply smiles at the praise and answers your question.

Tip 958. Consider Third-Person Praise.

In a staff meeting, the manager stands in the doorway and comments, "Where's Sylvia? That woman has the stamina of five people. She made 32 appointments last week. Will somebody find out what her secret is and let the rest of us in on it?" Somebody will be sure to pass on to Sylvia what the manager said about her performance. Third-party praise builds morale because it's even more believable when it's delivered as "fact" to someone else.

Tip 959. Deliver "Eavesdropped" Praise.

Deliver your praise to a second person within earshot of the one who's being praised. You'll eliminate the person's need to respond and increase the value of the compliment because it was shared. For example, one colleague talks "around" a friend who's seated at the table with others. "Somebody should tell Carlos the campaign is over. He's still beating the bushes for new customers. Would you believe he reeled in three new accounts last week?" Carlos doesn't have to respond; he can smile modestly and bask in the glow of the conversation around him.

Tip 960. Don't Overpraise.

In the workplace, few people veer even close to this situation, but there is danger in lavishing praise on others at the expense of helpful criticism. Much has been said about building or maintaining others' self-esteem—so much that some people who are responsible for the career development of those they supervise feel uncomfortable in passing on any criticism of poor performance at all. Giving only praise in an attempt to help people progress is like driving your car without a reverse gear. Sometimes you need to back up. Praise does generally accomplish more than negative feedback, but not to the total exclusion of necessary feedback.

Tip 961. When Receiving a Compliment, Don't Match It.

You will sound insincere if you return the exact compliment that someone gives you: "I like your new hairstyle." Response: "Well, yours looks nice also." While the attempt to acknowledge the remark gracefully is understandable, the matching compliment will diminish the other person's gift of words to you. If you sincerely feel that a matching compliment is in order, at least change the phrasing: "You beat me to the punch; I was going to tell you how much I liked..."

Tip 962. Don't Respond to Praise with a Put-Down.

Eliminate these responses: "Tom actually is the person who should get all the credit." "It was really nothing." "I was lucky, that's all." "Oh, I'm not so sure it was of any consequence." "I try." "It was no big deal." "Oh, that? I do that all the time." "Well, I see you finally noticed."

When you brush a compliment aside, you're implying that the other person has made a mistake in offering it. You're insinuating that the person misjudged the accomplishment or effort and gave the praise to the wrong person, at the wrong time, in the wrong situation. At best, when you give such a response, you make the one who offered the praise feel that he has done something to embarrass you rather than honor you. At worst, the other person will take your remark as a rebuff.

Tip 963. Accept Praise Graciously.

Never simply shrug and let a compliment "roll off" as if it were unnoticed, expected, or unappreciated. If praise embarrasses you and you feel at a loss for words, a simple acknowledgment is enough: "Thank you." "I appreciate your noticing." "I like to hear that." "That makes me feel really good." "How nice of you to say that." "Thanks for mentioning that. It makes me feel good that you noticed." "Thank you. I'm glad you're pleased with the results." "Yes, I did have to double-step to get the project finished. Thanks for the acknowledgment of the extra effort." "Thank you. I'm pleased it turned out so well."

Gifts of praise arrive too infrequently. Enjoy them.

20

Delegating and Giving Instructions so "Nothing Falls Through the Cracks"

People learn what you teach them; not what you intend to teach them.

—B. F. Skinner

Educators take something simple and make it complicated. Communicators take something complicated and make it simple.

—John C. Maxwell

An expert is someone who is one page ahead of you in the manual.

—David Knight

There seems to be some perverse human characteristic that likes to make easy things difficult.

—Warren Buffett

Everybody gets so much information all day long that they lose their common sense.

—Gertrude Stein

Facts mean nothing unless they are rightly understood, rightly related, and rightly interpreted.

—No attribution

If at first you don't succeed, destroy all evidence that you tried.

—Fahnestock's Rule for Failure

As coworkers, colleagues, and customers, we instruct people on how to market using social media, how to calculate lease payments, and how to merge conglomerates without chaos. Granted, some tasks are easier than others, but they all involve certain principles of explaining the unknown to a novice or newcomer. The following tips cover everything from media and message to motivation and mastery.

Tip 964. Pay Attention to Telltale Signs of Poor Instructions.

Listen to the conversations around you in staff meetings, in the workroom, or at home to identify trouble spots in instruction giving:

- "Does anybody have any questions about what I just explained?" (You get only blank stares.)
- "Does anybody have any questions about what I just explained?" (Answer: "Would you say it again?")
- "Nobody told me that."
- "Why didn't you mention that before we started the project?"
- "If there's any way to screw it up, these people will."
- "What do you mean 'delegate'? I can do it better and faster myself."
- Repetitions of the following: "Would you tell me *again* how to set the timer (run this machine, run these numbers, adjust these buttons, calculate these figures)?"

If these sound familiar, you have a problem with instructions.

Tip 965. Understand the Magnitude of a Foul-Up.

Until people understand what a low-tech blunder can mean in a high-tech office, they won't be motivated to give instructions the attention they deserve. After we have had to clean up our messes globally and culturally, we all eventually learn.

Tip 966. Motivate People to "Listen Up" by Focusing on Benefits.

It's generally more difficult to do things that you hate to do or that you don't consider relevant to your personal success than to do something that you enjoy or that will make you a billion dollars. Even when you're giving instructions, motivation matters. Make the project understandable, relevant, and important to others' personal success. Dwell on the personal benefits of the acquired knowledge or skill.

Tip 967. Understand the Difference Between Being Directive and Giving Direction.

Being directive involves giving orders and telling people exactly what to do and how to do it: "Please get me that Wilson report and put last month's sales figures into a spreadsheet that I can read easily."

Giving direction involves oversight and guidance. Direction includes setting goals, setting expectations for outcomes and results, sharing strategies to reach those outcomes, and setting parameters for time frames and resources.

You may need to be directive in some situations—for example, in a safety situation or with an untrained and inexperienced employee. But for the most part, people prefer direction rather than directives.

Tip 968. Decide Whether to Delegate Projects by Goals or Tasks.

A goal: "See what you can do to improve traffic flow around this office." A task: "Order some shelving that takes less floor space than what we now have." Neither approach works all the time with all the people. To determine the best approach, consider both the person and the project.

Goals such as, "Develop a strategy to increase our market share by 3 percent this year" can excite the seasoned marketing director eager to please, or can frustrate the inexperienced sales rep.

Tasks, on the other hand, may be equally worrisome or welcome: "Call Joan Frazier to ask how many people she expects to attend the luncheon, and then order engraved invitations. Get them in the mail by October 15. Then reserve a ballroom at the Hyatt, and select a salad menu, something under 20 dollars per person." To your new administrative assistant, such detailed instructions may be reassuring, but to the corporate meeting planner, they would be insulting or frustrating.

Tip 969. Clarify Whether People Can Refuse to Accept the Assignment.

If we have learned anything from Jim Phelps of *Mission Impossible*, we have learned the importance of accepting a mission. Some projects and tasks are doomed from the get-go because people say yes and do no. Some people hate to say no. So when they hear what they perceive to be a request from a peer—say, a team leader or a committee chair—they accept the assignment, but then do nothing. Because the person assigning the task or delegating the project isn't a mind reader and doesn't have a check-back built into the system before a critical due date, the project never gets off the ground.

A preventive step: Give people the freedom to say no when they have a choice in the matter. Emphasize that you *prefer* that they say no and do yes than that they say yes and do no.

Tip 970. Organize Well.

You can organize by topic, location, chronology, importance, or frequency of the task. Organization of your instructions is the beginning of clarity.

Tip 971. Give an Overview of the Goal.

State your overall intention. If all else fails, the person can always follow the spirit of your instructions, if not the letter of the law. A mission might be, "Make our star performers feel that they're special to our executive team."

Tip 972. State the Measurable Results.

How will the follower know that he has been successful? What is the tangible final product? A conference in a resort location to which the star performers can bring a guest?

Tip 973. Outline Any Procedure You Have in Mind.

Don't make the process a guessing game. If you have a certain procedure or process in mind, say so. Give the steps, actions, and explanations. Should the person assigned select the star performers by the numbers, or will someone else determine the guest list? Should she handle all the arrangements, or should she use a local meeting planner in the Caribbean? Should she make a personal site visit to several places before deciding on a location, or should she go with a local referral?

Tip 974. Tick Off the Timeline.

State the deadline—either for the project as a whole or for various interim steps. When do you expect all the details to be complete? When do you expect the star performers to receive an announcement about the event? When is the meeting to be held?

Tip 975. Share the Budget.

I'm not suggesting that you go into too much detail, but don't keep the budget a mystery. Mention the money available—upper and lower limits. You don't want to have in mind a budget for a sit-down dinner and discover that the meeting planner took your instruction to "watch the meal expenses" to mean a box lunch on the beach.

Tip 976. Warn People About the Worry Factors.

Mention things that the follower may encounter during the project that may create confusion and worry. With your advance warning, you'll lessen his apprehension when obstacles surface, when some steps take longer than anticipated, or when negotiations or changes in plans may be appropriate. End your recital of the worry factors with a clear definition of failure. What is inappropriate for the sales meeting? At what points or when what decisions or problems arise should the person report back to you for help?

Tip 977. Give Followers a Context.

"Make yourself comfortable when you plan to give visitors a tour of the building." Does this mean jeans and a T-shirt or a halter top, or does it mean walking shoes rather than high heels and lightweight fabrics rather than wools?

A manager asked his assistant to find the middle initial of a former chairman of the board. After searching online files to find the appropriate annual report without success, she spent two hours to retrieve files from their offsite storage location and finally located the retired official's middle initial. Upon her return, feeling rather proud of her resourcefulness, she announced her discovery to the boss—only to find out that his intended use was a gag birthday card for the retiree, whom he planned to play golf with on the weekend.

Whenever you're giving employees instructions to do a task, also give them the goal and context of the task so that they can make intelligent decisions along the way concerning things you can't anticipate.

Tip 978. Use Both Words and Pictures for Best Results.

If your instructions need to be repeated often, consider whether they should be in words (better for precision) or in pictures (better for speed). For best results, use both.

Tip 979. Give All the Pieces of the Puzzle.

I just returned from a 10-minute trip to a client's office that took 35 min-utes. Why? Here were the directions: "As you exit the rental car parking lot, you'll be on 1272. At the second signal light, turn left onto Magrauder Avenue. Then take the first left from Magrauder onto Bennet Street. Drive until the street dead-ends into the dock. Our plant is the building adjacent to the dock."

The problem? The client forgot to tell me that Bennet Street was called Division Street at the Magrauder intersection. It's difficult to remember how confusing something used to be before you learned it. To put it another way: It's difficult to give instructions for something that you understand intimately and have known for a long time. One omitted detail can mean the difference between success and failure. "I thought you'd surely know that blah, blah, blah" is a lame excuse for such omissions.

Tip 980. Avoid an Excess of Detail.

Too much is too much. "You'll be on Foster Street, and you'll come to a flashing light, then a stop sign. There's a Chevron station on your left, a Shell station on your right. I think there's a Burger King just past that. You've gone too far if you see the Burger King 'Drive-thru.' There's a driveway marked with a sign FOR DELIVERIES ONLY that angles off to the left, so don't be confused by that. Just keep going to the right, past all the parking spots and the dumpster off in the vacant lot." Detailed direc-tions like that confuse, not clarify.

Tip 981. Prefer Clarity to Brevity.

Brevity is good; clarity is better. Never sacrifice a few words or sentences in order to be brief. Screen space, paper, and air are cheap. Errors are expensive.

Tip 982. Remember That Your Objective Is Not Necessarily to Simplify, but to Clarify.

Your instructions do not need to be given in six-word sentences composed of one-syllable words (although there's nothing wrong with simple words and short sentences). When people question the instructions they receive, the problem is vagueness more often than complexity. Be precise and explicit.

Tip 983. Ask, "What Do You Understand?"

Never ask the more common, "Do you understand?" People generally respond to such a question in the affirmative or with a head nod. After all, who wants to admit, "No, I'm really a slow learner—I didn't get it at all." A better question is, "Tell me—*what* do you understand about the project at this point?" Or, "How do you think you'll proceed on the project at this point?" Or, "What will be your approach to this project?" Generally, the idea should be to have them voice aloud what they understand so that you can verify that they really do understand and further explain what they don't.

Tip 984. Limit "Use Your Own Judgment" Statements to the Exceptions.

A manager tells her employee, "Use your own judgment in shipping these supplies to our plant supervisors—I know you're busy this week." Can the shipments wait a couple of weeks? A month? Two months? Does that mean that the employee should use overnight mail—no matter what the cost? Such vague instructions beg for confusion. Instead, give precise guidelines for the most common situations and then use the catchall "use your own judgment" for the exceptions that no one can anticipate.

Tip 985. Clarify Whether Something Is a Must or a Preference.

"Wear protective lenses when entering the warehouse." Is this a guideline or an enforced safety regulation? Will employees feel less glare if they wear protective lenses, or will their eyesight be endangered if they don't wear them? "Take a taxi to the hotel." Does this mean that employees should not ride the free shuttle if it happens to be passing as they exit the airport terminal? Or, is taking a taxi a must because time is of the essence and the shuttle makes three interim stops?

Tip 986. Remember That the "Don'ts" Don't Necessarily Dictate the "Dos."

A sign on the mall doorway reads: "Do not enter through this door." So does that mean that you should enter through the doorway adjacent to the one with the sign, or does it mean that you should go to the other side of the store? "Do not force this lever when paper becomes jammed." So how do you remove the jammed paper? Can you jiggle the lever? Should you lift the lever? Should you find another lever or button to manipulate? Let's say the vice president instructs the sales team: "Don't offer to prepare a time-consuming proposal for our clients unless they specifically ask for one." Is it okay to prepare a proposal if you can use an old boilerplate and prepare one quickly?

Tip 987. Don't Make False Claims or Promises.

"After you apply two or three coats, the shine will become hard and durable." If followers apply three coats and don't see a hard shine, they'll think they've done something wrong and will often redo or undo the previous steps. "You'll have a newly wallpapered room in an hour" numbs the imagination of the worker who has been at the task all day.

Tip 988. Don't Insult Your Followers.

Watch phrases such as, "You should be finished in 10 minutes." "Everybody says it's as easy as falling off a log." "These instructions are idiot-proof; we've finally worked all the bugs out, and you should have no trouble." Do you think your followers will admit to having any questions or doing it wrong?

Tip 989. Use Correct Grammar; the Meaning Often Depends on It.

At the Dallas–Fort Worth airport, a sign at one of the restaurants reads NO SMOKING AREAS AVAILABLE. Does this mean that the restaurant has no areas where patrons can smoke? Or, does it mean that it has areas designated for nonsmokers? To solve this case of the missing hyphen, insert one appropriately: "No-smoking areas available."

"Turn the lever and depress the cylinder that opens the air chamber." Is this one action or two? Do you turn the lever and depress the cylinder simultaneously, or do you take one action after the other? Or, is depression of the cylinder the result of turning the lever?

Proper grammar produces clear writing. If instructions on technical procedures sound fuzzy, check the grammar.

Tip 990. Avoid Hostile Repetition of the Same Words.

If someone does not understand your instructions, don't assume a patronizing or irritated tone and repeat the same words: "As I told you earlier, the equipment needs to be cleaned thoroughly." If you "told him earlier," don't tell him again in the same words. Assume that the question is a good indication that the follower doesn't understand what "cleaned thoroughly" means. Use different words to express what you mean by "cleaned thoroughly": Wiped with a damp cloth? Sprayed with a water hose? Or scrubbed with a disinfectant?

Tip 991. Curb a Superior Tone.

Sometimes the person giving the instructions assumes a superior, smarter position—and often models the classroom-teacher tone from grade-school days: "Now, listen carefully as I call out the correct answers to this quiz." "Now, line up against the wall, and wait until I tell you to go." "Wait until I give you permission to leave." To prevent taking on that tone, keep the rebellious student in mind as you word your instructions or delegate projects to colleagues.

Tip 992. Be Approachable for Reruns.

Let others know that it's okay to ask you additional questions as they proceed with a project—or even before they begin. Comments like, "As you get into this, be sure to let me know if you discover I've left out something," or, "If something I said was unclear, be sure to ask me again rather than wasting your time or becoming frustrated," lets your followers know that you're accepting some of the responsibility for the clarity and success of your instructions.

Tip 993. Duck Boomerangs.

If delegated projects and tasks frequently bounce back to you, consider that a symptom of a problem that requires further investigation. Start by looking back through these tips to make sure that you typically provide adequate information up front when you delegate. As a further step, ask the person who routinely bounces the project or task back to you these questions: "What *specific* questions do you have for me? What can I do to help you complete this project *on your own? Which aspects* of the project or task aren't clear to you? Tell me *exactly what you've thought through* and where you're stuck."

Such questions force the other person to understand that the responsibility for follow-through rests with her. A direct statement cements the expectation: "I expect you to resolve the issue." "This is your project to complete." "I could do this project, but I've assigned it to you, and I trust you with it. Let me know when it's complete."

Regifting has become an accepted practice. But redelegating to your boss should *not* be standard practice.

Tip 994. Take into Account the Frequency of the Task.

If you're telling someone how to complete a series of tax forms, you should expect that you'll have to tell him again each year for several years. Why? He doesn't do the task often enough to remember it. When you know that there'll be a time lapse between repetitions of the task that you're teaching, plan for forgetting. Leave an example, model, or written instructions for a refresher. One time around won't do it.

Tip 995. Choose the Appropriate Medium.

If the instructions are simple and concise, you may give them once orally. If they're complex and will need to be referred to over and over, consider an online job aid, a video post on the intranet or your YouTube channel, or a live demonstration. Consider whether the instructions should be light and entertaining or matter-of-fact. Sometimes the delivery and the medium motivate people to understand the message.

Tip 996. Build Instructions into the Product or the Process.

Either make information accessible or forget it. Through the years, my husband and I have used this "build-it-in" principle to create fun for our children's (and now grandchildren's) Easter egg hunts. We hide the candy-filled basket and plant clues on cards hidden around the house and the yard. The children tackle the whole treasure hunt, instruction card by instruction card. The first card leads them to the second clue instruction card, which they retrieve to read the clue and search for the third card and clue. Even in serious work situations, built-ins help. If your information is complex enough to record for later use, then record it so that people can find it. Build instructions into the item or process.

Tip 997. Realize That Understanding Doesn't Necessarily Lead to Action.

People may understand a project or a task completely and still take no action. That's where motivation moves into the picture. No amount of explaining, verifying, double-checking, nagging, planning, repeating, or clarifying will do the trick. Skip to the persuasion chapter in this book to address the motivation issue.

Tip 998. Categorize the Follower's Personality and Attitude and Adapt Your Style.

Instruction takers fall into these various categories and personality types:

- "Don't go so fast" (slow learner)
- "I got it; I got it" (fast learner, impatient)
- "I don't need instructions" (kinestic learner)
- "I just don't get it" (overwhelmed, confused)
- "I'm all thumbs" (lacks confidence to try)
- "While I'm thinking about it, I've got a question about Barcelona" (unfocused)
- "I'll never need to know that" (sees no benefit, unmotivated)
- "Who are you to tell me?" (resistant learner)
- "Where will you be if I need help?" (lacks confidence, helpless)

Plan your pep talk, your order, your offer, and your phrasing accordingly.

Tip 999. Pinpoint Your Own Style and Modify What Doesn't Work for You or the Other Person.

Delegators fall into several general categories. Do you see yourself in any of the following types?

- "I don't have time to explain" (impatient)
- "Just let me put out this fire and I'll be back" (unfocused)
- "Just believe me—it works; do it" (dictator)
- "Then you... Oh, I forgot to mention... Back to the... and while I'm thinking of it... Second, you try..." (disorganized)
- "Now don't do anything until I tell you" (controlling, sees only one way to do things)

- "Just do as I do" (unknowledgeable in instructing or delegating)
- "Forget how I do it myself—just listen to what I'm telling you" (theoretical)
- "You're really going to love this" (motivator)
- "Even *you* can learn this" (demotivator)
- "You don't need instructions, do you?" (impatient self-starter)

Identify your delegation habits and hang-ups, and you'll learn how "you are here" maps in malls became such a hit.

21

Minimizing Cross-Talk Between Men and Women

Men and women belong to different species and communications between them is still in its infancy.

—Bill Cosby

A study in the Washington Post says that women have better verbal skills than men. I just want to say to the authors of that study: "Duh."

—Conan O'Brien

My first wife divorced me on grounds of incompatibility, and besides, I think she hated me.

—Oscar Levant

As soon as you cannot keep anything from a woman, you love her.

—Paul Geraldy

In the last 50 years, a great deal of research has been done on gender communication issues. The result? Men and women communicate differently. You knew that. Some researchers had previously theorized that all the observed differences could be explained by the differences in power and status in our culture. For example, they argued, when women have more power and status in the workplace, their language will change. To some extent, that has been true. Powerful people of either gender speak more confidently than lower-status people with no power. It stands to reason.

Nevertheless, major differences in the communication styles of men and women remain. In addition to my own research, these differences have also been investigated and reported by Robin Lakoff, Lillian Glass, John Gray, Deborah Tannen, Patricia Arburdene and John Naisbitt, Patricia Heim, and Barbara Annis, to name the most noteworthy researchers.

As you read the following tips, keep in mind that all differences in communication are a matter of degree and that particular differences may not exist in all men or all women. We are individuals first, of course, with our own idiosyncrasies and ways of conversing. This chapter presents tendencies and techniques—not universal truths for members of either gender.

QUESTION OR OBJECTION?

As females grow up in our culture, they are taught not to be con-frontational—not to make a scene or be aggressive or pushy. Although in the 18 years since the first edition of this book was published, women have become more assertive in their language, they still struggle against the label and perception of aggressiveness. They still want to be consid-ered "nice."

So how do they express opposition to an idea? Often they use ques-tions to redirect someone's thinking. They also, of course, use questions in the traditional way—to solicit information, to build consensus around an idea, or to develop their staff members and help them rethink their positions, plans, or ideas.

Men, on the other hand, do not always recognize indirect messages or pick up on nuances in words or body language. In short, they don't always accurately "read between the lines" to understand the meaning of a woman's question. The results: (1) Women ask questions that are meant in a variety of ways, and men may ignore their implied objections and feel-ings. (2) Women ask questions that are meant only to solicit information, to which men may react defensively.

Tip 1000. (for women) State Your Objections Directly.

Not: "Do you really think we should leave early?" *But:* "I don't think we should leave early." *Not:* "How much higher did you say Vendor A's bid is?" *But:* "I think Vendor A's bid is too high."

Tip 1001. (for men) Verify Whether Questions Are Solicitations of Information or Objections, Then Respond Appropriately.

If you're not sure how to take a question, probe before answering. Here's an example:

WOMAN: Have you already signed the contract for the new equipment?

MAN: Not yet. I'll get to it later in the week.

WOMAN: Didn't John have some concerns about the terms?

MAN: He cleared those up in the last meeting.

WOMAN: Do you think we should just forget about the staffing priorities, since this new equipment purchase will eat up all our cash this quarter?

MAN: I'm sensing maybe you're not sure that buying the equipment is a good decision. Do you still have some reservations there?

WOMAN: Well, yes, ... I do. I think that ...

Once objections are in the open, you can deal with them more effectively.

DETAILS OR BIG PICTURE?

Women generally push for details for three reasons: to show concern about a person or situation, to vicariously participate in an experience or conversation, and to verify assumptions and check for accuracy. Men tend to gather details just long enough to get the big-picture message and then dump them as trivial, not worth remembering.

The results: (1) When men don't ask about or share the details of a situation, women sometimes think that they don't care about the people involved. (2) Women sometimes think that men intend to be secretive and distant. (3) Women sometimes doubt men's conclusions because they fear that men have missed some of the important details. (4) Men sometimes think that women "waste time" on the details rather than get to the main point. (5) Men think some details are irrelevant to their conclusions.

Tip 1002. (for women) Get to the Point in Meetings.

If a discussion of the details is not germane to the point in a team meeting, be aware of men's impatience with them. State your big-picture assessment and offer the details as an option. If no one solicits the details behind your conclusions, omit them and save yourself the trouble.

Tip 1003. (for women) Ask for Details to Verify Meaning.

In "sticky" situations, continue to probe for details to verify meanings and reach accurate conclusions. For example, when you're trying to verify the state of mind of an unhappy customer, dig out the details of the conversation that you missed in order to double-check your sales plans.

Tip 1004. (for women) Discuss Details to Show Concern.

Continue to ask questions and discuss situations that friends and colleagues toss out as means of showing support and interest. Whether or not men reciprocate when the situation is reversed should not inhibit your own caring attitude.

Tip 1005. (for women) Don't Jump to the Conclusion That Men Don't Care About a Situation Simply Because They Don't Ask for or Give Details.

Realize that men may fail to discuss details simply because they are not in the habit of doing so.

Tip 1006. (for men) Use Women's Inclination to Discuss Details to Verify Your Understanding of a Problem or Situation.

Realize that big-picture messages may be inaccurate if the process of selecting and sifting details is hurried. Take advantage of women's preference for detailed analysis of a problem to make sure that the solutions you generate are solutions to the right problem.

Tip 1007. (for men) Pay Attention to Details to Show Concern.

For example, to a female engineer, a discussion of the colors of the new lobby decor may mean that you understand and care that the success of the renovation project will be important to her career—and satisfy the customer's specifications.

SMALL TALK OR BIG TALK?

Women often talk to build rapport with others. When that's the case, the information exchanged is secondary to the connection. They may talk about personal topics, such as relationships, family, experiences, and social activities, or about business issues. To women, an important aspect of conversation is simply "connecting" emotionally with another person. Women also talk to explore their own feelings and opinions, as well as to come to a decision. Consequently, they consider most subjects worthy of conversation.

Men, on the other hand, tend to view conversation as a means of exchanging information or solving problems. They discuss events, facts, happenings in the news, or sports—generally topics not directly related to themselves. Other subjects, such as "routine" matters, may, in men's estimation, not warrant conversational effort.

Results: (1) Women toss out conversational topics, and men respond only minimally or not at all. As a result, women sometimes think that men do not care about them personally. (2) Some men may think that women talk too much about "trivial" subjects.

Tip 1008. (for women) Continue to Signal Men About What's Important Enough for Conversation.

By the phrasing you choose, let men know that you expect a response when you pose a question or make a comment.

Tip 1009. (for women) State Outright That You Are Interested in Conversation Just for the Sake of Connection.

Make a direct statement that you want conversation in the same way you might state that you want an opinion on a staff problem. Example: "Have you got a minute for a cup of coffee? I need to talk to somebody besides my computer for a change. Tell me about the project you're working on."

Tip 1010. (for men) Expand Your Repertoire of Conversational Topics to Include "the Routine."

If conversation is good just for the sake of the camaraderie it generates, then any topic is as good as any other. Don't pressure yourself into thinking that every topic you introduce or every response you make has to be profound. Routine will do. The act of talking may be most important to your colleague or customer.

Tip 1011. (for men) Explain Your Desire to "Connect" Despite Your Lack of Conversation.

If you simply can't think of any information to share or appropriate responses to a woman's comments, say so directly, but offer encouragement in the process: "I'm enjoying listening to your account of the meeting. Tell me more," or, "I'm talked out, but don't let that stop you. If you have time, I'd really like to hear how your project turned out." Then listen.

FACTS OR FEELINGS?

Women talk more about people than about things. In our culture, females grow up with permission to express their frustration, disappointment, or pain. They express their feelings, get them out, and move on to other things. Males have been taught to suppress such feelings; unlike women, they hold on to those feelings longer under the surface. Yes, even after four decades of discussion about "the sensitive male," men's conversations still lean toward the factual rather than the personal. "Personal" does not necessarily mean "intimate," but rather simply off-the-record comments about personal activities, likes, dislikes, fears, hopes, or plans. Men talk more about things than about people.

Neither type of conversation—facts or feelings, people or things—is better; the issue involves sharing conversation for whatever relationship you want to create: friend or acquaintance.

Result: (1) Women share feelings to create a bond or intimacy in the relationship. When men don't reciprocate, women think men are intentionally creating distance. (2) Women do not often consider colleagues or customers close friends if they have never discussed personal topics and issues.

Tip 1012. (for women) Share Both Facts and Feelings.

Model the sharing that you want. Continue to talk about both facts and feelings in conversation so that men will feel comfortable and encouraged to reciprocate.

Tip 1013. (for women) Don't Assume That When Men Do Not Share Feelings, They Are Trying to Create Distance.

Attribute a man's reluctance to share personal information—for example, his regret that he missed his son's ball game because of work-related travel—to discomfort rather than to disinterest in building camaraderie.

Tip 1014. (for women) Talk More About Things With Men.

You can always start with the day's newspaper headlines and trade facts or opinions to build rapport. Although such a discussion may not feel "personal" to you, having common opinions and interests will build a bond with a man.

Tip 1015. (for men) Share Feelings to Create Camaraderie or Intimacy in Personal Relationships.

Examples of personal information include things like plans for an upcoming family activity, enjoyment of a hobby, disappointment about how the economy is affecting your family, frustration over difficulties in working on a project, opinions on ethical situations, or plans for your career and your family.

Tip 1016. (for men) Reveal Feelings to Build Loyalty in Customer or Colleague Relationships.

If you've ever lost a customer contract that you considered "safe," reevaluate the relationship. You may have considered a female customer to be a loyal friend simply because the two of you talked. She, on the other hand, may have considered the relationship tenuous because you discussed only "official" business during your calls and visits.

Tip 1017. (for men) Talk More About People and Feelings with Women.

Women are interested in relationships and in the well-being of others around them. Ask how others they know or work with are progressing on various projects, plans, or pursuits.

EMPATHY OR SOLUTION?

When a woman dumps a problem, she wants empathy along with a solution. In fact, being resourceful and creative herself, she may not want a solution at all. She wants to know that someone understands her frustration, disappointment, pain, or predicament. Again, one of women's basic drives is emotional connection with other people.

But when a man hears a problem, he goes about trying to solve it: Try this. Try that. Try the other. Why? Because men win admiration by solving problems. In fact, women often complain that men take on a father role and start treating them like daughters in their attempt to "fix things." In those cases, women feel "dismissed" and are infuriated rather than pleased by the suggested solution.

The reverse is true. When a man has a problem, he wants a specific suggestion for solving it. What does a woman give? What she'd want in return—empathy.

Results: (1) Women grow frustrated when they want empathy and get lectures and solutions. (2) Men grow frustrated when they want solutions and get either empathy or criticism.

Tip 1018. (for women) When Mentioning a Problem, Be Specific About Whether You're Soliciting Support or a Solution.

Examples: "Got a minute? I need to blow off a little steam. That inventory system is archaic. It cost me two hours of overtime yesterday." "I'm so angry I could bite nails and not even taste the iron. Listen to what Troy said about..." Make it clear that you're just passing on information, not asking for answers: "Yeah, yeah, I know how to handle him. I just didn't want to have to terminate him. I'm just complaining to a 'safe' person, you know what I mean?"

Tip 1019. (for women) Interpret Solution Giving as Supportive.

Consider a man's attempt at solving a problem as being a sign of empathetic support. After all, solutions take as much time as expressions of "ain't it awful?"

Tip 1020. (for women) When a Man Mentions a Problem, Offer Options, Not Just Empathy or Criticism.

Examples: "Well, as I see it, you've got two choices..." "Have you thought about talking to Julian in HR about hiring some help?"

Tip 1021. (for women) When a Man Mentions a Problem, Don't Editorialize With "Shoulds" and "Oughts" About Past Actions and Future Actions.

When your assessment of a man's predicament indicates that the whole problem could have been avoided, the temptation is to tell him "helpful" things for next time. Example: "Next time, rather than just signing a blank authorization, you should call to ask if you can examine the written documentation before you purchase the software." Such a comment makes the other person feel stupid, as if he is being criticized for the current problem—a challenge to a man's need for admiration.

Tip 1022. (for women) Make Sure Men Know You Are Not Necessarily Blaming Them When You State a Problem.

You may consider the following comment simply a statement of fact to which you expect a commensurate empathetic statement: "I ran out of gas this afternoon in the company car." Because men see themselves as problem solvers, a likely response might be: "Well, it's not my job to check it before we sign you out. We expect the user to do that." To lessen the defensiveness, add a lead-in to such comments: "I didn't check the gas gauge before I left in the company car, and I ran out of gas." The pressure is off.

Tip 1023. (for men) When You Mention a Problem, Be Specific About What Kind of Response You Want.

Examples: "I forgot the name of the furniture broker that Arthur prefers. Do you know who might have that name?" "I've had to work overtime four nights in a row because I couldn't figure out a way to schedule all the dinner breaks for my people in the shorter days. Do you use a computer scheduling package?" The idea is to end the problem statement with a request for a solution.

Tip 1024. (for men) Interpret Empathy Giving as Supportive.

Giving empathy takes as much time as giving suggestions. Accept it, and then ask for suggestions specifically.

Tip 1025. (for men) When a Woman Mentions a Problem, Offer Empathy, Not Just Solutions.

Examples: "Well, I gather you think he treated you unfairly under the circumstances. You must be concerned that Bryan won't come through with the raise you needed." End of thought. End of discussion—unless she specifically asks for more help.

Tip 1026. (for men) When a Woman Mentions a Problem, Don't Editorialize About How to Solve All Future Problems.

Squelch the temptation to add: "You know, you should never have let Bryan gloss over that morale problem in his department a year ago. And if it comes up again, you should just…"

Tip 1027. (for men) Understand That When a Woman States a Problem Involving You, She Is Not Necessarily Blaming You.

A statement of a problem is a statement of a problem, not an accusation. Don't feel as though you're being cited as the source.

QUESTIONS: RAPPORT BUILDING OR INTRUSIVE?

Women use questions to stimulate conversation. They sometimes ask questions just to express interest in others and to get to know them. They hope men will reciprocate with questions of their own in return; thus, they can build camaraderie, making their working relationship more enjoyable.

Men, on the other hand, don't feel such a driving need to connect emotionally. If they don't see a reason for the conversation, they may choose not to respond or to respond only minimally. Men initiate fewer questions just to encourage others to talk.

Results: (1) Women think some men remain aloof and are noncommunicative. (2) Men think some women invade their privacy.

Tip 1028. (for women) Offer Information About Yourself and Make a Man's Reciprocal Response Optional.

If you want to strike up a conversation with a brief acquaintance or a stranger, start with statements rather than questions.

Tip 1029. (for women) If You Choose to Ask a Series of Questions, Make Them Broad and General Rather Than Narrow and Personal.

Try to add a lead-in that explains why you're asking questions that may seem unusual.

Tip 1030. (for men) Interpret Questions as a Show of Interest.

The information shared is less important than the overture of conversation.

Tip 1031. (for men) Learn to Either Self-Disclose Nonthreatening, Nonconfidential Information or Toss the Question Back to the Woman and Show Interest in Her Response.

If you prefer not to share what you think or feel personally about an issue, offer a broad, general response: "Most people I've talked with do support the policy changes. What do you yourself think about the plans announced yesterday?"

HELP OR HUMILIATION?

Men tend to put the person with the information, skill, or know-how in a superior position. Information or skill equates to power or authority. As boys grow up, they use one-up statements to gain status: "Well, my big brother knows how to tie that kind of knot." "My dad knows how to get free tickets to the game." "My uncle knows all the senators by their first names." To a man's way of thinking, having "inside" access or information puts someone in a position of power and respect.

That's not necessarily true of women. As children, girls grow up gaining approval by being helpful, by getting pats on the head for knowing the answers. Therefore, women like to *give* information to be helpful, and they assume that everyone else does also. Women do not necessarily equate having information or a key skill with power or status. When others offer help to a woman, she feels valued or loved—not necessarily insulted or inferior.

Results: (1) Men often resist having to ask for help or information. (2) Women become impatient and resentful when men cause delays or problems by resisting help.

Tip 1032. (for women) Respect Men's Needs to Solve Their Problems Independently of Others.

They need to feel self-sufficient.

Tip 1033. (for women) Offer Help in a Casual, Offhand Way.

If a man refuses to ask for directions when you're driving somewhere, toss out your own experience: "Last year when our group drove to this conference, we got lost because Highway 2244 had so many detours. What we eventually had to do was..." Pass on your information as personal experience and hope that men use it.

Tip 1034. (for men) Don't Equate Help or Information With Status.

Will Rogers was the first to admit: "Everybody is ignorant, only on different subjects." Try to separate ego from information.

Tip 1035. (for men) Weigh Speed, Accuracy, and Results Against Delays and Status.

Remind yourself of your ultimate goal and consider whether asking for help or information is a necessary step in accomplishing your mission.

SYMPATHY: SUPPORT OR PUT-DOWN?

Women love to have company in their misery. They share misfortunes, great and small, to elicit support and build camaraderie. When others, in turn, respond with similar stories of their own misfortunes, women feel encouraged and "not alone" in their predicaments. Misfortune makes best friends.

Men have a different view. Unless the relationship with the other person is already a close one, most men do not feel comfortable sharing their troubles. Because they seek to gain admiration, misfortune—particularly those that they can't control, such as poor health or the loss of a job—remind them they are *not* in total control of their lives. Misfortunes and related comments may be blows to a man's self-esteem.

Results: (1) Women offer sympathy freely to men, thinking that their sympathy is supportive. (2) Men sometimes feel humiliated by a sympathetic comment, as if someone were "rubbing salt in the wound."

Tip 1036. (for women) Test for Receptivity and Sensitivity Before Offering Sympathy.

If you don't know someone particularly well, broach the subject generally. If a man doesn't mention a problem, don't bring it up yourself. Or, prefer to offer sympathy in general to others of a group. Example: "With layoffs so common these days, people are really in a tight spot. It's always more difficult to look for a job when you don't have one."

Tip 1037. (for men) Interpret Sympathy as a Sign of Caring Rather Than Humiliation.

Consider it salve, not salt, in the wounds.

TO BE LIKED OR RESPECTED?

Given a choice between being liked and being respected, many women would prefer to be liked. It's not that they don't enjoy admiration; it's just that being thought pleasant, open, caring, and likable score higher. Women also find it easier to work with people that they like personally.

As leaders, managers, and team members, women work to build consensus. Their conversations sound like the following: "So what do *you* think, Miriam?" "Well, we certainly agree on that point." "You're certainly right about that." "Let's see where we can get together here."

Men like to be liked, too. But being liked has little to do with gaining respect for their ideas and competing for the dollar or the door prize. Men can argue and shout at one another over the terms of a proposal, then relax together on the golf course a half hour later. They are comfortable with competition. They vie for respect by outproducing, outperforming, and outthinking others. Their conversations sound like the following: "Well, I don't see it that way." "You're dead wrong on that point." "We'll never agree on that issue." "I disagree wholeheartedly." "Okay, so you do it your way, and I'll do it mine."

Results: (1) Women hate not being liked. (2) Men hate not being respected.

Tip 1038. (for women) Learn to Swim in a Competitive Environment.

Men often equate your willingness to compete for your idea, project, or budget with your commitment to it. From a man's viewpoint, if you don't fight for your work or your ideas, they must not be worth fighting for.

Tip 1039. (for women) Learn to Work with People You Don't Necessarily Like.

Separate personality from performance. If necessary, keep reminding yourself how much you're making per hour when you're working with a disagreeable person.

Tip 1040. (for men) Value Cooperation.

Diversity contributes great value in the workplace. Prefer to gain through cooperation what might disappear in a competitive atmosphere.

Tip 1041. (for men) Don't Equate a Woman's Commitment to or Passion for an Idea With Her Willingness to Compete to Gain Acceptance of That Idea.

Evaluate ideas on their own merit, not on someone's delivery of them or her willingness to parade them repetitively throughout a discussion.

OPINIONS: TAKE 'EM OR LEAVE 'EM

Women ask for men's opinions as part of their attempt to explore their own feelings and come to conclusions. They may or may not make their decisions based on the opinions offered by others. When persuading their colleagues or their staff to come to a decision, women generally prefer building consensus rather than pulling rank. Men ask for opinions less often. And when they give opinions, they often state their opinions as fact and consider the effort wasted if women do not act or make a decision based on those opinions. When persuading their colleagues to come to a decision, men generally prefer dictating a solution rather than "wasting time" to build consensus.

Results: (1) Men think women waste their own and others' time "shopping" for opinions that they don't use. (2) Women sometimes think male bosses "run over" them with decisions. (3) Men get frustrated when they can't tell whether their female boss is stating an opinion or a command. (4) Women get frustrated when male subordinates don't comply with what they themselves think are clear directives.

Tip 1042. (for women) When Requesting an Opinion, Make It Clear That You Intend Only to Evaluate the Opinion and Come to Your Own Conclusions.

Tip 1043. (for women) Determine Whether to Build Consensus or Dictate a Decision on a Case-by-Case Basis.

Tip 1044. (for women) Make Sure Your Subordinates Know When You're Giving an Opinion or Making a Request Versus Stating a Decision or a Directive.

Tip 1045. (for men) Offer Your Opinions Without Expectation or Obligation That a Woman Will Act or Decide Based on Them.

Tip 1046. (for men) Work to Build Consensus When You Want Buy-In From Others on a Decision and Want Others to Feel Valued for Their Input.

Tip 1047. (for men) Make Sure Your Subordinates Know They Have a Choice in a Situation if You Mean Your Opinion as a Preference Rather Than a Directive.

DIRECTNESS OR INDIRECTNESS?

Much training in the past two decades has focused on assertive language for women. As a result, women today do state what they want clearly. But because women tend to prefer consensus rather than competition and like to avoid confrontation where possible, they often choose tactful phrasing. Their messages can be indirect, discreet, and at times manipulative.

Women tend to give fewer directives and use more courtesy words with those directives. (Examples: "The approach is not exactly foreign to our designers," meaning, "They are familiar with it." "Mary may not be available to handle the project," meaning, "Mary doesn't want to handle the project." "Jerry, I have complete confidence in the way you deal with such customers—I trust you completely to make these kinds of decisions," meaning, "I hope you'll keep taking care of these headaches without bothering me about them.")

Men's language tends to be direct and powerful. It can also be blunt and even offensive. Men generally give more directives, with fewer courtesy words. (Examples: "Tom blew the deal with that client because of his stubborn refusal to negotiate on the delivery." "I will not approve that expense—it's totally unnecessary." "That's a half-baked idea if I ever heard one. You're dead wrong.")

Tip 1048. (for women) Use Straightforward Language if You Want to Make Sure Your Message Gets Heard.

Tip 1049. (for women) Be Objective and To-the-Point so as Not to Dilute Performance Feedback to a Colleague or Subordinate.

Tip 1050. (for men) Use Tact and Show Respect for the Individual Even When You're Emotionally Upset and Even When You Have Someone Else's Best Interest at Heart.

Tip 1051. (for men) In Social Settings, Use Less Directive Language When Expressing a Preference.

TO OVERLAP OR INTERRUPT?

Women overlap each other's speech as a show of encouragement to and identification with the other person speaking. In fact, two women can sometimes talk at the same time they're hearing the other person. This often expressive, passionate overlapping says, "I know exactly what you mean! That's so true!" Women allow more interruptions or overlapping. Men focus, even when they talk. Either they talk or they listen—but not both at the same time. When men overlap, that overlapping is most often an attempt to interrupt.

Results: (1) When a woman overlaps conversation, she is showing support. (2) When a man's conversation is overlapped, he considers it rude and irritating.

Tip 1052. (for women) Continue to Overlap Another Woman's Speech to Show Support and Identification With What's Being Said.

Talking at the same time to agree with the other person says, "I'm right with you."

Tip 1053. (for women) Don't Overlap a Man's Speech Unless You Intend to Interrupt Him.

Allow a man to finish his statement before you jump in and add your opinion or information.

Tip 1054. (for men) Don't Interrupt a Woman's Speech as a Power Play.

You are interrupting rather than supporting when your volume is louder, when your body language intimidates, or when your tone shows either hostility or superiority.

NAGGING

Women tend to nag more than men. Because of their nurturing instinct with children, they often feel compelled to train, to improve, to help. If others don't follow their "nurturing," their tone often becomes whiny, petulant, or angry.

Men nag less because their attention is focused more on their own behavior and performance than on that of others. Men don't mind women nagging them if they interpret such remarks as being affectionate. ("Honey, don't forget your overcoat—I don't want you to get another cough and be sick for the weekend.") They resent nagging that they interpret as being disapproving or "telling them what to do." ("Would you clean up the mess you made with the newspapers and mail on the dining table?")

Tip 1055. (for women) Nag Less; Show Caring in Other Ways.

Tip 1056. (for women) Offer Appreciation for Behavior You Want to Encourage Rather Than Disapproval for Behavior You Dislike.

Tip 1057. (for men) Appreciate the Reason Behind Affectionate Nagging.

SHOWING AFFECTION

Women generally show affection openly. They compliment people and express pleasure directly. They laugh and cry more often than men do. When arguing, women bring up past wrongs because they see the relationship as fluid and evolving; they accuse more and hold grudges longer. They apologize more readily and easily. They do not see arguments as a contest, and they can bear the burden of being wrong. Women are motivated when they feel liked or loved.

Men tend to show affection less directly, through action. They compliment people less, and instead use sarcasm and teasing to show liking. They laugh or cry less often than women. When arguing, men stick to the problem at hand, accuse less, hold fewer grudges, and forgive sooner. They apologize less and with difficulty. Men often see disagreements as a contest and insist on being right, on winning. Men are motivated when they feel needed, admired, or appreciated.

Tip 1058. (for women) Stick to the Issues at Hand When Arguing to Solve a Current Problem.

Tip 1059. (for women) Forgive More, and Forgive More Often.

Tip 1060. (for women) Don't Try to Nag or Shame a Man into Showing Affection More Openly.

Tip 1061. (for women) Express Appreciation Frequently to Men for Their Work and Results.

Tip 1062. (for men) Consider Past Issues and Events When Trying to Understand Current Difficulties in a Relationship.

Tip 1063. (for men) Apologize More, and Apologize More Directly.

Tip 1064. (for men) Show Affection More Openly Through Direct Compliments and More Emotional Intonation.

JOKE TELLING AND HUMOR

Women tell fewer jokes and stories than men do. When they use humor, they more often tell self-deprecating anecdotes. Put-downs directed toward them or toward others, even in jest, often make women feel uncomfortable. Under stressful conditions and tight deadlines, they feel compelled to be serious and "to quit kidding around" in the workplace.

Men tell more jokes and stories than women do. Rather than using self-effacing humor, men usually direct their humor toward others. They use put-down humor and teasing with those they like and respect as well as with those they don't like and don't respect. In stressful situations, they often "clown around" to break the tension and lessen embarrassment.

Tip 1065. (for women) Recognize the Value in Humor, Even in Serious Discussions.

It's rare that a situation or group cannot benefit from a moment of levity to lessen tension and improve relationships.

Tip 1066. (for women) Practice Telling More Amusing Stories in Safe Environments Until You Gain the Confidence to Tell Them More Often in Larger Groups.

Master the techniques of storytelling in general as a means to increase your personal presence and expand your influence. Storytelling has become an essential art form for professionals who act as spokespersons for their organizations.

Tip 1067. (for men) Avoid Offensive Sexual Humor.

Not only will this improve your communication with the opposite gender, but also it will keep you out of court.

Tip 1068. (for men) Verify That Your Humor at Others' Expense Does Not Make Them Feel Uncomfortable.

Ask yourself if you would feel comfortable as the butt of your own joke or story. If not, it's probably inappropriate.

ACCOMPLISHMENTS

Women tend to downplay their achievements so as not to create jealousy among their peers and generate distance or difficulty in a relationship. Because they enjoy working through consensus, they often share the credit with team members. As a result, their skills may be underestimated and their achievements go unnoticed.

Men tend to announce their achievements so as to gain respect among their colleagues. They e-mail, tweet, post their accomplishments on Facebook, pass on testimonials from customers and peers, and generally present themselves well. As a result, their skills win recognition and reward.

Tip 1069. (for women) Find Ways to Display Your Skills and Achievements so as to Win Rewards in the Workplace.

Tip 1070. (for men) Continue to Gain Respect for Your Accomplishments.

Tip 1071. (for men) Recognize and Reward Women's Achievements.

SELLING AND PERSUADING

Female salespeople tend to relate to men in one of four ways: the coquette, the daughter-to-father appeal, the mother-to-son advisor, or an equal colleague. Women sometimes have difficulty selling to a man when men raise objections; they are uncomfortable challenging a man's opinions, suppositions, or reservations in buying.

When a woman is selling to a man and the man listens passively with little facial expression, the woman may become concerned that he's disbelieving or is uninterested in what she's saying or selling. Her sense of timing falters; she doesn't know whether to back up or speed up to change his mind.

Male salespeople tend to relate to women in one of four ways: the flirtatious flamboyant, the father-to-daughter advisor, the ambitious young man wanting to make good and to please, or an equal colleague.

A man has difficulty selling to women when he challenges the customer's objections bluntly or directly. A female customer shows discomfort when the buying conversation takes on a competitive tone. A male salesperson sometimes loses his sense of pacing when a female customer nods and smiles throughout the presentation, indicating that she's following what he's saying. He speeds up, thinking that she's agreeing and is giving buying signals. Then, when he asks for the order, he discovers that she has objections that he didn't recognize and skipped over hurriedly when he misread the body language.

Tip 1072. (for women) Avoid a Flirtatious Manner to Prevent Creating Suggestions Concerning Other Interests.

Tip 1073. (for women) Don't Make the Buyer Feel Obligated if You Don't Want to Be Perceived as Less Powerful and Damage Your Chances for Negotiating Your Terms.

Tip 1074. (for women) Respect a Man's Ego When Explaining Your Product or Service; Show Confidence in His Intelligence and Quick Understanding.

Tip 1075. (for women) Handle Confrontational or Blunt Statements as Requests for Further Evidence of What You're Saying, Not as Personal Affronts.

Tip 1076. (for women) Depend on Your Own Proven Sense of Timing in Presenting Your Product or Service; Don't Interpret Matter-of-Fact Language and a Nonexpressive Face as Boredom or Disagreement.

Tip 1077. (for women) Avoid a Matronly Tone as if Scolding, Demanding, or Condescending.

Tip 1078. (for men) Forgo a Flirtatious Manner to Prevent Creating Suggestions Concerning Other Interests.

Tip 1079. (for men) Put Aside a Fatherly Tone to Avoid Inciting a Woman's Inclination to Plead or Pout, Thus Damaging Your Own Negotiating Power.

Tip 1080. (for men) Don't Disregard a Woman's Intelligence with a Condescending Tone in Explaining Products or Services.

Tip 1081. (for men) Avoid a Pleading or Oversolicitous Tone so as Not to Damage the Buyer's Confidence in Your Product or Weaken Your Negotiating Strength.

Tip 1082. (for men) Guard Against a Competitive, Challenging Tone When a Female Customer Voices Objections and Reservations.

Tip 1083. (for men) Depend on Your Proven Sense of Timing in Presenting Your Product or Service; Don't Interpret Nods and Smiles as Premature Buying Signals.

AIRTIME

Women tend to talk more in private; men talk more in public situations. Women hold the floor for shorter periods of time; men's contributions last longer. Women tend to carry on conversations (exchanges or dialogues); men's talk tends to focus on one-way speaking (reporting facts and stating opinions). Men interrupt more than women do; women allow more interruptions.

Tip 1084. (for women) Insist on Finishing Your Comments When You Are Interrupted.

Tip 1085. (for women) Take More Opportunities to Speak in Public, Share Your Expertise on Panels, and Become an Active Networker.

Tip 1086. (for men) Share More Airtime if You Want to Be Perceived as Less Authoritarian or Less Opinionated.

LISTENING

Women tend to listen to others to relate and to build rapport, and they respond more willingly than men. They show more facial expression, smile more often, nod more often, use more eye contact, and generally acknowledge and accept conversational topics that men introduce. They use more tentative language and often answer questions with questions.

Men generally enjoy talking more than they enjoy listening. They tend to listen only to gather information or to solve a problem. Their face often shows little or no expression other than a frown or squint. When they are spoken to, they often grunt or give no response at all, and they make little or no eye contact when they are listening. They often refuse to accept conversational topics introduced by women, responding with silence or changing the subject back to their interests. They use more forceful language and tend to answer questions with opinions stated as facts.

Tip 1087. (for women) Speak Up or Change the Subject When You've Listened More Than "Your Fair Share."

Tip 1088. (for women) Take Care Not to Mislead with Smiling and Nodding; Men Often Take Such Responses as Agreement with and Interest in What They're Saying.

Tip 1089. (for women) Use More Forceful Language; Avoid Tag Questions; Answer Questions with Facts or Directly Stated Opinions.

Tip 1090. (for women) Realize That When a Man States an Opinion, He Is Not Necessarily Closed to Opposing Opinions or Facts.

Tip 1091. (for men) Respect the Fact That a Woman Is Not Necessarily Talking to Make a Point, but Rather to Explore Feelings or Relieve Stress.

Tip 1092. (for men) Acknowledge a Comment Directed to You.

Tip 1093. (for men) Encourage Women to Speak Up When They Disagree or Have Their Own Interests to Discuss.

Tip 1094. (for men) Identify Opinions as Such Rather Than Stating Them as Irrefutable Facts.

Tip 1095. (for men) Don't Continually Change Conversational Topics Offered by Women.

BODY LANGUAGE

Women tend to pull themselves in and hold their arms and legs close to their bodies. They make small, easy gestures toward rather than away from their bodies. They hold their fingers apart and use circular hand movements. When they are listening, they usually lean forward. Generally, they move more fluidly, with the trunks of their bodies turning as their head, arms, and feet do. They gather their possessions closely around them so as not to infringe on others' territory and often sit more quietly and rigidly.

Men take up more space than women, using big, angular, forceful gestures out and away from their body. They hold their fingers together and often point. They extend their arms and legs and make their possessions (books, papers, briefcases) an extension of themselves to protect their territory. They may lean back when they listen, tend to shift their positions occasionally, and appear to be in control of their environment.

Tip 1096. (for women) Take Up More Space.

People who take up more space seem more confident, relaxed, and powerful. "Withdrawing into yourself" may make you seem less competent and knowledgeable.

Tip 1097. (for men) Be Careful Not to Intimidate People by Size and Bigger-Than-Life Gestures and Motions.

Avoid taking up more than "your fair share" of space in a workstation or meeting environment so as not to appear arrogant or aggressive.

WORD CHOICE

Much research has been done on the language and word choice of both genders. Dr. Robin Lakoff, a pioneer in this area, has written most extensively on this subject. Others' research has confirmed many of her early conclusions and has also raised questions about earlier hypotheses, relating some issues to power and position in the workforce rather than simply to gender differences.

The following differences between the genders, however, still stand: Women use more intensive adverbs (*so, just, very, much*), more expressive adjectives (*gorgeous, electrifying, devoted, awesome*), more emotional words (*furious, lovingly, thrilled*), and more diminutives (*tiny, cute, precious*). Their color vocabulary is more extensive (*teal blue, periwinkle blue, baby blue, aqua*). Women tend to use tentative language. In general, they use less slang, more precise diction, and better grammar than men.

Men use more game analogies, stronger profanity, and more expletives than women do. They tend to use more forceful, confident language. They generally use more slang and colloquialisms, less precise diction, and more improper grammar than women.

Tip 1098. (for women) Use More Nouns and Verbs Than Adjectives and Adverbs When You Want to Sound More Factual Than Subjective.

Tip 1099. (for women) Use Direct Language When You Want to Sound Authoritative, Competent, and Confident.

Tip 1100. (for men) Use Questions, Pausing, and a Milder Tone When You Want to Sound Less Dictatorial and More Approachable.

METAMESSAGES

Metamessages surround words and give them their complete meaning: tone of voice, actions, body language, and context.

Women are more intuitive than men. They take words and examine them for nuances of meanings. They talk about talk and contemplate the how and why of what was said or left unsaid; they are fascinated by human interactions and motivations. Women pay a great deal of attention to tone of voice when they're spoken to. Their own tone tends to be excited, upbeat, emotional, friendly, light, and soft. Women use inflection to emphasize feelings and key points. When they sense a problem in a relationship, they're inclined to bring it up and discuss it, "to work things out." They deal with stress by talking about it. In other words, the complete message—words and meanings—registers on a woman's mind.

Men tend to take words at face value. They don't necessarily concern themselves with how or why things are said, and they gloss over the reasons behind someone's actions if those reasons don't change "reality." Men are less attentive to tone when they are spoken to. Their own tone is more matter-of-fact or blunt, with little intensity. Men use volume to emphasize key points. If men sense a problem in a relationship, they're inclined to ignore it and hope that it will disappear. Men deal with stress in a relationship by withdrawing. In other words, men tend to focus primarily on the words of a message.

Tip 1101. (for women) Prevent "Reading into" Words More Than Is Intended.

Tip 1102. (for men) Don't Miss Real Messages by Concentrating Only on the Words.

Tip 1103. (for men) Welcome Discussions to Improve Relationships.

22

Crossing the Cultural Gulf

If you talk to a man in a language he understands, that goes to his head. If you talk to him in his language, that goes to his heart.

—Nelson Mandela

The highest form of ignorance is when you reject something you don't know anything about.

—Wayne Dyer

Share our similarities, celebrate our differences.

—M. Scott Peck

If err we must, let us err on the side of tolerance.

—Felix Frankfurter

Cultural differences create hotbeds of miscommunication between CEOs and their employees, between managers and their staffs, between salespeople and their customers, between coworkers, and within teams. Even though "diversity" has been a frequent topic of training seminars and speeches, graduate school curricula, and management symposiums, there's still a big gulf between an *awareness* of differences and an *appreciation* of differences. Appreciating the differences comes more slowly, but brings greater rewards. These tips should help provide practical steps.

Tip 1104. Identify Whether You're Dealing with a Content or a Context Culture.

A client recently called with this consulting challenge: "We need help in getting all our people on the same page when it comes to putting together their presentations for our executive team. The problem is that we have regional marketing directors from more than 20 countries. And when they send in their reports on our various product lines, they sound totally different. Take the Germans, for example. They load their reports with data, data, data—very precise, but no conclusions. They're very literal. We Americans take our numbers, spin the story, draw conclusions, and make recommendations. Now, we've got a new chief marketing officer, and he and the board have to make some key decisions based on these reports. How do we get everyone on the same page? You'd never know we're working for the same division of the same company! And that's just for starters—the *written* reports. When they deliver their reports, well, that's another problem altogether."

She continued to detail the problems—many of which stemmed from the difference between context and content, among other differences.

In high-context cultures, much of the meaning of a message is implied. Interpretation is based on the relationship, body language, silences, and actions. In high-content cultures, the meaning is explicit, precise, and specific. Content cultures deliver their messages through spoken or written words.

You can understand the frustration when high-content cultures demand that everything be documented in databases and e-mails, and high-context cultures prefer face-to-face communication and relationship building to move a transaction forward.

So when is a deal done? In a high-context culture, the relationship and a personal promise carry far more weight than a formal contract. In a high-content culture, a deal isn't final until all parties have signed on the dotted line—and maybe it has been notarized in front of witnesses! If you don't understand the different expectations, you can lose good sleep.

The first time I had occasion to do business in an Arab country, the client representative contacted my company by e-mail to lead a series of workshops. We sent a proposal, the client accepted it, we agreed on the details quickly, and we set a date for my travel. But the client never signed and returned our contract. The closer we got to the departure date, the more concerned I became. "No signed contract, no travel" was my position.

My American sponsor continued to assure me that the business had not evaporated. "Get on the plane; I have a relationship with them."

The departure date drew closer. Still no signed contract. I called my American distributor again. "The contract is a minor detail. I've spoken to the CEO. They are moving ahead with the training. Get on the plane."

It was a six-figure contract, so I got on the plane. I did the work, the client was pleased, and all went well. We became friends, and I returned again the following year for more assignments. Had I waited for the client to operate as my high-content culture dictated, I might still be waiting.

Tip 1105. Dress with Sensitivity to Modesty.

"When in doubt, don't" is always a good rule of thumb. Err on the side of dressing conservatively so as not to embarrass yourself and your country. In Muslim countries, women should cover their arms and neck and wear hems at midcalf or lower. Pantsuits are preferred. In Latin American countries, knee-length skirts and pantsuits rule the day—even for casual activities. Likewise, the Japanese dress in conservative styles for business. Colors matter as well. In China, white is the color of mourning, while in the United States, it's black.

In various places of worship, pay attention to postings about dress outside the building and to what other worshippers wear so as not to offend on a highly sensitive issue.

Tip 1106. Choose the Right Time and Place to Discuss Business.

In Asian cultures, people dine first and strengthen friendships before doing business. In Western cultures, people may begin business over cocktails. Americans discuss business almost anywhere and interpret others' refusal to do so as lack of interest or lack of aggressiveness.

Tip 1107. Come to Agreement About the Meaning of Time.

What is seen as punctuality and good manners in one culture may mean rigidity and disregard for human nature in another culture. Swedes demand that a two o'clock meeting begin at two o'clock. Mexicans and Greeks see no such urgency if "something comes up."

Tip 1108. Determine the Appropriate Ceremony for Exchanging Business Cards or Personal Profiles

The business card ritual merits careful attention. Westerners tend to exchange business cards at the end of a meeting, and they may make notes on each other's cards as reminders. If the card simply provides a reminder of the person's title, phone number, or address, the receiver may simply slip it into a briefcase without looking at it in the other person's presence. And in many circles, the business card has been replaced altogether by online profiles on LinkedIn, Twitter, or Facebook.

In Japan, businesspeople present their cards to each other upon first meeting. Ceremonially, the person of highest rank in a group gathering presents his card first, then others follow. The Japanese extend their cards with both hands so that the printing is readable to the receiver, and they expect the receiver to read the card carefully and nod their approval of the title and/or the company before tucking the card away. Both a failure to read the card and the act of writing on the other person's card are considered rude.

Tip 1109. Get the Greeting Right.

The handshake has become almost the universal greeting around the globe, but even that has nuances from culture to culture. In the United States, Canada, and Australia, handshakes can be expressive, with several pumps and a variation of grips. The Latin Americans and the Arabs offer a lighter, but lingering handshake. Across Europe, there are subtle variations: the British give you three to five strong pumps, whereas the French and Germans are done after a lighter pump or two. Asians and Africans offer what Americans consider a limp hand.

In addition to the handshake, some groups add a kiss. This may be a single kiss, a double kiss, or a triple kiss.

The Japanese and South Koreans greet by bowing rather than shaking hands. In India, they use the namaste (palms pressed together in a praying gesture). In Islamic cultures, they greet with a salaam (touch the heart with the right palm and then raise the arm upward and outward).

Getting the greeting correct sends a gracious message that you intend to fit into the culture. After all, you see greetings demonstrated many times a day while you're visiting the country.

Tip 1110. Give Gifts to Either Express, Establish, or Strengthen a Relationship.

Gift giving serves different functions in different cultures. In most business settings in the United States, gift giving has become a taboo—an ethical concern and even cause for legal action. In other cultures, gift giving opens the door for business relationships. In still other cultures, gifts express appreciation for an ongoing relationship.

In India, the value of a gift doesn't matter, but color and respect do matter. Gifts wrapped in red, green, and yellow bring luck. And if someone gives you a gift, remember to show your respect by waiting until later to open the gift—when not in the gift-giver's presence.

In Asian cultures, business gifts express appreciation. Generosity is the name of the game. Just don't give anyone in China a white, blue, or black gift—or a clock.

Tip 1111. Watch Where You Step or Stand.

I'm speaking literally here. People from different cultures require more or less physical space to feel comfortable. If you stand too close to them, you may violate their sense of personal space; if you stand too far away when interacting with them, you may create unnecessary emotional distance.

In general, Americans feel most comfortable interacting at what sociologist Edward T. Hall refers to as *social distance*: 4 to 12 feet. But in many cultures, people feel most comfortable interacting at distances half that far apart—2 to 6 feet.

As a rule, people in South American countries and Arab countries stand the closest to other people. Asians feel most comfortable at the greatest distance from other people. Americans stand farther apart than people in Latin and Arab countries, but closer than Asians.

Beware of "backing someone into a corner" or "running away from" someone without realizing his comfort zone for standing to socialize or discuss business.

Tip 1112. Recognize That Respect May Be Shown in Numerous Ways.

Anglos stand up to show respect, Fiji Islanders sit down to show respect, and Japanese bow to show respect. Some people raise their faces and their eyes to show respect; others lower their faces and their eyes for the same reason. Some people shake hands to show respect; others refrain from doing so to show deference and humility. In addition to the Western handshake, traditional greetings and a show of goodwill may be expressed by hugs, nose rubs, kisses, hands together in a praying position, or a nod. Americans show respect and cordiality by using first names; Germans seldom use first names in business dealings. All in the name of respect.

Tip 1113. Maintain or Avoid Eye Contact Depending on Your Relationship and Status.

In Middle Eastern and Latin American cultures, to show respect, an employee may look down or away from his boss. In Southeast Asia, the rule is to avoid prolonged eye contact until you've established a firm relationship with a person. In Anglo cultures, people maintain eye contact to show interest and attention. Anglos may also use strong eye contact to show aggression or power. Avoidance of eye contact in Anglo cultures suggests low self-esteem, shyness, evasiveness, dishonesty, disrespect, disdain, or boredom. The rules of eye contact vary greatly.

Tip 1114. Determine If Questions About Personal Life Are Appropriate.

In the United States, business acquaintances may ask general questions about one's personal life: "Do you play much golf?" "Does your family live in this part of the country?" In some African cultures, even on first meeting, it is appropriate to ask specific, personal questions: "Do you have boys or girls?" "Is your father rich or poor?" In Arabic countries, such family and personal matters are totally off limits to business acquaintances.

Tip 1115. Touch or Refrain from Touching, as Appropriate.

People in some cultures stand close and feel offended when those of other cultures pull away; other talkers keep a comfortable distance and feel invaded when colleagues come too close. Touching is taboo in some cultures (British, Canadian, Australian, German, Japanese, Asian, Indonesian, Indian, and Pakistani) and welcomed in others (Spanish, Italian, French, Greek, Russian, Latin American, Jewish, and Arabian). The touchers hug, embrace, and pat each other to show goodwill, affection, concern, or trust. The nontouchers refrain for the same reasons.

Tip 1116. Treat Silence as Both Golden and Guarded.

Understand how the people you're visiting interpret silence. For example, the Japanese feel comfortable with silence and discreetness, particularly with confidential information. They particularly admire someone who gives careful thought before answering questions or making a point. Americans cover silences as if they are unwelcome and unwarranted. They admire fluent speakers who move quickly from idea to idea without pause in an organized manner. Americans talk to *resolve* differences; Japanese keep silent to *avoid* differences. Americans talk to share feelings; Japanese keep quiet to share feelings. For Americans, silence represents a breakdown in communication; for the Japanese, silence represents harmony in communication.

Tip 1117. Identify Whether Politeness Is a Mask or a Goodwill Gesture.

In some cultures, people bow, smile, nod, and agree so as not to offend. Courtesy may cover very different feelings of estrangement and formality. In other cultures, people are not overly concerned with offending; therefore, a show of courtesy generally indicates goodwill.

Tip 1118. Verify That the Stories You Tell Illustrate Shared Values.

If you're trying to make either a serious or a humorous point, verify that your illustration does in fact make your point. For example, if you tell a story describing an "absent-minded" professor, you may intend the professor to be the butt of the joke, while your listener may revere the professor because of his age. In a meeting, you may make a joke about the length of time it takes a customer to make a buying decision. You may mean to imply that the time was wasted, while the listener infers that valued time was spent on a thorough analysis.

Other examples: You tell a story about a purchasing agent who always buys from his neighbors and friends, implying impropriety and possibly kickbacks; however, in your colleague's culture, people always do business with friends and neighbors rather than with strangers. Or, you may tell a story glorifying individual ruggedness and resourcefulness, while a listener from another culture values group decisions and a team spirit.

You as storyteller have to understand varying, even conflicting, values and illustrate them appropriately rather than holding them up to mockery.

Tip 1119. Adapt Your Humor.

Punch lines don't always translate from one culture to another. Your listeners may be baffled, bored, or buffaloed. The slightest difference in word choice, use of slang, or even timing may send your punch line straight over others' heads. What's more, they may consider you a "fuzzy thinker."

Tip 1120. Remember That Laughter May Not Be All Fun and Games.

In most cultures, laughter and giggles indicate good humor, goodwill, joy, and amusement. But in some cultures, laughter and giggling may mask pain or embarrassment. My Okinawan cleaning lady met me one day after work with a bad case of the giggles; she was embarrassed over having broken a cherished vase. To me, it was no giggling matter; it was years later after a study of cultural differences that I "got it."

Tip 1121. Use Appropriate Sports Analogies.

People everywhere either watch, participate in, or know about sports. But which sports are popular vary from country to country. Take the point you want to make and transport it to the appropriate field, court, pole, pool, stadium, floor, arena, or ring.

Tip 1122. Select the Right Pronoun for "You."

In modern English, the second person *you* means one or many, familiar or formal, friend or foe. In other languages, the appropriate pronoun depends on a person's age, sex, occupation, and social and professional status.

Tip 1123. Avoid Acronyms and Initials.

Letters that have a meaning in one culture may confuse others and may even spell something offensive in another culture.

Tip 1124. Use Technical Terms When Appropriate.

Technicians understand the technical terms associated with the equipment and processes they use. Don't, however, confuse the use of technically accurate terms with the inappropriate use of jargon when speaking to laypersons. This misuse of jargon has nothing to do with the fact that listeners are from another culture.

Tip 1125. Avoid Idioms, Slang, and Colloquialisms.

The mark of a well-traveled person or a seasoned tour guide is her ability to understand idioms and colloquialisms in a foreign language. Some years ago, we vacationed in Mexico, and we hired a driver for a few days to show us the places of historical significance that we'd missed on earlier trips on our own. Wanting to impress us with his facility in both Spanish and English, the tour guide demonstrated it: He used an idiom or colloquialism every few minutes.

Clearly, his skill with languages is not the norm for most of us. In fact, my college friend Tim, who speaks seven languages and works at the UN, has always amazed me. Forget those people; they're off the charts. The majority of first-language speakers have difficulty mastering their own language.

Americans refer to "springs" of water; Mexicans refer to the "eye" of the water (*ojo de la agua*). You'll have great difficulty explaining these tidbits to those from other cultures: "Put the shoe on the other foot." "He's robbing Peter to pay Paul." "It's raining cats and dogs." "Why don't you put your own house in order?" "Don't give me so much lip." "You'd better make hay while the sun shines."

Some people may not even realize that they've been insulted with these comments: "Well, everybody knows that!" "Even you should be able to run this machine." "I'll explain it again—for all the good it'll do." "Look who's talking."

Tip 1126. Speak Slowly for Second-Language Speakers.

Mastering the first language takes study. Mastering multiple languages takes even more mindshare. Make it a little easier for second-language speakers by speaking slowly.

Tip 1127. Whistle, Hiss, or Applaud Appropriately to Show Approval or Disapproval.

Americans boo or hiss at a performer to show displeasure and whistle to show approval. Europeans hiss when they want silence and whistle when they're displeased. Americans, Europeans, and Asians applaud to show approval. Americans lift a fist to show contempt or anger; Russians lift a fist to show determination to try harder or improve.

Tip 1128. Be a Student of Expressiveness.

People in some cultures are expressive over the slightest pain or joy, with wild gesturing and body movement, varying intonation, and dramatic facial expressions. Those living in other cultures may experience the deepest pain or joy with no outward expressions at all—no gesturing, expressionless faces, monotone voices, and stillness. Consider the stoic faces of the Japanese people as they dealt with the aftermath of the 2011 tsunami that hit their country. Can you imagine the difficulty physicians have in diagnosing and treating pain from an expressive hypochondriac or a stoic victim?

Tip 1129. Translate Yes and No with Care.

In various cultures, all the following gestures can mean yes: a raised head and chin, a nod forward, rocking the head from shoulder to shoulder four times, wagging the head from side to side, a backward nod with raised eyebrows, or a smile.

Noes may be communicated by a finger wagging from side to side, a palm-down hand shaking from side to side, a backward tilt of the head, a hand waved in front of the face, or a clicking tongue. When you're traveling, these yes and no gestures are the first things you need to master; otherwise, you may be buying more than you can pay for or selling more than you own.

Tip 1130. Make Gestures and Movements with Care.

Making a circle with the thumb and forefinger means "OK" or zero in the United States; however, it conveys zero or worthlessness in France, money in Japan, and an obscenity in Russia and some South American cultures. A pointed finger, which is perfectly acceptable to Americans, is considered rude by Asians, Africans, and Belgians. Remembering to point with my closed palm and thumb was a challenge to me as a seminar leader in Malaysia.

Waving is an insult in Greece and Nigeria, but a welcome in most Western cultures. Snapping your fingers is considered vulgar in Belgium and France; it's a pastime in the United States. Pointing the soles of your feet in the direction of a Thai will offend, but propping your feet up on the desk of a Canadian may show camaraderie and relaxation. The thumbs-up sign that Americans and several other cultures use when they want to say "Great job!" will offend Australians and Nigerians. Flashing two fingers in the air to form a V means "victory" to Americans—but if the palm is facing outward, the gesture will be considered vulgar in England, New Zealand, and Australia.

Be alert to the gestures of others, and be aware when people of other cultures seem to be offended by your gestures. If you plan to visit a particular country, study a travel guide for appropriate or inappropriate gestures.

23

Syncing Your Body Language with Your Words

When one is pretending, the entire body revolts.

—Anaïs Nin

Deafness has left me acutely aware of both the duplicity that language is capable of and the many expressions the body cannot hide.

—Terry Galloway

When the eyes say one thing, and the tongue another, a practiced man relies on the language of the first.

—Ralph Waldo Emerson

The shortest distance between two people is a smile.

—Victor Borge

Watch out for the man whose stomach doesn't move when he laughs.

—Cantonese proverb

There's so much to say, but your eyes keep interrupting me.

—Christopher Morley

She learned to say things with her eyes that others waste time putting into words.

—Corey Ford

Wear a smile and have friends; wear a scowl and have wrinkles.

—George Eliot

What you see is what you get—on most computers and with most colleagues. Body language is so much a part of communication that the picture would be out of focus without attention to voice, visual presence, and verve.

In fact, salespeople, professors, negotiators, managers, coaches, doctors, nurses, lawyers, teachers, speakers, police officers, and security agents could not do their jobs without a fundamental knowledge of body language and how it either supports or negates spoken words.

The better your grasp of what your body says, the more consistent the message you send will be. (For a discussion of how body language contributes to your personal presence, see my book *Creating Personal Presence: Look, Talk, Think, and Act Like a Leader*. And if you'd like to assess and expand your own personal presence, go to www.bkconnection.com/personalpresence-sa.)

Tip 1131. Avoid Typing Your Personality with Your Voice.

If you were participating in a corporate skit, how would you play the part of a complainer? (Whiny, nasal voice?) How would you play the part of a crook? (Raspy, harsh tone?) How would you play the role of an incompetent nerd? (High-pitched, rapid, quivering voice?) How about the role of a sexy coquette? (Breathy, slow speech?) An impatient teen? (High-pitched, fast-paced, shallow?)

All other things being equal, movie producers accept or reject actors based on how their appearance and their voice match the characters they're to portray. You may be typed for life by the impression that your voice creates. Become aware of how you sound to others—your volume, pitch, speaking rate, tone, intensity, and other qualities.

Tip 1132. Lower Your Pitch to Sound Authoritative and Credible.

We generally use musical terms to categorize voices: soprano, alto, tenor, baritone, and bass. People with high-pitched voices give the impression of being nervous, immature, lacking in confidence, emotional or even hysterical. People with low-pitched voices sound confident and competent.

You can modify your voice once you become aware of your pitch. For the most part, your posture and breathing control how you sound. Standing or sitting erect, expanding your diaphragm, and breathing deeply will help you lower your pitch. Voice coaches, self-help recordings, and books can tell you exactly how to effect and practice this change. If you want to make it to the boardroom, adopt the lower, hushed tones most often heard there.

Tip 1133. Speak at a Slower Rate to Convey Seriousness and Deliberation.

A slow rate of speech implies well-chosen words and underscores the importance of the message. The pace gives a listener time to contemplate what's being said and attach the appropriate significance to it.

Tip 1134 Speak at a Faster Rate to Convey Excitement, Enthusiasm, and Energy.

A faster rate creates interest and demands attention. The pace makes listeners work hard at hearing and translating what's being said, but it eliminates opportunities for their minds to wander. They have to "listen up" to keep up.

Tip 1135. Use the Appropriate Volume.

Loudness has become synonymous with aggression, unruliness, and even vulgarity. A soft volume suggests shyness, nervousness, and even incompetence. Stay away from these two extremes.

Tip 1136. Avoid Playing with Toys When You Talk.

Don't try to talk with a pen, pencil, paper clip, toothpick, or gum in your mouth. Other annoying habits include scratching your head, jerking a knot in your tie or scarf, jingling money or keys, strumming your fingers, twirling your pen or stapler or letter opener, clearing your throat, or snapping your fingers. Besides making it more difficult to understand you, these trinkets and mannerisms detract from a professional image.

Tip 1137. Make Your Laughter Contagious.

People generally laugh to show amusement, excitement, happiness, or even relief. They also, unfortunately, can communicate nervousness or embarrassment with a laugh. When you laugh, make it intentional. Genuine interest, amusement, and happiness often become contagious. People in control of their emotions and the situation spread laughter and goodwill.

Tip 1138. Smile with Your Mind, if Not Your Mouth.

For years, novelists have tried with mere words to distinguish false from true smiles. In some of my own novels, I've used statements such as: "Her smile rose and faded like the window shade," or, "Her smile was in her eyes." When you feel a smile, it shows in the rest of your face—the lines around your eyes, your pupils, your forehead, your cheeks. Likewise, when you're faking a smile, it shows: The timing isn't right. Genuine emotions and expressions fade quickly, whereas false ones linger. The wrinkles don't follow the smile.

Flash a genuine, not a fake, smile. In some situations, inappropriate smiling may convey innocence. But some smiles, smirks, and giggles may say that you're more uncomfortable than amused. Those who study politicians for a living insist that inappropriate smiling contributes to their impression of lying and fakery.

Tip 1139. Establish a Baseline Before You Attach Deep Meanings to Body Language.

We've all read books and heard talks about what various gestures mean: Arms folded across the chest indicate a defensive attitude. Leaning forward means interest. Shrugged shoulders mean indifference. Narrow eyes and a set jaw mean defiance. A smile and nodding mean agreement. But few gestures convey meaning in and of themselves; you have to interpret them in clusters.

The gestures and attached meanings mentioned here do generally hold true, but the real meaning of a gesture comes only with *context* and as exhibited by a *particular* individual. Just as in spoken messages, one boss's "excellent" on a performance appraisal is another boss's "satisfactory." Interpreting nonverbal language accurately involves paying attention to the variations and the habits of any particular individual. Mitch may *always* sit with his arms folded across his chest—when he's bored and when he's elated. Sally may frequently strum her fingers—whether she's impatient or whether she's nervous.

Before you decide to risk much on reading a customer's or colleague's body language, establish what's normal for that person. Chat with her on a neutral subject to get a reading on what's normal before you try to interpret how she reacts to something controversial that you may want to communicate. One man's smile may be another man's belly laugh.

Tip 1140. Remind Yourself That People May Give False Nonverbal Cues.

People who smile and laugh at your jokes may be bored to tears; people who look at you with a blank stare may be very interested in what you have to say. I recall one seminar I conducted several years ago at which one female engineer rested her head in her hands and kept her eyes downcast while doodling on a piece of paper the entire time. No amount of eye contact on my part, gesturing, or raising and lowering my voice could stir her to look up.

After the first six hours, I gave up on trying to pique her interest. Dreading what her final evaluation of the seminar would say, I was surprised to read her comment: "Best seminar I've ever attended in my 14 years with the company. This should be a required course for all employees." So much for reading body language.

Some people just never let their emotions travel to their face.

Tip 1141. Stand Rather Than Lean.

Your control of a group or a situation can be won or lost by the image you present as you stand, walk, or sit. Visualize those who lean as if they hardly have the energy to hold themselves upright. Message sent: I'm fearful, intimidated, weak, wimpy, sick, or tired.

Good posture conveys self-confidence and competence. Stand with your shoulders back and your arms comfortably relaxed at your side, weight balanced on both feet. For more suggestions on appropriate posture and gestures when speaking before a group, see my earlier book *Speak with Confidence: Powerful Presentations to Inform, Inspire, and Persuade* (McGraw-Hill).

Tip 1142. Sit Straight Rather Than Slump or Sprawl.

The slumpers look as though they've melted from an ice cream stick into a puddle. They slouch their shoulders and let their chest cave inward. The sprawlers take on the look of a wet noodle draped over the back of a chair. They give the appearance of the Energizer Bunny waiting to be recharged. The message sent: I'm worn out, wasted, and wanting out.

To show interest in a conversation, sit relaxed with your shoulders straight, leaning slightly forward in your chair.

Tip 1143. Walk Rather Than Stalk, Slink, or Shuffle.

The stalkers pace back and forth like courtroom lawyers addressing a jury. The slinkers swish and sway from side to side like models on a runway, dipping their heads and peeping up from side to side for approval. The shufflers shift their weight from one foot to the other, back and forth, back and forth,... peel the heel,... never miss a beat. The message sent: I'm performing, I'm nervous, and I need your approval.

Walk with purpose at a comfortable stride and good energy. Imagine yourself standing behind a curtain about to go onstage to collect an award. They call your name, and you walk eagerly forward to center stage. That's the walk of purpose and competence.

Tip 1144. Avoid Winding Yourself into a Corkscrew.

Walking around among a group of strangers at a networking event, you'll frequently see the crossed-legs stance (ankles crossed), often accompanied by crossed arms as well. The posture says, "I'm nervous, closed, and defensive." But what did you expect? I mentioned that it was a roomful of strangers.

Tip 1145. Avoid the Celebrity Sprawl.

Envision a sexy guest on a late-night talk show. She's half-sitting, half-lying, with one hip sideways on the chair and the other raised off the chair. Message sent: I have interest in you other than business.

Tip 1146. Keep an Appropriate Distance.

Edward T. Hall has done extensive research on the proper distances for various relationships and conversations. Patting someone on the back, letting a friend cry on your shoulder, and reading a report over someone's shoulder involve *intimate* distances—within touching range. *Personal* distance, from 1 to 4 feet, is appropriate for conversations that you don't want to have overheard, like a problem shared in confidence. *Social* distance, about 4 to 12 feet, is comfortable when you are conversing with others and you don't mind whether people overhear you—at a networking event or in a sales presentation to a customer. *Public* distance, farther than 12 feet, is when we tell children, "Don't shout; he'll see us and come over in a minute." We use public distance to establish formality and control when speaking before a group.

Speaking and conversing from the correct distance gives you control, authority, and rapport. Speakers who want to maintain authority step up on a podium away from individuals and in view of the larger group. When they want to build trust with a group and establish an easy, open, informal dialogue, they move closer, often among the audience members. Space is no less important for you when you're communicating one on one—especially when you're communicating with those of another culture, gender, or age.

For example, women tend to sit next to people that they like; men tend to sit facing people that they like. Have you noticed that if women want more space, they tend to put things (a coat, a briefcase, or papers) on the seat beside them to prevent others from joining them? When men have the same intentions, they block the seat in front of or behind them. Children and older people prefer to sit and stand closer to others than people of middle age. Extroverts stand and sit closer to others; introverts stand and sit farther away.

Awareness of these differences prevents you from making others feel as if they're being either "invaded" or ignored. People tend to trespass on our territory in one of three ways: (1) They "clutter" our space with their things. (2) They use and seem to take over what's ours. (3) They step inside our personal bubble of space. For example, a salesperson who "towers" too close to a customer may intimidate her.

Generally, the closer the relationship and the more comfortable people are with each other, the less personal space they need between them. The more discomfort or stress there is in the relationship, the more space they need. Be aware of all these trespasses in another's territory and the discomfort and anger that they may create.

Tip 1147. Show Interest by Moving Closer or Standing Up.

Notice that in a conversation, when people get interested in an idea, they tend to lean forward, talk faster, gesture more, and even stand and move toward the other person. If the other person backs up, the pursuer sometimes doesn't even notice. Instead, he keeps leaning or walking forward. If your intention is to generate enthusiasm, go with your natural inclination to move forward, but be aware of any negative reaction.

Tip 1148. Arrange the Layout so That People Respect Your Personal Space.

If people seem to "lean over" and around you as they work, reconsider the layout of your work space, equipment, or desk items. Are they functionally placed so that people who interact with you can reach what they need without invading your space? Either use the "obstacles" to reinforce the personal space you need or remove them to create an open, inviting space for others to enter.

Tip 1149. Monitor the Mirroring Effect to Build Rapport.

When a colleague or client mirrors (matches) your body language, that's her nonverbal way of saying that she's in sync with you—she likes you or she agrees with you. When that happens, you're ready to move the conversation or the transaction another step forward—make the decision, close the sale, end the meeting, ask for the favor, or whatever.

On other occasions, you may want to do the mirroring. To build rapport, match your colleague's speaking pattern and body language (his facial expression, his posture, his body orientation/direction, even his breathing pattern).

Tip 1150. Lean Forward to Create Connection.

Whether you're sitting or standing, leaning backward signals to the other person that you dislike her, disagree with her, or have negative feelings of some kind. Leaning back can also be an attempt to dominate; you're saying, "Meet me more than halfway." But leaning forward to listen to someone or talk with him shows interest and builds rapport.

Leaning forward and lowering your voice often encourages others to speak intimately—to share their feelings more openly. Police interrogators use this leaning technique, coupled with a lowered, empathetic voice, to encourage confessions.

In a sales situation, buyers may voice objections that they might not otherwise express. In a meeting with a colleague, they might admit having reservations about a decision that they would not mention in a different, less-intimate seating arrangement.

Tip 1151. Nix the Negative Signals.

If you disagree with someone or doubt what she's saying, consider voicing your opinion tactfully at the appropriate time rather than screaming the message with negative body language. Be cautious about the following negative signals and positions, which an adept student of body language can read easily:

- Leaning backward with your hands clasped behind your head (considered an arrogant, know-it-all posture)
- Leaning your chin on your hand with an index finger on the side of your face (critical of what's being said, disbelieving)
- Rubbing the back of your neck (disbelieving, doubtful)
- Picking imaginary lint off your clothing (disagreeing, but holding back)
- Folding your arms across your chest (disagreeing and defensive)
- Tapping your fingers on a table or desk (impatient)
- Pursing your lips (disagreeing)
- Pressing your lips tightly together (angry, frustrated, or holding back information, comments, or emotions)
- Rolling your eyes (sarcastic shrug)

Tip 1152. Touch with Sensitivity.

Pats, squeezes, brushes, strokes, and hugs happen every day in the workplace. Some become the basis of sexual harassment charges; others convey sorrow and comfort at the death of a colleague. Touching underscores much of what we intend to communicate to colleagues: friendliness, empathy, consolation, excitement, commitment, sincerity, and goodwill. If you feel that people recoil at your touch or if you feel hesitant to touch others when the occasion calls for it, ask a trusted friend to help you sort through the confusion.

Sensitivity often extends to others' work space, desk accessories, and clothing as well. Picking up desk gadgets, twirling jewelry, or flipping a tie or scarf can frustrate people as much as if you'd slapped them across the face or pinched them in a peculiar place.

Tip 1153. Use Eye Contact to Show Respect.

The person with more authority has the privilege or responsibility of making and breaking eye contact. If you continue to stare belligerently after someone has broken eye contact and "dismissed" you, your behavior may be considered defiant and rude.

Tip 1154. Use Eye Contact to Build Rapport With Others.

Locking eyes with another individual can say to the other person that you're interested in him, that you think he's important, that you believe in what you're saying, or that you believe it's important that *he* hear what you're saying.

On the other hand, *withholding eye contact* can say to others that you don't think they're worth getting to know, you're not interested in them, you're lying, or what you have to say is of little consequence.

Darting eyes send another message. Generally, people consider darting eyes a sign of lying. But they also signal nervousness, anxiety, insecurity, and even defensiveness—as if someone's looking for an escape route.

Wide eyes may mean two things. Typically, someone's eyes grow wider when she's surprised and happy. Consider the photos of kids on Christmas morning! But also recall the cliché, "he had the look of a deer caught in the headlights." Wide eyes can signal a negative surprise—shock or fear of physical harm.

For most purposes, you want to maintain steady eye contact without staring. If you're talking to several people at once, maintain random sustained eye contact, looking at first one and then another, holding a gaze for five to seven seconds before moving on to another person in the group.

Eye contact is so powerful in our culture that we summon waitresses or taxi drivers by "catching their eye." We reprimand a child with a glance. We show love by gazing into the lover's eyes. Your eye contact can be the most powerful tool you have for building rapport—or your most dangerous weapon in destroying relationships.

Tip 1155. Adopt a Handshake That Matches Your Personality.

A limp handshake conveys shyness or aloofness; a macho handshake suggests aggressiveness and a sense of competition. A "quickie" handshake tells others that you don't want to get involved or even that you have something to hide; a longer handshake shows interest. A prolonged handshake signals more than a business interest. So, for routine occasions, offer the routine handshake: not too firm, not too limp, not too long, not too brief. Just right.

Make palm-to-palm contact. The web of your hand should touch the web of the other person's hand. When you break away, never look away. Again, that creates the impression of hiding something. A firm, confident handshake makes a favorable impression.

Tip 1156. Nod Your Head To Show That You're "Home."

If you've ever heard people complain that they felt they were talking to a "brick wall," they were probably reacting to a lack of nodding from the listener. In Western culture, a nodding head is very important. In various situations, it says, "I understand," "I like you," "I agree with you," or "I identify with you." If you have the feeling that people seem aloof when you're present, be aware of the absence of head nodding on your part. If you want to, you can literally nod your way to friendship.

Tip 1157. Beware of Nodding Yourself into Submission.

Let an alarm go off, and heads snap to attention. Literally, people are turning an ear toward the noise in order to hear better. If you're taking questions from a group, turning your head to one side and even dipping your head slightly is a visible sign that you're "giving them an ear" and intend to be responsive with your answer.

On the other hand, a head that is tilted sideways is also a gesture of submission. The gesture can mean, "Do I have your approval on what I just said?" Unless that's what you intend, keep your head in a straight-on, neutral position.

Tip 1158. Open Your Hands to Be Persuasive.

The expression "he's holding his cards close to the vest" refers to a secretive attitude. Holding your hands and arms close to your body as you gesture gives the same impression—that you have something to hide. Exposing your palms and opening up your arms to leave the front of your trunk open to another person likewise demonstrates candor and trust. The more you assume an open body posture with wide arms and hands, the more persuasive you are with your listeners.

Tip 1159. Don't Point with Your Finger.

People often associate this gesture with an authoritarian in their life—a scolding parent, teacher, or boss. A wagging finger in their face turns people off.

Tip 1160. Tell Your Body What Mood You're *Supposed* to Be In.

When you feel sexy or romantic, your voice takes on a different pitch, your breathing rate changes, your eyes flirt, and your gestures and movement become more fluid. When you feel laid-back and informal, your voice seems to yawn with little or no energy, your eyes dim, and your movements become less controlled and more random. That coordination between mood and body works well—unless the mood is inappropriate for the time, place, or relationship.

Make sure your body language mirrors the image and mood that you want to project. Change your body language, and you literally have the power to change your mood.

24

Presenting Yourself Online Through Social Media

The more elaborate our means of communication, the less we communicate.

—Joseph Priestley

Clarity is a rarity.

—Thomas Dismukes

It seemed rather incongruous that in a society of super-sophisticated communication, we often suffer from a shortage of listeners.

—Erma Bombeck

Good communication does not mean that you have to speak in perfectly formed sentences and paragraphs. It isn't about slickness. Simple and clear go a long way.

—Thomas Dismukes

Social media has been called the world's biggest cocktail party. So let's stay with that metaphor for a moment. Unless you're attending solely for the purpose of pushing products and services on unsuspecting peers (not recommended), you walk in with the intention of fitting in. You expect to see people whom you already know and strengthen your relationship with them. You hope to meet new people who will enrich your life in the future. Where these people are concerned, you can offer help in the form of introductions to others, answers to questions, and ideas and information in your area of expertise.

When you walk into the typical cocktail party, you don't expect a formally planned evening, with everyone being given 10 minutes on stage to introduce himself and present a question for the group to give input on, or with a panel of experts to present information, with Q&A to follow. Instead, the conversation flows freely among ever-changing mix-and-match groups.

That's where the cocktail party metaphor breaks down. Typically, it's taboo to bring up heavy business topics during a cocktail party. The party represents a time to get to know others socially—personality, family, hobbies, and interests apart from work. So LinkedIn, Twitter, Facebook, and blogs resemble a cocktail party—but also a formal networking event and an advisory group rolled into one platform. That is, "attendees" to the party formally introduce themselves beforehand by way of written profiles and tell you their interests in connecting.

That difference makes *all* the difference in how you think about connecting online.

Tip 1161. Pick Your Media.

When you walk into a party, it's generally a good idea to pause for a moment and take in the scene to decide which direction you want to head. The same is true of the social media party.

If you're not already connecting online, don't assume that you're the only one on the planet who isn't going to the prom. According to a 2010 Deloitte & Touche survey, 32 percent of employees do not yet use social networks for fear that what they do or say online may somehow hurt their career. This is all the more reason for you to be reading this chapter. That's like saying, "I'm not going to my best friend's wedding because I may behave badly, embarrass him and myself, and even get arrested. So I'll just stay home." (A better choice might be to behave well.)

If you're not already conversing on social media, survey your options. You may not want to join all the groups and conversations that are going on there.

LinkedIn is the place where you'll find professionals carrying on business conversations: introductions to other business colleagues, questions and answers to help you make good business decisions, recommendations on suppliers and resources, input on research projects, and announcements about events that you may want to attend.

Facebook for business is about loyalty: those people who already know and love you "like" your Facebook fan page. For individuals, it's about staying in touch with friends and family in one-to-many updates rather than one-to-one e-mails or calls.

Twitter represents a trade-show aisle, with everyone mixing and mingling at lightning speed. People tweet messages that others consider valuable; listeners "follow" to hear more. Other people tweet questions; experts tweet answers to be helpful, hoping to build a relationship and maybe win a customer. Business representatives "listen" for complaints to fix problems and listen for opportunities and trends that lead to innovative new products or services.

Blogging beats standing on a street corner with a megaphone—I think. (I've been blogging for about seven years. So far, so good. I've never tried standing on a street corner, but it doesn't look like much fun.) Bloggers have expertise or an opinion to share, generally in one topic area. They may blog daily, weekly, or monthly. Some bloggers provide substantive comments, information, or analysis. Other bloggers give little more than the time of day. Well, hardly. They may or may not invite comments or questions from their readers.

The website Ping.fm lets you post your comments there and automatically rolls your posts to all the other social network sites. Atomkeep.com keeps all of your social network profiles synced so that when you change something in one place, you can tell the site which profiles you'd like to update with the new information. Other software packages have similar features that allow you to update or post simultaneously. For example, HootSuite and TweetDeck allow you to post a tweet on Twitter and then roll the post to Facebook as well.

Pick the media that suits your purpose.

Tip 1162. Join the Right Conversation.

On any of the sites, you need to find the right group and join the conversation that makes sense for you. For example, when I was getting ready to hire a vice president of sales and marketing for our company, I e-mailed a group of colleagues on LinkedIn, asking if they knew of someone appropriate for the position. That would not have been an appropriate message for Twitter.

If you want to engage on Twitter, you can use hashtags (#) to search on key words of interest to find others of like mind. For example, I search on these key words: "#presentationskills," "#writingskills," "#communication," "#interpersonalskills, " "#executivepresence," "#leadershipcommunication."

To answer a question, you can search on "#yourkeyword#?" (add a space and a question mark after the key word) to offer input.

Tip 1163. Create Your Profile With Your Purpose in Mind.

Decide whether your conversations online are going to be primarily for business or primarily for pleasure. That's not to say that work conversations can't be enjoyable. But when you go out to lunch with clients or colleagues, you probably don't wear your swimsuit, and you probably don't discuss your brother-in-law's recent run-in with the police. That swimsuit and that brother-in-law may be part of your life, but rarely are they appropriate for work.

Similarly, when you set up your profile, consider topics, photos, and opinions that you'd share as a company representative. If you list your title and organization, you become one face of that organization. Listing personal interests, hobbies, books, or music makes you a well-rounded person—but it can also create controversy and erect barriers.

If your purpose for the profile is business, when in doubt, leave it out.

Tip 1164. Make Your Profile Rich in Key Words and Easy to Skim.

If you want to be found (and that's why you're socializing, right? Who wants to go to a party and stand in the corner by yourself?), make sure your headline sums you up well. Obviously, you can't write your life story in 120 or 140 characters (or whatever the limit is for whichever site your listing is on). But consider what words others will search for to find you—either to talk to you about a specific subject or to do business with you.

Then, as you fill in the details in your full profile, think lists, not paragraphs. Start items with verbs and nouns, not adjectives. Use headings for emphasis. Use all the tools available to personalize your profile listing (background color, fonts, photos). People don't warm up to interacting with a poster and a logo. Don't be missing in action.

Tip 1165 Give Serious Thought to Why You're Hiding Your Profile.

One of the most discussed concerns on the social media scene has been privacy—what data various sites have about you and what they're sharing with those who want to market to you. But that's an entirely different issue from your decision to hide your profile from public view.

What do you think when you hear an organization's name, but you can't find it anywhere online? I know what I thought when I received calls from two would-be clients recently—one a hedge fund and the other an investment firm. My assumption: They were either shady businesses or too small for me to bother with a callback. What do you think when a business has no phone? When someone wears dark sunglasses and refuses to remove them inside a building?

Something seems questionable when profiles remain private.

Tip 1166. Follow the Influencers.

You probably already know the gurus in your industry. Either connect to them directly on LinkedIn or ask for an introduction through mutual acquaintances. Join their groups and participate in their conversations. Follow them on Twitter to see what trends they're discussing.

Tip 1167. Follow Those Whom the Influencers Follow.

To get to the real sources of wisdom, see whom the gurus read, recommend, interview, and quote. For example, the guru in your industry may have 32,000 followers—but he may be following only 120 people. Check out those 120 to get to the wellspring of ideas: the raw data, the studies, the polls, and the analysts who draw the conclusions—people from other industries who feed into your industry.

Tip 1168. Pay Attention to Quality Over Quantity.

Every year my next-door neighbors host a Christmas party for approximately 800 to 1,000 guests. (Okay, I don't have access to the actual guest list to count. But for the entire four hours, they as hosts stand at the door and greet people coming and going.) The party is so large that as guests arrive, the hosts hand out "programs" listing the entertainment so that guests can find their way to the various courtyards, buffets, and activities inside and outside. When my husband and I return home after the party each year, we always comment to ourselves, "What a fabulous party. But how could it be any fun for them? All they got to do was say 'hello' and 'good-bye' to friends as they came and went."

There are two reasons I've never thrown a party for 1,000: budget and beliefs. The same is true for social media connections: I believe the payoff from high-quality connections is much greater than that from quantity.

Never be fooled by fly-by-night scammers who promise you 7,000 followers by linking here or there. Instead, focus on followers who have the same interests.

I've been talking primarily about LinkedIn, Facebook, and Twitter. Granted, you can connect in myriad places—either by posting your profile or rating or commenting on someone else's blog, video, speech, photo, slides, or podcast: YouTube, Flikr, Slideshare, Brainshark, FastPitch, Ning, Amazon Author Central—the list could go on for several lines.

If you try to be everywhere, you'll soon be the corollary of the office gadabout, who can't get her work done because she's "connecting" online with everyone.

Tip 1169. Search for the Right Connections.

Here are some free tools to help you search, connect, listen, and capture what you hear:

- www.search.twitter.com
- www.Tweetscan.com
- www.Twellow.com
- www.twemes.com
- www.blogsearch.google.com
- www.google.com/alerts
- www.LinkedIn.com/search

Tip 1170. Be Careful Not to Clutter Your Stream.

Beware of trash. Whether you're looking at Facebook or Twitter, you can link to so many people who are blasting out so many messages that you miss those that you want to see. That defeats the purpose altogether of connecting online to stay up to date. Clutter on your screen is just as bad as circulars in your mailbox. You can't find the first-class mail that interests you.

Tip 1171. Stop, Drop, and Roll if It's on Fire.

In her excellent book *Share This!* Deanna Zandt tackles the topic of out-of-control buzz on social media sites. If you're already active, you've experienced the phenomenon. It's like the old game of gossip, where someone whispers a secret in your ear, and you tell it to the next person, who tells it to the next person, who tells it to the next, and on around the circle until the final message becomes garbled beyond recognition.

That version plays out on social network sites faster than lightning. Zandt recalls the advice that we all heard as kids: if you're on fire, "stop, drop, and roll." If your news stream is on fire, stop, drop, and *think*. Pause for a moment to process the information. Does it sound reasonable? Verify it before passing it on. If you pass on too many of those inaccurate messages, you can burn down your reputation quickly.

Tip 1172. Learn to Listen Before You Leap into Conversations.

Learn from the big guys how to use social media for business advantage. Rather than shouting, "We're the best," at the top of their lungs to anyone who's nearby, the Fortune 500 companies have their representatives listening to what customers say about them. They search for questions about their products or services and provide helpful answers. They listen to complainers and try to turn them into cheerleaders by resolving their issues. They listen for feedback on the current product and look for opportunities to improve and innovate.

Three recent cases come to mind. A few months ago, I had a Kohler sink that cracked—a tiny two-inch hairline crack. I contacted Kohler's customer service department from its website and asked what the company would do about it. It responded within a few hours with a clearly written, customized apology, asking for photos and a receipt. I sent the photos, but I had no receipt because the sink had been in the house since it was constructed—four or five years earlier. Kohler promptly sent a second e-mail, with a letter for me to take to a local retailer for a replacement. Amazed at the prompt, no-hassle response, I blogged about it—which rolled up to my Facebook page, to my LinkedIn page, and to my Author Central.Amazon.com page.

Second case: The folks at Brainshark "listened" to me blog and tweet about poorly designed visuals and offer principles to improve presentation structure and design. They suggested that I try out their multimedia tool to build learning content and presentations. I was thrilled with their software. As a result, among a group of about 100 or more entrepreneurs looking for such a tool, I had occasion to pass on Brainshark's name.

A third case: At the same meeting of business owners, a CEO commented on the Sears brand and its guarantee of satisfaction, giving his personal experience about Sears's listening on the Internet and replacing his defective refrigerator. And now I'm telling all my readers about all three companies.

Does listening rather than shouting your message pay off? You be the judge.

Tip 1173. Read Before You React.

Set up a free account with Google Reader or through your Microsoft Outlook and sign up for the RSS (real simple syndication) feeds for all of your key words. Read them to hear what others are saying before you say something that's really last-decade and embarrassing. No, I'm not playing politician here and suggesting that you listen to all the polls and then make up your mind about an issue. In fact, you may read what others are saying, then voice a contrarian opinion or present facts that tell a different story. But reading first keeps you from doing embarrassing things like announcing "breaking news" three days after the online buzz has passed or giving an amateurish opinion the day after the industry guru has just posted the definitive white paper.

Tip 1174. Give Information, Plus Insight.

Whether you're blogging or tweeting, think tour guide. Consider past situations when you've been fortunate enough to have an experienced tour guide—possibly through the Smithsonian, the Louvre, or another center of interest. Guides don't just function as signposts: "Here's an eighteenth-century military uniform." "There's the kitchen." "Turn left and then walk straight ahead and you'll see the *Mona Lisa*."

Instead, the tour guide provides intriguing anecdotes about historical figures, illustrations of how equipment was used in past centuries, and statistics to put past feats into perspective so that you can compare them with current frames of reference. The tour guide's insight elevates the information from dry to dramatic. Serve your followers on the Internet in the same way. Aim not to be just a signpost to this or that article, book, or video, but a savvy person with opinions about the information you're sharing with your connections. Add insight.

Tip 1175. Think Value.

Some people play in the tweet stream for a pastime. The same people link on LinkedIn for laughs. And they friend on Facebook for fun. Those statements were truer several years ago when the sites were newer than today. Nowadays, the Twitter stream has trash, LinkedIn has spammers, and Facebook can become frivolous.

So if you want to be heard and stand out from the crowd, communicate something of value. "It's a bad hair day" lacks inspiration. "Waiting in line at the airport" doesn't contribute to people's lives. "Life is what you make it" doesn't provoke deep thought. "How about those Cowboys?" may stir up discussion in Dallas, but it's not exactly a life-changing issue. Consider contributing to the stream of communication with value statements and provocative questions, not polluting it.

Tip 1176. Identify What Expertise You Can Contribute to the Conversation.

Don't be shy about sharing. What would you give an opinion about at a networking event with your colleagues and clients? They're listening online. For starters, provide helpful tips in your areas of expertise. For example, I tweet communication tips—and that's a fairly broad umbrella: business or technical writing, presentation skills, interpersonal skills, personal presence, running effective meetings, listening, organizational communication, resolving conflict, persuasion. You get the idea. Your expertise might be anything from kayaking, to coyotes, to cooking.

Other ideas for valuable comments:

- Your recommendations for travel—places to visit, hotels, restaurants, shops, museums, sports facilities, or other attractions
- Your recommendations on great books, movies, speakers, or learning products
- Your opinions on current events and how they affect our lives
- Provocative questions on current events and trends
- New insights from some self-development program you've participated in
- New research: polls, surveys, test data
- New ideas, strategies, or trends as you see them developing
- Predictions about your industry, social changes, or moods in the country or your workplace

Tip 1177. Create and Leverage Your Own LinkedIn Group.

As a group owner, you'll have several benefits. Others will see you as a connector, a person of value. All those who join your group will go to your profile to check you out. You'll have instant access to everyone on the list with just one click. You can take a quick poll, ask for input on a puzzling

issue, or find an immediate resource. And a final benefit: prospects, suppliers, and great job candidates will find their way to you.

Describe and summarize your group in a compelling way because this
is how others will decide whether or not to join when they are searching
for like-minded people. Pay attention to key words in your summary that
others in your field and industry are likely to use to find you. Then search
for others who may be interested in joining and invite them. Because you
own the group, be present. Start the conversations. Ask provocative questions that generate interest and engage people. Suggest articles and other
resources that the group might find valuable.

Here are a few ways I've used LinkedIn: When debating the creation
of a new product, I polled my connections to ask their opinions about
whether it should be an audio or a video series. On another occasion, I've
asked them for bilingual contractors to lead workshops in foreign countries. On still other occasions, I've posted a job opening, asking if they knew
of a great candidate for a general manager.

Tip 1178. Seed, Feed, and Weed.

Like good marriages or exceptional project teams, vibrant networks
don't just happen. Authors John Hagel III and John Seely Brown, blogging for *Harvard Business Review*, suggest that networks don't just grow
themselves without active involvement. Network owners need to carefully tend and *seed* them with interesting people, tossing out intriguing
comments and questions that motivate people to contribute and engage.
They should recognize and reward (*feed*) those who contribute the most
value. And when negative people interrupt the conversation to self-pro-
mote, the network owner should *weed* them from the group and show
them the door.

Tip 1179. Compliment a Company That Does Things Well.

When you get good service somewhere, recognize the organization or its
representative. Chances are it has a Google Alert, and your tweet or post
will pop up on the organization's screen. A colleague of mine commented
on a product that she liked, and a week later, she had a year's supply
delivered to her door. But don't leave the comment at that. Interpret it
for your readers. What's the takeaway for them? What's the model or attitude to emulate?

Tip 1180. Link Everything if You Routinely Have a Message of Value to Get Out.

If you go to the trouble to post a comment, get your money's worth out of the thinking time. Leverage your effort, link your sites, and let them go. You can distribute your blogs to social bookmarketing sites. You can post about your blog on Facebook and LinkedIn. You can tweet about key points from your blog. You can link your tweets to roll up to your Facebook page and LinkedIn. Others can retweet your tweets.

Tip 1181. Don't Confuse Value with Profundity.

That's not to say that every time you want to tweet or add a comment on someone's blog post, you have to be so profound as to cause people to grab a pen and capture the thought for posterity. Reminding people to be grateful for good health when you've just lost a loved one certainly isn't a new thought. But it serves to remind people to cherish what's important. Telling someone why you enjoyed a movie may not be profound, but may increase his understanding and enjoyment of the movie.

Don't let the "value proposition" cause you to hesitate in joining online conversations. As in face-to-face discussions, just try not to bore people with inane comments.

Tip 1182. Add "Me Too" Statements to Build Solidarity.

You may shy away from posting a comment in a chat room or a blog basically to show agreement with what someone else has already said. But consider the value of repetitive comments. They show the strength of a particular stand, opinion, idea, or cause. In fact, such comments serve as the basis for trend analysis. Politicians scan them to determine support for legislation. Executives look at them in deciding the level of support for and commitment to a policy change. Manufacturers search them to determine when to raise or lower prices and when to modify an unpopular customer service policy.

Even if the idea has been expressed by someone else, putting in your two cents' worth can pay off in getting the point across emphatically.

Tip 1183. Ask Provocative Questions.

Value comes in the form of a thought-provoking question as well as a declarative sentence. Think how many people have pondered the age-old question: "If a tree falls in the forest and nobody is there to hear it, does it make a sound?" (Or the related joke that's bound to offend some of my own gender, but which I still think is funny: "If a man speaks in the forest and no woman is there to hear him, is he still wrong?")

Granted, you won't get very far with stale questions such as these. But try tossing out a thoughtful question about a current trend, asking for opinions on a controversial issue or policy, or asking for suggestions for solving prevalent problems. The BP oil spill generated thousands of suggested solutions—some of which brought significant recognition and financial reward to those who offered answers or piggybacked on others' thinking.

Tip 1184. Make Your Writing on the Wall Clear and Crisp—and Go for Clever.

Not everyone is a born novelist, poet, or rapper. So that "clever" criterion may be a stretch. But you can learn to write clear, crisp, correct comments and questions. Your writing represents your face on the screen and your attention to detail on the job. I'm not talking about a typo. If you have clumsy thumbs and you're tweeting from your cell phone on a jerky elevator, you may miss a key. Rather, I'm talking about misused words, nonsensical phrasing, ungrammatical sentences, and other grammar goofs that raise eyebrows and cause confusion. Such things create an image in the minds of thousands of "friends" and "followers."

Tip 1185. Avoid Sounding Hysterical.

If you want to avoid sounding like a 16-year-old, drop the emoticons and avoid the overuse of exclamation points. ☺ Forget it! Got it? No emoticons! No TWEETs that YELL! And TEXTS? What about texts? Those, too!!! No, I'm not hyper, angry, or on speed. Really!!! I'm just over 19!;-)

Tip 1186. Feel Free to Mix Business with Pleasure.

Even if you're interacting on behalf of your organization, make it personal. Otherwise, your firm could hire a computer to send out automated responses. If your firm sells widgets, your comments don't have to be limited to widgets. Think wider. A comment about the excellent service you received from the local supermarket—along with insight to make it relevant—certainly has its place in social conversation. Your opinions, recommendations, and commentaries that provide insight into people's personal or work lives add value. Just don't whine and drivel about your dining room chairs. That's boring.

Tip 1187. Respond to People Who Contact You.

If someone asks you a question, answer it. If someone retweets one of your messages, thank her.

Tip 1188. Avoid Automated Functions to Connect.

Some Twitterers use autoreply and autofollow. But personal connection is the purpose. Why bother if you're on autopilot?

Tip 1189. Make Retweets Easy; Leave Room.

When I first started tweeting, I didn't realize why so many people replaced my perfectly clear English tweets with texting phrases. You know the kind: U R gr8t! Then I realized that I wasn't leaving them enough room for the retweet. After the autoretweet began @diannabooher:, they'd already lost 18 characters out of the allotted 140 spaces. Now when I tweet, I plan not to exceed about 120 characters. That makes it easy for people to click and retweet without struggling to rephrase my original comment.

Tip 1190. Recommend Colleagues, Clients, and Suppliers.

Part of the value that you bring to the conversation is your positive experience with others—others whom those you are communicating with may not know but who can meet a current or future need. Spend 10 minutes a week posting a recommendation for someone on LinkedIn; or reviewing her white paper, article, e-book, or book on Amazon; or rating her video or YouTube. The person will be surprised when she sees the comment or gets the notice in her inbox—and will often reciprocate. But even if she doesn't, you've strengthened your relationship with your colleague.

Tip 1191. Refuse to Be an Online Jerk.

As at any face-to-face party, you will have a few obnoxious guests. They come only to hand out business cards and give their elevator pitch. They never listen to what anybody else says; all their conversation centers on themselves. When they do occasionally break into an ongoing conversation, it's with a hostile comment, a critical opinion, and a know-it-all tone to "correct" someone. They win as many friends and followers as the face-to-face jerk at the cocktail party. Don't join them, link to them, or model yourself after them.

25

Communicating Common Courtesy: Etiquette Matters

Good manners will open doors that the best education cannot.

—Clarence Thomas

Manners are a sensitive awareness of the feelings of others. If you have that awareness, you have good manners, no matter which fork you use.

—Emily Post

Manners are of more importance than laws.

—Edmund Burke

Politeness is an easy virtue, costs little, and has great purchasing power.

—Amos Bronson Alcott

Kind words can be short and easy to speak, but their echoes are truly endless.

—Mother Teresa

Politeness is to goodness what words are to thoughts.

—Joseph Joubert

Good manners—the longer I live, the more convinced I am of it—are a priceless insurance against failure and loneliness.

—Elsa Maxwell

"**I**t's not polite to sing at the table." Although my mom taught me that rule of etiquette as a child, it never made much sense to me. Actually, if the truth be known, I'm betting that many a mom sang as she flew "airplanes" disguised as spoons into her petulant preschooler's mouth.

On the other hand, "Write thank-you notes when you receive a gift" makes perfect sense. It's always in good taste to show gratitude. And based on common sense, "Chew with your mouth closed" certainly ranks near the top of the etiquette list. Who wants to look into a mouthful of slobber and goulash while somebody talks?

So over time, common sense dictates what constitutes acceptable behavior among civilized, educated people. Those who behave outside the norms create negative impressions of themselves. If you go too far outside the norms, people begin to punish you by withdrawing invitations, withholding promotions, and limiting their interactions with you.

In case your invitation to the royal wedding of Duke William and Duchess Catherine of Cambridge got lost in the mail, you may be a little foggy on the current protocol for formal events. Well, never mind.

Because there are complete books on proper dining etiquette, wedding etiquette, business correspondence, and so forth, the focus here is solely on etiquette issues involving interpersonal communication in the broadest sense.

PHONES

Tip 1192. Sit Up to Speak Up.

People can see you when you speak—and they don't need a video camera to do it. They hear your posture in your voice. When you slouch in your chair, the trunk of your body caves in, making it difficult for you to breathe from your diaphragm. Your breathing grows shallow. Your voice becomes weaker because it has no air behind it, and you sound lethargic. So if you want to project a commanding presence on the phone, sit up straight, smile, and speak clearly into the phone. Better yet, stand to talk. For radio interviews, I stand—even for an entire hour show. The energy, quality, and tone will present an entirely new image that says, "I'm paying attention to you." A slouching posture translates into boring conversation.

Tip 1193. Never Cough, Sneeze, Blow Your Nose, or Sniff into the Phone.

If you're talking when the urge strikes, cover the mouthpiece or speaker, or turn your head away. Then offer an apology for the lesser noise that leaks through to the listener. If you're on a conference call, the mute button takes care of this problem.

Tip 1194. Put the Paper Shuffling Aside.

My book editor once said to me about my literary agent at the time, "Dianna, every time I talk to him, I get the distinct impression that he's reading the morning newspaper." People can hear inattentiveness. Whether you're flipping papers, clicking computer keys, or looking for your car keys, listeners can tell that you're not giving them your full attention. Not only is there noise in the background, but there's also the second or two delay in your responses—much like the delay on TV when you hear foreign correspondents respond to interview questions via satellite. Either focus on your caller or ask to call him back later.

Tip 1195. Never Munch, Chew, or Slurp While You're on the Phone.

The caller can hear every crunch, crackle, slush, smack, sip, snort, and pop of your soda, chips, candy bar, carrot sticks, gum, granola bar, or yogurt to go. Again, the message is, "You as caller are less important than my stomach."

Tip 1196. Turn Off Your Background Noise Makers.

Callers do not want to hear your music makers in the background (your radio, your iPod, or your iTunes selection) coming through while they're trying to carry on a conversation with you.

Tip 1197. Warn Callers Up Front About an Abrupt Ending.

When someone calls you just before a scheduled conference call, webinar, or meeting, let her know how long you have to talk from the get-go rather than ending abruptly just as you are getting into an important discussion with her—or worse, in the middle of a negative discussion or sensitive issue. "Oh, Teevah, nice to hear from you. I am just about to get on a conference call in three minutes. What's up?"

If she continues to talk past that time, interrupt with, "Sorry. As I said, I've got to catch that call now. Please get back to me later. Thanks." You've prepared her, and the abrupt ending doesn't sound contrived.

Tip 1198. Never Leave a Caller on Hold Longer Than 15 Seconds.

If you don't believe that's an eternity for a caller, try it yourself. Put down this book, set a timer to ring in 15 seconds, and turn away from the phone, the computer, and anything else that would distract you. Stare out into noth-ingness, just like your callers do while they wait for you to come back on the line with an answer for them or to finish up another call.

If you're going to be away longer than that, come back on the line, tell the caller what you're doing, and ask him if he'd like to continue to wait or if he would prefer that you return the call later. Leaving a caller on hold is like leaving guests standing at your front door ringing the doorbell while you tidy the house.

Tip 1199. Leave an Informative Voice Mail Greeting.

When I was consulting at IBM, employees there used to refer to those who called to check their voice mail greetings as "the phone police." At some point, the executive team had noticed that when employees were out of the office, they often recorded vague, incomplete messages that left callers wondering whether to expect a callback within the hour, the week, or the month. What's more, the greetings often referred callers to another employee and number as a backup, but when the caller phoned the backup person, he had also left a similarly vague greeting. The phone police had as their mission to make sure that all employees left informative, up-to-date greetings.

To make your greetings informative yet concise, include these essen-tials: (1) your name, (2) when the person can expect a callback (that is, are you in the office that day or out of the country for three weeks?), and (3) an alternative way to reach you or another contact person for emergencies. Your greeting should not run more than 15 seconds. Time it.

Tip 1200. Leave a Clear, Complete, Concise Message.

State your name, your phone number, a one-sentence summary message, and what action you want from the caller. Then circle back to fill in any neces-sary details to make the message more complete and the action easier to carry out. End by restating your name and phone number, spelling your name if it's unusual. Finally, make sure you articulate. Nothing irritates the listener more than having to replay a message three times to try to capture the phone number and a garbled, difficult-to-spell name.

Tip 1201. Lower Your Voice on a Cell Phone in Public Places.

Walking through airports these days, I often chuckle to myself as I survey a scene that looks like a mental hospital, with patients wandering about aimlessly, talking aloud to themselves. (No offense intended to those of you who have loved ones institutionalized. I've had occasion to visit such a place, where my grandfather had to spend the last two years of his life after a car accident and head injury left him totally out of his mind and uncontrollable at home.)

People rush from gate to gate while they talk to their broker on their headset in a booming voice, gesturing wildly as they push through the crowd. People stand in line at the cafeteria and talk to their best friend about the details of their divorce. People in the restroom stand at the lavatory with a flushing toilet behind them, carrying on a conversation with their boss about a status report. Salespeople sit in the restaurant at breakfast and talk to their affiliate in Switzerland about why the shipment hasn't reached him. Even if you are dining alone and the cell phone provides companionship, the guests at the next table do not care to join you.

A colleague of mine grew so frustrated at a fellow passenger that she took matters into her own hands. Noticing that other travelers were as tired as she was of hearing this passenger carry on loud conversations with his broker about all his investments, his doctor about his abscessed foot blister, and his sales reps about their week's appointments, she walked over to the adjacent waiting area and dialed his cell phone (he'd been giving out the number loudly for callbacks). When he answered, she delivered this message: "Your fellow passengers seated around you at Gate 67 would appreciate it if you would shut up!"

Loud personal calls in public places are neither classy nor common courtesy. Movie theaters flash an animated cartoon on the screen before the featured movie to remind moviegoers not to add their own soundtracks with a crying baby or a ringing phone. Other public venues with hosts on the scenes comment on the same common courtesy, ... which may be less and less common.

When you must use your cell phone in a public place, keep the volume low and intimate.

CONFERENCE CALLS, TELESEMINARS, AND WEBINARS

Tip 1202. Mute Yourself on a Conference Call, Webinar, or Teleseminar

Unless you're speaking, use the mute button to block background noises. Otherwise, other callers on the line can hear all sorts of strange, interrupting noises: barking dogs, construction crews working next door, people popping into your doorway to say hello, your opening your purse for a tissue or a pen, paper shuffling, computer keys clicking.

I was once on a teleseminar in which someone's heavy breathing became so loud that the host asked a couple of times for all of us to mute ourselves. Finally, when the loud breathing didn't grow quieter, the host had to announce point-blank, "Someone is breathing heavily into the phone and making it difficult for others to hear. Please put yourself on mute." Evidently that caller had fallen asleep, because it took three such direct pleas before the caller muted himself.

Tip 1203. Announce Yourself at the Appropriate Time on a Conference Call.

Like the baby bear's porridge, you want to announce yourself just right. Not too early. Not too late. Just right. Don't announce yourself immediately when you enter because you may interrupt the ongoing chitchat among other early arrivers. Neither do you want to lurk in the silence without announcing yourself. That's like eavesdropping from outside the door. Enter the call, wait for a few seconds until there's a lull in the conversation, and then announce your name.

Tip 1204. Repeat Your Name When There Are Multiple Strangers on the Line.

You can't tell the players without a program. So with multiple people on a call, before you speak each time, restate your name. It's difficult to keep straight who said what when you can't see faces. However, because your colleagues may forget to do so, you may want to make yourself a voice chart during the "introductions" part of the call. Jot down any distinctions about a person's voice to help you recognize who's talking. For example, Jennifer—southern drawl; Nick—Boston accent; Ava—screechy pitch; Heather—hoarse; Bilton—tentative tone/shy.

INCLUSIVE, CONSIDERATE LANGUAGE

Tip 1205. Expand Your World Beyond "Normal" and Everybody Else.

Take care about putting people into categories that make them feel that they fall outside the norm. After all, unless you've done a survey or have data at hand, keep in mind that the norm changes frequently. Avoid labeling those with disabilities as "invalids," "handicapped," "crippled," "mute," "dumb," or "wheelchair bound." Instead, simply say, "You'll recognize Sheila when you meet the group in the lobby. She has cerebral palsy," or, "Mark is without speech," or, "Tony uses a wheelchair for mobility."

Tip 1206. Think "People Before Label" When You Are Aware of a Physical Difference.

You would never say, "You'll need to talk to the Japanese guy, Hachiro." Instead, you'd say, "You'll need to talk to Hachiro." You might or might not mention that he's Japanese, depending on whether you wanted to help someone pick him out in a crowd of people of other nationalities. Likewise, avoid classifying people by their disability. *Not:* "Walter is a *disabled person*, so we'll need to make sure that we have wheelchair access to the stage." *But:* "Walter has a disability, so we'll need to make sure that we have wheelchair access to the stage."

Tip 1207. Don't Turn Up the Volume or Speak More Slowly to Those with Physical Limitations.

Avoid speaking to those with physical disabilities at a louder volume (unless, of course, they have a hearing impairment) or by speaking more slowly than you would to someone with no physical disability. This odd reaction reflects more on the speaker than on the individual with a disability.

Tip 1208. Relax and Be Reasonable.

Recently, after I left the stage where I was speaking, a group of well-wishers from the audience lined up to ask questions. One woman in a wheelchair waited at the end of the line until all the others had left the room. An attractive woman of about fifty, she introduced herself as a manager in a pharmaceutical company.

Here was her question and comment: "How can I put people more at ease when they're around me? At staff meetings, when I accompany them on a sales call to a client, or when we all go out to lunch, people just seem nervous—as if they don't know what to do and don't want to offend. We come near to a door, and they look at me in a panic, like: 'What should I do?' Should they open it for me, or not? Ask me? Push me through it? If I drop papers all over the floor, should they pick them up for me or not? How can I get them to relax and treat me just the way they would treat any other person—just to use common sense?"

Indeed. And I imagine that her situation is not all that uncommon. If you're unsure what someone needs, simply ask as you would any other person: "Need help with that?" Or simply respond to the situation as you would with anyone else and follow the other person's lead for the future.

Hearing Impairments

Remember that those with a hearing loss can function in even the most challenging situations. The senior pastor of our megachurch of more than 10,000 members has a 95 percent hearing loss and wears hearing aids in both ears. Invited to address groups at venues around the globe, he is an incredible speaker who speaks with no noticeable difficulty. By reading lips, he can facilitate meetings with several people talking at once. You can make life less challenging and avoid offending by remembering these key tips.

Tip 1209. Face the Person as You Speak.

Not all people with hearing impairments read lips, but most do. They have to see your face to read your lips, so don't turn away or walk around as you speak.

Tip 1210. Keep Your Hands Away from Your Mouth.

Keep your lips in clear view.

Tip 1211. Avoid Eating, Drinking, or Chewing Gum While You're Talking.

These extra mouth movements complicate lip reading.

Tip 1212. Speak Clearly and Distinctly, but Don't Exaggerate or Slow Your Lip Movements.

Exaggerated articulation or a slower-than-normal speaking rate makes lip reading more, not less, difficult.

Tip 1213. Never Increase Your Volume or Lean Into a Hearing Device to Speak.

Those who wear a hearing device can adjust the volume as necessary to hear your normal speaking voice. Leaning into the device causes it to squeal.

Visual Impairments

Vision loss spans a wide spectrum, from tunnel vision to total blindness. Keep these tips in mind when interacting with those who have a vision impairment.

Tip 1214. Announce Yourself as You Approach.

Example: "Hey, Chris. This is Arturo. Scott's tagging along with me here. Tried to leave him at the coffee shop back there, but he's got a bad habit of following me. What are you up to today?" The exception, of course, is if the person will recognize your voice.

Tip 1215. Say Your Name When You Speak Up in a Meeting.

This allows the person to follow the interactions among several participants in the group.

Tip 1216. Let the Other Person Know When You're Leaving or Walking Around.

Either say, "Good-bye," as you leave or simply announce what the sighted person can readily see that you're about to do. "Jack, I'm going to walk over to the buffet table, refill my plate, and see if I can't irritate my boss a moment about that Wilton project. I'm leaving you in good hands here with Sherrie and Alex."

Tip 1217. Offer to Help With Tasks Where Sight Is Called For.

Example: "Would you like me to enter on your Favorites list those websites the speaker mentioned this morning? That way you'll have them when you and your wife start to complete the forms we have to turn in."

Tip 1218. Give Safety Warnings.

Example: "Jerome, there's a huge flower pot about four feet ahead of you. You can go around to the right."

Tip 1219. Guide Them, When Asked, by Offering Your Elbow.

When you arrive at your destination, give them some orientation by placing their hand on a desk, chair, wall, or table and then describing the area around them.

Tip 1220. Guide Their Hand for Signatures.

Take the person's hand and place it on the correct spot when he needs to sign a document. Place a straight-edged tablet beneath the signature line for alignment.

Tip 1221. Never Move Items Around in Their Offices or Homes.

A person without sight has rooms memorized. She knows where objects on her desk, in the bedroom, and in the kitchen are located, and she knows how many steps it takes to get from one room to the next or from the desk to a favorite chair or bookshelf.

Mobility Limitations

As a junior high school student, Richard didn't seem to mind that his classmates played roller derby with him in his wheelchair. Bohunk, his best friend and the key guilty party, served as the ringleader of the rowdy crowd, so Richard tolerated it all in good fun. Being the only kid in school with this novelty prop, Richard was understandably popular. But what Richard tolerated from his friends at age 12 is far from acceptable etiquette among adults.

Keep these tips in mind as you interact with those who have mobility limitations.

Tip 1222. Never Separate the Person from His Mobility Aid.

Don't move the walking cane away from the chair or table. Don't roll the wheelchair away from the desk or out of the aisle. Don't push the walker over by the window. The person will tell you if he wants the item moved.

Tip 1223. Don't Violate Someone's Personal Space.

Don't fiddle with or "try out" someone's wheelchair, walker, brace, cane, or prosthetic. Doing so is like asking to use her comb or her toothbrush.

Tip 1224. Don't Lean or Hang on a Person's Wheelchair or Walker.

Your leaning affects his maneuverability and balance and may damage the equipment.

Tip 1225. Don't Push Someone in a Wheelchair Unless She Asks You to Do So.

The person may not be prepared to move. A sudden movement, jerk, or turn may be startling or even painful. Additionally, your help may be no more welcome than taking the shoulder of any other colleague and pushing her in a direction in which she did not intend to go at a time when she did not intend to go.

Gender Inclusiveness

Tip 1226. Avoid Using the Generic "He" or "She" Exclusively for Both Genders.

A comment like the following excludes approximately half the population: "A client has to certify that he has completed the safety video before we can take him on a tour of the facilities." To include both genders in your language, you have several choices:

- Use nouns rather than pronouns. ("A client has to certify that the representative has completed the safety video before we can take anyone on a tour.")
- Use plural nouns and pronouns. ("Clients have to certify that they have completed the safety video before we can take them on a tour.")
- Use second-person pronouns. ("You have to certify that you have completed the safety video before we can take you on a tour.")
- Substitute the article *a, an,* or *the* for the pronoun—or omit the pronoun altogether. ("A client has to certify completing the safety video before we can do the tour.")
- Alternate between *he* and *she* in your speech and writing rather than using one pronoun exclusively for both genders.

Tip 1227. Select Nouns That Represent Both Genders.

Not: Policeman. *But:* Police officer.

Not: Service men. *But:* Service men and women.

Not: Postman. *But:* Postal workers.

Not: Repairman. *But:* Service agent.

Not: Stewardess. *But:* Flight attendant.

Tip 1228. Allow the Host to Pay for a Business Lunch, Regardless of Gender.

If you're hosting and you feel uneasy about this, arrive early and provide your credit card to the waiter so that your bill never even arrives at your table.

Tip 1229. Help Another Person Put On or Take Off a Jacket, Regardless of Gender.

Tip 1230. Assist Someone Who Is Carrying or Manipulating Heavy Books, Bags, or Other Items, Regardless of Gender.

Tip 1231. Stand to Greet Someone, Regardless of Gender.

Tip 1232. Shake Hands When Greeting or Saying Good-Bye in Business, Regardless of Gender.

Tip 1233. Open the Door for Yourself and Others if You Reach the Door First, Regardless of Gender.

Tip 1234. Express Gratitude Rather Than Glare if Someone Assists You, Regardless of Gender.

INTRODUCTIONS, TITLES, AND HANDSHAKES

Tip 1235. Understand Your Role as Host.

If you're the senior person representing your company, organization, department, team, or group, arrive first. Never send an assistant to play host. It's your role to meet and greet your guests and introduce them to one another.

Tip 1236. Understand Your Role as a Guest.

If you join a group after others have already been introduced, it's your responsibility to introduce yourself to the host and to other guests.

Tip 1237. Don't Be Partial with the Name Game.

In all but the most informal situations, introduce people using both first and last names. And by all means, if you use the first and last names of one person, use the first and last names of the other person. You can offend someone greatly with this slight in a mutual introduction: "Have you two met? Kyle Johnson, this is Belinda." If you use titles, do so for both people: "Mr. Ed Frazier, I'd like you to meet Ms. Su Lin Hughes, one of our suppliers."

Tip 1238. Introduce an Internal Person to a Client.

In making introductions, say the honored person's name first, then "present" the less-important person to him. For example, to your client, you might say, "Susan, I'd like to introduce my assistant to you, Abby Ferguson. Abby, this is Susan Sanders, CEO of Sagemont." If you stumble and say the wrong person's name first, you can always recover this way: "Abby, there's someone I want you to meet. Susan, I'd like to introduce someone to you—Abby Ferguson here is my assistant. Abby, this is Susan Sanders, CEO of Sagemont."

Tip 1239. Introduce a Junior Person to a Senior Person.

Example: "Bart, we have a new engineer on board that I'd like you to meet. Allison Tyzart. Allison, this is Dr. Bart Phileomeo, head of our R&D lab in Sacramento."

Tip 1240. Introduce a Younger Person to an Older Person—Unless Rank Is Involved.

Example: "Mr. Sanchez, I want you to meet the summer intern who's been writing all those press releases this month, Jason Jacobs. Jason, this is Carlos Sanchez, my long-time mentor here at Universal."

Tip 1241. Use the Proper Acknowledgment When You're Introduced.

"Hi" works for a child or a young teen, but for an adult, the proper response when introduced is "Hello" or "How do you do." It's not a question any more than "Dear Mrs. Smith" on a letter refers to your sweetheart. The phrase serves merely as a conventional acknowledgment, much like "you're welcome" after an act of kindness or "bless you" after a sneeze.

Tip 1242. Shake Hands When You Meet and Part.

With a close friend or a family member, hugs may be in order. But in business, it's customary to shake hands when you

- Meet someone outside your work environment in a public place.
- Enter someone's office or work area (unless you do so several times a week).
- Conclude a business deal.
- Conclude an interview.
- Leave a meeting (unless the meeting is regular and routine with the same people).
- Leave a social or business event.

Exception: When a celebrity or executive holds a much higher rank and approaching him to shake hands would seem too familiar or too aggressive.

SOCIAL AND BUSINESS EVENTS

Few things puzzle people as much as the rules of etiquette regarding social and business events—accepting and declining invitations, determining when to talk business, deciding what to wear, dining, gift giving, and the like. The following tips focus only on the communication challenges relating to these issues:

Tip 1243. Accept or Decline All Invitations Promptly.

When you wait longer than a week to reply when RSVPs are requested, the host may wonder whether you're waiting for a better offer to come along. Hosts must plan the menu, pay for the food for each attendee, and in some cases rent serving dishes and furniture for a specific number of guests. If the host has to contact you to ask whether you're attending, you have committed a major faux pas.

Tip 1244. Decline an Invitation With a Brief Explanation to Add a Touch of Class.

It's certainly acceptable to decline an invitation with a simple, "No, thanks, I will not be able to attend." Although you're not required to do so, adding a brief explanation about a conflict in your schedule (if it's truthful) adds warmth to the no. Of course, sometimes an online form that allows you only to click a button doesn't provide space for an explanation. In that case, sending an extra e-mail or note with an explanation that you will not be able to attend the event acknowledges your interest in the people or the cause behind the invitation.

Tip 1245. Dress to Show Respect for Your Host and the Other Guests.

Your attire conveys your attitude about yourself and toward other people. Think of a special occasion of your own: a wedding, your graduation, or a special anniversary party for yourself or your parents. You've spent a walletful of money to make it as nice as possible, to hire an entertainer, to rent the best venue, and to invite your best friends and all the important people in your life. And then one of your guests brings along a friend, who just happens to be on his way home from an Ironman competition. His running suit stinks. His shoes are wet with blood from bruised toes. His matted hair smells of mosquito spray. Which other guest do you want to seat him beside for the meal?

Tip 1246. Be Present When You Show Up.

When you attend an event, turn off all the gadgets and get in the spirit of the thing. What host wants to have guests who stand in the corner and hang on their cell phone all evening? Or who wants guests who pop in for 15 minutes, only to announce that they were late and are leaving early because they have more important places to be and people to see? If you're going to show up, join in. Don't make your attendance sound like an obligatory duty.

Tip 1247. Never Bring Unexpected Guests with You.

It may be that you've accepted an invitation to a social or business event, and then your own unexpected guest shows up on the day or weekend of the event. Never put your host on the spot by calling to ask if you can bring your guest along. And never simply fail to show up without explanation. The host has probably already paid for the food and planned space for a specific number of attendees. Instead, call the host and decline with your explanation.

Then wait to hear the response. If the host accepts your regrets, thank her and hang up. But if there's extra food, other last-minute cancellations, and plenty of room, the host may be gracious and extend the invitation to your guest. Go. You're all set.

Tip 1248. Never Complain About the Venue, the Food, or the Entertainment.

Even when you're attending a business affair, someone—a meeting planner, assistant, or assigned person whose regular job happens to be bookkeeping or bridge building—has planned the event. Whining about the wine, bad-mouthing the band, or making fun of the food puts you in a category of complainers who are not highly popular back on the job.

Tip 1249. Send a Thank-You Note, E-mail, Card, or Small Gift After the Event.

Be sincere, be specific about what you enjoyed, and be prompt. A note that arrives 10 days later looks like "my mom made me write it."

THE BEREAVED

One of the most difficult challenges is knowing how best to express your feelings in the face of sorrow, tragedy, or loss. In sympathy situations, friends, colleagues, and clients have the greatest need to hear from you. Don't leave them wondering about your lack of concern. Either speak to them personally, call, or write to say that you care. (If you write, you may want to go to www.sympathylettersonline.com for model notes and letters to customize for your situation. And by the way, these should be handwritten on your personal stationery.)

Tip 1250. Make a Straightforward Comment About Your Feelings—Your Sadness, Your Shock, Your Sorrow, or Your Concern.

Examples: "I was so shocked to hear of the news that . . ." "I want to express my deepest sympathy about the loss of your mother." "I am so sorry to hear about the fire." "I know that going through this bankruptcy situation has taken its toll on you and your staff."

Tip 1251. Mention Something Positive That You Remember About the Situation or the Individual.

In the case of death, if you did not know the deceased personally, recall something you've heard others say. Examples: "I know you depended so much on your father's advice. I've heard you say so many times how knowledgeable he was about ... " "I remember how much his calls to me meant back in my early days here at the organization." "I've heard you say so many times how you enjoyed vacations together and golf outings."

In the case of a natural disaster, you might say something like this: "I'm sure you were glad that no one was home." "I know you must feel fortunate that you were able to save some of your things." "Your business has always had an excellent reputation. I feel certain that your customers will return whenever you are able to rebuild."

Tip 1252. Express an Understanding of the Extent of the Loss or the Pain, but Avoid Gruesome Details.

When mentioning a positive (see the previous tip), never minimize a loss or the pain that someone feels. Anyone who has suffered a loss wants to know that you are trying to understand. However, you don't want to go into so many details that you cause the person to recall the tragic loss or situation again. Examples *to avoid*: "All those photos destroyed—you'll never have all those cute baby pictures again." "Divorces can get nasty, I know. But it can't get much worse than what this jerk has already done to you!" "You're young. You can always have another baby."

Tip 1253. Be Brief and Be Sincere.

You don't need to go into all the details of a situation—how you heard the news or what so-and-so told you. Your caring concern in an "I-am-so-sorry" comment or note speaks volumes to your colleagues.

Tip 1254. End the Interaction or Note with a Comforting Phrase That Reflects Your Concern and Your Relationship.

Examples: "My heart goes out to you during this difficult time." "You're in our thoughts and prayers." "We'll be thinking of you in the weeks ahead." "We share in your loss of Tom." "Please know that I am concerned about you." "With deepest sympathy for your loss."

Bibliography

Abrams, Kathleen S. *Communication at Work: Listening, Speaking, Writing, and Reading.* Englewood Cliffs, N.J.: Prentice-Hall, 1986.

Adams, Marilee, Ph.D. *Change Your Questions, Change Your Life: 10 Powerful Tools for Life and Work.* San Francisco: Berrett-Koehler, 2009.

Adler, Ronald B. *Communicating at Work: Principles and Practices for Business and the Professions.* New York: McGraw-Hill, 1992.

_____. *Talking Straight.* New York: Holt, Rinehart and Winston, 1977.

Alberti, Robert E., and Michael L. Emmons. *Your Perfect Right: A Guide to Assertive Living.* San Luis Obispo, Calif.: Impact Publishers, 1986.

Alessandra, Tony, Ph.D., Michael J. O'Connor, and Janice Alessandra. *People Smart: Powerful Techniques for Turning Every Encounter into a Mutual Win.* La Jolla, Calif.: Keynote Publishing, 1990.

Allen, Donald E., and Rebecca F. Guy. *Conversation Analysis: The Sociology of Talk.* The Hague, Netherlands: Mouton & Co., N.V., 1974.

American Management Association. "Executives Say the 21st Century Requires More Skilled Workers." American Management Association 2010 Critical Skills Survey. http://www.amanet.org/news/AMA–2010-critcal-skills-survey.aspx. New York: AMACOM, April 15, 2011.

Anderson, Allen R., and Cara J. Abeyta. *Face-to-Face Interactions: Experiencing the Dyadic Communication Process.* Dubuque, Iowa: Kendall/Hunt, 1988.

Anderson, Kare. *Getting What You Want: How to Reach Agreement and Resolve Conflict Every Time.* New York: Dutton/Penguin Books, 1993.

Annis, Barbara. *Same Words, Different Language: How Men and Women Misunderstand Each Other at Work and What to Do About It*, 2nd ed. New York: Barbara Annis & Associates, Inc., 2010.

Arliss, Laurie P. *Gender Communication.* Englewood Cliffs, N.J.: Prentice-Hall, 1991.

Atwater, Eastwood. *"I Hear You": Listening Skills to Make You a Better Manager.* Englewood Cliffs, N.J.: Prentice-Hall, 1981.

Auger, B. Y. *How to Run Better Business Meetings.* St. Paul, Minn.: Minnesota Mining and Manufacturing, 1979.

Augsburger, David. *Caring Enough to Confront.* Ventura, Calif.: Regal Books, 1981.

_____. *Caring Enough to Hear and Be Heard.* Ventura, Calif.: Regal Books, 1982.

Aviel, David. "The Manager's Response to Cultural Barriers." *Industrial Management,* vol. 32, May/June 1990: 9–14.

Axtell, Roger E. (ed.). *Do's and Taboos Around the World,* 3rd ed. White Plains, N.Y.: Parker Pen Company, 1993.

Baker, Stephanie. *I Hate Meetings.* New York: Macmillan, 1983.

Baldoni, John. *Great Communication Secrets of Great Leaders.* New York: McGraw-Hill, 2003.

Bandler, Richard, and John Grinder. *Frogs Into Princes: Neurolinguistic Programming.* Moab, Utah: Real People Press, n.d.

Banville, Thomas G. *How to Listen—How to Be Heard.* Chicago: Nelson-Hall, 1978.

Barrack, Martin K. *How We Communicate: The Most Vital Skill.* Macomb, Ill.: Glenbridge Publishing Ltd., 1988.

Barton, Michael. "Manage Words Effectively." *Personnel Journal,* vol. 69, January 1990: 32–37.

Baskin, Otis W., and Craig E. Aronoff. *Interpersonal Communication in Organizations.* Santa Monica, Calif.: Goodyear Publishing Co., 1980.

Bauby, Cathrina. *Understanding Each Other.* San Francisco: International Society for General Semantics, 1976.

Bender, Peter Urs. *Secrets of Power Presentations.* Toronto: Achievement Group, 1991.

Berent, Irwin M., and Rod L. Evans. *The Right Words: The 350 Best Things to Say to Get Along with People.* New York: Warner Books, 1992.

Berg, Karen, and Andrew Gilman. *Get to the Point: How to Say What You Mean and Get What You Want.* Toronto: Bantam Books, 1989.

Bernstein, Albert J., and Sydney Craft Rozen. *Dinosaur Brains: Dealing with All Those Impossible People at Work.* New York: John Wiley & Sons, 1989.

_____. "Preventing Turf Wars." *Executive Female*, vol. 13, January-February 1990: 22–24.

Bhide, Amar, and Howard H. Stevenson. "Why Be Honest if Honesty Doesn't Pay?" *Harvard Business Review*, vol. 68, September-October 1990: 121–130.

Birdwhistell, Ray L. *Introduction to Kinesics.* Louisville, Ky.: University of Louisville Press, 1952.

_____. *Kinesics and Context.* Philadelphia: University of Pennsylvania Press, 1970.

Bittner, John R. *Each Other.* Englewood Cliffs, N.J.: Prentice-Hall, 1983.

Bohan, George P. "Build, Don't Battle." *Training & Development Journal*, vol. 44, February 1990: 15–19.

Bolton, Robert. *People Skills.* Englewood Cliffs, N.J.: Prentice-Hall, 1979.

Booher, Dianna. *Booher's Rules of Business Grammar: 101 Fast and Easy Ways to Correct the Most Common Errors.* New York: McGraw-Hill, 2008.

_____. *Creating Personal Presence: Look, Talk, Think, and Act Like a Leader.* San Francisco: Berrett-Koehler, 2011.

_____. *E-Writing: 21st Century Tools for Effective Communication.* New York: Simon & Schuster/Pocket Books, 2001.

_____. *Executive's Portfolio of Model Speeches for All Occasions.* Englewood Cliffs, N.J.: Prentice Hall, 1991.

_____. *From Contact to Contract: 496 Proven Sales Tips to Generate More Leads, Close More Deals, Exceed Your Goals, and Make More Money.* Chicago: Kaplan/Dearborn, 2003.

_____. *Great Personal Letters for Busy People: 501 Ready-to-Use Letters for Every Occasion,* rev. ed. New York: McGraw-Hill, 2006.

_____. *Personal Presence Self-Assessment.* San Francisco: Berrett-Koehler, 2011.

_____. *Speak with Confidence: Powerful Presentations That Inform, Inspire, and Persuade.* New York: McGraw-Hill, 2003.

_____. *To the Letter: A Handbook of Model Letters for the Busy Executive.* New York: Jossey-Bass, 1988.

_____. *The Voice of Authority: 10 Communication Strategies Every Leader Needs to Know.* New York: McGraw-Hill, 2007.

_____. *Winning Sales Letters.* New York: Jossey-Bass, 1990.

Bormann, Ernest G., and Nancy C. Borman. *Effective Small Group Communication.* Edina, Minn.: Burgess Publishing, 1986.

Bostrom, Robert N. *Communicating in Public: Speaking and Listening.* Edina, Minn.: Burgess Publishing, 1988.

Bowden, Mark. *Winning Body Language: Control the Conversation, Command Attention, and Convey the Right Message?Without Saying a Word.* New York: McGraw-Hill, 2010.

Bramson, Robert M. *Coping with Difficult Bosses.* New York: Carol Publishing Group, 1992.

Braude, Jacob M. *Proverbs, Epigrams, Aphorisms, Sayings and Bon Mots: Complete Speaker's and Toastmaster's Library.* Englewood Cliffs, N.J.: Prentice-Hall, 1965.

Bright, Deborah. *Criticism in Your Life.* New York: Master Media Limited, 1988.

Brounstein, Marty. *Coaching & Mentoring for Dummies.* New York: Wiley Publishing, 2000.

Brownell, Judi. *Building Active Listening Skills.* Englewood Cliffs, N.J.: Prentice-Hall, 1986.

Burg, Bob. "Act Your Way Into Really, Really Liking Them: Tips on Dealing with Difficult People." *SUCCESS Magazine*, December 2010: 19–21.

Burley-Allen, Madelyn. *Listening: The Forgotten Skill.* New York: John Wiley & Sons, 1982.

Butler, Pamela E. *Self-Assertion for Women.* San Francisco: Harper & Row, 1981.

Campbell, Susan M. *Beyond the Power Struggle.* San Luis Obispo, Calif.: Impact Publishers, 1984.

Carnegie, Dale. *How to Win Friends and Influence People.* New York: Simon and Schuster, 1936.

Carnes, William T. *Effective Meetings for Busy People: Let's Decide It and Go Home.* New York: McGraw-Hill, 1980.

Caroselli, Marlene. *The Language of Leadership.* Amherst, Mass.: Human Resource Development Press, 1990.

Carroll, Nannette Rundle. *The Communication Problem Solver: Simple Tools and Techniques for Busy Managers.* New York: AMACOM, 2010.

Carter, Arnold. *Communicate Effectively.* Gretna, La.: Pelican Publishing, 1978.

Carter, Jay. *Nasty People.* Monmouth Junction, N.J.: Unicorn Press, 1983.

Carter, Kathryn, and Carole Spitzack (eds.). *Doing Research in Women's Communication.* Norwood, N.J.: Ablex Publishing, 1989.

Case, Anne, and Christina Paxson. "Stature and Status: Height, Ability, and Labor Market Outcomes." *Journal of Political Economy*, vol. 116, no. 3, 2008: 499–532.

Chaiken, Shelly. "Communicator Physical Attractiveness and Persuasion." *Journal of Personality and Social Psychology*, vol. 37, no. 8, 1979: 1387–1397.

Chapman, Elwood N. *Your Attitude Is Showing.* New York: Macmillan, 1993.

Cheney, Paul. *The Digital Handshake: Seven Proven Strategies to Grow Your Business Using Social Media.* Hoboken, N.J.: John Wiley & Sons, 2009.

Cialdini, Robert B., Ph.D. *Influence: The Psychology of Persuasion*, rev. ed. New York: Harper Business, 2006.

Coffin, Roy A. *The Negotiator.* New York: AMACOM, 1973.

Cohen, Allen R. *Influence Without Authority.* New York: John Wiley & Sons, 1990.

Cohen, Arianne. *The Tall Book.* New York: Bloomsbury, 2009.

Cohen, Herb. *You Can Negotiate Anything.* Secaucus, N.J.: Lyle Stuart, 1980.

Coleman, Paul. "Cease Fire! Ending No Win Arguments and Becoming a Happier Couple." *Redbook*, vol. 177, August 1991: 92.

Comeau, John, and Gwen Diehn. *Communication on the Job: A Practical Approach.* Englewood Cliffs, N.J.: Prentice-Hall, 1987.

Conklin, Robert. *How to Get People to Do Things.* Chicago: Contemporary Books, 1979.

Connelly, J. Campbell. *A Manager's Guide to Speaking and Listening*. New York: American Management Association, 1967.

Copper, Carolyn. "A Certain Smile." *Psychology Today*, vol. 25, January-February 1992: 20.

Cory, Lloyd (comp.). *Quotable Quotations*. Wheaton, Ill.: Victor Books, 1985.

Cox, Taylor H., Sharon A. Lobel, and Poppy Lauretta McLeod. "Effects of Ethnic Group Cultural Differences on Cooperative and Competitive Behavior on a Group Task." *Academy of Management Journal*, vol. 34, December 1991: 827–847.

Crook, Thomas, and Christine Allison. "The Art of Remembering Names." *Reader's Digest*, vol. 141, July 1992: 71–74.

_____. *How to Remember Names*. New York: HarperCollins, 1992.

Crum, Thomas F. *The Magic of Conflict*. New York: Simon & Schuster, 1987.

Cuddy, Amy J. C. "Just Because I'm Nice, Don't Assume I'm Dumb." *Harvard Business Review,* February 2009.

Cunningham, Chet. *50 Secrets: How to Meet People and Make Friends*. Leucadia, Calif.: United Research Publishers, 1992.

Cushman, Donald P., and Dudly D. Cahn Jr. *Communication in Interpersonal Relationships*. Albany, N.Y.: SUNY Press, 1985.

Cyr, John E. *Psychology of Motivation and Persuasion in Real Estate Selling*. Englewood Cliffs, N.J.: Prentice-Hall, 1975.

Danow, Sheila, and Caroline Bailey. *Developing Skills With People*. New York: John Wiley & Sons, 1988.

Davis, Wynn (comp.). *The Best of Success*. Lombard, Ill.: Great Quotations Publishing Company, 1988.

Dawson, Roger. *The Confident Decision Maker.* New York: William Morrow and Company, 1993.

_____. *Secrets of Power Persuasion*. Englewood Cliffs, N.J.: Prentice-Hall, 1992.

Deep, Sam, and Lyle Sussman. *Smart Moves*. New York: Addison-Wesley Publishing, 1990.

_____. *What to Say to Get What You Want*. New York: Addison-Wesley Publishing, 1992.

Derlega, Valerian J. (ed.). *Communication, Intimacy, and Close Relationships*. Orlando, Fla.: Academic Press, 1984.

Diehm, William J. *Criticizing*. Minneapolis, Minn.: Augsburg Publishing House, 1986.

Diekman, John R. *Human Connections: How to Make Communication Work*. Englewood Cliffs, N.J.: Prentice-Hall, 1982.

Dilenschneider, Robert L. *Power and Influence: Mastering the Art of Persuasion.* New York: Prentice-Hall Press, 1990.

Dilley, Josiah S. . . . *And I Thought I Knew How to Communicate!* Minneapolis, Minn.: Educational Media Corporation, 1985.

Dillon, T. *The Practice of Questioning.* London: Routledge, 1990.

Dimitrius, Jo-Ellan, and Mark Mazzarella. *Reading People: How to Understand People and Predict Their Behavior—Anytime, Anyplace.* New York: Random House, 1998.

Ditmer, Bob, and Stephanie McFarland. *151 Quick Ideas to Improve Your People Skills.* Franklin Lakes, N.J.: Career Press, 2009.

Donaldson, Les. *Conversational Magic: The Key to Poise, Popularity and Success.* West Nyack, N.Y.: Parker Publishing Company, 1981.

Doyle, Michael, and David Straus. *How to Make Meetings Work.* New York: Wyden Books, 1976.

Drakeford, John W. *The Awesome Power of Positive Attention.* Nashville: Broadman Press, 1990.

Dunsing, Richard J. *You and I Have Simply Got to Stop Meeting This Way.* New York: AMACOM, 1978.

Earley, Christopher P. "Perceived Importance of Praise and Criticism, and Work Performance: An Examination of Feedback in the United States and England." *Journal of Management*, vol. 12, Winter 1986: 457–473.

Edwards, Richard T. "You Cannot Communicate unless You Are a Good Listener." *American Salesman*, vol. 35, October 1990: 28.

Edwards, Tryon (comp.). *The New Dictionary of Thoughts.* New York: Standard Book Company, 1974.

Eigen, Lewis D., and Jonathan P. Siegel. *The Manager's Book of Quotations.* New York: AMACOM, 1989.

Eisen, Jeffrey, with Pat Farley. *Powertalk!* New York: Simon & Schuster, 1984.

Ekmann, Paul. *Emotions Revealed: Recognizing Faces and Feelings to Improve Communication and Emotional Life.* New York: St. Martin's Press, 2003.

Elgin, Suzette Haden. *Gender-Speak: Men, Women, and the Gentle Art of Verbal Self-Defense.* New York: John Wiley & Sons, 1993.

_____. *The Gentle Art of Verbal Self-Defense.* New York: Dorset Press, 1980.

_____. *More on the Gentle Art of Verbal Self-Defense.* Englewood Cliffs, N.J.: Prentice-Hall, 1983.

English, Gary. "Curing the Meeting Blues." *Management Review*, vol. 79, June 1990: 60.

Erickson, Kenneth A. *The Power of Communication.* St. Louis: Concordia Publishing House, 1986.

Evatt, Cris. *He & She: 60 Significant Differences Between Men and Women.* Berkeley, Calif.: Conari Press, 1992.

Fast, Julius. *Subtext: Making Body Language Work in the Workplace.* New York: Viking, 1991.

Fast, Julius, and Barbara Fast. *Talking Between the Lines.* New York: Viking, 1979.

Finegan, Jay. "48 Hours with the King of Cold Calls." *Inc.*, vol. 13, no. 6, June 1991: 100–107.

Fisher, Dalmar. *Communication in Organizations.* St. Paul, Minn.: West Publishing Company, 1981.

Ford, Jeffrey, and Laurie Ford. *The Four Conversations: Daily Communication That Gets Results.* San Francisco: Berrett-Koehler, 2009.

Fox, Sue. *Business Etiquette for Dummies: Your Guide to Acting Appropriately Across the Globe*, 2nd ed. Hoboken, N.J.: Wiley Publishing, 2008.

France, Kim. "Sleeping with the Enemy: How to Fight with the Man You Love." *Mademoiselle*, vol. 97, October 1991: 146.

Frank, Milo. *How to Run a Successful Meeting in Half the Time.* New York: Simon & Schuster, 1989.

Freedman, Adam. "Why Trial Lawyers Say It Better," *Wall Street Journal*, January 29–30, 2011.

Friedman, Paul G. *How to Deal with Difficult People.* Mission, Kans.: SkillPath Publications, 1989.

Fugere, Brian, Chelsea Hardaway, and Jon Warshawsky. *Why Business People Speak Like Idiots: A Bullfighter's Guide.* New York: Simon & Schuster/Free Press, 2005.

Gabor, Don. *How to Talk to the People You Love.* New York: Simon & Schuster, 1989.

Gamble, Cheryl. "CFOs Cite Integrity as Most Important Trait." *T+D Magazine*, December 2010.

Garner, Alan. *Conversationally Speaking: Tested New Ways to Increase Your Personal and Social Effectiveness.* New York: McGraw-Hill, 1981.

Gates, Anita. "The Smartest Way to Give a Performance Review." *Working Woman*, vol. 16, May 1991: 65–67.

Gerstenzang, Peter. "Look Who's Talking Too Much." *Cosmopolitan*, vol. 212, March 1992: 110.

Girard, Joe. *How to Sell Yourself.* New York: Warner Books, 1981.

Gitomer, Jeffrey. *Social Boom! How to Master Business Social Media.* Upper Saddle River, N.J.: Pearson Education, 2011.

Glaser, Susan R., and Anna Eblen. *Toward Communication Competency: Developing Interpersonal Skills.* New York: Holt, Rinehart and Winston, 1986.

Glass, Lillian. *He Says, She Says.* New York: G. P. Putnam's Sons, 1992.

_____. *Say It Right: How to Talk in Any Social or Business Situation.* New York: G. P. Putnam's Sons, 1991.

Glatthorn, Allan A., and Herbert R. Adams. *Listening Your Way to Management Success.* Glenview, Ill.: Scott, Foresman and Company, 1983.

"Go Along and Get Along." *Economist*, vol. 317, November 24, 1990: 76.

Golde, Roger A. *What You Say Is What You Get.* New York: Hawthorn Books, 1979.

Goman, Carol Kinsey. *The Nonverbal Advantage: Secrets and Science of Body Language at Work.* San Francisco: Berrett-Koehler, 2008.

Goodman, Gerald, and Glenn Esterly. *The Talk Book: The Intimate Science of Communicating in Close Relationships.* Emmaus, Pa.: Rodale Press, 1988.

Goodson, Jane R., Gail W. McGee, and Anson Seers. "Giving Appropriate Performance Feedback to Managers: An Empirical Test of Content and Outcomes." *Journal of Business Communication*, vol. 29, Fall 1992: 329–341.

Gordon, Myron. *Making Meetings More Productive.* New York: Sterling Publishing Company, 1981.

Gorman, Ronald H. "Sell the Solution." *Personnel Journal*, vol. 69, September 1990: 37.

Gray, John. *Men Are From Mars, Women Are From Venus.* New York: HarperCollins, 1992.

_____. *Men, Women and Relationships: Making Peace with the Opposite Sex.* Hillsboro, Ore.: Beyond Words Publishing, 1990.

Greenburger, Francis, with Thomas Kiernan. *How to Ask for More and Get It: The Art of Creative Negotiation.* New York: Doubleday & Company, 1978.

Guirdham, Maureen. *Interpersonal Skills at Work.* Englewood Cliffs, N.J.: Prentice-Hall, 1990.

Hagel, John, III, and John Seely Brown. "Five Tips for Smarter Social Networking." *Harvard Business Review Blog, Guest Edition*, http://blogs .hbr.org/bigshift/2011/01/five-tips-for-smarter-social-n.html, February 2, 2011.

Hajdu, David. "Why Not Talk Like a Grown-Up?" *Cosmopolitan*, vol. 208, February 1990: 128.

Hamilton, Beatrice. "Hearing, Analyzing, Empathizing, and Succeeding in Management." *T+D Magazine*, vol. 44, August 1990: 16.

Hamlin, Sonya. *How to Talk so People Listen.* New York: Harper & Row, 1988.

"Hands On" (illustration), *Inc.*, vol. 12, October 1990: 150.

Haney, William V. *Communication and Interpersonal Relations: Text and Cases.* Homewood, Ill.: Irwin, 1992.

Hanks, Kurt. *Getting Your Message Across*. Los Altos, Calif.: Crisp Publications, 1991.

_____. *Motivating People*. Allen, Tex.: Argus Communications, 1982.

Hanna, Sharon L. *Person to Person: Positive Relationships Don't Just Happen*. Englewood Cliffs, N.J.: Prentice-Hall, 1991.

Harbaugh, Frederick W. "Accentuate the Positive." *Technical Communication*, vol. 38, February 1991: 73.

Harvard Business School Press and Society for Human Resource Management. *The Essentials of Power, Influence, and Persuasion*. Boston: Harvard Business School Press, 2006.

Hegarty, Edward J. *Making What You Say Pay Off*. West Nyack, N.Y.: Parker, 1968.

Helweg-Larsen, M. "To Nod or Not to Nod: An Observational Study of Nonverbal Communication and Status in Female and Male College Students." *Psychology of Women Quarterly*, vol. 28, no. 4, 2004: 358–361.

Henley, Nancy, and Barrie Thorne (comp.). *She Said/He Said: An Annotated Bibliography of Sex Differences in Language, Speech, and Nonverbal Communication*. Pittsburgh, Pa.: Know, 1975.

Hensley, Carl Wayne. "What You Share Is What You Get: Tips for Effective Communication" (speech transcript). *Vital Speeches*, vol. 59, December 1992: 115–118.

Hess, Ursula, Reginald B. Adams, Jr., and Robert E. Kleck. "Who May Frown and Who Should Smile? Dominance, Affiliation, and the Display of Happiness and Anger." *Cognition and Emotion*, vol. 19, no. 4, 2005: 515–536.

Holden, Lorraine. "Teamwork: A Delicate Balance." *Managers Magazine*, vol. 65, August 1990: 29–33.

Howell, William Smiley. *The Empathetic Communicator*. Belmont, Calif.: Wadsworth, 1982.

Hutchins, Robert M. (ed.). *Great Books of the Western World*. Vol. 9, *The Works of Aristotle, vol. II*. Chicago: William Benton, 1952.

Hybels, Saundra, and Richard L. Weaver II. *Communicating Effectively*. New York: McGraw-Hill, 1992.

Impoco, James, and Betsy Streisand. "The Great Divide: U.S.–Japanese Business Deals Are Often Unable to Bridge a Vast Cultural Gap." *U.S. News and World Report*, vol. 113, July 6, 1992: 52.

James, Jennifer. *You Know I Wouldn't Say This If I Didn't Love You*. New York: Newmarket Press, 1990.

Jamieson, G. H. *Communication and Persuasion*. London: Croom Helm, 1985.

Jandt, Fred E. *Conflict Resolution Through Communication*. New York: Harper & Row, 1973.

Johnson, David W. *Human Relations in Your Career.* Englewood Cliffs, N.J.: Prentice-Hall, 1991.

Jones, G. Brian. *Men Have Feelings, Too! A Book for Men (And the Women Who Love Them).* Wheaton, Ill.: Victor Books, 1988.

Jones, Norman. *Keep in Touch: How to Communicate Better by Responding to the Feeling Instead of the Event.* Englewood Cliffs, N.J.: Prentice-Hall, 1981.

Kane, Kimberly F. "MBAs: A Recruiter's-Eye View." *Business Horizons*, vol. 36, January-February 1993: 65–71.

Kaplan, Burton. *Strategic Communication.* New York: HarperCollins, 1991.

Kaplan, Michael. "The Secrets of Super Sales People." *Working Woman*, vol. 15, May 1992: 92–96.

Karrass, Chester L. "There's Plenty of Give and Take in Making Concessions." *Purchasing*, vol. 109, October 11, 1990: 55.

Katz, Sally N. "Power Skills for Executive Meetings." *T+D Magazine*, vol. 45, July 1991: 53.

Kaufman, Joanne. "Hot Copy." *Ladies Home Journal*, vol. 108, July 1991: 43–44.

Key, Mary Ritchie. *Male/Female Language.* Metuchen, N.J.: Scarecrow Press, 1975.

Kiefer, George David. *The Strategy of Meetings.* New York: Simon & Schuster, 1988.

Kirkpatrick, Ronald L. *How to Plan and Conduct Productive Business Meetings.* New York: AMACOM, 1987.

Kizilos, Peter. "Fixing Fatal Flaws." *Training*, vol. 28, September 1991: 66, 68–70.

Kotker, Zane. "The 'Feminine' Behavior of Powerless People." *Savvy*, March 1980: 36–42.

Kouzes, James M., and Barry Z. Posner. *Credibility: How Leaders Gain and Lose It, Why People Demand It.* San Francisco: John Wiley & Sons/Jossey-Bass, 2003.

Krafft, Susan. "How to Break Bad News." *American Demographics*, vol. 13, July 1991: 43.

_____. "Killing the Messenger." *American Demographics*, vol. 13, July 1991: 40–41.

Kramer, Cheris, Barrie Thorne, and Nancy Henley. "Perspectives on Language and Communication." *Signs*, no. 31, Spring 1978.

Lakoff, Robin Tolmach. *Language and Woman's Place.* New York: Harper Colophon Books, 1975.

_____. *Talking Power.* New York: Basic Books, 1990.

Langs, Robert. *Unconscious Communication in Everyday Life.* New York: Jason Aronson, Inc., 1983.

Lee, Irving J. *How to Talk with People.* New York: Harper & Row, 1952.

Leeds, Dorothy. *Smart Questions: A New Strategy for Successful Managers.* New York: McGraw-Hill, 1987.

Legge, Peter. *The Power of Tact: It's Not What You Say or Do, It's How You Say and Do It.* Burnaby, British Columbia, Canada: Eaglet Publishing, 2008.

Leritz, Len. *No-Fault Negotiating.* New York: Warner Books, 1987.

LeRoux, Paul. *Selling to a Group: Presentation Strategies.* New York: Barnes & Noble Books, 1984.

Lesly, Philip. *How We Discommunicate.* New York: AMACOM, 1979.

Letich, Larry. "Ins and Outs: Ignoring the Psychological Side of a Small Meeting Can Be Hazardous to Its Success." *Meetings & Conventions*, vol. 25, August 1990: 4–8.

Lichtenberg, Ronna. *Pitch Like a Girl: How a Woman Can Be Herself and Still Succeed.* New York: Rodale, 2005.

Lindskold, Svenn. *You and Me: The Why and How of Interpersonal Behavior.* Chicago: Nelson-Hall, 1982.

Linkemer, Bobbi. *How to Run a Meeting.* New York: American Management Association, 1987.

Long, Lynette, Louis V. Paradise, and Thomas J. Long. *Questioning: Skills for the Helping Process.* Monterey, Calif.: Brooks/Cole Publishing Company, 1981.

Lovas, Michael, and Pam Holloway. *Axis of Influence: How Credibility and Likeability Intersect to Drive Success.* New York: Morgan James, 2009.

Lukaszewski, James E. "Bridging the Communication Gap." *Sales & Marketing Management*, vol. 143, August 1991: 62–66.

Luntz, Frank. *Words That Work: It's Not What You Say, It's What People Hear.* New York: Hyperion, 2007.

Lusardi, Lee A. "When a Woman Speaks, Does Anybody Listen?" *Working Woman*, vol. 15, July 1990: 92–95.

Madonik, Barbara Haber. "I Hear What You Say, but What Are You Telling Me?" *Canadian Manager*, vol. 15, Spring 1990: 18–21.

Margerison, Charles J. *If Only I Had Said....* London: Mercury Books, 1987.

Martel, Myles. *Mastering the Art of Q and A: A Survival Guide for Tough, Tricky and Hostile Questions.* Homewood, Ill.: Dow Jones-Irwin, 1989.

Martinet, Jeanne. *The Art of Mingling.* New York: St. Martin's Press, 1992.

_____. "Who Says You Can't Be a Good Mixer?" *Cosmopolitan*, vol. 213, November 1992.

Maude, Barry. *Communication at Work.* London: Business Books Limited, 1977.

Maxwell, John C. *Be a People Person.* Wheaton, Ill.: SP Publications, 1989.

Mayo, Clara, and Nancy M. Henley (eds.). *Gender and Nonverbal Behavior.* New York: Springer-Verlag, 1981.

McCabe, Bernard P., Jr., and Coleman C. Bender. *Speaking Is a Practical Matter.* Boston: Holbrook Press, 1976.

McCallister, Linda. *I Wish I'd Said That!* New York: John Wiley & Sons, 1992.

McCroskey, James C., Virginia P. Richmond, and Robert A. Stewart. *One on One: The Foundation of Interpersonal Communication.* Englewood Cliffs, N.J.: Prentice-Hall, 1986.

McGill, Michael E. *The McGill Report on Male Intimacy.* New York: Holt, Rinehart and Winston, 1985.

McKenzie, E. C. *14,000 Quips & Quotes.* New York: Greenwich House, 1984.

McLaughlin, Margaret L. *Conversation: How Talk Is Organized.* Beverly Hills, Calif.: Sage Publications, 1984.

McLellan, Diana. "Who's Smiling Now?" *Washingtonian*, vol. 25, February 1990: 108–111.

Mead, Richard. *Cross-Cultural Management Communication.* New York: John Wiley & Sons, 1990.

Mehrabian, Albert. "Communication Without Words," *Psychology Today*, September 1968: 53–55.

_____. *Silent Messages.* Belmont, Calif.: Wadsworth Publishing Group, 1971.

Mehrabian, Albert, and Morton Wiener. "Decoding of Inconsistent Communications." *Journal of Personality and Social Psychology*, vol. 6, no. 1, 1967: 109–114.

Meyer, Paul J. *The Art of Creative Listening.* Waco, Tex.: Paul J. Meyer, 1980.

Mills, Harry. *Artful Persuasion: How to Command Attention, Change Minds, and Influence People.* New York: AMACOM, 2000.

Molcho, Samy. *Body Speech.* New York: St. Martin's Press, 1985.

Moran, Robert. "Watch Your Body Language." *International Management*, vol. 45, May 1990.

Murnighan, J. Keith. *Bargaining Games.* New York: William Morrow and Company, 1992.

Myers, Pennie, and Don Nance. *The Upset Book.* South Bend, Ind.: Academic Publications, 1986.

Nelson, Carol. "If It Isn't Direct, It Doesn't Follow." *Direct Marketing*, vol. 52, March 1990: 66.

Nelson, Sara. "Why Men Can't Take Criticism." *Glamour*, vol. 90, August 1992: 152.

Nelton, Sharon. "The Womanly Art of the Deal." *Nation's Business*, vol. 81, January 1993: 60.

Nierenberg, Gerard I. *The Art of Negotiating.* New York: Cornerstone Library, 1977.

_____. *The Complete Negotiator.* New York: Nierenberg & Zeif Publishers, 1986.

_____. *Creative Business Negotiating.* New York: Hawthorn Books, 1971.

_____. *How to Give & Receive Advice.* New York: Simon & Schuster, 1975.

Nierenberg, Gerard I., and Henry H. Calero. *How to Read a Person Like a Book.* New York: Simon & Schuster, 1971.

_____. *Meta-Talk.* New York: Pocket Books, 1975.

Nierenberg, Juliet, and Irene S. Ross. *Women and the Art of Negotiating.* New York: Simon & Schuster, 1985.

Nirenberg, Jesse S. *Breaking Through to Each Other: Creative Persuasion on the Job and in the Home.* New York: Harper & Row, 1976.

_____. *Getting Through to People.* Englewood Cliffs, N.J.: Prentice-Hall, 1963.

_____. *How to Sell Your Ideas.* New York: McGraw-Hill, 1984.

Noonan, Peggy. *Simply Speaking: How to Communicate Your Ideas with Style, Substance, and Clarity.* New York: Regan Books, 1998.

Osborn, Denise. "Managing Meeting Disrupters." *Manage*, vol. 42, May 1991: 8–12.

Parkinson, J. Robert. *How to Get People to Do Things Your Way.* Lincolnwood, Ill.: NTC Business Books, 1986.

Parlee, Mary Brown. "Conversational Politics." *Psychology Today*, vol. 12, May 1979: 48–56.

Payne, Stanley L. *The Art of Asking Questions.* Princeton, N.J.: Princeton University Press, 1951.

Pease, Allan, and Barbara Pease. *The Definitive Book of Body Language: The Hidden Meaning Behind People's Gestures and Expressions.* New York: Random House/Bantam Dell, 2004.

Penn, C. Ray. "A Choice of Words Is a Choice of Worlds" (speech transcript). *Vital Speeches*, vol. 57, December 1990: 116–117.

Pettit, John D. "Interpersonal Skills Training: A Prerequisite for Success." *Business*, vol. 40, April-June 1990.

Phillips, Bob. *The Delicate Art of Dancing with Porcupines.* Ventura, Calif.: Regal Books, 1989.

Phillips, Gerald M. *Help for Shy People.* Englewood Cliffs, N.J.: Prentice-Hall, 1981.

Pietsch, William V. *Human Be-Ing: How to Have a Creative Relationship Instead of a Power Struggle.* New York: Signet, 1975.

Postman, Neil. *Crazy Talk, Stupid Talk.* New York: Delacorte Press, 1976.

Potash, Marlin S. *Hidden Agendas.* New York: Delacorte Press, 1990.

Pritchett, Price, and Ron Pound. *Team ReConstruction*. Dallas, Tex.: Pritchett Publishing Co., 1992.

Prochnow, Herbert V. *Speaker's & Toastmaster's Handbook*. Rocklin, Calif.: Prima Publishing & Communications, 1990.

Reck, Ross R., and Brian G. Long. *The Win-Win Negotiator: How to Negotiate Favorable Agreements That Last*. New York: Pocket Books, 1987.

Reeves, Elton T. *How to Get Along with Almost Everybody*. New York: AMACOM, 1973.

Reiman, Tonya. *The Yes Factor: Get What You Want. Say What You Mean. The Secrets of Persuasive Communication*. New York: Penguin Group/Hudson Street Press, 2010.

Richmond, Virginia P., James C. McCroskey, and Steven K. Payne. *Nonverbal Behavior in Interpersonal Relations*. Englewood Cliffs, N.J.: Prentice-Hall, 1987.

Ricks, David A. *Big Business Blunders: Mistakes in Multinational Marketing*. Homewood, Ill.: Dow Jones-Irwin, 1983.

Roane, Susan. *How to Work a Room*. New York: Warner Books, 1989.

Rogers, Carl R., and Barry Stevens. *Person to Person: The Problem of Being Human*. Lafayette, Calif.: Real People Press, 1967.

Rosenbaum, Bernard L. "Making Presentations: How to Persuade Others to Accept Your Ideas." *American Salesman*, vol. 37, February 1992: 16–19.

Runion, Meryl, and Wendy Mack. *Perfect Phrases for Leadership Development: Hundreds of Ready-to-Use Phrases for Guiding Employees to Reach the Next Level*. New York: McGraw-Hill, 2011.

Russell, Anne M., and Lorraine Calvacca. "Should You Be Funny at Work?" *Working Woman*, vol. 16, March 1991: 74–78.

Sandberg, Jared. "People Are Hugging a Lot More Now and Seem to Like It," *Wall Street Journal*, March 15, 1993: A1, col. 4.

Sands, Ken. *The Peacemaker*. Grand Rapids, Mich.: Baker Book House, 1991.

Sandstrom, Teena. *Working Better Together: A Human Relations Guidebook for Office Professionals*. Round Rock, Tex.: Professional Training Associates, 1990.

Sanford, John A. *Between People: Communicating One-to-One*. New York: Paulist Press, 1982.

Sanzotta, Donald. *The Manager's Guide to Interpersonal Relations*. New York: AMACOM, 1979.

Satran, Pamela Redmond. "When Not to Talk About It." *Redbook*, vol. 178, March 1992.

Schabacker, Kirsten. "A Short, Snappy Guide to Meaningful Meetings." *Working Woman*, vol. 16, June 1991: 70–74.

Schulte, Lucy. "How to Negotiate Your Way Into Almost Anything." *Mademoiselle*, vol. 98, May 1992: 198.

Scott, Bill. *The Skills of Negotiating.* New York: John Wiley & Sons, 1981.

Sedgwick, John. "Talking." *Boston Magazine*, vol. 84, September 1992: 45.

Seltz, David D., and Alfred J. Modica. *Negotiate Your Way to Success.* Rockville Centre, N.Y.: Farnsworth Publishing, 1980.

Sharif, Karim. "Customs Problems." *Los Angeles Business Journal*, vol. 14, August 3, 1992: 30–31.

Shields, Donald J., Lela K. Bullerdick, and Donald G. Shields. *Effective Communication for Professionals.* Dubuque, Iowa: Kendall/Hunt Publishing Company, 1989.

Simon, George F., and Deborah Weissman. *Men and Women: Partners at Work.* Palo Alto, Calif.: Crisp Publications, 1990.

Simon, Sidney B. *Negative Criticism.* Allen, Tex.: Argus Communications, 1978.

Smith, Gerald Walker. *Hidden Meanings: A Psychological Dictionary.* New York: Peter H. Wyden Publisher, 1975.

Smith, Wen. "Why 'Bye-Bye' Is a No-No." *Saturday Evening Post*, vol. 264, September-October 1992: 36.

Snell, Frank. *How to Hold a Better Meeting.* New York: Harper and Brothers, 1958.

_____. *How to Win the Meeting.* New York: Hawthorn Books, 1979.

Sondak, Arthur. "What's Your Conflict Barometer." *Supervisory Management*, vol. 35, May 1990.

Sparks, Donald B. *The Dynamics of Effective Negotiation.* Houston: Gulf Publishing Company, 1982.

Stark, Amy. *Because I Said So.* New York: Pharos Books, 1992.

Stenzler-Centonze, Marjorie. "EE's Next Challenge: People Not Products." *EDN*, vol. 35, August 23, 1990: 39.

Stewart, John (ed.). *Bridges Not Walls.* New York: McGraw-Hill, 1990.

Stewart, Nathaniel. *Winning Friends at Work.* New York: Ballantine Books, 1985.

Stewart, Susan. "The Truth About Lying." *Current Health*, October 2, 1992.

Stiebel, David. "What to Do When Talking Makes Things Worse." *Journal of Public Management*, vol. 72, August 1990: 20–21.

Strayhorn, Joseph M., Jr. *Talking It Out.* Champaign, Ill.: Research Press Company, 1977.

Stubbs, Lucy. "Speak for Yourself." *New Statesman and Society*, vol. 3, May 25, 1990: 24.

Swets, Paul W. *The Art of Talking so That People Will Listen.* Englewood Cliffs, N.J.: Prentice-Hall, 1983.

Tannen, Deborah. "How Men and Women Use Language Differently in Their Lives and in the Classroom," *Education Digest*, vol. 57, February 1992: 3–6.

_____. *That's Not What I Meant.* New York: Ballantine Books, 1986.

_____. *You Just Don't Understand: Women and Men in Conversation.* New York: William Morrow and Company, 1990.

Thomsett, Michael C. *The Little Black Book of Business Speaking.* New York: American Management Association, 1989.

Thorne, Barrie, Cheris Kramarae, and Nancy Henley (eds.). *Language, Gender, and Society.* Rowley, Mass.: Newbury House, 1983.

"Tips That Can Enhance Your Business Lunch." *Profit-Building Strategies for Business Owners*, vol. 20, September 1990: 16.

Tropman, John, and Gersh Morningstar. *Meetings: How to Make Them Work for You.* New York: Van Nostrand Reinhold, 1985.

Truitt, John. *Phone Tactics for Instant Influence.* New York: Dembner Books, 1990.

Tucker, Raymond K. *Fighting It Out with Difficult—If Not Impossible—People.* Dubuque, Iowa: Kendall/Hunt Publishing Company, 1987.

Uris, Dorothy. *Everybody's Book of Better Speaking.* New York: David McKay Company, 1960.

Van Fleet, James K. *Lifetime Conversation Guide.* Englewood Cliffs, N.J.: Prentice-Hall, 1984.

_____. *Power with People.* West Nyack, N.Y.: Parker Publishing Company, 1970.

_____. *Twenty-Five Steps to Power and Mastery Over People.* West Nyack, N.Y.: Parker, 1983.

Vargas, Marjorie Fink. *Louder Than Words: An Introduction to Nonverbal Communication.* Ames: Iowa State University Press, 1986.

Verderber, Rudolph F. *The Challenge of Effective Speaking.* Belmont, Calif.: Wadsworth, 1988.

Verderber, Rudolph F., and Kathleen S. Verderber. *Inter-Act: Using Interpersonal Communication Skills.* Belmont, Calif.: Wadsworth, 1980.

Voges, Ken, and Ron Braud. *Understanding How Others Misunderstand You.* Chicago: Moody Press, 1990.

Walters, Barbara. *How to Talk with Practically Anybody About Practically Anything.* New York: Dell, 1970.

Walther, George. *Phone Power: How to Make the Telephone Your Most Profitable Business Tool.* New York: G. P. Putnam's Sons, 1986.

Walton, Donald. *Are You Communicating? You Can't Manage Without It.* New York: McGraw-Hill, 1989.

Warschaw, Tessa Albert. *Winning by Negotiation.* New York: McGraw-Hill, 1980.

Wassmer, Arthur C. *Making Contact.* New York: Dial Press, 1978.

Watson Wyatt Worldwide 2009/2010 Communication ROI Study Report. "Capitalizing on Effective Communication," http://www.towerswatson.com/research/670, December 2009.

Weaver, Richard L., II. *Understanding Interpersonal Communication.* Glenview, Ill.: Scott, Foresman and Company, 1987.

Weeks, Dudley. *Conflict Partnership.* Orange, Calif.: Trans World Productions, 1984.

Weiner-Davis, Michele. "The Strategy That's Guaranteed to Improve Your Marriage." *McCall's*, vol. 119, January 1992.

Weisinger, Hendrie. *The Critical Edge: How to Criticize Up and Down.* Boston: Little, Brown and Company, 1989.

Weisinger, Hendrie, and Norman M. Lobsenz. *Nobody's Perfect: How to Give Criticism and Get Results.* Los Angeles: Stratford Press, 1981.

Weiss, Donald H. *How to Deal with Difficult People.* New York: AMACOM, 1987.

Wells, Theodora. *Keeping Your Cool Under Fire.* New York: McGraw-Hill, 1980.

Wetzler, Scott. "Sugercoated Hostility." *Newsweek*, vol. 120, October 12, 1992: 14.

Wiesendanger, Betsy. "A Conversation on Conversation with Deborah Tannen." *Sales & Marketing Management*, vol. 143, April 1991: 38–43.

Wiksell, Wesley. *Do They Understand You?* New York: Macmillan, 1960.

Williams, Jonathan. *Quote, Unquote.* Berkeley, Calif.: Ten Speed Press, 1983.

Wilson, Gerald L., Alan M. Hantz, and Michael S. Hanna. *Interpersonal Growth Through Communication.* Dubuque, Iowa: William C. Brown Publishers, 1989.

Winawer, H. H. *Expression Is 9/10 of the Flaw.* Holladay, Utah: Double HH Publications, 1983.

Wisniewiski, Jeanine G. "Wicked Words: Getting to the Roots of Words." *English Journal*, vol. 79, April 1990: 78–79.

Wolk, Robert L., and Arthur Henley. *Yes Power.* New York: Peter H. Wyden, 1969.

Woodall, Marian K. *How to Talk so Men Will Listen.* Chicago: Contemporary Books, 1993.

Woolf, Bob. *Friendly Persuasion: My Life as a Negotiator.* New York: G. P. Putnam's Sons, 1990.

_____. "Ways to Win." *Reader's Digest*, vol. 138, May 1991: 23–28.

Wortman, Art (ed.). *Will Rogers: Wise and Witty Sayings of a Great American Humorist.* Castle Press, 1969.

Wright, Milton. *The Art of Conversation and How to Apply Its Technique.* New York: McGraw-Hill, 1936.

Wurman, Richard Saul, and Loring Leifer. *Follow the Yellow Brick Road*. New York: Bantam Books, 1992.

Yamada, Haru. *American and Japanese Business Discourse: A Comparison of Interactional Styles*. Norwood, N.J.: Ablex Publishing, 1992.

Yanow, Morton. "Mutual Agreement: Tactics for Negotiating." *Whole Earth Review*, Spring 1992.

Zack, Devora. *Networking for People Who Hate Networking: A Field Guide for Introverts, the Overwhelmed, and the Underconnected*. San Francisco: Berrett-Koehler, 2010.

Zander, Alvin. *Making Groups Effective*. San Francisco: Jossey-Bass Publishers, 1982.

Zandt, Deanna. *Share This! How You Will Change the World with Social Networking*. San Francisco: Berrett-Koehler, 2010.

Resources By Dianna Booher:
Available From Booher Consultants

BOOKS: SELECTED TITLES

Creating Personal Presence: Look, Talk, Think, and Act Like a Leader

The Voice of Authority: 10 Communication Strategies Every Leader Needs to Know

Booher's Rules of Business Grammar: 101 Fast and Easy Ways to Correct the Most Common Errors

From Contact to Contract: 496 Proven Sales Tips to Generate More Leads, Close More Deals, Exceed Your Goals, and Make More Money

Speak with Confidence: Powerful Presentations That Inform, Inspire and Persuade

E-Writing: 21ˢᵗ Century Tools for Effective Communication

Good Grief, Good Grammar

To the Letter: A Handbook of Model Letters for the Busy Executive

Great Personal Letters for Busy People

The Complete Letterwriter's Almanac

Executive's Portfolio of Model Speeches for All Occasions

Your Signature Work®: Creating Excellence and Influencing Others at Work

Your Signature Life®: Pursuing God's Best Every Day

The New Secretary: How to Handle People as Well as You Handle Paper

Winning Sales Letters

Get a Life Without Sacrificing Your Career

Ten Smart Moves for Women

Get Ahead, Stay Ahead

The Worth of a Woman's Words

Well Connected: Power Your Own Soul by Plugging into Others

Mother's Gifts to Me

The Esther Effect

Love Notes: From My Heart to Yours

First Thing Monday Morning

Fresh-Cut Flowers for a Friend

The Little Book of Big Questions: Answers to Life's Perplexing Questions

MULTIMEDIA PROGRAMS

Communicate with Confidence®: Quick Tips with Dianna Booher
Communicate with Confidence®: Communicate Your Way to the Top
Sales Sizzlers®
Effective Writing
Effective Editing
Good Grief, Good Grammar
More Good Grief, Good Grammar
Ready, Set, NeGOtiate

WORKSHOPS

Presentations That Work®
Strategic Writing™
Email Matters®
Technical Writing
Developing Winning Proposals
Good Grief, Good Grammar
Communicate with Confidence®
eService Communications
Customer Service Communications
Listening Until You Really Hear
Resolving Conflict Without Punching Someone Out
Meetings: Leading and Participating Productively
Negotiating so That Everyone Wins

For More Information

For more information, please contact:

Booher Consultants, Inc.

Phone: 817-318-6000 or 800-342-6621

mailroom@booher.com

Primary: www.Booher.com

E-store: www.BooherDirect.com

Blog: www.Booher.com/BooherBanter

Twitter: @diannabooher

Facebook: Facebook.com/DiannaBooher

About the Author

Dianna works with individuals and organizations to improve their productivity and effectiveness through better communication: oral, written, interpersonal, and cross-functional.

As an internationally recognized business communication expert, she's the author of 45 books, published in 24 countries and in 17 foreign languages, as well as numerous video series, audio series, and e-learning programs.

She's the founder of Booher Consultants, a communication training firm based in the Dallas–Fort Worth metroplex. The firm provides communication consulting, coaching, and training to some of the largest Fortune 500 companies and government agencies, among them IBM, Lockheed Martin, BP, Chevron, Conoco-Phillips, USAA, Northwestern Mutual, Principal Financial, JPMorgan Chase, PepsiCo, Bayer, the Internal Revenue Service, the U.S. Department of Veterans Affairs, the Army & Air Force Exchange Service, and the U.S. Navy.

Dianna has been interviewed by major national media, including *Good Morning America, USA Today,* Fox, CNN, Bloomberg, *Fortune, Forbes,* the *Wall Street Journal, Investor's Business Daily,* NPR, the *New York Times,* and the *Washington Post. Successful Meetings* magazine has named Dianna to its list of "21 Top Speakers for the 21st Century."

Dianna and her husband live in the Dallas–Fort Worth metroplex.